Barriers to Entry

Paul Ross

Barriers to Entry

Overcoming Challenges and Achieving
Breakthroughs in a Chinese Workplace

Paul Ross
Boynton Beach, FL, USA

ISBN 978-981-32-9565-0   ISBN 978-981-32-9566-7   (eBook)
https://doi.org/10.1007/978-981-32-9566-7

This Palgrave Macmillan imprint is published by the registered company Springer Nature
Singapore Pte Ltd.
The registered company address is: 152 Beach Road, #21-01/04 Gateway East, Singapore
189721, Singapore

To my grandmother,
Annette Margolis
who envisioned this book 50 years before it was written

FOREWORD

The globalization of Chinese firms has a number of dimensions: People, Information, Goods and Services and Capital. Focusing on the movement of people, Paul writes from the unique vantage point of someone who has worked in China for a long period of time and been a member of the workforce in a multinational Chinese enterprise.

Paul and I first crossed paths at the *China Goes Global* Conference I co-founded more than a decade ago. The genesis of the conference was a recognition of the growing appetite Chinese firms were showing for expansion into markets outside of China. This led to our first book on the subject, *Globalization of Chinese Enterprises*, (Palgrave Macmillan, 2008) that we edited with John R. McIntyre, Professor of International Business in the College of Management at Georgia Tech.

Paul, who was back in the U.S. at the time and eager to keep on top what was going on in China, saw the *China Goes Global* conference as a way to stay connected and meet others who had a similar interest. As a way of engaging with the conference and with what we were doing, he offered to pitch in anywhere assistance was needed and by doing that had the opportunity to absorb new ideas and share insights he had developed through his own experience.

With more than two decades of experience in the telecommunications industry under his belt and a decade spent living and working in China, Paul brought industry and practical experience to the discussion. In the subsequent years he attended the conference, running panel discussions and then eventually submitting research papers on topics that caught his attention, he maintained a commitment to engaging in a serious, interpretive study of what real Chinese companies were doing in the real world.

We considered Paul a 'practitioner' because he had come from industry, a profile that is an exception in most academic conferences. However, as time went on, and we got to know him better, we came to realize that he had an academic bent. It was this combination—the profile of a 'practitioner' and the heart of an academic—that was a source of insight and gave him a unique perspective.

The book that Paul has written on the experience of foreign staff in Chinese companies combines extensive secondary research with first-hand observation based on the experience he has gained over the years he has spent in a Chinese working environment. It adds a novel dimension to our understanding of Chinese enterprises, their culture, and the nature of their workplaces much of which previously was based on conjecture and assumption. It is also highly applicable to the situation of an increasing number of people around the world who are today or, in the near future, will be working in a Chinese firm.

That the employment of foreign staff in Chinese firms is a global phenomenon I can attest to from my own vantage point in Norway where I currently teach. In less than a decade, Chinese firms have invested billions of dollars in Norwegian firms in sectors such as Transportation, Chemicals, Metals, and Energy. As a result of this development, there are today plenty of Norwegians who work for Chinese firms and are engaged with Chinese management.

This movement of talent across borders is a significant and important, but often overlooked aspect of China's globalization in the twenty-first century. This book serves as a timely source of insight into the Chinese enterprise as well as a well-informed guide for those who want to better understand the phenomenon of foreign employees in Chinese firms or who may one day in the not too distant future find themselves employed by a Chinese firm.

Kristiansand, Norway   Ilan Alon Ph.D.
2019   President of the Chinese
                                Globalization Association
                           http://www.chinagoesglobal.org

PREFACE

Before I had a chance to work in a Chinese company myself, I had heard many comments about what kind of experience it was: "Management in a Chinese company was top-down". "Chinese bosses were tyrants", and the food served in the company canteen was "inedible". Undeterred by the words of caution, most of which of were imparted by commentators who had never set foot in a Chinese company themselves, I accepted a position at the Shanghai Bell Company and started work promptly on May 8, 2011, a day that marked the beginning of nearly 3000-day journey that would culminate in the writing of this book.

Founded in 1984, the Shanghai Bell Company was regarded, at the time, as a leading light for China's nascent hi-tech industry and a symbol of the country's future aspirations. Today, more than three decades after its founding, the company's place on the list of China's state-owned enterprises remains unchanged. What has changed are the types of products it sells, the profile of the companies it competes with, and the shape of the markets it addresses. In the more recent past, the company has entered into successive partnerships with a number of foreign companies—the French telecommunications equipment provider Alcatel, then Alcatel-Lucent, and most recently Nokia.

Over the months and then years I spent at Shanghai Bell, first in the company's marketing department and then in the export division, I went from standing out as a novelty at meetings, training sessions and team-building activities to fitting in as coxswain on the company's Dragon Boat and moderator at the company's book club. And if I didn't entirely fade into the company's woodwork, I became embedded in its operational fabric, a vantage point from which I could, undisturbed and unobstructed, make observations about how the company worked and record impressions about my experience as a foreign employee. Over a lengthy period of time, I found that incidents and events that at first seemed random and inadvertent began to emerge into discernible patterns and fit into larger themes. My impressions and observations would eventually take form as the source of this book's content and the themes and patterns I discerned would eventually take shape as its outline.

The source of the book's inspiration, quite distant in both location and time from the book's source of content, was incongruously a room on the fifth floor of a dormitory at Wuhan University in central China's Hubei Province where I lived for the better part of a year more than a quarter of a century ago. Through a program organized by my school in the U.S., I was engaged as an English teacher at the University and assigned, by default and fiat, to a private apartment in a building dedicated to the housing of foreign staff. Eager to learn more about life in China and disappointed to find that Chinese were not permitted to live in the building where I was housed, I requested permission to move into a dormitory on campus and share a room with Chinese students, appealing for support directly to the president of the university, Liu Daoyu. Against the better judgement of his staff and in the face of opposition from the rest of the administration, President Liu took the unprecedented step of approving my request and making possible what would prove to be a unique and unforgettable experience.

As disconnected as Wuhan University and the Shanghai Bell Company are by time and place, it was only as I began to write this book that I realized how closely connected they were by experience. As I reflected on that experience, it became clear to me that the spirit of curiosity and adventure that had motivated me to move into a student dormitory at Wuhan University was the same one that prompted me to seek an opportunity for employment with the Shanghai Bell Company a quarter of a century later.

For their patience, friendship, and support I am indebted to the executives at the Shanghai Bell Company I worked for and the colleagues I worked with. I am indebted in even greater measure to President Liu Daoyu of Wuhan University who at a delicate time in China's most recent history took the bold step of letting a young American student move into a Chinese dormitory and in taking that step forever changed that student's life.

Boynton Beach, USA   Paul Ross

ACKNOWLEDGEMENTS

It goes without saying that a project of this scope and complexity is the work of many hands and, no matter how sincere and heartfelt my expression of gratitude for the support I have received may be, I realize that it will never be enough to compensate those to whom I am most indebted. In recognizing here the experts, family, and friends whose contributions were most meaningful and significant I hope to be able to repay at least some small part of that debt.

Professor Ilan Alon, a world-renowned expert in international strategy and business and an inspiring teacher currently at the University of Agder in Norway, who recognized the value of the topic I proposed from the very beginning and made a convincing case for turning it into a book. Ilan's enthusiasm was the fuel that got the project got off the ground and his guidance was what got it going in the right direction. Bill Araiza for applying his prodigious talents as a writer and editor and his extensive experience as a professor and scholar to critiquing my early drafts. His careful reading and thoughtful comments showed me how I could take the raw material I shared with him and turn it into chapters that someone would find worth reading. Oded Shenkar, Professor of Management at Ohio State University's Fischer College of Business, a leading expert in International Business and Chinese Management who was a consistent and reliable source of advice on any and every aspect of the project and whose words of encouragement and wisdom gave me the courage I needed to move forward. Jim Cheng, Director of the C. V. Starr East Asian Library at Columbia University, who made sure that I had the resources I needed—books, articles and people—even when I myself had given up any hope of ever being able to find, much less get access to them. Richard Smith, professor emeritus of Rice University and eminent scholar of Chinese intellectual and social history who welcomed my inquiries with open arms and, without the slightest hesitation, shared the wealth of knowledge he had acquired over a long and fruitful career. Mr. Gao Jiacheng currently completing an advanced degree at Shanghai's East China Normal University who, with very little guidance or direction, gamely took up the challenge of reading through hundreds of pages of unfinished and unwieldy chapters to produce a coherent index for the book.

Bill Sees at Columbia University, Zhang Wenxian at Rollins College and Joshua Seufert at Princeton University for their generosity in granting access to library services, sharing invaluable references, and providing archival support; Professors Zhang Yanli at Montclair State University, Li Mingjie at East China Normal University and Mike Ryan at Georgetown University, for input on topics as diverse as Chinese social trends, etymology, and trade policy. "China Hands" Matt Shofnos at Alibaba and Pat McAloon, Director of the Heartland China Association, whose insights into the operations and culture of Chinese companies were indispensable. Old and dear friends, Joel Epstein, Lin Boyang, Dee Rogers, Rosey Jaffe, Rob Amen, Frank Bilstein, and Josie Shen whose unstinting support and encouragement throughout the project was a source of strength and hope. And my brother, Phil, and his family in Jacksonville—Ruthie, Manny and Evan who provided "Uncle Paul" with a much needed portal back to his own country during the eons he was living in a place that seemed like a galaxy "far, far, away".

The Palgrave Macmillan team of publishing guides and editorial gurus: Marcus Ballenger in New York who was willing to take a second look at the half-baked proposal for this book that arrived unsolicited on his desk. Jacob Dreyer in Shanghai who endeared himself to me at our first meeting in the Westin on Henan Road by showing up with a well-worn copy of Dante's *Inferno* under his arm and demonstrated an equally thorough familiarity with the works of German philosophers as with the policies of Chinese Government officials. His breadth of knowledge and his own experience as a writer made him the ideal editor for a first-time author whose book covered a wide range of topics and domains. Anushangi Weerakoon in Singapore and Abarna Antony

Raj and Sooryadeepth Jayakrishnan in Chennai who oversaw the book's production and whose patience, grace, and consummate professionalism made them the perfect partners for an author who was inexperienced, disorganized, and often tardy.

Finally, I am especially thankful to my father whose boundless curiosity, spirit of adventure, and intense interest in other cultures was what inspired me to go to China in the first place. And his passion for imagining what could be was what inspired me to think that I could one day write a book about what I saw when I got there; To my mother, who has always been there for me no matter what. As I got deeper into the project and began to have doubts about whether I would ever be able to finish, she stepped up, pitched in, and helped out wherever help was needed, from tracking down photo usage rights held by organizations halfway around the globe to, a little closer to home, brewing up a cup of hazelnut coffee when she sensed I was losing momentum. To Catherine, who, without one word of reproach or sign of protest, changed plans, cancelled appointments, and sacrificed time we should have spent together so that I could keep working on my book project and bring it to successful conclusion. If nothing else, this project made me even more keenly aware of how unworthy I am of her unconditional love and infinite patience.

CONTENTS

LIST OF FIGURES

List of Tables

CHAPTER 1

Introduction

Against the backdrop of local panhandlers selling knock-off handbags at the entrance to a bustling shopping center in a Shanghai suburb, the lanky South African pushing foreign language programs for a local training company cuts a striking figure.

With a killer smile and patter delivered in Chinese he has honed to perfection over weeks of seven to eight-hour days, David immediately puts potential customers at ease. "I'm a bit of a novelty," he grins, breaking away for a minute to make his pitch to a group of middle-aged Chinese women who see fluency in English as the key to their children's future success.

As unconventional as David's role selling services for a Chinese company may appear, his experience is far from "novel". In fact, David is just one of a growing number of non-Chinese who are employed by Chinese companies and report to Chinese management.

Just a train ride away from Shanghai in the Southern Chinese city of Foshan a group of young professionals from the U.S., Europe, and South America is hard at work in the offices of the city government. They have been hired by the Government's investment office to write brochures, develop videos, and craft value propositions that showcase the city's advantages and serve as the base for pitches to overseas investors (Bland 2015).

At first blush, hiring a team of recently-graduated foreigners to work in a government office seems like a bold and unlikely step for a

Chinese city to take, but Foshan has a history of taking bold steps and a reputation for adopting a pragmatic approach to overcoming challenges. The city was one of the first to catch the wave of entrepreneurial activity unleashed by the economic reforms the Chinese Government initiated in the early 1980s, a wave the city's inhabitants rode to prosperity in the years that followed. Three decades later, confronted with slowing growth, rising wages, and increasing competition, Foshan was again taking steps to position itself for the next phase of economic evolution, leveraging innovation to transform itself from a manufacturer of cheap consumer goods into a purveyor of profitable, value-added services. Effecting such a large-scale transformation, Foshan's leaders recognized, would require a new approach that included tapping sources of investment outside of China. Although hiring foreigners was a departure from the past that some more conservative voices in the government considered much too radical, those who set their sights on the future maintained that the potential benefit the foreigners could deliver—developing marketing materials and crafting value propositions that would appeal to overseas investors —far outweighed the risk and therefore was an experiment worth undertaking.

Few would argue with the claim that an "experiment" such as this was a bold step, but there are some who would question whether the "departure from the past" it represented was so radical. In fact, the phenomenon of foreigners working for Chinese and Chinese Government offices, in particular, has a long history.

Historical Background

In the latter part of the nineteenth century, Robert Hart, a British citizen was employed by the Qing court to administer the empire's sprawling tax and customs system. Nearly three hundred years before Hart, Johann Adam Schall von Bell (1591–1666), a Jesuit priest from Italy, served the Ming and Qing courts as scientific adviser, emissary, and interpreter. And if the definition of "foreigners" is taken more broadly to include non-Western peoples, the historical record shows that as far back as the Tang Dynasty, if not earlier, Sogdians, Turks, and the representatives of various other Central Asian peoples—were employed by Chinese as entertainers, domestics, and even soldiers. Filling in the spaces between these well-documented cases are accounts of numerous, yet lesser-known, medical practitioners, military advisers and science experts, who have at different times in China's long history been engaged in the service of Chinese imperial offices and government bureaus.

Accounts that chart the history of foreigners in the employ of Chinese, although not numerous, have been written. Jonathan Spence's "To Change China: Western Advisers in China", for example, chronicles the exploits of foreign missionaries, soldiers, doctors, teachers, engineers, and revolutionaries who have served China over the course of nearly four centuries.[1] Anne-Marie Brady's more overtly political "Making the foreign serve China", picks up where Spence left off and tells the story of foreigners who came to contribute to the post-1949 Chinese Government, paying particular attention to the ways in which the Government took advantage of their contribution and, more often than not, manipulated it to achieve its own ends.[2] As rich and varied as these accounts are, not one of them considers the most recent development in the history of foreigners in the employ of Chinese. Yet it is precisely in the current era that the greatest departure from the past and the most significant transformation in this relationship has occurred.

CURRENT VIEW

In this most recent phase of development, an unprecedented explosion in commercial activity and corresponding increase in the number of Chinese enterprises across all sectors has created new employment opportunities for Chinese and non-Chinese alike. Coincident with the increase in the number of foreigners working for Chinese corporate entities, there has been an expansion in the variety of roles they occupy as well as the scope. Many of these are commercial positions that are commensurate with the operations of an enterprise and quite different from the largely bureaucratic or imperial-related profiles of the past. An even more fundamental change, and arguably the most consequential, is that the vast majority of foreigners working for Chinese companies today are not adventurers, fortune-seekers, and revolutionaries who have traveled to China seeking fame and riches. They are salespeople, product managers, technicians, and other professionals who very likely have not made the

---

[1] Spence, Jonathan, *To Change China: Western Advisers in China*, Penguin, 2002 (reprint).

[2] Brady, Anne-Marie, *Making the Foreign Serve China: Managing Foreigners in the People's Republic*, Rowman & Littlefield, 2003.

journey all the way to China, but have been hired by Chinese companies in the cities, towns and countries where they live. Data points such as the ones below provide ample evidence for this real and growing trend.

> 82% (17,600) of workers employed by the Chinese National Petroleum Corporation (CNPC) in Africa are local hires. To support its operations in Zambia, the Chinese National Minerals Corporation has hired 12,500 local workers. ("2013 Report" 2013)

> In the U.S., Chinese investments support about 80,000 domestic jobs, a five-fold increase in the past five years and a recent study by the Rhodium Group, a U.S. research firm, predicts that a doubling of Chinese investment in the US by 2020 will generate on the order of 200,000-400,000 additional jobs. (Anderlini 2015)

> Hi-tech giant, Huawei has announced that it will add 5,500 employees in Europe over the next 5 years and plans to double the number of European scientists and engineers to 1,700 in three years to realize its regional R&D ambitions. ("Huawei to Hire" 2014)

These references and others like them form the outline for a new chapter in the history of foreigners employed by Chinese that is just now unfolding. To fully appreciate the story that is being told in this chapter, however, it is instructive to take a closer look at some actual cases.

Huawei: Shifting the Paradigm

Held up as a model for the global expansion of Chinese firms, telecommunications equipment provider Huawei today claims customers in more than 170 countries around the world and thanks to the sustained demand of those customers for its products Huawei has since 2011 recognized more revenue from its overseas business than it has from its business in China. Over the same period of time, the ranks of Huawei's foreign staff have swelled to more than 20,000.[3] The employees who fill out those ranks work in capacities whose diversity and range far exceeds that of roles occupied by foreigners at any time in the past.

---

[3] *Source* "Caring for Employees" section in: Huawei Sustainability Report (online) 2018, https://www.huawei.com/us/about-huawei/sustainability/win-win-development/develop_love [The report states that the company employs more than 28,000 staff outside China and assumes "a localization rate of 70%"].

In 2012, for example, Huawei hired Donald Purdy, a high-profile U.S. cybersecurity strategist and former Homeland Security official, as the company's Chief Security Officer to implement broad-based security training, build security into the company's product development process, and establish strategy and oversight committees across the company (Nakashima 2012). C. T. Johnson, a 45-year-old U.S. finance expert, joined the company as corporate financial controller in 2013. and then went on to lead a division within the company that negotiates sales contracts with customers (Osawa and Chu 2013).

The cases of Purdy, Johnson and hundreds of other employees like them is what makes Huawei such a compelling and instructive example for how the employment of foreigners in Chinese companies has evolved. However, to appreciate the full scope of the phenomenon and be able draw meaningful conclusions, it is instructive to consider a broader sample of cases based on the experience of workers employed in different industries and situated in different geographies.

GLOBAL EMPLOYMENT REPORT CARD: A MIXED RECORD

19 October 2012—Douglas Mwila, 24, had his ear sliced using a metal object by his supervisor Guo Haisheng at China Jiangxi while on duty.

All Africa Global Media

16 September 2016—An angry Chinese small-scale miner, Zeng Wuachin, has sacked his personal driver for allegedly stealing frog meat from his stew.

Ghana Star

29 June 2011—Last month cook Patrick Makaza quit his job at the restaurant saying he had been beaten by his bosses. "Working for these men from the East is Hell on Earth," he explained (Moyo 2011).

Mail & Guardian

Failing

The experience of Africans working for Chinese management as portrayed in the local press is typically highly-charged and conflict-ridden. The image of the Chinese boss these accounts promote is often that of an uncivilized and insensitive brute who insists on overtime for no pay, is not above stealing his employees' lunches, and has even been known to slice off the ear of a poor African worker or two along the way. Graphic reinforcement for this unkind image that has been established in print can be readily found in videos circulating widely on the Internet. One such video opens on the shocking scene of Ethiopian workers lined up in tight rows like a platoon of soldiers at the entrance to a Chinese company's manufacturing site on the outskirts of Ethiopia's capital, Addis Ababa. As the scene unfolds, the workers march forward under the watchful eye of a Chinese supervisor who shouts marching orders into a bullhorn. Although the scenes introduced in the video, like the accounts that appear in the press, are so extreme that they stretch credulity, they cannot be entirely dismissed as pure fabrication either given the well-documented evidence of confrontations, some fatal, that have occurred between local workers and Chinese management over the past few years.[4]

There are some who contend that such a confrontational relationship between management and workers is inherent to the risky and often dangerous operating environment in the extractive industries that many Chinese companies in Africa represent. It would be tempting, therefore, to conclude that the experience of Africans working for Chinese is unique to Africa and largely dependent on the nature of the work and the composition of the industries represented. However, records of incidents involving Chinese companies in other geographies and representing other industries suggest there are other factors that need to be taken into consideration.

Fuyao: Labor Unrest
When the Fuyao Glass Industry Group, a Chinese supplier of glass used in automobiles, bought and refurbished an old GM plant in Dayton, Ohio, it hired more than one-thousand five-hundred workers from the area to staff the new facility and at the time was widely praised for injecting new life into an otherwise moribund local economy. However, less than two years later, workers who eagerly joined the company when it opened found themselves locked in a contentious relationship with the company's management. What began as a trickle of isolated "incidents" involving disagreements between local workers and Chinese management soon became a steady stream of formal "cases" that raised concern

[4]Fifty-one miners at the Chambishi mine in Zambia in 2005, were killed in a blast that was attributed to mismanagement by the Chinese company managing the mine. In 2006, a violent protest broke out at the same mine over poor wages (Yang 2008). In 2012, Workers killed a Chinese manager during a dispute over pay at the Collum coal mine in Sinazongwe, Zambia (BBC online—August 5, 2012).

among members of the community, attracted media coverage, and eventually appeared as an issue to be addressed on the agendas of local government officials.

One manager claimed he was dismissed because he was not Chinese and pointed out that with his departure the director of Human Resources would be the only member of the executive team who was not Chinese (Scheiber and Bradsher 2017). Those who remained complained that Chinese management demonstrated little interest in even engaging with the Americans let alone sharing responsibility for decision making. A growing number of workers on the factory floor complained of conditions so unsafe that some even filed formal complaints. Finally, local media reported instances of employees who had allegedly been disciplined because they had not applied for leave far enough in advance. The increase in the number of such cases and the severity of the claims on which they were founded eventually attracted the attention of the Occupational Safety and Health Administration (OSHA) and convinced the agency to initiate a formal investigation into the incidents reported. The investigation revealed that management was so focused on increasing speed and wringing out efficiencies that it compromised worker safety by instructing workers to cut corners on standard operating procedures. Based on this and other similar reports, the office that carried out the investigation came to the conclusion that Fuyao was guilty of negligence and fined the company $100,000 (Gnau 2017). The growing labor unrest also attracted the attention of the United Auto Workers of America (UAW) and prompted the union's leadership to initiate a campaign in support of Fuyao's local workers ("Glass plant workers file details dangers" 2017). In response, the company's embattled CEO, Cao Dewang, defended the actions of his management team claiming that the quality of the work did not meet company standards and that local workers had consistently failed to follow management direction ("Chinese Tycoon Rebuts" 2017).

Maxwell Alves Solicitors: Discrimination
In London, papers filed with an employment tribunal detailed a racial discrimination suit brought by attorney Robert Smith against his former employers, Maxwell Alves Solicitors. Mr. Smith alleged unfair dismissal after the firm's Chinese management informed him that they had no work for his "kind" and demonstrated a clear preference for hiring

Chinese lawyers (Taher 2014). Mr. Smith surmised that his dismissal had been precipitated by his intervention in an argument between the head of the firm and a senior director during which he had pronounced their behavior "disgraceful". By intervening in such a direct way, he believed he had inadvertently made the firm's principals feel as though he was trying to undermine their authority. The firm claimed they made him redundant because he did not speak Chinese.

Following a review of these filings, reports, and statements we can identify a number of consistent themes and common sources of contention that characterize the experience of foreigners working in Chinese companies.

1. Chinese companies put a premium on speed and push employees to cut corners at the expense of standard operating procedures.
2. Management in Chinese companies demonstrate an insensitivity towards racial diversity and a lack of respect for the cultures of the localities where they operate.
3. Local staff are consistently excluded from decision making and don't feel that their views are taken into account.
4. Common to all geographies is the perception that Chinese companies are highly-hierarchical and managed in a command-and-control fashion.

The conclusion one draws from these vignettes is that, no matter whether you are an Ethiopian factory worker, an American machinist, or a British solicitor, if you are faced with the prospect of working for a Chinese company and a Chinese boss, it is very likely that the relationship will be a contentious one and that it quite possibly will degrade to a point where, to paraphrase the Zambian cook quoted earlier in this chapter, working with the "men from the East" is like "Hell on Earth."

This less than favorable image of Chinese management that has been promoted has, in quite a number of cases, hampered the efforts of Chinese companies to hire local staff and take advantage of their contributions. If even half the tales of Chinese mismanagement and accounts of poor working conditions circulating are any indication, it is easy to understand why local candidates Chinese companies would like to employ might be less than enthusiastic about considering such an opportunity. Rebalancing this perception is a key challenge that nearly all Chinese companies face in recruiting and retaining qualified foreign talent.

As compelling as these accounts are and as real the consequences, their strident tone leads one to question their veracity and wonder whether there isn't another side of the story to be told that could be the source for a more balanced assessment.

Passing

In contrast to the lurid accounts of abuse and mistreatment that are routinely presented for public consumption, discussions with many Africans who work for, or have worked for, Chinese firms reveal a more nuanced picture.

The video that depicts the working conditions at the Chinese company operating in Ethiopia as closer to a bootcamp than a place of employment nevertheless concludes with interviews of Chinese managers and Ethiopian workers that are professional in tone, strictly focused on the company's operations, and do not sound any notes of conflict or dissatisfaction. The Chinese interviewed describe the challenges they face maintaining sufficient quality control and production efficiency. The local Ethiopian workers emphasize the value of the experience working in the company and the opportunity it offers for skill development and training.

Huajian: A Stepping Stone

This is in line with the reports from quite a number of African workers, especially recent graduates, who actively seek out employment opportunities in Chinese companies because they view Chinese companies as a source of skill development and a stepping stone to a better career. Young Ethiopian workers who claimed they could get a higher salary elsewhere nevertheless chose to work at Chinese shoe manufacturer Huajian's factory outside of Addis Ababa because they saw an opportunity to develop new techniques for making shoes, get experience operating more advanced machines, and even learn how to speak some Chinese (Tang 2016, page 114). Echoing the sentiments of the Ethiopian shoe manufacturers, a young Senegalese engineer explains that he purposely sought out employment at a Chinese company because "the Chinese have a very strong work ethic; you get to learn a lot more than you would at a Senegalese company" ("African Workers Share" 2013). This is a particularly attractive proposition for a younger generation of educated Africans who see employment at a Chinese firm and the prospect for professional training it offers as a key stepping stone on the path towards realizing a longer-term dream of starting a company. It is very common for young African engineers to start their own companies after they have completed a two or three-year stint at a Chinese company and acquired requisite skills and experience.

There are quite a number of other videos and related sources circulating on the Internet that also tell a story very different from the one that features Ethiopian staff marching in formation before a Chinese boss who is barking orders into a bullhorn.

Tides and Times: All in the Family

Asked to share his thoughts on working for Chinese management in one such video, an American manager at the Chinese-owned Tides and Times Group explains that the company's Chinese president, Jimmy Lee, "counts us all as family." Greenfield Industries of South Carolina, another company under Chinese ownership, enjoys a relatively 'harmonious' corporate environment where Chinese management and local employees appear as "partners in building a successful future".

During the cameo interviews with local employees that anchor these videos there are a number of recurring themes that come to the surface: "The company is like a family" is one of the more prominent. Not only do workers enjoy close relations with each other and with Chinese management, but the company actively promotes family values and offers generous policies that support this family-friendly culture. The local employees interviewed also emphasize the Chinese company's contribution to the local economy, highlighting in particular its effectiveness in generating opportunities for employment.

Thailand: A Long-Term Commitment

Expressing sentiments similar to those of their American and African counterparts, employees working for a Chinese company in Thailand note that under Chinese management the work tends to be rushed and deadlines short, tendencies that lead to concerns about quality. "Increasing speed seems to be more important than insuring quality," observed one Thai line manager (Bunchapattanasakda and Wong 2010, page 279). In addition to raising general complaints about the low level of understanding for the local culture and a lack of sensitivity for cultural differences, some staff complain that Thai employees are very rarely invited to meetings with Chinese managers and feel excluded from decision-making. Yet in spite of these grievances, the Thai employees expressed confidence in the company's future, felt they were adequately supported by the Chinese management, and especially valued Chinese management's commitment to the long-term.

Like the Thais, German employees whose firms have been acquired by Chinese firms consistently express their appreciation for the Chinese commitment to the long term. This positive evaluation stands in marked contrast to the less than favorable assessment many Germans have of American firms whose management they disparage for their myopia and obsession with short-term profit. Even though the Germans employed in Chinese firms find some aspects of the Chinese style of management a bit out of the ordinary and sometimes annoying, such as the more fluid sense of time and less than well-defined working hours that characterize the Chinese workplace, they, by and large, have adopted a "business–as–usual" attitude and demonstrate a willingness to make accommodations ("anpassen") to maintain the status quo and get along with Chinese management. A manager at a German company now under Chinese ownership remarks, "you have to be very flexible when you work for the Chinese. It's not uncommon for schedules to change on the fly" (Sobel 2013).[5]

These testimonies and accounts sourced from different locations around the world suggest that, initial impressions to the contrary (and not very positive impressions, at that), the experience of foreigners working for Chinese companies is quite varied and, furthermore, that the relationship between foreign workers and Chinese management is to some extent shaped by local culture and geography. Gaining a better understanding for how these factors influence that relationship and shape the experience of foreigners working for Chinese management requires a more structured approach that makes use of a framework and methodologies suited to the purpose.

---

[5] My translation of the following: "Man muß sehr flexibel sein, wenn man für die Chinesen arbeitet, denn es kommt bei ihnen häufig vor, daß die Zeitpläne kurzfristig verändert werden".

GENESIS OF A FRAMEWORK

Even the most cursory investigation of areas where cultures and companies intersect and influence one another is bound to turn up the name of Dutch sociologist, Geert Hofstede. A pioneer in the field of organizational culture, an area of study that considers the effect of national culture on corporate organizational behavior. Hofstede took initial steps towards developing the models and the insights on which the tenets of organizational culture are based while serving as Director of Personnel Research at IBM in the early 1980s. Through rigorous analysis of the responses to thousands of surveys he distributed to employees in company locations around the world, Hofstede developed novel insights into the interplay between national and corporate cultures. He then distilled his insights into a multi-dimensional model that formalized understanding of cultural difference.

In its basic form, the model comprises four dimensions—*Power Distance, Individualism, Uncertainty Avoidance, Masculinity*—each one of which makes use of a scoring system devised to measure the extent to which a given culture prizes or privileges a specific cultural value. The brief overview of the model's dimensions that follows presents the essential characteristics of each respective dimension.

The *Power-Distance* dimension profiles the way in which power in a society is distributed; The *Individualism-Collectivism* dimension captures the degree of interdependence a society maintains among its members; The *Masculine-Feminine* dimension characterizes the way in which values are distributed between genders; The *Uncertainty Avoidance* dimension gauges a society's tolerance for ambiguity and degree of comfort in unstructured situations. The basic four-dimensional model was eventually supplemented with two additional dimensions: the *Short-term vs. Long-term* dimension that considers the degree to which societies maintain links with their past and prioritize social goals while dealing with the challenges of the present and future and the *Restraint vs. Indulgence* dimension that describes a culture's socialization process with a focus on how members are raised and is defined by the extent to which people try to control basic desires and impulses.

The China Cultural Dimension

Evaluating Chinese social characteristics through the lens of Hofstede's model yields a cultural mapping that provides quantitative context for some familiar cultural traits and national characteristics (see Chart 1.1).

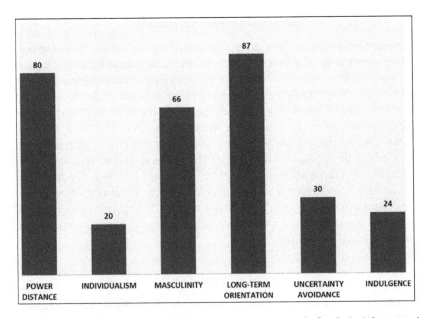

Chart 1.1   China's cultural fingerprint (*Source* www.hofstede-insights.com/country-comparison/)

China's scores on the *Long-Term, Power Distance,* and *Masculinity* dimensions, among the highest among cultures studied,[6] are characteristic of a culture whose members are pragmatic, exhibit a propensity to save, and have a high degree of perseverance. It is also a society whose members have a healthy respect for authority and are flexible enough to adapt easily to changed conditions. At the other end of the spectrum, the scores China exhibits on the *Individualism* and *Uncertainty Avoidance* dimensions are among the lowest of all cultures evaluated, mark China as a highly collectivist society that privileges personal relationships. China's particularly low score on the *Uncertainty Avoidance* dimension implies a society whose approach to laws and rules is fluid and flexible enough to accommodate and adapt to actual conditions.

[6]Notably Malaysia, Philippines and Saudi Arabia on the Power Distance dimension and Mexico and Japan on the Masculinity dimension.

Methodology and Application

The most common application of these methodologies in a Chinese corporate context is as a practical aid for the China-based foreign executive who wants to be more effective at managing a staff of local Chinese employees. Accordingly, the comparison of cultural characteristics on which the aid is based is exclusively between the culture of the executive's country of origin, usually a Western country, and local Chinese culture. A companion study that considers how this cross-cultural framework could be applied to the case of the Chinese executive tasked with managing foreign staff does not exist. With an eye towards addressing this omission and gaining deeper insight into the conditions that define the experience of local employees working for Chinese companies we will apply the framework and methodologies introduced here to some of the cases presented previously.

Cross-Cultural Analysis

A cursory review of the cases considered leads to some initial conclusions about the differences in the way employees from different countries and cultures relate to Chinese management and experience working in a Chinese corporate environment.

The relationship that Germans and Thais working for Chinese companies have with Chinese management in the cases considered is clearly less confrontational than that of employees in African countries and in the U.S.. Common to both Germans and Thais is the value they place on the perceived commitment of Chinese firms to the long-term, a quality to which the American and the African employees ascribe less value and to which they consequently pay less attention. Using this preliminary view as a baseline, we can now take advantage of the framework presented to better understand what accounts for these differences. *Long-Term Orientation* and *Individualism* stand out as dimensions that have the potential to yield the greatest insight:

Long-Term Orientation
A comparison of countries along the *Long Term Orientation* dimension (see Chart 1.2) reveals that the positions of the Germans and Chinese are remarkably similar and, moreover, are quite a bit higher than those of any of the other cultures considered. The close positioning of the

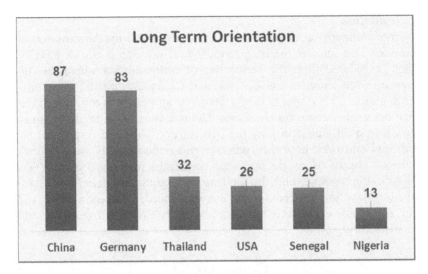

Chart 1.2 Long-term orientation comparison (*Source* www.hofstede-insights. com/country-comparison/)

two countries on this dimension provides some explanation for why the long-term orientation of Chinese companies strikes a particularly sympathetic chord with German (as well as Thai) employees and why the German assessment of Chinese management is more favorable than that of those who are members of other cultures. This alignment of values is further reinforced by the coincidence of scores (66) that the Chinese and Germans record on the *Masculinity* dimension, implying a common emphasis on ambition, achievement, and accomplishment.

In contrast to Germany and Thailand, the position of African countries[7] relative to China on these dimensions lies at the opposite end of the spectrum. On the *Long-Term Orientation* dimension, most notably, none of the African countries considered has a score greater than 30. At 13, Nigeria's score, for instance, is less than a quarter of China's. The magnitude of this disparity is one indication for why the experience of Africans in the employ of Chinese companies is so plagued with misunderstandings, misalignment of expectations, and conflict.

[7]A random sampling of countries where China has commercial interest and companies operating.

Individualism

As large a disparity as exists between the Chinese and the Africans in how they view and valorize the long-term, the relationship is almost reversed when considered from the perspective of *Individualism* where the difference in the scores of the US (90) and China (20) on this dimension is significant. This disparity is reinforced by an equally significant difference between the two on the *Power Distance* dimension implying, most obviously, a difference in how the two cultures view and respect formal authority and even how they perceive and define "truth" and "rules". This is a source of insight into why Americans workers at a plant like Fuyao's, for example, find the Chinese willingness to circumvent established production procedures to increase speed so objectionable and why the Chinese find the Americans work habits so irresponsible and unsatisfactory.

COUNTERPOINT

In testimony submitted on behalf of the aggrieved attorney, Mr Smith, legal representatives asserted that their client was so humiliated by his sacking that he had to take antidepressants to cope. Under the circumstances, a jury could be excused if they dismissed this and other similar claims as the exaggerations of a disgruntled employee and the posturing of a team of legal advisers eager to make a case for greater restitution. However, a jury briefed with the insights that a cross-cultural framework such as Hofstede's yields might temper their judgement with the understanding that the relationship between foreign staff and Chinese management can indeed be quite intense and that claims such as those made by Mr. Smith and his advisors may not be entirely the product of unfounded exaggeration. However, before applying insights gained from study of Hofstede's model to arrive at a more informed judgement on the Smith case, the jury must be made aware of the framework's inherent shortcomings and take them into careful account before proceeding.

Although Hofstede's cultural model and methods have been widely adopted and applied, a more thorough study of China's past and a closer examination of its present surface facts and conditions that Hofstede's model and others like it do not adequately account for or accurately describe.

The Chinese Rebuttal

"A Critique of Hofstede's Cross Cultural Research As It Applies To Chinese Culture" (Chen 2008) points to specific facts of Chinese social history that challenge some of the basic assumptions on which Hofstede's model is based. As a general principle, the 'Critique' asserts that a number of the cultural characteristics Hofstede's model depicts as standing in opposition to one another can actually coexist and that Chinese society presents a ready case for this 'coexistence'. "Individualism" and "Collectivism", for example, positioned as an opposing pair of values at the ends of a dimension on which Hofstede's model is based, coalesce in Chinese society to constitute an important part of its unique nature. The authors of the 'Critique' find support for their assertion in Chinese social history and structure. They first trace China's evolution from an agrarian-based society that defined the country throughout most of its history into a more collective-oriented culture that still characterizes the country today, a characteristic that, when considered on its own, justifies the values attributed to it within the dimensions of Hofstede's model and its position on the Collectivist continuum. However, the authors emphasize that beneath this collectivist exterior lies a strong individualist streak that is firmly anchored in the family unit that forms the nucleus of the Chinese social structure. It is this blend of Individualism and Collectivism that distinguishes Chinese culture from other cultures and keeps it from being neatly classified within the constraints of Hofstede's theoretical construct. As illustration, the authors consider the position of China's culture in relation to those of Japan and the U.S., countries that the authors situate at opposing ends of the Individualism-Collectivism spectrum. They reason apophatically that because Chinese society is not as extreme in its individualistic tendency as the U.S. and is not as extreme in its collectivist tendency as Japan, it must, by definition, fall somewhere between the two and, by default, incorporate elements of both. However, because these two aspects in Chinese society are so tightly fused it is impossible to say with any certainty where along the continuum between Individualism and Collectivism Chinese society should be situated. What is more likely, the authors conclude, is that China can't be positioned anywhere within the "Individualism-Collectivism" dimension as defined because in China's case making such a distinction between Individualism and Collectivism is neither relevant nor applicable.

A Dose of Reality

Taras and Steel (Taras and Steel 2009) arrive at a similar conclusion but through an approach that is more grounded in the present than the past and in which China figures as an examplary case rather than as an exclusive one. In the well-documented individualism and independence of China's Millenials, Taras and Steel find ample evidence for their claim that a number of key assumptions on which Hofstede's model is based are flawed. In fact, it is not so much because of their behavior that China's Millenials figure so prominently in Taras and Steel's thinking and makes them such a compelling case, it is because of the magnitude of the difference in behavior that separates them from their parents' generation as well as the pace at which that change has occurred. Hofstede's model is predicated on the assumption that cultures and the values they represent are relatively static and slow to change. Taras and Steel insist that cultures are dynamic constructs that change in response to changes in the environment and hold up China's Millenials and their behavior patterns as proof. This cultural mutability for which China's Millenials are a reference point poses a direct challenge to the some of the basic underpinnings on which Hofstede's model is founded (Taras and Steel 2009).

China's Millenials as a group form what sociologists refer to as a "cohort", a well-established construct in which members develop common characteristics as the result of a shared social history (Taras and Steel). New cohorts are generated regularly (e.g. Baby Boomers, Generation X, Generation Y, etc.) and the existence of one such as China's Millenials represent is an incontrovertible indicator of cultural change.[8]

Hofstede also assumes that the explanation for individual and national phenomena observed is to be found in a country's underlying cultural values (e.g., Highly individualistic American society as the driver for the accumulation of such substantial personal wealth in the U.S.). Taras and Steel posit that cultural values change under the influence of socioeconomic developments and in a direction that is highly predictable. Chinese Millenials are the poster children for Taras and Steel's claim that Individualism results from economic growth not the other way around, as Hofstede would have it (Taras and Steel 2009, page 10).

Finally, Taras and Steel hypothesize that societies converge around some common set of values as they modernize and, once again, look to

---

[8] Ibid., page 9.

China as a clear and convenient proof point for this convergence. They observe consistent change towards lower Power Distance and higher Individualism and Achievement Orientation worldwide, especially in a country such as China that has experienced such dramatic economic and political change in its recent past (Taras and Steel 2009, page 8).

The issues these critiques raise and the conclusions they present are a reminder of the difficulty inherent in trying to distill the characteristics of a complex culture with thousands of years of history and over a billion inhabitants into a neat set of quantitative measures.

Considered together, constructs such as Hofstede's and critiques such as Taras/Steel's have something to say about cross-cultural relations that is of value and practical use to the foreign employee in a Chinese firm. Hofstede's model and associated methodologies are a convenient way to conceptualize and characterize complex cross-cultural interactions and, as a frame for the experience of foreign employees in Chinese companies, offer some insight into the forces that shape the relationship with a Chinese employer. Taras and Steel's pragmatic and practical approach, based as it is on concrete cases drawn from contemporary society balances the abstractions and generalizations that are the unavoidable shortcoming of a model such as Hofstede's. In plotting out a rough course by which foreign employees can orient themselves as they navigate the unfamiliar and often challenging territory of a Chinese workplace, the chapters that follow look to Hofstede as a source of general direction and to Taras/Steel as a source of practical and real-world examples of issues foreigners working for Chinese are likely to encounter.

Outline

The chapters that follow fit into a coherent structure that comprises three parts:

Foundation reviews what foreigners employed in Chinese organizations do, where they work, and how they contribute.

Experience presents the different aspects of a foreign employee's experience in the Chinese workplace and highlights associated challenges.

Activities describes activities foreign employees engage in day-to-day and the role those activities play in determining the employee's success on the job.

Foundation

Many of the professions that foreigners employed by Chinese represent are the direct result of China's most recent economic, political, and social transformation. Pilots, Athletes, and Super Models are a few representative professions, each one of which has its own unique profile and conditions. However, it is through identification and analysis of what connects them—career-focused, consumer-oriented, and compensation-driven—that broader conclusions about the experience of foreigners in the employ of Chinese and the evolution of Chinese society in the twenty-first century can be drawn.

Chinese enterprises with global reach, another exponent of China's economic transformation, have emerged as the largest employer of foreign talent due in large part to the aggressiveness with which they have expanded into markets around the world. Hundreds of foreign staff work in the headquarters of Chinese companies. Thousands more work in representative offices overseas. Whether in China or abroad the roles that foreign employees play in Chinese enterprises have become increasingly varied and the contributions they make indispensable.

Experience

Building on the **Foundation** that established what foreign employees do and where they do it, Experience considers how they do what they do and what they experience along the way. Work-life balance, career development, and job definition, all challenges common to employees in companies around the world, take on a different complexion in a Chinese enterprise. Exclusion and isolation appear in a variety of forms are and an unavoidable part of a foreign employee's experience in a Chinese company. There are a number of approaches and techniques foreign employees can employ to address these challenges and overcome them.

Activities

The **Activities** section complements the exploration of a foreign employee's day-to-day experience in a Chinese workplace that was the focus of the **Experience** section by describing more concretely the types of activities a foreign employee engages in and serves as a guide that a foreign employee can follow to increase effectiveness and success in a Chinese workplace. Highlighted are corporate events and their relevance to the foreign employee's job as well as corporate communications and techniques the foreign employee can take advantage of to become a more effective communicator in a Chinese organization.

A View to the Future

The chapter that concludes the study considers the shape that the future of employment for foreigners in Chinese organizations might take. Emerging trends shaped by demographics, technologies, and national policies will recast the nature of the work that foreigners do, how they relate to the Chinese who employ them, and perhaps even redefine what it means to be "foreign". However, before engaging in any further speculation about the future and the impact these emerging trends may have we will, as a next and most immediate step, make a foray into the past.

REFERENCES

"2013 Report on China-Africa Trade and Economic Relationship", Chinese Academy of International Trade and Economic Cooperation.

"African Workers Share Experiences at Chinese Factories", *Chinafrica*, March 27, 2013.

Anderlini, Jamal. "Surge in U.S Workers Employed By Chinese Firms", *Financial Times*, May 15, 2015.

Bland, Ben, "Young Foreigners Embedded in Local Government", *Financial Times*, November 16, 2015.

Brady, Anne-Marie, *Making the Foreign Serve China: Managing Foreigners in the People's Republic*, Rowman & Littlefield, 2003.

Bunchapattanasakda, Chanchai, and Wong, Pisit, "Management Practices of Chinese Managers in Chinese MNCs Operating in Bangkok", *Cross Cultural Management: An International Journal*, Vol. 17, No. 3, 2010, pages 268–282.

Chen, Dongping, "yi zhongguo wenhua wei shijiao de huofusitaide kua wenhua yanjiu ji qi pingjia", Vol. 1, 2008, Nankai University Business School in Jianghuai Luntan, pages 123–127.

"Chinese Tycoon Rebuts Untrue New York Times Report About His American Factory", *China: Xinhua*, June 20, 2017.

"Glass Plant Workers File Detail Dangers at Fuyao" (online), UAW.org, May 16, 2017.

Gnau, Tom, "OSHA Levies New Safety Violation Against Fuyao", *Dayton Daily News*, June 20, 2017.

"Huawei to Hire 5,500 More Workers in Europe", *South China Morning Post*, June 11, 2014.

Moyo, Jason, "Working for Chinese Is 'Hell on Earth'", *Mail & Guardian*, June 29, 2011.

Nakashima, Ellen. "Huawei Hires Former Defense Contractor Official", *Washington Post*, July 10, 2012.

Osawa, Juro, and Chu, Kathy. "Huawei Hires Foreign Executives in Global Push", *Wall Street Journal*, November 24, 2013.

Scheiber, Noam, and Bradsher, Keith, "Culture Clash at a Chinese-Owned Plant in Ohio", *New York Times*, June 10, 2017.

Sobel, Dmitri, „Mein Chef ist ein Chinese", *Express*, February 26, 2013, www. express.de.

Spence, Jonathan, *To Change China: Western Advisers in China*, Penguin, 2002 (reprint).

Taher, Abul, "My Chinese Bosses Sacked Me for Being British", *Mail on Sunday*, February 27, 2014.

Tang, Xiaoyang, "Does Chinese Employment Benefit Africans? Investigating Chinese Enterprises and Their Operations in Africa", *African Studies Quarterly*, Vol. 16, Nos. 3–4, December 2016, pages 107–128.

Taras, Vasyl, and Steel, Piers, "Beyond Hofstede: Challenging the Ten Commandments of Cross-Cultural Research", in Nakata, C. (ed.) Beyond Hofstede: Cultural Frameworks for Global Marketing and Management, Palgrave Macmillan, Chicago, IL, July 2009.

Yang, Chloe, "Corporate Social Responsibility and China's Overseas Extractive Industry Operations: Achieving Sustainable Natural Resource Extraction", *Foundation for Environmental Security and Sustainability* (FESS), Issue Brief, 2008.

CHAPTER 2

History Lessons

Chinese history is a rich source of insight that has direct relevance for the experience of a foreigner employed by a Chinese firm today and a source of lessons that foreign employees can apply to meet the challenges they are likely to encounter in a Chinese workplace. Undertaking a review of history is worthwhile because it is only with historical context that the present can be properly evaluated and understood. However, the task of identifying applicable lessons and finding relevant insights over the period of time that Chinese history spans and the sheer number of events, people, and places it encompasses is a daunting one that can only be accomplished by establishing a solid foundation, identifying common denominators and finding relevant models.

Western accounts of foreigners in the employ of Chinese typically take as their starting point the arrival in China of the Jesuit missionary Matteo Ricci in the seventeenth century. Given the contributions Ricci made in areas as diverse as astronomy, mathematics, and geography and the impact he had on generations of Westerners who followed in his footsteps, Ricci certainly bears mention. However, if one takes "employment" in its strictest definition Ricci was not, technically-speaking, "employed" by the members of the imperial court whom he advised and instructed. Moreover, if the definition of the term 'foreigner' is broadened to include non-Chinese, in general, then the record of foreigners in the employ of Chinese can be extended back hundreds of years before Ricci's arrival to at least the Tang Dynasty, if not before.

© The Author(s) 2020
P. Ross, *Barriers to Entry*,
https://doi.org/10.1007/978-981-32-9566-7_2

FOUNDATION

As far away in time as it is from the current era, the Tang Dynasty (618–907 A.D) is, in many respects, surprisingly close in spirit. A vibrant and open society, the Tang engaged foreigners on a large scale and employed them in many different capacities. It is in this diversity of roles that foreigners occupied, in areas as disparate as the military, entertainment and commerce, that the Tang can be seen as a kind of template for the range of positions foreigners would hold in the years to come. It serves as a base on which to develop an understanding for the experience of foreigners in the employ of Chinese and the dynamics that conditioned the relationship between Chinese Employer and foreign Employed.

COMMON DENOMINATORS

The only way to understand and make sense of the experience of foreigners in the employ of Chinese over the hundreds of years of history that have elapsed between the end of the Tang Dynasty and the beginning of the twenty-first century is to find a focus and commonalities. A thematic approach makes it possible to organize, rationalize, and ultimately draw valuable and relevant conclusions. Through this approach it is possible to see more clearly where the twenty-first century fits into the story of foreigners in the employ of Chinese and understand how those who are employed by Chinese in the current era differentiate themselves from their predecessors.

MODELS

Much can be learned from the experience of others with an eye towards identifying the steps they took that led to their success or, conversely, the missteps that brought about their failure. In the case of foreigners in the employ of Chinese, the challenge one faces is not of having too few relevant cases from which to choose, but rather of having too many. The most applicable ones are those that are a source of insight and illustration of lessons learned that are as valid to the situation of the foreign employee in a Chinese enterprise today as they were then.

> The Western courtesan with features like a flower
> Stands by the wine warmer and laughs with the breath of Spring
> Dancing in a dress of sheer silk gauze, she asks

"You won't be going anywhere, sir, surely not before you are drunk" (Whitfield 2015, page 146)

MODEL EMPLOYEES: THE SOGDIANS

Entertainers

The 'Sogdian Whirl', all the rage at the height of the Tang Dynasty in the eighth century, was a twirling dance, typically performed on a red felt carpet, that incorporated many of the gestures, facial expressions, and eye movements associated with traditional Indian dance. Its prëeminent practitioners were entertainers from Kucha, a cultural oasis and commercial hub on the ancient Silk Road, whose geographic location, according to the prevailing Tang cosmology, qualified its inhabitants as 'Western'. Drawn to the imperial capital Chang'An (today, Xi'an) for the opportunities of employment the city offered, Kuchan musicians, dancers, and singers were common fixtures in the bars, teahouses and pleasure quarters that were the Tang Dynasty's centers of entertainment. Kuchans were also frequently engaged as performers at the Tang imperial court (Photo 2.1). The Xuanzong emperor (712–756), a patron of the arts and an accomplished performer in his own right, purportedly retained a corps of 30,000 entertainers, a large number of whom came from Kucha and other towns that dotted the Central Asian plateau.

The residents of Kucha were a people of Iranian ancestry known as 'Sogdian' whose territory stretched across parts of today's Uzbekistan and Tajikistan. Contemporary accounts of the Sogdians suggest that they enjoyed a reputation for commercial prowess that was on a par with that which they enjoyed for their ability to entertain:

Entrepreneurs

These people are skillful merchants...They excel at commerce and love profits; from the time a man is twenty, he goes to neighboring kingdoms. (Lung 2011)
(Lerner [2001, page 222] translation of Xintangshu 221: 6243–6244 in Lung 2011, page 151)

As itinerant merchants, the Sogdians plied an expansive network of trade routes that brought them into contact with a wide range of peoples who

Photo 2.1 Sogdian dancers (*Credit* Heavenly devas dancing on small carpets like the early Silk Road dancers, showing the Sogdian Whirl fully appropriated into the high style of Tang dance and art—the dance is refined into technical precision and Chinese silk billows with a light touch; Mogao Cave 220, Dunhuang. Tang dynasty [618–907], mural painting. After Wang Kefen, *Chinese Dance: An Illustrated History*, Beijing Dance Research Institute, 2000, image 517)

were the subjects of these 'neighboring kingdoms'. To facilitate the business transactions on which their far-reaching commercial activities depended, the Sogdians developed superior communications skills that included mastery of a number of local languages as well as a highly-tuned cross-cultural sensitivity. Because these skills were so highly valued, Sogdians who possessed them were frequently sought out as intermediaries by others whose capabilities in these areas were less well-developed. One of the largest employers of Sogdian talent was the Tang military whose officials often engaged Sogdians as emissaries whom they tasked with communicating, interpreting, and negotiating on their behalf with representatives of the nations arrayed along the Empire's borders. One such emissary, the Sogdian Shi Jiezhi, served the Tang military in this capacity on a number of occasions and the accounts of his missions, pieced together from extant sources, offer valuable insight into the nature of the relationship that existed between the Tang and the foreigners in their employ.

The available records reveal that sometime towards the end of the Summer of 842 Tang officials engaged Shi Jiezhi to approach a group of Uzbeks who had pitched their camp at a location whose proximity to the Empire's border was a little too close for the military's comfort. Acting under direct authority of the Tang military command, Shi Jiezhi was dispatched on a mission to request that the Uzbeks withdraw to a distance that the military deemed more acceptable. The trust that the Tang military officials placed in Shi Jiezhi and the confidence they demonstrated in his ability to carry out such a delicate mission is attested to in an official letter of introduction addressed to the Uzbek tribe's chieftan (Qaghan) that Shi Jiezhi was entrusted to deliver:

> Shi Jiezhi has long been at the capital.... We praise his insight on current exigencies...The Qaghan himself should judge [the current situation] by questioning [Shi Jiezhi] and quickly choose a good plan. (Lung 2011, page 141)

Shi Jiezhi apparently completed this mission to the satisfaction of his Tang employers as he was subsequently dispatched on a similar mission less than a year later. However, no sooner had Shi Jiezhi embarked on this second mission, then the Tang officials who had engaged him began to express misgivings. They raised concerns about his ability, wondering whether the message they had given him responsibility to transmit would indeed be delivered as intended and, once delivered, whether it would be presented in a manner befitting the circumstances. They also raised questions about his loyalty—suspecting that he might be sympathetic towards those whom he was meeting and could therefore be tempted into entering an alliance with them. The concern raised about the emissary's professional qualification is one that is a common and often unavoidable occupational hazard for any intermediary and stems from the inability of those dependent on the intermediary's services to have any direct means of validating whether his actions have, in fact, been carried out in accordance with expectations.[1] The concern about the emissary's

---

[1] Feldman in his consideration of the case of an intermediary between two parties of different cultures notes that the role of the intermediary very often is to "absorb cultural conflict" which often involves doing something inconsistent with one or both cultures behind the scenes. In: Feldman, Steven, *Trouble in the Middle: American-Chinese Business Relations, Culture, Conflict, and Ethics*, Routledge, London and New York, 2013.

integrity, by contrast, was more unique to the specific circumstances under which Shi Jiezhi was engaged and followed from the presumption of a natural affiliation between Uzbeks and Sogdians, a common misperception in the Tang that was perpetuated by a perceived racial similarity. What the case of Shi Jiezhi illustrates is just how tenuous the relationship between Chinese and foreigners in their employ can be and how consequential the role that ethnic bias can play in determining the level of trust on which the strength of that relationship depends.

As unjustified as we may find the Tang officials' prejudicial treatment of Shi Jiezhi and as unfounded as we may believe the grounds on which they based their mistrust, we must first consider the frame of reference within which they were formulating their judgements and the broader context that shaped their relationship with the Sogdians in their employ before calling them to account and leveling accusations. Were the Tang officials to be accused of prejudice and reprimanded for a lapse in judgement there is no question that they would turn to the historical record and in their defense recall events that took place a few decades before that Summer of 842.

Soldiers

Arguably the most well-known Sogdian in the history of the Tang Dynasty[2] (or the most notorious, depending on perspective) was a general in the Tang army named An Lushan who led a revolt in the middle of the eighth century that ultimately brought the Tang Empire to the brink of collapse. An Lushan's rise through the ranks of the Tang army to become one of its most well-known and well-respected commanders could hardly have been more improbable. Born in impecunious circumstances a world away, geographically and socially, from the corridors of imperial power he would later come to inhabit, An Lushan in his youth was better known for his insubordination and volatile temper than for his leadership ability. These character traits, not surprisingly, did little to endear him to his superiors and, on at least one occasion, very nearly cost him his life. That An Lushan, in spite of such an inauspicious beginning and the impediments posed by his less than ideal conduct, nevertheless managed to work his way into the upper echelons of Tang society and secure a place for himself in the highest ranks of the Tang military can be

---

[2] In fact, he was reputedly half-Sogdian and half Turkic.

attributed in equal parts to his own aptitude, seemingly innate, for cultivating relationships with those in positions of power and influence and to
the support of mentors who were willing to overlook his humble origins
and low social rank and were perceptive enough to glimpse flashes of talent that his character flaws otherwise obscured. An Lushan came to an
untimely end at the hands of his son in 757 and the rebellion he led was
ultimately suppressed by forces loyal to the emperor. However, even in
failure, he managed to secure a prominent place for himself in the annals
of Chinese history.

If An Lushan's rags-to-riches story was unique, his presence as a foreigner in the Tang military complex was not. His peers Ge Shuhan and
Shi Siming were just a few of the generals in the Tang army who claimed
Turkic, Tadzhik, and Uzbek ancestry. The presence of rank-and-file soldiers who hailed from across Central Asia was further evidence of just
how firmly entrenched non-Chinese were in the administration of the
Tang government and in the execution of its military affairs.

Model Employees—Summary

The Uzbek soldiers who served the Tang military in remote outposts on
the Empire's borders, the Kuchan performance artists who entertained
the Tang emperor on felt-covered stages, and the Sogdian envoys who
acted on behalf of Tang officials in negotiating agreements with the leaders of 'neighboring kingdoms' reflect the diversity of roles that foreigners occupied in the employ of Chinese more than a thousand years ago.
Moreover, the record of their experience offers valuable insight into the
nature of their relationship with the Chinese who employed them and
the forces within which it was forged. In essence, the ways in which the
Tang employed foreigners to communicate, negotiate, and even enter
into combat with other foreigners form, in their entirety, a complete
template for the range of roles that foreigners would come to play in the
service of military officers, imperial functionaries, government administrators, and even entertainers over the centuries that followed. In addition, the dimensions of the relationship between Chinese Employer and
foreign Employed, the fickle nature of trust, the cultural mispercep-
tions, and the influence of ethnic (racial) stereotyping as illuminated in
the Tang, reveal themselves as consistent thematic threads that weave
their way through the story of foreigners in the employ of Chinese as it
unfolds over the next thousand years.

SAVING SOULS, SAVING LIVES, SAVING CHINA

The few studies that tell that story, or even some part of it, typically proceed chronologically, detailing the exploits, accomplishments, and missteps of particularly noteworthy figures as they make their entrances and exits on and off the stage across which the *Sturm* and *Drang* of Chinese history has played itself out. The advantage of such a strictly chronological approach is its effectiveness in illuminating trends and charting the course of their evolution over an extended period of time. However, it is a method that is less well-suited to surfacing issues of greatest relevance to the foreigner who is trying to navigate the unfamiliar territory of a Chinese organization. Adopting an approach that is thematically-based as alternative has the advantage of providing a convenient way of rationalizing the diverse experiences of foreigners in the employ of Chinese and identifying common denominators that connect those experiences across lengthy periods of time and across the different ages by which that time is delineated. A number of potential candidates offer themselves for consideration: A theme based on professions, for example, might present a historical canvas that is peopled with soldiers hailing from different cultures and countries who at periodic junctures in China's past have served in the ranks of China's armies and followed its leaders onto the battlefield. Conversely, a culturally or ethnically-grounded theme might feature the experiences of representatives from a specific geography, say Europeans, across the full range of capacities in which they served Chinese officials and superiors (e.g. European soldiers, artists, doctors, etc.) Unfortunately, because of the inherent temporal or geographic limitations their definition imposes, these themes disqualify themselves from further consideration: A history of foreign soldiers in the employ of the Chinese military would reach its conclusion well before the beginning of the current era (i.e. starting with the economic reforms China initiated in the 1980s) and in so doing would exclude aspects of the story that are most relevant to this study and of greatest interest to foreigners who are in the employ of Chinese today. Similarly, using the experience of a specific cultural or ethnic group, say Europeans, as the lens through which that history is viewed would, even at its periphery, have a blind spot where the Tang Dynasty is concerned. It is an oversight that would result in omission of a critical part of the historical foundation on which the story of foreigners in the service of Chinese is based.

As alternative, a theme based on the basic motivations that prompted those who came to China to leave familiar surroundings and enter the service of a people with whom they had many cultural incompatibilities holds some promise. The most obvious advantage this more conceptually based theme has over the others previously proposed is that is not bound by time or place and is common to all foreigners, as applicable to a Sogdian entertainer performing in the tea houses of Chang'An in the eighth century as it is to an American marketing professional working for a Chinese hi-tech company in the twenty-first century. Additionally, it offers a solid base from which to evaluate the most recent developments in the story of foreigners in the employ of Chinese and situate them in larger perspective. Indeed, it is precisely through the source of their motivation that those who are employed by Chinese in the twenty-first century differentiate themselves most clearly from their predecessors. Within this larger thematic there is a diversity of motivations that can be conveniently grouped into three categories: (1) Saving Souls; (2) Saving Lives; (3) Saving China.

Saving Souls

Mephistopheles: Here, an unwearied slave, I'll wear thy tether,
And to thine every nod obedient be:
When there again we come together,
Then shalt Thou do the same for me.

Faust: When on an idler's bed I stretch myself in quiet.
There let, at once, my record end!
Canst thou with lying flattery rule me,
Until, self-pleased, myself I see,—
Canst thou with rich enjoyment fool me,
Let that day be the last for me!
The bet I offer.   Goethe, Faust Part 1, Act IV

Anteing up a human soul as pledge for the promise of access to greater knowledge is a wager whose unique expression of the human condition formed the basis for more than a few literary works before achieving its apotheosis in Goethe's Faust. However, before Goethe or any of his literary forbears ever conceived of taking this exchange-of-souls-for-knowledge model and turning it into a literary construct, Jesuit missionaries had already adopted it as a guide for their missionary activities and put it into effective practice. The Jesuits may at times have concerned themselves with the potential threat Science posed to their belief system and even considered its basic premises antithetical to their most firmly held convictions, but they were astute enough to realize that it was also a discipline that could be turned to advantage in achieving missionary goals. This application of scientific expertise in the service of fulfilling missionary ambitions lies at the heart of the Jesuit experience in China.

Many of the missionaries who were dispatched to China in the seventeenth century were well-versed in the latest scientific developments of the age and upon arrival leveraged the knowledge they had acquired to gain entrée into the Chinese imperial court by gaining the confidence of the mandarins who were its functionaries. Once inside, the missionaries made themselves indispensable by imparting their scientific knowledge to those whose souls they hoped to save in exchange.

As well-publicized as their exploits have been, the Jesuits were far from the first foreigners to be employed by the Chinese for their scientific acumen. Gautama Siddha,[3] an Indian mathematician-astronomer who achieved prominence for his contributions to Chinese astronomy in the Tang Dynasty, was just one of many Indian mathematicians active in the Tang court. The high regard in which the Indian experts were held was due in large part to the level of accuracy they were able to achieve in the measurement of astronomical phenomena (e.g. eclipses). The premium placed on these achievements was motivated by considerations that exceeded their purely scientific value. The improvement in predicting eclipses that these more precise measurements enabled, for example, had direct consequence for the Emperor whose legitimacy in some part depended on the accuracy of their prediction (Deshpande 2015, pages 215 and 219).

Foreign scientists continued to be employed in the Yuan Dynasty and maintained a presence at court through the Ming and into early part of the Qing Dynasty. However, over the course of the centuries that these dynasties spanned, the profiles of these experts changed. Where once the greatest number of those who presented themselves for employment touted experience acquired in centers of learning that were located in India and Persia, over the course of time they increasingly referenced locations in Middle East as their places of origin, reflecting

---

[3]The name appears in different renderings; "Gautama Siddha" corresponding to the original Indian and "Qutan (Qudan) Xita" its sinified version. In fact, Siddha/Xita was one of a long line of Indian astronomers who, according to sources, was born in the Tang capital, Chang'An (Deshpande 2015, pages 218–219).

a broader shift in the center of economic, political, and scientific gravity that occurred as Arab science entered its golden age. Jalal al-Din, an accomplished Muslim astronomer who was active in China during the Yuan Dynasty, was an exemplar of this shift. Numerous references to the presence of 'Mohammadan' scientists at the Ming were further evidence of the transformation that had taken place (Spence 2002, page 25). However, by the middle of the Ming Dynasty, even with the contributions of these scientists, the predictions on which imperial legitimacy depended were less reliable and the calculations on which they were based plagued by discrepancies and inaccuracies. This condition would eventually be exposed by Matteo Ricci and subsequently exploited by the Jesuit missionaries who came after him.

Johann Adam Schall von Bell (1591–1666) and Ferdinand Verbiest (1623–1688), who followed in Ricci's footsteps and took the example he set as their guide, were arguably the scientist-missionaries who achieved the greatest success in exploiting these inconsistencies by demonstrating the superiority of methods they had honed in Europe. Public competitions whose goal was to improve the accuracy of astronomical predictions by pitting scientists against one another, provided the scientist missionaries with the opportunity they needed to showcase their skills. Through the results they achieved in these demonstrations Schall and Verbiest attracted the attention of the Wanli, Tianqi, and Chongzhen emperors successively and achieved a level of trust that earned them appointments as directors of the Astronomy Bureau in the early part of the Qing Dynasty (Schall from 1644 to 1668; Verbiest from 1673 to 1688).

In addition to leveraging their scientific acumen, Schall and Verbiest took great pains to adapt to the local culture as part of their effort to enhance relations with their Chinese patrons and earn their trust. It was an endeavour that was reflected in nearly every aspect their daily conduct. They both made significant effort to learn Chinese, eventually reaching a level of fluency high enough to be able to compose lengthy treatises in the language and engage in discourse on a wide range of subjects. A contemporary account of Schall noted that he "worked hard at the Chinese language, studied the Confucian Classics, wore the long robes of the Chinese scholar, and lived in considerable style" (Spence 2002, page 14), all measures that were nominally undertaken to win over Chinese hosts as a necessary precondition for converting them. Ironically, the greater the success Schall and Verbiest achieved and the more prominent they became the more resistance they encountered from local scientists who, most likely out of jealousy and concern for their own positions, devised ways to undermine them. They were also criticized by some of the more conservative members of their own order who felt that they had gone too far in embracing the local culture and in the process had forsaken the principles on which their own religion was founded.

By the middle of the Qing Dynasty, the Jesuit presence had clearly begun to wane, a consequence of the court's shift towards isolation from the West and away from the influence of its representatives. An accompanying paranoia made the members of the court increasingly critical of the Jesuits' activities and suspicious of the motives that lay behind them (Winston and Bane 2010, page 6). Those missionaries who were still employed maintained a status in the bureaucracy that was a far cry from the exalted posts Schall and Verbiest had held and their contribution to scientific advances was equally diminished.

Saving Lives

Comrade Bethune's spirit, his utter devotion to others without any thought of self, was shown in his boundless sense of responsibility in his work, and his boundless warm-heartedness towards all comrades and the people. Every Communist must learn from him.

(Mao Zedong, 21 December 1939)

With these words Mao Zedong eulogized the Canadian doctor Norman Bethune who came to China in middle age and sacrificed his time, his health, and, ultimately, his life in the service of the Chinese Communists and the Chinese people. Despite his affiliation with the Communists and support for their cause, Bethune's service was more mission-driven than ideologically motivated in line with his conviction that he could change the lives and destinies of others through his work. Indeed, Bethune's dedication to his work was legend. He regularly logged eighteen-hour days and once recorded completing a total of seventy-one minor and major operations over a forty-hour period (Spence 2002, page 223). Those who worked with him observed that the heavier the task that was placed before him the greater was the energy that he seemed to draw from it. Given his capacity for work and the number of lives he saved, it is little wonder that Bethune was so highly praised by the Communist leadership and that his health was so compromised.

Jakob Rosenfeld, like Bethune, was a doctor who served the Communist army and saved the lives of its soldiers but whose service was not ideologically motivated. However, where Bethune came to China because he was driven by a sense of mission, Rosenfeld, an Austrian-Jewish refugee from Nazi oppression, came to China as a consequence of circumstance (ability to obtain a visa).

Bethune and Rosenfeld, like other foreign doctors who came to China in the late nineteenth and early twentieth centuries, were assigned to support the army because the greatest need for medical care and attention at a time of such great turmoil and conflict was on the battlefield. As an adjunct to their military service, these foreign doctors dedicated their time to serving the villagers and peasants who lived in the poor regions the troops moved through. While carrying out his mission to establish mobile hospitals for the army, Bethune, for example, provided the local people he encountered with basic medical care and even taught them how to treat themselves (Spence 2002, page 224).

The zeal with which Bethune carried out his duties made him no less a missionary than Ricci, Schall, and Verbiest, but the mission that inspired him did not involve service to a higher power or lofty ideal. On the contrary, it was much more mundane service to the poor and downtrodden that was his mission. His base of operations was a makeshift operating room near the frontlines not a chamber at an imperial court. He professed his admiration for the courage, optimism, and idealism of the Communists, but in doing this he was not driven by a specific ideology but from a conviction that: "that is where the need is greatest; that is where I can be most useful".

In deferring to pragmatism and humility as a guide for their actions rather than religious conviction or idealism, Bethune and Rosenfeld epitomized a class of foreigner that included doctors, soldiers, and even farmers who distinguished themselves from others who came to China both in the object of their service ("whom they served") and their motivation ("why they served").

Saving China

Mentioning soldiers and farmers in the same breath would, under most circumstances, seem to be an unlikely pairing. However, it doesn't seem quite as extraordinary when one considers that for much of the world's history, and in this regard China's history is no exception, a good many rank-and-file soldiers were nothing more than farmers in uniform. Within the context of this study it is not just the shared experience of military service that connects soldiers and farmers, it is their common goal of saving China even though their motivations for trying to save China could not have been more different.

Soldiers

As early as the Tang Dynasty, the military, as we have seen, distinguished itself as one of the more aggressive Chinese employers of foreigners and, in the centuries and dynasties that followed, proved to be one of the most consistent. The military's engagement of foreign troops was especially pronounced in times of conflict and upheaval as it was at these junctures that the country was in most dire need of support and correspondingly demonstrated the greatest willingness to consider reinforcements from outside, especially those who knew how to handle a gun and win wars. The latter half of the nineteenth century, judging by the lengthy list of military conflicts—the Opium War, the Boxer Rebellion and the Taiping Rebellion—was one such period. It was into the breach created by this turmoil that foreign mercenaries, soldiers of fortune, and advisers leapt. One such foreign military adventurer whose exploits in China left an indelible mark was Charles Gordon and in return for those exploits China left its mark on him through the epithet "Chinese" that was appended to his given name and used as a reference for the rest of his military service.

Judging from this moniker one might conclude that Gordon had 'gone native' during his tenure in China, abandoning country and countrymen to serve in the Chinese army and devote himself to fighting battles on behalf of the Chinese state. The reality, however, was much more complex. Gordon certainly fought for the Chinese and led Chinese troops into battle, but at the same time he maintained his allegiance to the British Army, who considered him a British officer serving under the umbrella of the Qing army. In this arrangement, Gordon reported directly to Li Hung Chang ("Li Hongzhang" in pinyin transcription) a military leader and high-ranking civil servant who eventually became the Governor of Zhili Province (today, Hebei Province). This dual allegiance was, in fact, just one of the many dualities that defined Gordon's experience in China and was a source for many of the apparent contradictions that characterized his behaviour, his exploits, and his leadership.

A chronically shy and lonely person by nature, Gordon came to China in 1859 to support enforcement of the Tianjin Treaty, an agreement, signed the year before Gordon's arrival in China, that brought the first phase of the Second Opium War to a close. In his first job building barracks for the local garrison Gordon may not have made much of an impression, but when he took a tour of duty on the battlefield, he was transformed into a brash, brave, and daring warrior. Gordon's performance on the battlefield did not go unnoticed and after he had completed a couple of successful tours of duty, the regiment's senior officers gave him troops to command. The troops Gordon inherited were a band of poorly-trained Chinese foot soldiers and poorly-disciplined foreign mercenaries who together formed the euphemistically named "Ever-Victorious Army".

As commander, Gordon set about instilling the discipline on which the effectiveness of his men depended and demonstrating a fearlessness on which they could draw for inspiration. His positive view and healthy respect for the Chinese people was another trait that enabled him to capture the minds and win the hearts of the troops and was key to achieving success on the battlefield.

The Ever-Victorious Army's opponent in battle was the army of the Taiping Heavenly Kingdom, a group of rebels who established an occupational state in the Northern Chinese port city of Tianjin and earned Gordon's respect through their bravery and shrewdness. After defeating the Taiping in a battle near Suzhou, Gordon gave the officers his word that he would guarantee them safe conduct as a condition for their surrender, a sign of the high regard in which he held them. When Gordon's Chinese superiors, acting in compliance with an Imperial decree, subsequently had the Taiping leaders put to death Gordon regarded it as an insult to his personal honor and expressed his dissatisfaction in no uncertain terms to Li Hung Chang. According to some sources, he even threatened to take Li's life over the incident.

To make amends, the Chinese, once again acting on Imperial decree, brought Gordon gifts that included ten-thousand taels of silver,[4] and Taiping battle flags in recognition and compensation for his capture of Suzhou. Much to the consternation of both his Chinese and the British

---

[4]A *tael* is worth approximately $30 in today's currency based on the assumption that its value was equivalent to that of a 35 kg of rice at the time.

superiors, Gordon summarily rejected the gifts offered on behalf of the Emperor on principle, writing simply: "Major Gordon...begs his Majesty to receive his thanks for his intended kindness and to allow him to decline the same" (Boulger 1896, page 111). As much as Gordon's heart beat with the pulse of a mercenary, the blood it pumped was that of an 'Englishman' whose allegiance to principle and sense of honor were even, or perhaps especially, in full display on the battlefield. Nevertheless, little more than a year later the same honor-bound Charles Gordon, now reasoning like a mercenary, had no qualms about accepting payment of £100,000 from Li, effectively a payoff, in return for his agreement to disband the Ever-Victorious Army.

Prior to his departure, Gordon yet again made requests for all sorts of gifts that stretched the bounds of permissibility. Nevertheless, the emperor eventually acceded to these requests as the following note from a functionary attests:

> The Emperor has by a special Edict conferred on you the Hwang Ma-Kwa, or yellow jacket, and also presented with you four sets of Tetuh's uniform which you remember you said you would like to have.
>
> (Lewis 1964, page 77)

These gifts were certainly valuable in their own right, but it was the edict issued by the Emperor himself that was perhaps even more meaningful recompense because it was a clear and meaningful sign of just how significant Gordon's contribution had been and the degree to which his service had been recognized and respected. Incongruously, but at the same time perfectly in character, Gordon ultimately gave most of the gifts he received to friends and family, leaving the epithet "Chinese" as perhaps the only "spoil of war" he took with him when he left China in 1864.

Farmers

> I've taken part in two of the greatest things of the 20th century — the development of the atom bomb and the Chinese Revolution. Who could ask for anything more than that?
>
> (Joan Hinton, 2002[5])

---

[5] This statement made during an interview with NPR in 2002 and referenced in: Purnell Forest, "Joan Hinton '42: Traversing the 20th Century," The Bennington Free Press, May 17, 2013.

Joan Hinton, who began her career as a nuclear physicist in the U.S. and ended it as a dairy farmer in rural China, was one of the more unique figures in the history of foreigners employed by Chinese and, unquestionably, one of the most idealistic. Recruited into the Manhattan Project, the epicentre of U.S. atomic research in 1944, while she was still a graduate student, Hinton embarked on what to all appearances was a career of promise designing nuclear reactors. However, after witnessing the destruction wrought by the atomic bombs dropped on Japan during the Second World War, she experienced a disillusionment with the program and what it stood for that was so profound it led her to terminate her employment in 1948 and then secure passage on a ship bound for China later that year. All appearances to the contrary, Hinton's decision to depart for China was not a manifestation of some mental derangement or response to extreme stress. It was prompted by the prospect of reuniting with the two most important people in her life, her older brother, William and her boyfriend, Erwin Engst. Engst, an agriculture expert, had gone to China the year before to support agricultural development projects and joined her brother who had been dispatched there in 1945 as a representative of the U.S. Office of War Information. In addition to the prospect of reuniting with her boyfriend and her brother, what particularly attracted Hinton was the opportunity to witness at first-hand the advance of the Communist movement that the letters they sent described in increasingly vivid detail. The promise that a peasant revolution held for the creation of an egalitarian society appealed in equal part to her adventurous spirit and her idealistic nature (Photo 2.2).

Following her arrival in China at the end of the 1940s, Hinton first worked briefly for Sun Yatsen's widow, Soong Ching-Ling, then spent part of the following year in Yan'an before finally going to work on a state farm in Shaanxi Province. She would eventually be joined by her brother who, after completing his assignment with the Office of War Information, came to Shaanxi Province under a U.N.-sponsored program to provide farmers in rural China with training in modern agricultural methods. In Long Bow, the village where the Hintons eventually took up residence, Bill Hinton became known for his skill in repairing tractors. In Western academic circles he became known for his skill in observing and documenting the social transformation of rural China under the newly installed Communist government. Hinton's observations and the notes he took to record them formed the base for two widely-read books, *Fanshen* and its companion *Shenfan*.

Photo 2.2   Joan Hinton (1921–2010) (*Source* Bennington College [https://www.bennington.edu])

Whether it was toiling in the fields or participating in village commit-tee meetings, the Hintons impressed those for whom they worked with their devotion to Communism and their commitment to China. Their devotion to Communism was so zealous that it led them to oppose the economic reforms China initiated in the 1980s on grounds that the reforms contravened the basic tenets of Socialist doctrine. Their commit-ment to China was so deep that it led them to insist on being treated like any other Chinese citizen regardless of the privations they might have to endure as a result. A poster the Hintons and a few other like-minded foreigners drafted at the height of the Cultural Revolution and tacked to a wall of Beijing's International Studies University was the tangible and very public expression of their conviction. It was also a tangible expression of the foreign experience working for Chinese. The poster's deceptively spare title, "Five Have Nots and the Two Haves", captured the essence of the exclusion and social dislocation that foreigners liv-ing and working in China endured. The five "Have Nots" was a refer-ence to the activities in which all Chinese were expected to participate

(but from which foreigners were notably excluded).[6] The "Two Haves",
by contrast, were privileges—a standard of living that was higher than
that of the average Chinese and special treatment for which only foreigners qualified. As such, these privileges were no less effective a condition
as the "Have Nots" in ensuring that foreigners' "Otherness" was maintained and their exclusion from the larger Chinese society guaranteed.

Summary

After reviewing the record of foreigners in the employ of Chinese, histo-
rians such as Spence and Brady come to the conclusion that the story it
tells is a "cautionary tale" whose protagonists were manipulated by the
Chinese they served and thwarted in realizing their ambitions. Even if we
accept Spence's and Brady's basic assessment as valid, it is clear from the
account presented here that considers the experience of these foreigners
from the perspective of their motivations that some foreigners employed
by Chinese fared better than others and made contributions that were
well-received and had a positive outcome. In fact, cases of outright failure or unqualified success are few and far between. More common was
a tenure such as Bethune's that was marked by both success and failure. Highlighting Bethune's death as a proof point, Spence and Brady
might depict Bethune's service in the Communist army as another chapter in the "cautionary tale" of foreigners in the service of Chinese. The
Communist leadership, taking Mao's eulogy as representative, regarded
Bethune's tenure as an unqualified success and were grateful for his contribution. Spence himself gives Bethune credit for "technical brilliance"
and furthermore recognizes that it was this "brilliance" coupled with
extreme dedication that enabled Bethune to gain entrée into a society
that "would have otherwise rejected him".

For the insights into the ingredients for success and causes of failure
it provides, this analysis of Bethune's case makes it a valuable reference
for foreign staff in Chinese organizations who are determined to achieve
success and desperate to avoid failure. With Bethune as a starting point

---

[6]The "Five Have Nots": Physical labor, Thought reform, Engagement with workers and
peasants, Class struggle, Production struggle.

we will highlight a number representative cases that can supplement
Bethune's and form a basis for drawing broader conclusions. As criterion
for judging a foreigner's success (or failure) in meeting the expectations
of the Chinese for whom they worked and a basis for selection, we will
consider expressions contained in official statements, such as the eulogy
that Mao Zedong delivered on the occasion of Bethune's passing.

SUCCESS CASES

The Artist

In recognition of his diligence, we conferred the rank of 'third order' ['san
pin'] on the foreigner Lang Shining, who served the court from the time
of the Emperor Kangxi. (Nie 2016, page 21)

With this succinct statement, the Qianlong emperor in the Qing Dynasty
marked the passing of the Jesuit missionary Giuseppe Castiglione
(known at court by his Chinese name "Lang Shining"), an extraordinary
gesture that attested to the magnitude of the contribution Castiglione
had made not only to the cultural enrichment of Qianlong's own court
(1711–1799), but to those of his father and grandfather, the emperors
Yongzheng (1678–1735) and Kangxi (1654–1722) respectively over an
active career in China that spanned more than forty years.

The 'contribution' for which the Qianlong emperor and his court
held Castiglione in such high esteem was an astoundingly diverse and
prolific creative output that included portraits of the imperial family,
still life images, copper engravings, and even the design of Western-style
pavilions for the Old Summer Palace.

A native of Milan, Castiglione was born in 1688 and from an early
age demonstrated a talent for painting that qualified him for a spot
as apprentice in the prestigious Milanese workshop of Filipo Abbati
(Musillo 2016, page 1). Castiglione complemented his artistic calling with a religious one when he made the decision to enter the Jesuit
order in 1707. Over the next ten years he matured both as a painter
and as a priest serving first in Genoa where he executed a series of
paintings for the local Jesuit Novitiate and then in Coimbra, Portugal
where he painted murals to decorate the Jesuit College Chapel (Musillo
2016, page 43). It was on the basis of this experience, both artistic and

religious, that Cadtiglione was eventually selected to serve as a missionary in China. Following his arrival in China in 1715, Castiglione received an appointment at the Qing court. Such appointments were highly valued by the Jesuit missionaries because of the access they afforded to potential converts who were in positions of power and influence. Castiglione was certainly not the first Western missionary painter to serve at the Qing court nor would he be the last, but he stood out for the length of his tenure in China, the privileges he enjoyed during that tenure, and the profile of the projects to which he was assigned.

Castiglione eventually achieved the designation of imperial painter, a broadly-defined post whose scope of activity, commensurate with his growing reputation, expanded over time to include not only the painting of imperial portraits, but also the design of fountains in the Lofty Gardens Pavilion, and even oversight for the construction of the Western-style palaces situated in the imperial gardens of the Old Summer Palace. These projects showcased the full extent of Castiglione's talent and versatility as an artist and, at the same time, attested to the level of trust and esteem he was accorded. Remarkable enough in their own right, these achievements appear even more remarkable when considered in the context of other similarly-appointed European artists many of whom, after failing to win favor at court and secure sufficient support from the Chinese who engaged them, suffered premature termination of their appointments and subsequent repatriation back to the countries from which they had come.[7] Castiglione's success in avoiding a similar fate can be attributed to a number of factors that, when taken together, fall under the rubric of embracing local culture and a willingness to accommodate local conditions. The most apparent of the adaptations Castiglione undertook included discarding his traditional religious garments in favor of dress befitting a member of the Chinese court. He also devoted himself to the study of Chinese, a language he would eventually come to speak, read, and write fluently. However, the adaptation he made that was arguably the most consequential for ensuring his longevity and success as an imperial painter was his willingness and ability to adapt his artistic techniques and artistic style to suit the local Chinese aesthetic. In so doing, he demonstrated his respect for the traditions that informed

---

[7] cf. the case of Venetian painter, Michele Arailza, who was expelled from the Qing court in 1723 for not having "enough skill in painting to satisfy His Majesty" (Musillo 2008, page 56).

the art his Chinese counterparts practiced and his commitment to meeting, if not exceeding the expectations of the emperor he served.

The Qianlong emperor's unadulterated reaction to one of Castiglione's earliest attempts to render the royal family was that the otherwise well-executed portraits were blemished by "traces of dirt". His reference was to the *chiaroscuro* technique that Castiglione, steeped in European aesthetic, had so liberally applied. The emperor found the dark shadings especially concerning because of the bad omen they portended. (The reaction of a supervisor in a Chinese enterprise to a similarly applied artistic device featured in Chapter 8—"Metaphorically Speaking", suggests that the judgement rendered here is informed by a more general culturally-determined aesthetic and is not merely a reflection of Qianlong's personal sensibilities.)

Despite the less than positive nature of his initial assessment, the emperor, nevertheless, recognized Castiglione's talent. Loathe to throw the proverbial baby out with the bathwater, the emperor proposed that Castiglione work alongside Chinese painters so he could gain a better understanding of and appreciation for Chinese art and the aesthetic principles that governed it.[8] In contrast to many other European painters who bridled at being instructed to "learn" from local Chinese artists, Castiglione, with the characteristic humility that was such an essential factor for his success, readily agreed to the proposal and set to work learning the craft of Chinese painting from the masters the court employed.[9]

Castiglione eventually succeeded in evolving a unique style that met the expectations of his Chinese patrons and at the same time maintained some degree of European compositional sensibility. Some have suggested that Castiglione might have had an easier time than other Western painters in making the adaptations necessary to accommodate the Chinese style because of his training in the Milan school, a style of painting whose techniques bore some resemblance to those used by the Chinese

[8] Tang Jianjun, an expert from the China Academy of Chinese Poetry, Calligraphy, and Painting.

[9] Musillo notes that a posthumous biography of Castiglione—*Memoria Posthuma Fratris Josephi Castiglione*—highlights the role that "prudence" and "obedience" played in enabling Castiglione to gain the Emperor's trust (referenced in: Musillo, Marco, "Reconciling Two Careers: The Jesuit Memoir of Giuseppe Castiglione, Lay Brother and Qing Imperial Painter" (2008, page 56).

court painters. For example, *tempera a guazzo*, a tempera in which the colors were mixed with animal-based glue and then applied with water that Milanese painters favored was similar in consistency to the Chinese pigments that were similarly mixed with animal-based glues and then solidified into cakes, ground on ink stones and diluted with water. The tempera's application on silk after its preparation was complete, a technique commonly used in China, was also adopted in the Milanese area (Musillo 2015, page 321).

Although this training in Milan might have been some advantage, Castiglione clearly had to demonstrate extraordinary sensitivity and apply significant creativity in adjusting his Western aesthetic principles to suit Chinese taste. For example, in response to the emperor's antipathy towards the use of *chiaroscuro*, Castiglione reduced the intensity of the light he used when executing portraits of imperial family members so that no part of the face was obscured in shadow and the features were rendered more distinct. The portraits that Castiglione produced employing this technique display a three-dimensionality and skin texture but without relying on the use of a strong *chiaroscuro*. As he made these adaptations and found novel ways to accommodate the Chinese aesthetic, Castiglione also had some influence on the Chinese painters he worked with and quite a number of Qing court paintings of the time reflect a clear Western influence, particularly evident in the use of techniques such as contrast of light and shade and perspective, as well as choice of subject matter such as the depiction of contemporary events.

The Teacher

In the middle of a courtyard at the Beijing Foreign Studies University, the Chinese capital's premiere institution dedicated to the teaching of foreign languages, stands the statue of David Crook, a Briton who was the school's first dean. The statue was erected to honor Crook for the contributions he made as teacher, educational administrator, and member of the Chinese Communist Party during the more than four decades he lived and worked in China.

By any measure, Crook, who spent almost as much time on the front lines as he did in the classroom, was no ordinary educator. Then again, the path he followed prior to his arrival in China and prior to his engagement as a teacher, was just as unconventional. As a young man Crook had by turns worked as a furrier in New York's garment district, served as an airman, and even a spy (for the Soviet Comintern) in the Spanish Civil War. However, no matter how varied the roles he played nor how sharp the twists and turns on the path he followed, Crook maintained a spirit of idealism that was indefatigable and a belief in Communism that was unshakeable. However, it was his sense of humility and his willingness to endure and even embrace hardships that were as harsh if not harsher than what his Chinese colleagues endured that most impressed the Chinese and was the basis on which the unprecedented trust of the Communist leadership he enjoyed was founded.

After the Communists came to power in 1949, Crook continued to teach English at the Peking First Foreign Languages Institute laying the foundation for the establishment of an institution that would come to be known as the Beijing Foreign Studies University, a training ground for students who would eventually become senior statesmen in the new China's diplomatic service.

During the Cultural Revolution, Crook, like many other foreigners living and working in China at the time, suffered the fate of imprisonment. Where others saw prison as the end of the road, Crook regarded it as just another twist; one more test of his faith in Communism and commitment to China, proof of which was the statement he made upon his release from prison:

> I did not blame the Cultural Revolution for my fate, although I realized that its turbulence had caused me to be branded as a foreign spy, and swept me into a seven by fifteen-foot cell. I did not blame the guards, who peered at me day and night through the Judas-hole in the double door of massive timber and iron bars. (Crook 1990)

In making this pronouncement, Crook made it clear that, despite all the hardships he had endured, he harbored no ill will towards the Chinese Government and maintained his faith in the Party. "My five years in prison did not undermine my admiration for the past-achievements of the Chinese Communist Party and the People's Government". "A revolution is not a dinner party," Crook concluded quoting Mao Zedong whose vision he, true to form, remained committed to in spite of the ills that had befallen him (Crook 1990).

The Administrator

Trusted Counsellor of the Chinese Government
True Friend of the Chinese People
Modest, patient, sagacious and resolute
He overcame formidable obstacles and
Accomplished a work of great beneficence for China and the world

Thus read the inscription on a statue of Sir Robert Hart that stood for many years across from the Custom House in Shanghai commemorating his forty-year tenure as Inspector General of the Chinese Customs Service during the latter part of the Qing Dynasty (Bickers 2014).

As Inspector General, Hart's job, simply described, was to administer the Qing emperor's customs system. In this position, Hart was responsible for applying taxes and collecting duties from foreign merchants who were bringing goods into China. In the course of carrying out the duties his post prescribed, Hart rose to a level of prominence that established him as one of the most influential foreigners in China at the end of the nineteenth century. However, the real measure of Hart's power and of the influence he wielded was the veritable empire he presided over, an extensive network of customs offices, battalions of "indoor" and "outdoor" staff, a fleet of ships, and even schools dedicated to the training of interpreters.

Irish by birth, Hart left his native country in 1854 at the age of 19 when he entered the British Foreign Service and was posted to the British Consulate in Ningbo, a city located on China's East coast, about a hundred-and-fifty miles South of Shanghai. He eventually left the Foreign Service in 1859 to join China's Customs Service, serving first as Deputy Commissioner of Customs in Canton and then taking over as Inspector General four years later. The Customs Service that Hart inherited was under the purview of the Tsungli (written "Zongli "in pinyin transcription) Yamen, a Government organization that, according to the official description of its mission, had been established expressly to administer all of China's foreign affairs (Meng 1962, page 3). In practice, however, it effectively functioned as an intermediary between the highest level of Imperial authority and the representatives of foreign countries based in Beijing (Meng 1962, page 3).

In his capacity as head of the Chinese Customs Service, Hart was representative of a larger group of professional administrators and

bureaucrats whose appearance in China in the latter half of the nineteenth century was a function of the unique conditions (economic turmoil, political instability, and intervention from foreign forces) that
prevailed in the country at the time. In executing the duties of his office,
Hart trod a fine line between his employers, Prince Kung ("Gong", in
pinyin transcription) and the Chinese mandarins who administered the
Tsungli Yamen, and the foreign merchants from whom he was required
to collect duties. If he were perceived as leaning too far in the direction of the foreigners, especially the British with whom he was affiliated
through his previous service and by virtue of his nationality, Hart ran
the risk of having his loyalty questioned by the Chinese and losing their
trust. If he were perceived as leaning too far towards the Chinese, he ran
the risk of earning reprisals from the foreign merchant community and
objections from the government representatives of the countries those
merchants represented. It was a delicate balancing act that the historian
Robert Bickers has aptly characterized as "the tenuous position of the
foreign Inspector General, a non-Chinese director of an agency of the
Chinese State" (Bickers 2006, page 694).

This circumstance of dual allegiance, typically entailed direct employment by a Chinese state bureau and indirect, or "dotted line", reporting
to a foreign organization, an organizational arrangement that in today's
business parlance would be referred to as a "matrixed reporting structure". Hart's case was certainly not unique. There are quite a few cases
of foreigners employed by Chinese organizations both before and after
Hart whose scope of employment was circumscribed by such an arrangement. Verbiest and Schall who served as directors of the Astronomy
Bureau in the Ming Dynasty concurrently maintained their status as
missionaries under the Jesuit leadership. Joseph Stilwell in the twentieth
century, profiled later in this chapter, was at the same time Chiang Kai-
Shek's Chief Staff and a general in the U.S. Army. And as we will see in
subsequent chapters, this is an arrangement that continues to define the
experience of foreigners (e.g. star athletes) in the present time. Common
to all these cases is that the tension inherent in this dual allegiance has
posed a challenge all foreigners faced with this circumstance have struggled with and their success or failure in working for Chinese is directly
linked to how able they were at mitigating this tension and maintaining a
satisfactory balance.

The method Hart's predecessor Lay employed, if not to resolve this
tension entirely at least to lessen its impact, was to shroud the true

direction of his allegiance in ambiguity. Hart himself left no question as to where his responsibilities lay and had no reservations about making his position known publicly as a memo he drafted to the staff of the customs service shortly after taking up the post of Inspector General attests: "It is to be distinctly and constantly kept in mind that the Inspectorate of Customs is a Chinese and not, a foreign, Service" (Wright 1950, page 261).

Needless to say, official statements such as this one as well as other less formal gestures Hart made in both his professional and personal lives struck a sympathetic chord with the representatives of the Qing Government in whose service he was employed.

The consistently respectful and deferential demeanor Hart maintained from his very first meetings with the Qing officials was an essential element of the foundation on which the cooperative working relationship he maintained with them over an extended period of time was built. Prince Kung's insistence on referring to Hart as "our Hart", an exclamation that expressed both familiarity and praise, was a subtle, yet no less powerful, sign of the success Hart had achieved in winning the acceptance and gaining the confidence of those he served. As a demonstration of the trust they placed in him the Chinese officials in their turn, refrained from intervening in the day-to-day operation of the Customs Service.

Both officially and personally Hart demonstrated a strong affinity for China and for its people. He made it clear to those who worked for him that "It is the duty of each of its [the Custom Service's] members to conduct himself towards Chinese, people as well as officials, in such a way as to avoid all cause of offence and ill-feeling". As part of that duty, he insisted that all employees of the Customs Service achieve a high level of fluency in Chinese. His contemporaries noted, anecdotally, that Hart appeared much more at ease with Chinese than with Europeans (Bickers 2006, page 695). In conversation he was even known to remark that he viewed China as his 'spiritual home' (Bickers 2006, page 695).

In consideration of these achievements, it is clear Hart possessed a diplomatic acumen that was as finely-honed as his prodigious administrative skill. However, the achievement to which he perhaps owed the greatest part of his success was the size of the contribution to the imperial coffers that the taxes and duties he collected accounted for. By 1898 the Customs Service under Hart's leadership accounted for a full third of the Government's entire revenue, an accomplishment whose true significance can only be fully appreciated when considered within the context of the amounts that were recorded over the course of Hart's tenure. The revenue attributed to the Customs Service rose from 8 million silver taels in 1865, not long after Hart took over as Inspector General, to 14.5 million two decades later. Three years before Hart left China Customs revenue had reached an even more stratospheric level of 30 million (O'Neill 2017).

Hart's departure from China in 1908 was accorded all the pomp and circumstance befitting a dignitary of his stature. Contemporary accounts of Hart's farewell described him "walking steadily down the lines of saluting troops while the bands played 'Home, Sweet Home'", a public affirmation of the success he had achieved as a foreigner in the service of the Chinese state.

FAILURES

The Soldier

If Hart's departure from China was notable for its pomp and circumstance, the conditions under which the American general Joseph Stilwell left China nearly half a century later could hardly have been more different. According to a contemporary account, Hart's farewell, was so moving that very few of those in attendance "could say 'Bon Voyage' dry-eyed" (Bredon 1909, page 25). When Stilwell took his leave of China, the leadership of the Nationalist government couldn't have been more pleased and tears that were shed, if any, were most likely to have been tears of joy. Shortly before his departure, Stilwell concluded: "It looks very much as though they had gotten me at last...," a telling statement whose tone of resignation hinted at the fractious relationships and frustrations that had marked his tenure in China during which he served as Chiang Kai Shek's chief-of-staff.

On paper at least Stillwell appeared to have the all the personal and professional ingredients on which success in the post on Chiang Kai Shek's staff depended and it was in recognition of his "fit" that those at the most senior level of the U.S. Government and military establishment endorsed his candidacy. What they found especially appealing about Stilwell was that, in addition to being a battle-tested and highly-decorated officer, he happened to have spent time in China during a formative period in his military career and while there had achieved some degree of fluency in the Chinese language as well as an understanding of Chinese culture. The favorable commendations he received notwithstanding, Stillwell's own assessment of his prospects for success was much less sanguine and perhaps more realistic. He, better than anyone else, understood that no matter how solid the endorsement was that he received from his superiors in the U.S. military, at the end of the day it was the support from the Chinese side that counted. He also recognized that knowledge of the country and understanding of its culture was not the only determinant of success nor even the most consequential and that it might, in fact, be a liability.

Stilwell's position was subject to an organizational arrangement that, like Hart's, could best be described as "tenuous". Its point of fragility lay at the intersection of interests promoted by representatives of a Chinese government on one side and those of a foreign government on the other that were very often orthogonal to one another. Where Hart and Stilwell's circumstances differed was in the relative weights each of them assigned to the two reporting lines. Hart, as he himself made clear, considered himself directly reporting to the Chinese authorities and he aligned his activities with their interests accordingly. Where Stilwell's responsibilities lay was more ambiguous. While it was true that he appeared on Chiang Kai Shek's "organizational chart" as the Generalissimo's Chief of Staff, the common understanding was that the terms under which the post had been offered was as a secondment to the Nationalist army. It was an arrangement that conveniently preserved Stilwell's status as a U.S. military officer and kept him firmly within the orbit of the American military complex and tethered to the U.S. Government officials who were counting on him to advance their interests in China. This arrangement with its allegiance tilted towards the American side, was a source of tension between Stilwell and the leaders of the Nationalist government who trusted him less and yet, ironically, expected more of him because of it. They reasoned that because he maintained his status as a US military officer he would be able to exert more influence in Washington and increase the probability of securing more support for the Nationalist cause. It was a misapprehension that left them sorely disappointed.

Stilwell also differed from Hart in the value he assigned to his employment in the Chinese organization and the importance that the post he occupied played in the development of his career. Hart was appointed Inspector General of the Customs Service relatively early in his career, success he had achieved by dint of hard work and adroit political manoeuvring. Stillwell, by contrast, was already well along in his career when he was nominated to serve as Chiang's Chief-of-Staff. It was not a post he aggressively pursued and, in fact, was an opportunity he initially hesitated to take advantage of when it was offered because he was very well aware of how difficult a job it would be. On balance, taking on such an assignment had very little upside for Stilwell given where he was in his career and what he had already accomplished. Hart enjoyed the trust of the Chinese who employed him and maintained complete authority over the organization for which he was responsible. Stillwell's authority was consistently called into question and the decisions he made were often ignored both by the officers who reported to him as well as by those to whom he reported.

To be fair, the challenges Stilwell faced were virtually insurmountable, exacerbated by expectations from both sides that even under the best of circumstances would have been all but impossible for him to satisfy. However, even taking these challenging circumstances into account, Stillwell took a number of steps that severely compromised any relationship with Chiang Kai-shek he might have had, diminished whatever stature and respect he might have enjoyed, and wiped out any possibility for success that may have existed.

Stilwell's mission, as he saw it, was to apply the wisdom and experience he had acquired over decades of service as a senior officer in the U.S. Army to improve the quality of the Nationalist military operation and increase its effectiveness. To this end, he devised detailed plans that he subsequently shared with Chiang Kai Shek and his military leaders. The plans were based on his assessment of the current state of the Nationalist army and contained his recommendations for how the army could be transformed. At first, the proposals were respectfully received and reviewed, but as time wore on, and the tone in which they were written became more insistent, they received less attention. In many instances, they were simply ignored. From Stilwell's perspective, he was carrying out the duties of the job to which he had been assigned. From the Chinese perspective, Stilwell was challenging Chiang's authority. This increased the level of tension that already strained their relations, Chiang because he perceived Stilwell was trying to tell him how to do his job (something inexcusable for a subordinate, let alone a foreigner, to be doing) and Stilwell because he felt that his advice was not being taken seriously and that his time was being wasted.

Although it is clear Chiang had his own agenda and was not an entirely trustworthy or transparent partner, his actions did have some justification and can be better understood when one considers them within the context of the recommendations Stillwell's memos contained and appreciates the magnitude of the 'improvements' to military operations Stilwell was proposing. In some cases, the "improvements" were tantamount to a complete overhaul of critical parts of the Nationalist military organization. Through the proposals he made for reforms to the military Stilwell demonstrated a lack of sensitivity or understanding for the complexity of the power structure that guaranteed Chiang's position. If Chiang were to implement the reduction in the number of divisions, redistribution of resources, and removal of inefficient commanders Stilwell advocated it would have almost certainly put his own power base at risk and might very well have led to his downfall (Spence 2002, page 247). As if this lack of sensitivity for Chiang's position wasn't already bad enough, Stilwell committed a breach of diplomatic protocol and demonstrated a complete disregard for his position in Chiang's organization by referring to Chiang in a demeaning way.[10] Finally, he weakened his position with the Chinese who reported to him and lost their respect by insisting on living and even dressing like a rank-and-file soldier.

"My conscience is clear. I have carried out my orders," pronounced Stilwell at the end of his tour in the Nationalist army, but in carrying out his "orders" he failed to make adjustments that might have changed his fate and brought the Chinese what they most wanted—American funds, Allied support, and perhaps just as important—respect (Spence 2002, page 265).

The Revolutionary

Seen in its entirety, Sidney Rittenberg's nearly forty-year career in China follows the arc of a classic Greek drama—Meteoric rise as a revolutionary delivering impassioned speeches on the excesses of Capitalism to rapt audiences of Chinese peasants, workers, and government officials; Hubris that reaches its peak at the height of the Cultural Revolution when he becomes the leader of a faction that would take control of China's Central Broadcasting Bureau; A change in fortune and fall from grace

---

[10]It was Stilwell who first referred to Chiang Kai-Shek disrespectfully as "Peanut" in his correspondence.

when his exploits as an increasingly radical revolutionary catch up with him and eventually land him in Beijing's infamous Qincheng Prison for the better part of a decade.

When Rittenberg arrived in China with the U.S. Army in 1944, he was already an avowed Communist committed to righting social inequities and improving the lot of the oppressed masses. He was also a young man with a rebellious streak who had a penchant for taking contrarian positions, challenging the status quo, and making decisions that confounded even those who knew him well. His decision to join the Communist Party, for example, could be read as a renunciation of his comfortable upbringing as the scion of a well-to-do Southern family. In rejecting an offer to study at Princeton University, he was challenging social propriety and, on principle, rejecting the "bourgeois" value system that such an institution represented. Given Rittenberg's inclinations and personality traits, it is not surprising that during the time he was officially serving as a soldier with the U.S. Army in China, he was in reality dedicating an increasingly large part of his time to championing the cause of the poor and downtrodden Chinese he encountered. It was through his engagement in these activities that Rittenberg came to the attention of the Chinese Communist leadership who eventually invited him to join them, an offer Rittenberg readily accepted.

Rittenberg was one of just a few foreigners to join the Chinese Communists and one of an even smaller number to join Mao Zedong and the other Communist leaders in Yanan, a forbidding place in rural Shanxi Province that the Communists occupied and used as their base of operations. Rittenberg, very much in the mould of Crook and Hinton, earned a reputation during his time in Yan'an for his devotion to Communism and his dedication to the work that was assigned him. Most of this work involved translating documents and drafting correspondence on behalf of the Communist leaders to facilitate their communication with the outside world. By Rittenberg's own account, this job was a grueling one that tested his stamina and his commitment:

> I often worked all day long on translating the latest polemic. Then around 5 PM, as I was about to break for supper, a new version would suddenly arrive and I had to start all over again. Late in the evening more new versions or revisions would begin to pour in and I tried to keep up with them. The leaders worked from 9 PM until close to dawn. (Rittenberg 1993, page 81)

After the Communists came to power in 1949, Rittenberg became an increasingly visible actor on an increasingly larger stage. Undoubtedly, the largest stage he appeared on was the one from which Mao Zedong officially announced the establishment of the People's Republic of China on October 11, 1949. In photos taken of Mao addressing the masses who had gathered in Tiananmen Square to celebrate that historic occasion it is possible to make out Rittenberg seated on the dais in a place of prominence shoulder-to-shoulder with the leaders of the "New China" (see Photo 2.3).

If Rittenberg's rise was meteoric, his eventual fall was even more precipitous. The ten years he spent in Beijing's Qincheng Prison at the culmination of his fall afforded him ample time to reflect on his reversal of fortune and the missteps that had precipitated it. Heading Rittenberg's list of miscalculations was most certainly his decision during the Cultural Revolution to accuse Jiang Qing, Mao's consort and the putative leader of the Gang of Four, of betraying the Revolution's ideals.

Photo 2.3 Sidney Rittenberg with Mao Zedong (*Credit* www.revolutionary-movie.com)

As if denouncing Jiang Qing, who was then at the height of her power and renowned for her ruthlessness, wasn't bad enough, Rittenberg did so in open forum adding insult to injury and revealing just how blind to his circumstances his overconfidence had made him.

In addition to the very public denouncements he directed at high profile targets, Rittenberg made many less public, but no less damaging, denunciations of colleagues, friends, and everyday citizens that derailed careers and ruined livelihoods. Less grievous, perhaps, but no less shameful, was the advantage he took of his position and the benefits it afforded him. As a foreigner who had the ear of China's top leaders, Rittenberg could claim privileges that were well beyond the reach of the average Chinese citizen whose cause he insisted he was championing. In so doing, he revealed himself to be an even greater hypocrite than those he denounced.

For denouncing Jiang Qing Rittenberg was arrested and sentenced to prison and for destroying the lives of so many Chinese citizens his prison sentence was extended past the end of the Cultural Revolution, long after other foreigners who were similarly imprisoned had had their sentences commuted and been released. "Li Dunbai [Rittenberg's Chinese name] is a bad person who has committed serious political mistakes during the Cultural Revolution," offered Premier Zhou Enlai by way of official explanation for the severity with which Rittenberg's case had been treated and with this solemn pronouncement brought the last chapter in a cautionary tale to a sobering close (Rittenberg 1993, page 443).[11] Rittenberg himself had no illusions about the reason why he was imprisoned. "I had gotten too big for my britches," he acknowledged ruefully and, perhaps subconsciously thinking of Crook, reflected that he probably would have done better if he had become a teacher.[12]

Rittenberg and Crook certainly had much in common. They were both staunch believers in Communism and counted themselves among the few foreigners who had been granted membership in the Chinese

[11] In fact, Rittenberg had a reprise (reincarnation) of sorts in the 1980s at the beginning of the economic reforms when he became a consultant to Western companies eager to get a foothold in the nascent Chinese market and desperate to establish relationships with government officials on whom their success depended and with whom Rittenberg was on a first name basis.

[12] Rittenberg's comment in the documentary "The Revolutionary" (2012)—Stoutwater Pictures.

Communist Party. They were thoroughly committed to their work and were unstinting in their efforts to complete the tasks they were assigned. In the pursuit of ideals in which they believed, they had no qualms about flaunting convention. In fact, it was this unwavering dedication to their ideals that inured them to the criticism and opprobrium of others who were less committed and less tolerant. Despite these similarities, Rittenberg was no Crook and a closer examination of their differences yields insights that are the source for more broadly applicable conclusions about which factors were most decisive in determining whether a foreigner in the employ of Chinese succeeded or failed.

Where they differed most clearly was in the extent of the sacrifice they were willing to make to achieve higher ideals. For Crook, no sacrifice was too great; Rittenberg had his limits. Nowhere was this more evident than in how they lived and even where they lived. Rittenberg enjoyed the use of an apartment that was even larger and more luxurious than those occupied by most of China's senior leaders. Crook's quarters, situated in an unremarkable dormitory building on the Beijing Foreign Studies Institute campus contained only the barest of necessities. Rittenberg, as his poorly-conceived and very public criticism of Jiang Qing made clear, was prone to committing errors in judgement both in the assessments of situations in which he found himself as well as in the extent of his own capabilities. It was this overconfidence and arrogance that were the source of miscalculations that eventually led to his downfall and resulted in a lengthy prison sentence. Crook, by contrast, was the quintessence of understatement and maintained a sense of humility that, even under the most trying of circumstances, never wavered.

Each one of these cases has unique elements and highlights a different aspect of the foreign experience in the employ of Chinese. Considering them together we can draw a number of conclusions that have value and are applicable to the situations foreign staff working in Chinese organizations today encounter.

INGREDIENTS FOR SUCCESS

Dedication

Those foreigners who were honest and sincere in their efforts to support their host country and consistently put the interests and success of the Chinese they served above their own did exist, but they were few and far between. Because they were rare these foreigners were duly recognized for their dedication and commitment in the eulogies of emperors and government officials. In most cases, the sacrifice that those so recognized had made was their lives—literally, in the case of Bethune who worked himself to death or the foreign soldiers who lost their lives fighting in Chinese armies and figuratively, in the case of Castiglione, Hart, and Crook, each of whom spent their entire adult lives, living and working in China. It is perhaps pure coincidence, but an intriguing footnote none-theless, that those who were most successful during their tenure coinci-dentally all spent forty years in China. Whether coincidence or not, it is not so much the exact number of years that is consequential, but rather length of time and level of commitment that the number of years repre-sents. The natural conclusion that this review suggests is that achieving success requires a significant investment of time and effort. What elevates this conclusion above the mere platitude in whose guise it appears and distinguishes it from other similar statements, is the degree and scale of the investment (an entire adult life, thousands of hours studying Chinese language and preparing treatises, etc.) on which it is based. The other potential conclusion one could draw is that those who managed to remain in China for such a long time were only able to do so because they proved themselves ready, willing, and able to make the type of adap-tations and accommodations necessary.

Adaptability

The observation that flexibility and adaptability are essential ingredients for survival in a very unfamiliar environment would, at first glance, appear to be as much of a platitude as the conclusion that success depends on an investment of time and effort. What distinguishes the adaptations made by those profiled is the form they took. Some adaptations could be very visible and concrete such as achieving mastery of Chinese language and clothing oneself in local costume. However, these were more than sim-ply practical accommodations undertaken to facilitate living in a different and challenging environment. They were tangible expressions of a respect for the local culture and a commitment to the country and those who inhabited it. This significance was certainly not lost on the Chinese with whom these foreigners interacted and was a critical factor for their suc-cess in establishing and maintaining positive relations with the officials who employed them. What distinguished those foreigners who achieved the greatest success during their time in China was a willingness to go beyond making adaptations that were tangible, visible and, for the most part, cosmetic and take the much more difficult and challenging step of fundamentally changing the way they thought about things that were integral to their worldview and belief systems. Jesuit missionaries such as Verbiest and Schall stretched rules and even ignored fundamental principles of their faith in their efforts to integrate into the society in which they found themselves. Castiglione made significant adjustments to an artistic style and that had taken him years to develop and transformed an aesthetic sensibility that he had refined over a long period of time. All these adaptations taken together enabled them to increase their effectiveness and achieve results that guaranteed the privileged positions they occupied in the organizations of the Chinese who employed them.

Results

Common to all the cases of foreigners who achieved success in their employment was that what they did in executing the job to which they had been assigned resulted in tangible outcomes and delivered direct benefit to those who employed them. Most importantly, the efforts made and success achieved were in areas that were fully aligned with what the state, court, or empire needed or wanted whether that be making money, winning battles, or painting portraits. Hart significantly enriched the coffers of the Qing Government through his assiduous collection of customs duties and in recompense those responsible for the administration of the Government office under whose umbrella the Customs Service operated gave Hart ample leeway to run the organization as he saw fit. Gordon, at critical junctures, delivered decisive victories in battles against the Taiping rebels and was rewarded for his success with lavish gifts, substantial remuneration and, most importantly, imperial commendation. Castiglione produced portraits of imperial family members that showed their stature to best effect and, in recognition of his service and talent, was granted special privileges and was received favorably by the emperor who employed him.

"To do good work for China in every possible direction", Hart's formulation of the mission he defined for the Custom Service, succinctly expresses what made all of those who succeeded successful even though doing work that was "good for China" could involve significant inconvenience at a minimum and in most cases exacted a tremendous sacrifice.

SEEDS OF FAILURE

Over-Ruling

Failure to understand and adapt to local social conditions and cultural rules is perhaps the most common cause of failure among the foreigners working for Chinese considered here. Of the many factors that contribute to this failure one of the more illustrative, if not the most intriguing, is the appearance cultivated by those foreigners profiled, reflected most clearly in their manner of dress.

For the duration of his time in China, Stilwell insisted on wearing a rumpled uniform set off by an old campaign hat, standard issue G.I. shoes, and canvas leggings. It was a mode of dress that prompted one observer to liken Stilwell's appearance to that of an "itinerant vegetable peddler". It is conceivable that Stilwell's decision to adopt the style of dress he did was intentional and was one facet of the "tough, hard bitten, plain, fighting general" image he was making a concerted effort to cultivate. While this might have been an image that exemplified the kind of spirit the U.S. military prized and that resonated with the troops at home (Spence 2002, page 256), Stilwell's "omission of rank, badges, and the rest" only served to diminish his status in the eyes of the Chinese troops and leaders with whom he worked. From the Chinese perpsective, his way of dressing ill befitted a senior military official and made him look more like a poor rank-and-file soldier" (Spence 2002, page 254).

Even if they were not aware of the dictum "clothes make the man", the Jesuit missionaries Ricci, Schall and Verbiest fully embraced its spirit. Very early on they recognized that the way they dressed had a significant influence on their ability to carry out their work and build relationships with Chinese they encountered. They took great pains to adopt local dress because they understood that wearing such clothing was about more than making a fashion statement. Dressing in a manner befitting one's rank and station was a mark of status. The way they dressed, similar in effect to achieving mastery of Chinese language, communicated their intent and commitment while demonstrating their respect for the local culture. Making this accommodation was key to their success in cultivating relationships with those at a high level and advancing their missionary goals. Stilwell undoubtedly realized what was necessary and appropriate given his familiarity with Chinese culture. However, his refusal to play the role that was expected of him and demonstrate an appreciation for local custom by adopting the trappings of his rank and station was a sign of a general unwillingness to compromise fundamental principles and another source of failure (Photo 2.4).

Photo 2.4 Father Ferdinand Verbiest (1623–1688), Flemish Jesuit missionary in China during the Qing Dynasty (*Credit* Alamy Stock Photos—Science History Images)

Over-Reaching

The Dunning-Kruger effect describes an incidence of cognitive bias where those of low ability and low self-awareness imagine themselves to be much more capable than they actually are. It is a condition that manifests itself as a sense of superiority and over-confidence and is very applicable to the cases of foreigners who failed in the employ of Chinese.

Rittenberg, who was so convinced of the importance his contribution made to the Cultural Revolution and whose activities became so extreme that he was described as "redder than red", is a good example of this tendency and its consequence. Lay, Hart's predecessor in the Customs Service, presumed an importance and indispensability that prompted him to demand that he be granted expanded authority over customs revenues, a flotilla, and even use of a residence that was reserved exclusively for members of the imperial family (Spence 2002, page 110). The reality was that he had lost control over the organization he was meant to administer, a state of affairs that was already evident to those of whom he made his requests. In many of these cases, the sense of overconfidence led the foreigners suffering from it to believe that they were more capable in many ways than the Chinese who employed them and emboldened them to tell the Chinese what to do.

Over-Riding

Those foreigners, Spence notes, "who were the most convinced that their goals were good and that their advice was sorely needed" were the ones who complained most bitterly when the Chinese who employed them failed to act on their advice or ignored it outright. This as we will see remains a common complaint of those working for Chinese and for Chinese organizations and enterprises in the twenty-first century. Stilwell is the most obvious example, but there are plenty of others who found themselves similarly frustrated and rejected. Common to all of them, as Spence trenchantly observes, was "a desire not so much to help China, but to help themselves".

CONCLUSION

In reviewing the history of foreigners in the employ of Chinese, we can identify a number of themes that connect them and bridge their experiences across centuries and dynasties illuminating common denominators along the way.

One source of such trends are the professions that foreigners represented and defined what they did during their tenure in China. Foreigners who served as soldiers in the armies of emperors in virtually every era are an example, from An Lushan who was a high-level officer in the Tang military in the eighth century to Charles Gordon who led Chinese troops against the Taiping rebels under the Qing military command in the nineteenth century and Joseph Stilwell who served as Chief-of-Staff to Chiang Kai Shek in the twentieth century. Because Stilwell concurrently maintained his status as an American military officer while serving the Nationalist government in China he also represents another theme—foreigners employed by Chinese who at the same time maintained some allegiance to the country or organization with which they were affiliated prior to their service in China.

If we look back historically to the time before Stilwell we can identify similar cases of foreigners who maintained a second allegiance during their employment in China. Schall and Verbiest who served the Ming and Qing courts as scientists but maintained their affiliation with the Jesuit order are one such case. If we then look forward in time from Stilwell to the current era there are the cases, as we will see in the next chapter, of star athletes who play for Chinese teams and at the same time maintain their spots on the rosters of teams overseas. The tension created by this particular organizational structure is one that all those who are subject to it have to address. How successful they are at maintaining an appropriate balance depends on where their responsibilities lie, and the relative strength of their ties to the organizations by whom they are engaged and the push and pull they exert.

Common to all the foreigners employed by Chinese, regardless of background, motivation, or profession, is that they all at some point, whether as their primary role or as an adjunct, played a mediating role of translator culturally and linguistically between the Chinese who employed them and those who existed beyond Chinese borders. The Sogdians, by virtue of their role as emissaries and intermediaries, served as translators and interpreters between the Tang and the Central Asian peoples they encountered on their borders.[13] In the Ming and Qing dynasties Jesuits, such as the scientist-missionary Adam Schall, acted

---

[13] Even the rebel general, An Lushan, who purportedly was fluent in six languages, served as an interpreter in one of the outlying garrisons to which he was assigned in the early part of his military career.

as translators as necessary. "At a time when no mandarin in the Court spoke any foreign language and no foreign diplomat spoke Chinese or Manchu this was a task of peculiar importance" (Roland 1999, page 86). Sidney Rittenberg translated for Mao Zedong and the other Communist leaders when they needed to communicate with officials of other countries. Posted to Beijing for a number years during the Cultural Revolution the Hintons occupied their time editing and translating documents the Chinese Government deemed important.

In the next chapter that develops the story of foreigners employed by Chinese in the twenty-first century, we will see that the role of "translator", broadly defined, remains constant even as other themes and conditions are transformed or even abandoned when considered within the context of a Chinese enterprise.

REFERENCES

Bickers, Robert, "Purloined Letters: History and the Chinese Maritime Customs Service" *Modern Asian Studies*, Vol. 40, No. 3, 2006, pages 691–723.
Bickers, Robert, "Lost Monuments and Memorials of the Shanghai Bund 2: Statue of Sir Robert Hart, 1914" (online article post), October 13, 2014. https://robertbickers.net/2014/10/13/lost-monuments-and-memorials-of-the-shanghai-bund-2-statue-of-sir-robert-hart-1914/.
Boulger, Demetrious C., *The Life of Gordon*, 2 volumes, Fisher-Unwin, London, 1896 cited in Spence, Jonathan, *To Change China: Western Advisers in China*, Penguin, 2002 (reprint).
Bredon, Juliet, *Sir Robert Hart: The Romance of a Great Career*, Dutton, New York, 1909 cited in Spence, Jonathan, *To Change China: Western Advisers in China*, Penguin, 2002 (reprint).
Crook, David, From Hampton Heath to Tian'anmen—The autobiography of David Crook (online), 2009. http://www.davidcrook.net/simple/main.html.
Deshpande, Vijay, "Allusions to Ancient Indian Mathematical Sciences in an Early Eighth Century Chinese Compilation by Gautama Siddha" *Indian Journal of History of Science*, Vol. 50, No. 2, April 13, 2015, pages 215–226.
Feldman, Steven, *Trouble in the Middle: American-Chinese Business Relations, Culture, Conflict, and Ethics*, Routledge, London and New York, 2013.
Goethe, Johann Wolfgang von, Faust, Taylor, Bayard (trans.), *University of Adelaide (electronic version)*, December 2014.
Lewis, Jenny, "The Gordon Papers", *The British Museum Quarterly*, Vol. 28, 1964, pages 75–81 cited in Spence, Jonathan, *To Change China: Western Advisers in China*, Penguin, 2002 (reprint).

Lung, Rachel, *Interpreters in Early Imperial China*, John Benjamins, Amsterdam and Philadelphia, 2011.

Meng, S.M. "The Tsungli Yamen: It's Organization and Functions", Harvard University, East Asian Research Center, 1962.

Musillo, Marco, "Reconciling Two Careers: The Jesuit Memoir of Giuseppe Castiglione, Lay Brother and Qing Imperial Painter" *Eighteenth-Century Studies*, Vol. 42, No. 1, 2008, pages 45–59.

Musillo, Marco, "The Qing Patronage of Milanese Art: A Reconsideration on Materiality and Western Art History", in Brix, Donald (ed.) *Portrayals from a Brush Divine: A Special Exhibition on the Tricentennial of Giuseppe Castiglione's Arrival in China*, Taiwan National Palace Museum, Taipei, 2015, pages 310–323.

Musillo, Marco, *The Shining Inheritance of Italian Painters at the Qing Court 1699–1812*, Getty Research Institute, Los Angeles, 2016.

Nie Chongzheng, *Lang Shining de Huihua Yishu*, Meishu Chubanshe (Fine Art Publishing Company), Beijing, 2016.

O'Neill, Mark "Ireland's Imperial Mandarin. Referenced in Xing, Yi, 'The Story of Customs Official Sir Robert Hart'", *The Telegraph*, May 24, 2017 (original article published by the *China Daily*).

Rittenberg, Sidney, and Bennett, Amanda, *The Man Who Stayed Behind*, Simon and Schuster, 1993.

Roland, Ruth, *Interpreters as Diplomats: A Diplomatic History of the Role of Interpreters in World Politics*, University of Ottawa Press, 1999 (reference attributed to Chao 1954, 2–3).

Spence, Jonathan, *To Change China: Western Advisers in China*, Penguin 2002 (reprint).

Whitfield, Susan, *Life Along the Silk Road*, Second Edition, University of California Press, Berkeley, 2015.

Winston, Kenneth, and Bane Mary Jo, "Reflections on the Jesuits Mission to China", Harvard Kennedy School (Faculty Research Working Paper), February 2010, pages 1–37.

Wright, Stanley F., *Hart and the Chinese Customs*, Mulan, Belfast, 1950 cited in Spence, Jonathan, *To Change China: Western Advisers in China*, Penguin, 2002 (reprint).

CHAPTER 3

On the Runway

DEPARTURE FROM THE PAST

The departure from the past that the twenty-first Century represents in the story of foreigners employed by Chinese is nowhere better illustrated than in the Aviation, Sports, and Fashion industries. All three industries owe the prominence they enjoy in China today to the rise of the Chinese consumer whose increasing wealth and purchasing power has put the services these industries offer within reach and in the process has generated a whole host of new employment opportunities for foreigners who have the expertise and experience required to provide those services and satisfy demand.

The foreign athletes, pilots and models who are engaged in these industries distinguish themselves from the foreign doctors, scientists missionaries, and soldiers who preceded them in the employ of Chinese most obviously in the professions they represent. However, it is in the pursuit of their professional goals that the representatives of these new professions are different from their predecessors, both in how they perceive China and how they view the role that working for a Chinese organization plays in their personal and professional development.

The experience of these foreign professionals as they carry out their appointed tasks in airplane cockpits, sports stadiums and fashion shows would seem to have little in common with that of the average foreigner employed in a Chinese company (see Chapter 4—"Roles and Responsibilities"). However this difference, in reality, goes no deeper

© The Author(s) 2020
P. Ross, *Barriers to Entry*,
https://doi.org/10.1007/978-981-32-9566-7_3

than the uniforms they wear. The higher profile that their professional status confers merely serves to make a more universal transformation in the objectives, motivations, and experience of foreigners working for Chinese in the twenty-first Century more readily apparent and easier to visualize.

Many of the issues introduced here as the ones that athletes, pilots and models encounter will become recognizable in subsequent chapters as recurring themes that characterize the larger experience of foreigners working for Chinese management in Chinese organizations across industries and professions.

ATHLETES, PILOTS, MODELS

The broad cross-section of experience, ages, and countries that foreigners engaged in these industries represent is a platform that showcases the full spectrum of motivations, challenges, and adaptations that foreigners working for Chinese employers encounter and brings to light the conditions that shape their employment experience. At one end of this spectrum are seasoned pilots who are highly skilled but largely unknown and effectively invisible to the public at large. At the other end are young fashion models who are relatively unskilled and virtually unknown, but for that highly visible. Finally, there are foreign athletes who are skilled, highly visible, and, in many cases, quite well-known.

Demographically, the pilots, athletes and models working for Chinese organizations in their respective industries fit neatly into three distinct, yet complementary, age brackets. Fashion models, whose average age is 20, are the youngest of the three groups. Pilots are at the other end of the age scale, a difference in age that is even more pronounced given the demand of Chinese airlines for experienced pilots who are well-established and already well along in their careers. Athletes occupy a middle range that overlaps with fashion models at the low end and with pilots at the high end.

The three groups also distinguish themselves from one another in their geographic and ethnic diversity. The countries of origin for fashion models are overwhelmingly concentrated in Eastern Europe and CIS regions. Foreign athletes (soccer players, in particular) represent a much broader range of countries and a greater number of regions. Pilots are the most geographically diverse group with members who come from more than 50 countries worldwide.

These composite profiles make it possible to situate those who represent these professions demographically and tells something about who they are. To understand what they contribute and get a sense for the conditions that define what they do requires taking a look more broadly at the industries they represent: Sports, Aviation, Fashion.

Athletes

Of the sports in China that foreign athletes are engaged in, basketball and soccer employ the greatest number and have the most significant history.

The evolution of basketball in China, from its very earliest beginnings to its current state, has been shaped, guided, and promoted by foreign players, executives, and even members of religious orders. In fact, basketball made its first appearance in China towards the end of the nineteenth Century during the Qing Dynasty when it was introduced by foreign missionaries who played the sport in Tianjin where they were stationed. After this initial period of engagement, the involvement of foreigners ebbed as the tide of Chinese history changed course and the country presented a side of itself that was less than welcoming to foreign involvement. Coincident with the economic reforms the Chinese Government launched in the 1980s foreigners once again became engaged with the development of basketball in China directly, influencing not only how the sport was played but also how it was promoted. The first foreign players arrived in the mid-1990s not long after completion of reforms that led to the establishment of the Chinese Basketball Association in 1995. It was at about this same time that the National

Basketball Association became involved with the fledging Chinese Basketball Association in an advisory capacity and increased the profile of basketball in China by granting the rights to broadcast NBA games. These broadcasts fueled a promotional effort that attracted enormous audiences numbering in the millions. The debut of the Chinese basketball star Yao Ming in the U.S. National Basketball Association in 2002 was a catalyst for stimulating broader interest in U.S. basketball across China and opened a new chapter in the story of the connection of basketball in China with practitioners of the sport overseas.

Soccer in China has had a much longer history and, according to some, may even have originated in China. In its modern incarnation, soccer in China takes 1951, the year that the Chinese National Football League was established, as its starting point. For the next forty years, the league with its eight teams remained largely unchanged and attracted little attention. In the early 1990s, the League undertook a series of reforms that resulted in the creation in 1994 of what was portrayed as a more professional organization. However, in the years that followed the new league's establishment, its constituent teams became better known for the audacity of their point-fixing than the quality of their play, behavior that tarnished the League's image and eventually prompted its officials to take corrective action. The result of that action was the establishment in 2004 of the Chinese Super League (CSL) whose improved governance and European-style organization were selling points for foreign players who subsequently began to appear in greater numbers.

Most of the foreign basketball players who have joined Chinese teams come from the U.S. although they may not necessarily be U.S. nationals. Soccer players have much more diverse national and ethnic backgrounds. In the early years of the CSL, foreign players came predominantly from three regions: Eastern Europe, Africa and Latin America. As time went on, and the League's reputation improved, players from major European and South American Leagues began to appear. Today, Brazil, South Korea, and Australia are the three countries that contribute the greatest number of players to the CSL (see Chart 3.1).

In the case of both soccer and basketball, the arrangements under which foreign players join Chinese teams are subject to conditions that can be quite complex. Even though the jersey they wear may be that of a Chinese team, many foreign players maintain some connection to the team that engaged them before they came to China. There are some

COUNTRY OF ORIGIN	NUMBER OF PLAYERS (Cumulative)
Brazil	280
South Korea	160
Australia	100

Chart 3.1 Top three countries of origin for foreign players in the Chinese Soccer League

who even play for both their original team and the Chinese team that has engaged them at different times during the season. At the center of these arrangements are agents and intermediaries who involve themselves in virtually every aspect of the hiring process including recruitment, contract negotiation, and living arrangements.

Matt Beyer
Agent for American basketball players who want to play in China

- Founder of agency Altius Culture
- Represents approximately 20% of the Chinese Basketball League's foreign players
- Obtained Chinese sports agency license (2012)

Source Sin, Ben "How China Became the NBA's Farm System", *Men's Journal*, March 13, 2015

Pilots

Air travel in China has increased dramatically over the last five years from 319 million passengers in 2012 (Knoema 2017) to 549 million pasengers in 2017 (Xiang 2018). Consistent with this growth, more airlines have been established, more flights scheduled and more airports built. The supply of domestic pilots, however, has failed to keep pace with the tremendous demand this growth has created. At current projections, China will need to add 3000 pilots a year for the next 5 years to satisfy demand (Dennis 2016). It is a number that far exceeds the fewer than 1200 pilots who graduate annually from the country's training schools (Dennis 2016). Moreover, training pilots is a time intensive endeavor that can take five to six years. It can be another four to five years beyond graduation before a pilot attains the rank of captain.

Juneyao Airlines

Juneyao Airlines Co. Ltd. (Juneyao Airlines) is a subsidiary company of Shanghai Juneyao (Group) Co. Ltd, one of China's Top 100 Private Companies. adhering to the service concepts of "Juneyao Airlines, the Right Trip home", abiding by "Safety, Punctuality, Attentive Service"

Juneyao Airlines owns 500 million RMB registered capital. Based in Shanghai and operating hubs at Hongqiao and Pudong International Airports, Juneyao Airlines mainly operates domestic air transport of passenger, cargo and mail, business and tourist charter, as well as flights to Hong Kong, Macao and neighboring countries.

Juneyao Airlines started its maiden flight on September 25, 2006 and its flight routes originating from Shanghai. Juneyao Airlines targets at the middle and high level business and business leisure market. Juneyao airlines has ambitions to increase flights to Southeast Asia, Japan and Korea.

To make up for the severe shortfall in the number of pilots available, Chinese airlines have turned to foreign airlines as a source for experienced personnel and moved aggressively to hire pilots from overseas. The number of foreign pilots currently working for Chinese airlines is estimated to be in the range of 1500, a number that reflects a 30%

increase over the previous year. Nearly all Chinese airlines have recruited foreign pilots. However, the number of foreign pilots that newer, smaller Chinese airlines such as Spring and Juneyao (see profile) have employed is greater because their size and market position make it difficult for them to compete for the domestic flying talent available with the larger and more well-established airlines such as China Eastern.

Because the shortfall is so acute and the demand so urgent, Chinese airlines tend to hire foreign pilots with significant experience who can step in and take over the controls immediately. As a result, the average age of a foreign pilot is typically higher than that of the Chinese crew members who occupy the other seats in the cockpit. While this strategy has proven to be effective in meeting immediate needs, it may prove to be short-sighted if the airlines fail to develop sufficient local 'bench strength' in the meantime who can take over when these older foreign pilots begin to retire (Photo 3.1).

Photo 3.1 Captain Aurélien Schmitt (France) employed by China Eastern Airlines

Chinese airlines received approval to hire pilots from overseas beginning in 2007. With this approval in hand, the airlines turned first to South Korea as a source for pilots with requisite experience. Airline management reasoned that because of Korea's geographic and cultural proximity to China it might be easier for Korean pilots to adapt to the environment in China than it would be for pilots from other countries. Today South Korea is the country of origin for nearly a third of all foreign pilots employed by Chinese airlines, the largest source (Zhang 2018). However, to keep up with the explosive demand for air travel in the decade since they recruited the first cohort of Korean pilots, Chinese airlines have had to cast a much wider geographic net and today count pilots from a total of 53 countries on their staff rosters (Zhang 2018). After South Korea, Brazil and the U.S. round out the list of the three countries that are the largest sources of foreign pilots Chinese airlines employ.

Like foreign athletes who play on Chinese teams, most foreign pilots find their way to Chinese airlines through agents who, in addition to playing an active role in the recruiting and hiring process, also take responsibility for arranging payment for the pilots (usually in foreign currency) and managing their benefits (health care, etc.).[1] Similar to foreign basketball and soccer players, foreign pilots flying for Chinese airlines very often maintain some ongoing connection to the companies that originally employed them. In some instances, especially where a Chinese and foreign airline have an existing commercial relationship, pilots from the foreign airline may be "loaned out" to the Chinese partner airline for a given period of time. A number of Air France pilots furloughed during a business downturn found employment opportunities with Chinese airlines and were hired with the understanding that they would be rehired by Air France when conditions improved. Finally, a number of foreign pilots and crew members who are technically employed by Chinese airlines remain based in their home countries, an arrangement that can be accommodated because of the unique nature of the airline industry and is accommodated because pilots with experience are in such demand they can dictate favorable terms of employment and negotiate conditions that are in their best interest.

---

[1] One foreign pilot flying for China Eastern Airlines claimed to have simply applied for the job he eventually secured online this case is the exception rather than the norm.

Profile of Pilot Recruiting Agency

Risworth Aviation (www.risworthaviation.com) 30 years in business Database of 90,000 aviation professionals from 150 countries serves over 100 clients in 40 countries (including Chinese airlines)

Services include:

- Aviation Recruitment
- Crew Leasing
- Crew Training Support
- Aviation HR Consulting Services
- Market Intelligence

Models

According to some estimates, Western models appear in more than 50% of the ads that promote products in China's fashion, cosmetics, and beverage industries and see the highest demand for their services concentrated in the Yangtze River Delta among traditional centers of commerce that radiate out from the Shanghai core (Xu and Chen 2015, page 201). Hangzhou, one of the largest and most prosperous of these centers, is a useful reference point for the scope and source of the demand for foreign models. Nearly 80% of the events organized in Hangzhou that showcase consumer products are dedicated to clothing, a domain whose products foreign models are most commonly employed to promote ("Foreign Models" 2017). The explosion of e-Commerce in China over the last five years and the profusion of promotional channels such as video and live streaming has further fueled the already robust demand for their services ("Foreign Models" 2017).

The seemingly insatiable demand for use of foreign models in Chinese advertising and marketing campaigns can be attributed to a number of social and cultural factors: The foreign model represents a lifestyle (usually understood to be a Western lifestyle) that the Chinese consumer aspires to; is imbued with an aura of the exotic and therefore perceived as attractive for the departure he or she represents from the type of people the average Chinese consumer is likely to encounter in the course of their daily existence; conveys a general air of 'elegance' and 'refinement' that complements the products being promoted (Xu and Chen 2015; Schein 1994; Lee 2016).

Such strong demand and the wealth of opportunity it generates is a magnet for aspiring models who are resident in countries outside of China. Ukraine, Georgia, Russia and Eastern Europe are among the countries of origin that are the largest sources of foreign models who come to China for employment. Models from countries in Western Europe and North America are less well-represented, a function largely of the distance from their home countries and the disparity in compensation levels.

Similar to athletes and pilots, a foreign model who comes to China for employment is most likely to be engaged by one of more than seventy agencies that take care of scheduling models' assignments managing their housing, and, if they are lucky, organizing their transportation. As straightforward as this arrangement may appear and as similar to the one into which athletes and pilots enter, it is, in reality, a highly transactional relationship whose contours are often obscured by regulations that are poorly defined and loosely applied. "The relationship between models and agencies is not the like that between Employee and Employer," notes the head of one agency (Yan 2017). This tenuous relationship that exists between model and agency is further complicated by the relationships that the Chinese agency may maintain with the agency a model may have worked for in his or her home country. The overall lack of clarity around the assignment of responsibilities that results from these complex arrangements, gives the agencies the upper hand and often leaves the models exposed to abuse and exploitation.

SUMMARY

Pilots, athletes and models represent industries that have only recently become prominent in China and demand for their experience and skills still exceeds supply. The arrangements for the recruitment and employment of these foreign professionals in their respective industries usually involves agents and intermediaries. In many cases these arrangements are structured in a way that enables their beneficiaries to maintain relations in varying degrees with the organizations that originally employed them even as they fulfill their obligations with a Chinese employer. Seen within the historical context presented in Chapter 2—"History Lessons", this arrangement follows a tradition of dual-allegiances that has characterized the employment of foreigners in Chinese organizations for hundreds of years, from soldiers such as Gordon and Stilwell in the previous century to the scientist-missionaries Schall and Verbiest in the more distant past. Despite the similarities that exist in the way employment for pilots, athletes, and models in China is arranged, the conditions under which they are employed are quite different. Models, who are younger, less experienced, and more vulnerable are very often put in a position where they are taken advantage of and subjected to an existence that is precarious at its best. Older and more experienced athletes and pilots occupy a position of influence that enables them to take advantage of a luxurious lifestyle and generous benefits. The influence they wield has enabled them to do more than simply dictate favorable terms of employment. It has given them the wherewithal to shape and transform the industries they represent.

SHAPING INDUSTRIES

John Spencer is a name that probably none but a few sports aficionados would recognize. In China of the 1990s, however, Spencer was a phenomenon if for no other reason than the distinction he held of being one of the first foreign players to be recruited into the Chinese Basketball League. When Spencer joined the Jiangsu Dragons in 1996, basketball in China, and China itself for that matter, was at an early stage of development and still suffering from a shortage of even the most basic amenities. As appalled as Spencer was by the poor conditions in which Chinese players lived and trained, he was as impressed by the Chinese public's enthusiasm for the sport. He sensed there was potential for development and believed that he was uniquely positioned to contribute to realizing that potential. The form his contribution took included introducing a more physical style of play that was characteristic of basketball in the U.S. and a more strategic approach to the game than his Chinese teammates were accustomed to. The transformation that Spencer and others like him initiated, resulted in a dramatic increase in the number of foreign players active in both Chinese basketball and soccer leagues. The foreign players who followed in Spencer's footsteps would not only change the way the game was played in China, but, by adding momentum to Chinese basketball programs and attracting more attention, would transform it from a sport into a business (Kim 2017).

E.E. Bauer, like John Spencer, is relatively unknown outside of a limited circle of industry experts. However, his contribution was just as instrumental in transforming the way Chinese planes were flown as Spencer's was in transforming the way Chinese basketball was played. In 1980, Bauer, a Boeing executive, was appointed the company's first official representative in China and later worked for the Chinese Aviation Association where he promoted international safety measures and the adoption of standard maintenance procedures (Fallows 2013). As they transformed the Chinese aviation industry and basketball league, Bauer and Spencer also transformed the way China presented itself to the world and changed the perception of the role China could play in a foreign professional's development.

Shifting Perceptions

Paul Gascoigne's agent Wes Saunders recounted that one of the British soccer star's happiest moments during his brief tenure in the China Football League (CFL) was the day he reeled in a carp from the ornamental fish pond outside the guest house where he was staying using a bamboo pole as a makeshift rod. Like the carp dangling off the end of his rod, Gascoigne was very much a fish out of water in China and by indulging his passion for angling the aging star was perhaps subconsciously attempting to recreate the familiar in a very unfamiliar place.

To understand how Gascoigne had ended up in middle age playing for an unknown Chinese soccer team whose stadium sat at the end of the Silk Road, involved tracing out the trajectory of the arc that described his professional career. There was Gascoigne's meteoric ascendance through the English soccer leagues followed by an equally precipitous decline that eventually terminated in the Chinese Football League, a place from which, both his supporters and detractors agreed, he was fated never to return.

In 2014, little more than a decade after Gascoigne's departure from China, the Brazilian striker José Paulo Bezerra Maciel Júnior, known more familiary to friends and fans as 'Paulinho', found himself donning the unfamiliar red and white jersey of Evergrande, the Southern Chinese city of Guangzhou's professional soccer club. For Paulinho, the color scheme of the Evergrande jersey was as different from the white and blue of his home team, the São Paulo Corinthians, as his life in China was from that which he had known in Brazil.

A native of São Paulo, Paulinho made a name for himself early in his career for his contribution to the victories of his local team as well as for the goals he scored playing on Brazil's national team. Despite these early successes and the profile he enjoyed, Paulinho found that by 2013, aged 25, his career was foundering. That year he started in only three games for the Tottenham Hotspurs, a British team he had joined the year before. What concerned Paulinho even more than the reduction in playing time was his discovery that not one passenger recognized him when he boarded a public bus in his home town, the unmistakable indicator of a star in decline. Given the circumstances, Paulinho was more favorably disposed than he otherwise might have been to consider an offer that came one day from Guangzhou Evergrande. The lucrative €14 million fee Evergrande offered proved too good for Paulinho and Tottenham to refuse and, after some deliberation, he finally accepted the offer. Despite the effort he made to portray the deal with Evergrande in the best light possible, Paulinho failed to win over the pundits who remained convinced that a move to China, such as the one he was contemplating, would mark the premature conclusion of what had previously seemed a promising career. Against all odds, Paulinho would prove these naysayers wrong two years later on the day he boarded a plane for Europe to join legendary FC Barcelona who had paid €40 million to Guangzhou Evergrande to secure his services and bring additional depth to their midfield (Cororan 2017).

From Paulinho's perspective, the time in China had been well spent. Not only had playing for Guangzhou Evergrande been financially remunerative but, as he himself admitted, the increase in playing time he enjoyed as one of the stars of the Evergrande team had enabled him to hone his skills on the field and raise his confidence to a level that made him a viable candidate for a coveted spot on the FC Barcelona roster. For Guangzhou Evergrande the picture was less clear. From a purely financial standpoint, the team's management had benefited tremendously from the deal by recognizing a return that was nearly triple the initial €14 million investment they had made. However, this financial gain was offset by a sharp decline in attendance that Paulinho's departure precipitated. Officials of the Chinese Football League, less burdened by the financial considerations that occupied the team, were quick to position this latest development in Paulinho's career as incontrovertible proof that China's

Football League was successfully transforming its image from that of a terminal station for has-been European soccer stars playing out the twilight of their careers to an increasingly important stop on the career path of foreign players with potential who would find it conducive to improving their skills and kickstarting their careers.

In chronicling the fate of an aging star and the destiny of a rising talent, the story of Paul Gascoigne and Paulinho describes a shift in the way those outside China perceive the country and in the value they assign to an opportunity for employment with a Chinese organization. It also reflects a change that has occurred in the motivations that prompt foreigners to work for Chinese organizations and a transformation in the nature of their experience once they are employed within those organizations.

EXPANDING MOTIVATIONS

"As long as they said that money was where it was at I was sold and I was ready to go". American basketball star Josh Akognon's candid statement about the decisive role compensation played in his decision to come to China is consistent with that of other players for whom lucrative contracts and generous benefits are the primary driver and motivator. Even John Spencer, who asserted that the motivation for his decision to play basketball in China was a desire to contribute and "be part of something big", was nonetheless very much swayed by financial considerations. The $30,000-a-month contract the CBA offered Spencer to come back and play for a second year, although a pittance by current standards, was more than double what he earned the first year he played in China and was the decisive factor in his decision to return. Like foreign athletes, foreign pilots and models place compensation high on their list of considerations in making a decision to sign on with a Chinese airline or modeling agency. However, pilots and models are at opposite ends of the spectrum when the scale of compensation and related conditions are taken into account.

To attract foreign pilots Chinese airlines have demonstrated a willingness to pay double or even triple what those pilots would have earned in their home markets and those offers of compensation are supplemented with generous benefits packages. Although there are many factors that influence what a model can earn, a rough order of magnitude can be estimated from available data points. In 2016, a foreign model's average hourly fee was on the order of $800/hour (Yan 2016). More recent statistics suggest that a model can earn $1500/hour in Hangzhou for online shopping promotions and as much as $2000 an hour in Shanghai ("Foreign Models" 2017). According to industry practice, nearly half of what a model earns goes to the agency that represents them and most of what remains is used to cover basic living expenses (housing, transportation, food, etc.) (Hattam 2014). The viability of this business model depends on a model's willingness to accept conditions that are presented as "industry standards"—living in substandard housing, working long hours, and take on less than favorable assignments to make ends meet (Hattam 2014).

Because of the decisive role it plays in an athlete's, pilot's and model's considerations, compensation invariably occupies the lion's share of headlines and monopolizes the discussion. "We all know the reputation that the Chinese Super League has in Europe. The big names have arrived but the respect has not. Those who go there do so for the money" is a typical comment (Duerden 2017). This focus on compensation effectively obscures other factors that professsionals in these industries take into consideration when they are weighing a decision to work for a Chinese airline, sports team, or modeling agency. The case of Brazilian soccer players reveals that foreign athletes (as representative of professionals in the other industries referenced) have more than compensation on their minds when contemplating a move to a Chinese team. The actual decision-making process they follow is informed by a complexity that the average media headline is unable or unwilling to accommodate.

In any given year, Brazilians make up a third of the foreign players on teams in the Chinese Super League. However, their earnings have accounted for as much as sixty-percent of the total compensation that foreign players in the CSL receive, a detail that explains why articles that chronicle the exploits of Brazilian players tend to lead with a reference to their compensation. A more thorough analysis of statements the players themselves have made and interviews they have given yields ample evidence for the presence of factors other than compensation that enter into an athlete's considerations and are top of mind. Some of the more salient include:

1. Safety—21 of the world's 30 most dangerous cities are located in Brazil (Calderwood 2016). Large Chinese cities, by contrast, are some of the safest in the world. Beijing and Shanghai, for example, rank in the top third of all cities.[2]

2. Currency—Consistent with Brazil's unstable economic climate the Réal's value has experienced a dramatic decline that has been the genesis for headlines such as "Brazilian Real in Free Fall.[3] As a result of the magnitude of the devaluation of their country's currency, Brazilian athletes have a preference for compensation in a currency that is more stable and likely to retain its value (MacKenna 2016).

3. Consistency—A function of the overall economic climate in Brazil and, in some cases, poor management practice has an adverse effect on the financial health and stability of many Brazilian teams. This translates into delays in payment and significant uncertainty.

4. Transfer Fees[4]—Brazilian teams in poor financial straits are more likely and willing to consider trading players in return for lucrative transfer fees that other, better-financed teams such as those in China are willing to pay (see Chart 3.2).

Besides emphasizing the obvious potential for compensation employment in China promises, agents who canvass second and third tier cities across the Ukraine, Georgia and Russia in the search for new modeling talent paint a picture of a market that offers a number of advantages and benefits that together form the basis for a convincing and attractive value proposition. The market in China that the presentations of these agents describe is one:

1. That is more readily accessible than fashion centers such as New York, Milan, and Paris both because of its lower competitive intensity and its geographic proximity, both factors that rank high on the list of considerations for the aspiring model just starting out who is desperate to get a foothold in the industry and begin building a portfolio.

[2] Economist, Safe City Index 2017.

[3] For example, Bloomberg Leite and Oyamada, June 7, 2018.

[4] A 'transfer' in soccer refers to the transfer of a player's registration from one team to another. The 'transfer fee' is the fee paid for taking over those rights.

Player	Nationality	Transfer Fee
Hulk	Brazil	€ 55.80
Alex Teixeira	Brazil	€ 50.00
Jackson Martinez	Colombia	€ 42.00
Ramires	Brazil	€ 28.00
Elkeson	Brazil	€ 18.50
Gervinho	Cote D'Ivoire	€ 18.00
Ricardo Goulart	Brazil	€ 15.00
Paulinho	Brazil	€ 14.00
Demba Ba	Senegal	€ 13.00
Fredy Guarin	Colombia	€ 13.00

Chart 3.2 Transfer records for the top 10 foreign soccer players in the China Football League (*Source* Transfermarket 2016)

2. Where it is somewhat easier to obtain a visa than it would be in other markets.
3. Whose cost of living and related expenses are quite a bit less than they would be in North America and Europe.

In addition to highlighting the range of motivations that inform a decision to take advantage of an opportunity for employment in China, what the case of the Brazilian soccer players and Eastern European models also shows is that the specific factors a foreign candidate for an employment assignment in China takes into account depends in large measure on the stage of his or her career the candidate happens to be in, the industry they represent, and even the geography (country, region) they consider home. The soccer players and models profiled here tend to be in a relatively early stage of their careers and come from countries that are still developing and whose markets are not yet mature. To get a sense for the way in which the motivations of an experienced player coming from a more developed market might compare and the extent to which the factors that enter into a decision to join a Chinese team might differ we can consider the case of the American basketball star Josh Akognon introduced earlier.

Because he is so explicit in his public statements about the role that salary played in his decision to join a Chinese basketball team, Akognon gives the impression that the compensation package on offer is his only concern. However, considering his initial compensation-oriented response in full context leads to a more balanced assessment. "I realized that Marbury was playing there, so I started looking at it [the opportunity] more...," notes Akognon referring to Stephon Marbury, an NBA basketball star who came to play in China in 2010. In the decade since, Marbury has become a Chinese Basketball League star and a household name (Neumann 2017). In making reference to Marbury, Akognon is indicating that the quality of play is a differentiator he has duly factored into his considerations. Marbury's presence is, in essence, a stamp of approval for the caliber of play in the Chinese League and a proof point for the experience a foreign player can get by playing on a Chinese team with players of Marbury's stature. Akognon's assessment is further evidence of the transformation that has occurred in the perception of Chinese teams and leagues foreign players have. It is also a recognition that up-and-coming players like Paulinho can parlay the skills they build and the experience they gain playing in China into coveted slots on the rosters of top ranked European and South American soccer teams. The teams themselves increasingly consider the CSL a kind of proving ground for players with potential and a way to develop new talent for regular play.

Even though they are very well-compensated by any measure, pilots also do not necessarily regard compensation as the sole, or necessarily the most significant, determinant of a decision to join a Chinese airline. Pilots, in contrast to athletes and models, very often have families whose needs they have to take into account. Those with young children place a premium on security and safety when considering an opportunity for employment with a Chinese airline. There are others who prioritize the opportunities for travel that such an assignment might offer. Finally, most foreign pilots, similar to athletes and models, are motivated by the potential for professional development that an employment opportunity with a Chinese airline holds.

In summary, *compensation* and *experience* vie for leading position as the factors pilots, athletes, or models consider most important when deciding whether or not to take advantage of an employment opportunity in a Chinese organization. The previous discussion considered the effect that *compensation* has on the decision-making process. To complete the picture we will now take a closer look at the role that *experience* plays.

EXPERIENCE

Athletes

Brave Dragons, New York Times journalist Jim Yardley's account of foreign basketball players and an NBA coach who, against all odds, have been recruited by an obscure basketball team in Shanxi Province, the heart of China's rustbelt, offers a unique perspective on the momentous changes that have redefined Chinese society in the twenty-first Century. In its portrayal of the complex and often tense relations between Bob Weiss, the seasoned NBA coach, and the team's owner, Wang Xingjiang (a.k.a "Boss" Wang), the steel magnate with a passion for basketball who has hired him, *Brave Dragons* also provides a unique insight into the experience of foreigners in the employ of Chinese management.

"Boss" Wang turns out to be an impossible boss who can't resist second-guessing the professional coach he has recruited and bullying the foreign players who have joined him. There are a number of issues in particular that are the greatest source of frustration and pose the most significant challenge to both foreign players and coach alike:

- Employing a foreign expert (e.g. NBA coach) but then not taking his advice or letting him do the job he was hired for.
- Relegated to the sidelines, the expert still maintains his title and to all appearances is still in charge.
- Unexpected changes to the scope and definition of the job from what had been previously agreed upon.
- Applying different conditions to foreigners and Chinese that reinforce the divisions between them.
- Feedback on performance that is very personal in nature.

Experts Benched

Although he is applying routines and strategies that are time-tested and have proven effective in the NBA, Coach Weiss finds himself consistently overruled and eventually sidelined by "Boss" Wang who replaces the seasoned American coach with a much less experienced local coach. The results are so disastrous that Boss Wang eventually relents and restores Weiss to his original role.

Paper Titles

Even though the scope of his job has been reduced to carrying out largely administrative duties (e.g. calling timeouts), Weiss nevertheless retains his original title, still appears on the court during the game, and addresses media during the press conference afterwards. It's a set of circumstances that leaves Weiss baffled. At the conclusion of a discussion with the coach, Yardley notes, "the strangest thing to Weiss was that he remained head coach". However, it soon becomes clear that this is being done to ensure that Weiss's value as a figurehead is maintained. This fiction is sustained by the behavior of Weiss's replacement, the local coach Liu, who, Yardley notes, "still presented himself the dutiful student, the protégé, focusing intently whenever Weiss addressed the team…"

Unexpected Changes

Not long after his arrival Weiss learns that the scope of the job he is expected to do is different than what he had been given to understand it was when he agreed to join the team. And Weiss's case is not an exception. Robert Traylor (a.k.a "The Tractor") who arrives later in the season, encounters a similar change in conditions that he, unfortunately, does not accept with as much equanimity as Weiss. "They told me the deal was done. Now they're like, 'We'd like to see you practice for two or three days first'", an exasperated Traylor complains to Donta Smith, one of the other foreign players who has been recruited to join the team (Yardley 2012).

Different Strokes

The foreign players were treated differently from the Chinese players, a condition that reinforced the cultural differences that were already at play. By way of illustration, Yardley describes how, before every game, the Chinese players formed a circle at one end of the court before beginning their stretching routine while the foreigners did their own warm-up drills at the other end of the court. "It was as if they were different pieces of machinery," Yardley concluded. Chinese exchange student Fei Xing, in his account of a three-month internship he completed in the Belgian office of the Chinese telecommunications equipment provider, ZTE, describes a similar separation of Chinese and foreign staff that is reinforced by the layout of the office. Fei recalls that the Chinese staff sat in a large open space in the middle of the office while the local staff occupied a small office at the end of a hallway that extended off the main office space (Fei 2014, page 41). William Plummer's account of his time as Huawei's Director of North American External Affairs features descriptions of Chinese executives from company headquarters sequestering themselves in his office's conference room leaving the local U.S. staff to take up position in the corridors outside (Plummer 2018).

Ad Hominem

Post-game performance reviews are as much critiques of player's personalities as they are evaluations of their play. After the Brave Dragons lose an exhibition game, "Boss" Wang spends an hour singling out each player and dissecting his performance as well as his character. The Chinese players accept the ranting and raving of Boss Wang and some even argue that the feedback the diatribes contain are meant to be constructive. "He has good intentions and does it out of love for us," the Chinese players insist. The foreign players, Yardley notes, felt doubly "penalized" because they had to listen to Boss Wang deliver feedback "in a manner they found unacceptable and in a language they found incomprehensible".

Pilots

A series of videos that profile pilots from four different countries who are working in China is a convenient starting point for gaining some perspective on the experience of foreign pilots employed by Chinese airlines. The videos feature a young pilot from Hungary who takes viewers on a tour of the facilities at the airline where he works, a somewhat older Austrian pilot who speaks to the camera from the balcony of his apartment flanked by his wife and children, a seasoned British pilot who is preparing for an upcoming flight, and an American (Philippine) pilot who brings viewers into the home he shares with his newly-married Chinese wife.

Although their authorship is unattributed and the motivation for their production is not made explicit, the videos appear to have been conceived as promotional pieces whose intent, given the context in which they are presented, was to support recruitment of foreign pilots. However, If recruitment was indeed the intent of the videos, the

Top 5 Negative Aspects		Top 5 Positive Aspects	
Language barriers	Some captains don't speak English and this could cause lack of communication in the flight deck and sometimes misunderstanding	Good Pay Level	Best paid jobs are in China
Culture Shock	It's not easy to integrate into Chinese society	Flexibility	Good roster options
Lifestyle Change	Especially at early stage	Services	Most Chinese airlines have assigned staff to assist foreign pilots
Family Life	Family life needs to be adjusted, and there is an increasing number of pilots who bring their families to China with them	Nice Bases	Sanya, Shanghai, Shenzhen, Xiamen, Kunming and Hangzhou are among popular choices
		Good Working Environment	Working with professional people

Chart 3.3   2017 Foreign Pilot Employment Survey (foreign pilots employed by Chinese airline companies) (*Source* Tempo International Aviation Recruitment September 11, 2017 [https://tempointl.com/aviation-personel/])

contrived dialogue, akwardly staged scenes and poorly crafted messaging that characterizes their composition undermines their effectiveness. Instead of presenting the airlines as attractive employers of choice the videos have the opposite effect of casting them in a less than flattering light.

Judging by the degree of stylistic difference they exhibit and the absence of a common look and feel, the videos were, in all likelihood, produced independently of one another. However, if the lack of coordination in their original production is overlooked and the videos are placed next to one another in a loose ensemble, they appear to form a coherent scheme in which each one describes the experience and addresses the conditions of foreign pilots in different stages of their lives and careers:

1. The young pilot who leads a carefree life of travel to exotic destinations and workouts at the gym when he's not on the job.
2. The newly married pilot who is establishing a home and trying to find an appropriate work-life balance.
3. The established pilot who has a family with adolescent children.
4. The senior pilot who has a comfortable lifestyle that is conditioned by familiar and well-established routines.

In bringing shape to these distinct profiles, the videos capture some of the key themes that define the experience of foreign pilots working for Chinese airlines: quality of life, family, good working conditions with 'nice' colleagues, and compensation. That the parameters highlighted here are the most consequential in defining the experience of foreign pilots working for Chinese airlines is corroborated by the results from surveys conducted by industry organizations such as Tempo International (see Chart 3.3).[5]

[5] Tempo International Aviation Recruitment September 11, 2017 (https://tempointl. com/aviation-personel/).

Models

Consistent with the characterization of other aspects of a model's existence previously presented—commercial, professional, etc.—a model's experience is quite a bit different from that of pilots and athletes.

On Wednesday, October 25, 2014, Vlada Dzuba was admitted to Shanghai's Ruijin Hospital. On Thursday, the 14-year-old Russian fashion model was transferred to the hospital's intensive care unit. On Friday, she was pronounced dead. According to the Chinese agency representing Dzuba, the young Russian model had traveled on Monday to the town of Yiwu some 170 miles Southeast of Shanghai to prepare for a photo shoot that was scheduled for the following day. That night she began to feel sick, a condition that worsened until it became so acute that she had to be taken to the hospital. Family and friends suspected the cause of her death was overwork, a common occupational hazard for young foreign models in China. Citing an official medical report as evidence, the agency refuted the accusation of overwork, claiming instead that the young model had died from multiple organ failure caused by pyemia, a type of blood poisoning (Zhou 2017). Dzuba is certainly not the first foreign model working in China to die on the job nor is she likely to be the last,[6] but her case is instructive for the insights it provides into the dynamics of the working environment that foreign models encounter in China and the conditions that define their experience in the employ of Chinese modeling agencies and hi-end consumer product companies.

The glamorous lifestyle that foreign fashion models project while on the set masks the reality of a harsh life that is characterized by low pay, long hours, and a fluid work environment that one industry veteran characterized as a "hyper-sexual nightscape of drugs and promiscuity". This dichotomy that exists between the two spheres of a model's existence is mediated through the adjectives most commonly used to describe them. On the job, the foreign model posing seductively against the cornice of a colonial mansion in downtown Shanghai is perceived as 'exotic', 'fashionable', and 'elegant'. In her off hours, lying sprawled across a second-hand sofa that doubles as a makeshift bed, she is portrayed as

---

[6]Representative cases of suicides among foreign models include Ruslana Korshunova (2008), Daul Kim (2010), and Camila Bezerra (2014).

'innocent', 'impressionable', and 'young'. Given that the majority of foreign models working in China are under 20, with an age distribution that skews towards the 14 or 15 year-old end of the scale, use of such descriptors is well-justified.

Accounts such as Mara Hvistendahl's, *And The City Swallowed Them*, based on the murder in Shanghai of a young Canadian fashion model, capture the vulnerability of these young models and have raised the public's awareness of just how precarious their existence working in China is (Hvistendahl 2014). Specific cases like Dzuba's have gotten the attention of local authorities who have begun to impose stricter conditions and taken steps to enforce the responsibilities of intermediaries, agencies, and customers.

CONCLUSION

In their search for a common topic of interest, a group of China-based Korean pilots, Brazilian soccer players, and Ukrainian fashion models seated next to one another at a dinner party, might eventually discover that they had similar motivations for seeking employment in China. They would also come the realization that, regardless of profession, the scope and execution of their jobs was governed by rules that vary in their degree of specificity as well as in the rigor of their application, a condition whose effect was to make relations with their Chinese employers more transactional. This condition was exacerbated by the intervention of intermediaries (e.g. agencies and representatives). Finally, they would undoubtedly sympathize with one another over a common inability to find stability in their work lives given the brevity of the terms of their employment—typically a year or two for pilots and athletes and in some cases less than ninety days for models.

These aspirations and conditions of employment that models, pilots, and athletes working for Chinese employers today have in common are precisely what distinguishes them from those whose services were engaged by Chinese imperial courts, government bureaus, and military battalions in previous generations. The athlete whose decision to play for a Chinese basketball team in the twenty-first Century is motivated first and foremost by compensation would be incredulous to discover that the sources of motivation for many of the doctors, missionaries and revolutionaries who came to China in the twentieth, nineteenth, and eighteenth Centuries were ideals, faith and conviction.

However, even the player for whom financial considerations are top of mind when making a decision to join a Chinese team would also admit that there are other factors such as playing time, flexibility, and safety, that come into play. In fact, if he or she is a younger player with potential (e.g. Paulinho) they might even assign the experiential benefit to be gained (e.g. building skills and confidence) a value that is much closer in weight to that of the financial benefit. The assignment of greater importance to experience gained marks a clear shift in the perception that foreign players and their managers have of the employment prospects with Chinese employers—from the last stop on the line for an aging star reaching the end of their professional lives to the latest stop for up-and-coming talent. This transformation in the perception of China from "Last Stop" to "Latest Stop" on a foreign athlete's career development path is even more in evidence and more pronounced in the case of foreigners employed by Chinese enterprises, an area that will be explored more fully in the next chapter.

REFERENCES

Calderwood, Imogen, "The 50 Most Violent Cities in the World", *Daily Mail Online*, January 27, 2016. http://www.dailymail.co.uk/news/article-3419140/The-50-violent-cities-world-revealed-21-Brazil.html.
Corcoran, Huw, "Paulinho's $47M Move to Barcelona Is a Sign of Chinese Super League Potential", *Forbes*, August 25, 2017.
Dennis, William, "Chinese Airlines Scrambling to Hire Foreign Pilots", *AINOnline*, August 19, 2016.
Duerden, John, "How Paulinho Earned Seemingly Bizarre Barcelona Move", *Irish Times*, August 15, 2017.
Fallows, James, *China Airborne*, Vintage, 2013.
Fei, Xing, "Expat Training Effectiveness in Chinese MNCs: Four Case Studies", Louvain School of Management (Master's thesis), 2014–2015.
"Foreign Models Find Themselves in Demand as E-Commerce Grows in China", *Global Times*, November 3, 2017.
Hattam, Meredith, "My Life Working as a Model in China", *Fashionista*, January 13, 2014.
Hvistendahl, Mara, *And the City Swallowed Them*, Deca Stories, 2014.
Kim, Patrick, "China's Love for Basketball," *TutorMing China Expats & Culture Blog*, March 1, 2017. http://blog.tutorming.com/expats/why-the-cba-is-growing-fast.

Knoema World Atlas, China-Transportation 2017. https://knoema.com/atlas/China/Number-of-air-passengers-carried.

Lee, Elaine Y.J., "Why Do So Many Asian Brands Hire White Models?", *Highsnobiety*, May 2, 2016.

MacKenna, Ewan, "China Is the Latest Destination for Brazilian Stars", *New York Times*, February 1, 2016.

Neumann, Thomas, "What It's Really Like for Americans Playing Basketball in China," *espn.com*, June 17, 2017.

Plummer, William B., *Huidu—Inside Huawei*, June 2018 (self-published).

Schein, Louisa, "The Consumption of Color and the Politics of White Skin in Post-Mao China", *Social Text* (Duke University Press), No 41, Winter 1994, pages 141–164.

Sin, Ben, "How China Became the NBA's Farm System", *Men's Journal*, March 13, 2015.

Xiang, Bo, "China Contributes 549 Million Passengers to Global Aviation Industry in 2017", *Xinhuanet*, January 22, 2018. http://www.xinhuanet.com/english/2018-01/22/c_136915809.htm.

Xu, Xiaobing, and Chen, Rong, "The Role of a Model's Race in Influencing Chinese Consumers' Product Perception" *Asian Business & Management*, Vol. 15, No. 3, 2015, pages 201–225.

Yan, Alice, "China Is No Walk in the Park for Foreign Models Trying to Make a Buck", *South China Morning Post*, October 6, 2016.

Yan, Alice, "Shanghai Agency Denies Russian Teenage Model Worked to Death Under 'Slave Contract'", *South China Morning Post*, October 29, 2017.

Yardley, Jim, *Brave Dragons: A Chinese Basketball Team, an American Coach, and Two Cultures Clashing*, Vintage, 2012.

Zhang, Yi, "Number of Foreign Airline Captains Growing", *China Daily* (online), March 15, 2018.

Zhou, Wenting, "Infection Blamed in Death of Russian Model", *China Daily* (online), October 31, 2017.

CHAPTER 4

Roles and Responsibilities

TRANSFORMATION OF THE CHINESE ENTERPRISE

The Chinese company in its modern form emerged from a transformational period that extended roughly from the beginning of the decade before the turn of the twentieth Century to the end of the decade after (i.e. 1890–1910). As the catalyst for this transformation, Faure pinpoints the Company Law of 1904 that reduced imperial intervention in the establishment of commercial entities and thus paved the way for the privatization that was a precondition for the formation of the modern Chinese enterprise (Faure 2006, page 3).

Nearly a century after the introduction of the Company Law of 1904 the Chinese Government's "Going Out" initiative provided the stimulus for a new phase in the transformation of the Chinese company, from a commercial entity whose sphere of operation was almost exclusively confined to the Chinese domestic market to one with global aspirations and an increasing appetite for revenues from markets overseas. To feed that appetite Chinese companies have turned increasingly to foreign talent for support and in the process have become the largest employer of foreign staff.

The study that follows takes a closer look at how Chinese companies employ and engage foreign staff, how they position those staff within the company's organizational fabric, and how they envision the role that foreign staff play in overall corporate development. With an eye towards developing the base for a coherent framework, the study will present the cases of specific companies with attention to their internationalization

© The Author(s) 2020
P. Ross, *Barriers to Entry*,
https://doi.org/10.1007/978-981-32-9566-7_4

strategies and the composition of their leadership, two areas of greatest relevance to the foreign employee: *internationalization strategy* because of the bearing it has on the number of foreign staff a company needs to support its overseas efforts and the nature of the support that is needed; *leadership composition* because it is an indicator of how committed to the employment of foreign staff the company is and the potential a foreign employee has for long-term tenure in the company and career development.[1] It will also provide a profile of foreign staff ("Who they are") as well as describe the scope of their employment and the range of positions and functions that employment encompasses ("What they do").

THE CHINESE HI-TECH INDUSTRY: A LEADING EMPLOYER

Of particular interest and relevance for this study are companies that have not only demonstrated a commitment to expanding their business globally, but also a willingness to employ foreign talent and apply that talent to ensuring that the company's strategy achieves a successful outcome.

Given these criteria, an argument could certainly be made for consideration of Chinese State Owned Enterprises (SOEs). A number of these SOEs have been operating in markets outside of China for decades and over that time have built out an operating footprint that is global in scope. Moreover, although there is some debate about how many local workers Chinese SOEs actually employ in markets where they operate and lack of clarity around the capacity in which those workers are employed, there is no denying that SOEs are a source for cases of foreigners in the employ of Chinese companies that is valid and *a propos*. Despite their apparent "fit", however, these companies are subject to a number of constraints that make them less than ideal candidates for further consideration within the scope of this study: Their operations are largely oriented towards developing markets[2] and within those markets they are focused on a limited number of sectors such as infrastructure,

---

[1] Zaagman highlights and analyzes the connection between Chinese leadership composition and foreign employee experience in: Zaagman, Elliott, "Thinking About Working for a Chinese Company? First Find Out If It's A 'Lenovo' or a 'Huawei'", Supchina (online), October 9, 2017.

[2] In the more recent past Chinese state-run enterprises have become more present in developed markets, but in many cases the size of the operation is conservative and the staff they maintain is small. Consider Sinopec in the U.S. Viewed as a representative office

energy, and extractive industries. Finally, the number of foreign staff they employ in their headquarters offices, if any, is an exceedingly small number and the positions held by foreign staff locally are constrained with little evidence of foreigners in executive roles, if such potential even exists.

A much more promising pool of candidates is to be found among representatives of China's tech sector.[3] Of all Chinese companies, those in the tech sector have been among the most aggressive in exploring markets overseas and making development of business internationally an integral part of their core business and strategic plans.[4] Particularly relevant to this study are the steps companies in the sector have taken to employ foreign staff—both in company headquarters and in local field offices—and in a broad range of positions and functions. These companies have also recognized the potential value that foreign staff can contribute to long-term success and, in varying degrees, have developed programs that are designed to help them achieve that potential. Three firms that are particularly noteworthy for the effort they have expended in incorporating foreign talent into their operations and accounting for their contribution in strategic plans are—Alibaba, Huawei, and Tencent. Frequently referenced as models for the evolution of the Chinese multinational, each of these firms has taken a distinct and different approach to growing its international business and by association to employing foreign staff both in its China headquarters and in offices overseas.

ALIBABA

Company Profile

Alibaba was founded in the Southern Chinese city of Hangzhou in the late 1990's, at a time when the development of China's consumer culture and Internet infrastructure, although beginning to exhibit signs of

---

by the company and has about 100 staff, 60% are locals. Telecom operators like China Telecom have a similar model and maintain an office to facilitate, for example, bilateral traffic agreements, roaming agreements to serve China Telecom customers who may be visiting the U.S.

[3] Here to be understood in its broadest definition (including ICT, Internet based companies, Communications, etc.).

[4] Huawei, for example, generates more business from its overseas operations than it does from its domestic operations.

potential for significant growth, was still in a nascent stage. Fortuitously, Alibaba's business model positioned it at the confluence of these two trends, a position that enabled it to emerge in the early 2000s as a catalyst for the Chinese economic and commercial environment that was taking shape. Taobao, an Internet-based consumer shopping site Alibaba launched in 2003, exemplified the company's positioning at the avant-garde of an era distinguished by growth in personal spending, and entrepreneurial activity. Taobao was the earliest and, arguably, the most visible exponent of the company's business model. The company's successful listing on the New York Stock Exchange a decade later was another important milestone that paved the way to its current $480 Billion market value and its rise to prominence as the world's largest retail commerce company.[5] Although it was through the announcement of Alibaba's listing on the New York Stock Exchange that many foreign observers first became aware of the company's global aspirations, Alibaba had been building a base of customers outside of China for years prior to that announcement.

Internationalization Path

Alibaba first began to establish a presence in markets outside of China in 2014 with launch of an online retail service in the U.S. branded 11 Main. Today, the company generates approximately 10% of its revenues from outside of China and claims millions of customers in markets overseas, from the more than 60 Million buyers who connect with manufacturers and distributors in China using the company's AliExpress platform to the thousands of foreign brands and retailers who make use of TMall Global to reach Chinese consumers (Gray 2017; Sun 2018).[6]

The global strategy that Alibaba has conceived to realize its goals for expanding its presence in key markets around the world and serving international customers emphasizes retail commerce that is based on cross-border trade and is anchored by three pillars (see Chart 4.1).

[5] In terms of GMV in the twelve months ended March 31, 2017, on the basis of publicly available comparable transaction value data for the most recent fiscal year (Alibaba Annual Report 2017).

[6] Estimate of Alibaba's revenues from overseas is complicated by definition and complexity of the company's business (e.g. revenue from e-commerce exclusively, wholesale and retail, etc.). Two reports from 2017 to 2018 respectively estimate revenues at a little less than 10% (2017) and a little more than 10% (2018).

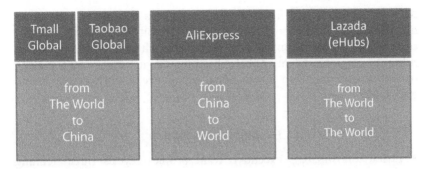

Chart 4.1 Alibaba corporate strategy—three pillars (*Source* Alibaba Annual Report 2017)

The execution of the strategy to date has focused on the first two pillars: "From the World to China" and "From China to the World" and largely involves making investments in companies that are geographically and commercially aligned with Alibaba's strategy.[7]

The company took a first step towards achieving the third pillar—"From the World to the World"—when it established its first eHub (see description below) in Malaysia in 2017. With a network of eHubs in place, the company will then be in position to realize its long-term global vision that entails building out a virtual and borderless electronic global commerce platform—the electronic World Trade Platform (eWTP) on the foundation established by the eHubs,

eHub
A one-stop service platform that will allow small businesses in one country to sell to consumers in another, with fast customs clearance, accessible payment and financing services, and access to efficient logistics through public-private partnerships in different countries.

---

[7]The company's acquisition of Singapore-based Lazada, an e-commerce platform developed specifically to serve customers in Southeast Asia is an example of how this strategy is implemented.

Recognizing that hard infrastructure and platforms can only be effective when their deployment is combined with soft people assets and that achieving its global vision will only be possible with the support and contribution of global talent, Alibaba has pursued an employment strategy that puts a premium on international experience at both executive and staff level.

Leadership Composition

A review of Alibaba's executive team profiles reveals three defining characteristics:

> More than a third have gained international academic experience through advanced education outside of China; Nearly two-thirds have worked for Western multinationals, especially in the Finance and Accounting sectors (e.g. KPMG and PWC); Nearly half the executive team are women, demonstration of a clear commitment to diversity.

Foreign Staff Profile

Foreign staff have been present in Alibaba from the earliest years of the company's operation.

In the two decades since, their number and the nature of their contribution has undergone an evolution that comprises a number of distinct phases. 1) Early Stage (2000–2006)—Alibaba engages a small group of foreign staff whose contribution to the company's development ranges from improving operational efficiency to engaging overseas investors; 2) Mid-Stage (2006–2013)—In an effort to make effective use of limited resources, Alibaba reduces the attention it pays to development of international markets in favor of focus on the China domestic market, a change in strategic orientation that reduces demand for foreign staff 3) Current Stage (2014–)—The company's renewed commitment to expansion of business outside of China is accompanied by local hiring and implementation of a formal management program for foreign employees at company headquarters—the Alibaba Global Leadership Academy (AGLA).

Early Stage (2000–2006)

In Alibaba's earliest years, the typical profile of a 'foreigner' who joined the company was an ethnic Chinese from Singapore or Hong Kong who, in many cases, had received an education in the U.S. The company's first non-Chinese hire, Porter Erisman, was an American with a Corporate Communications and Public Relations background, who joined the company in 2002. For the next six years Erisman led the company's international website operations, international marketing and corporate affairs as a Vice-President at Alibaba.com and Alibaba Group. Erisman's promotional and communications work complemented the efforts of others in the company who were charged with attracting and engaging international investors (Erisman 2015). The company's decision in 2006 to bring the compensation of foreign and local staff into closer alignment led to the departure of many foreign employees whose compensation was reduced as a consequence of the policy change. Their departure effectively marked the end of the company's earliest phase of engagement with foreign staff.

Mid Stage (2006–2013)
In the period that followed the earliest phase of engagement with foreign staff, the company concentrated its efforts and applied its limited resources almost exclusively to the development of the market in China. As a consequence of this domestic-market focus, cultivation of overseas markets languished and the demand for foreign staff weakened. Deviations from this general trend, such as the appointment of Tim Steinert (see profile below) as the company's general counsel in 2007, were few and far between.

Current (2014–)
Beginning in 2014, Alibaba undertook a number of initiatives to renew its commitment to customers outside of China and expand its presence overseas. The role of overseeing international expansion fell to Michael Evans (see profile below), a seasoned Wall Street executive hired in 2015 who embarked on a strategy of expanding investment in markets overseas and increasing the number of foreign staff. As an adjunct to the expansion of its overseas business and execution of its global market strategy, the company introduced a one-year management training program in 2016 that was designed to prepare young foreign employees for leadership roles in markets that were of strategic importance and considered vital to the company's future. The company's ambitions for the program, officially introduced as the Alibaba Global Leadership Academy (AGLA), were succinctly expressed in the slogan "Connect the World, Shape the Future" that featured prominently on the banners that accompanied the program's launch.

Foreign Executives[8]

J. Michael Evans

A member of the Canadian rowing team that won a gold medal in the 1984 Olympics and then a Wall Street executive who spent nearly 25 years at Goldman Sachs, Michael Evans joined Alibaba in 2015 as president of the Alibaba Group overseeing strategic initiatives in international markets. Although he joined Alibaba in official capacity only recently, Evans' engagement with company extends over more than a decade originating with his co-ordination of Alibaba.com's public offering in 2005 (Clover 2015).

Timothy A. Steinert

Tim Steinert has been General Counsel at Alibaba Group since July 2007. From 1999 until he joined the Alibaba Group, Steinert worked in the law firms Freshfields Bruckhaus Deringer. Davis Polk & Wardwell, and Coudert Brothers. He received a bachelor's degree in history from Yale College and a Juris Doctor degree from the Columbia University School of Law.

Although Evans and Steinert are the only two senior foreign executives currently employed by Alibaba, they are not the only high profile foreign executives to have served in the company's senior management ranks. Jim Wilkinson, for example, who joined Alibaba in 2014, established the company's international corporate affairs operations and international communications strategy. Before coming to Alibaba, Wilkinson was Executive Vice President of Global Communications at PepsiCo and prior to that had high profile experience in the U.S. Government, serving as chief of staff to former Treasury Secretary Hank Paulson, senior adviser to former Secretary of State Condoleezza Rice, and deputy communications director to President George W. Bush (Bradley 2016).

A review of the profiles of these executives yields a number of valuable insights into the role that foreigners, and specifically foreign executives, employed by Chinese companies play.

---

[8] This does not consider board members who are not in daily management roles.

Goldman and Guanxi

Closer study of these executive profiles reveals the presence of a close and consistent connection to Goldman Sachs, the U.S. investment firm. Michael Evans who spent most of his career at the firm and held positions at the most senior levels of the company including that of Vice-Chairman and Chairman of Goldman Sachs Asia is the most obvious link. However, the full extent of Goldman's presence can only be appreciated when one takes into consideration the profiles of foreign executives at other Chinese firms such as Tencent. James Mitchell, for example, Tencent's Head of Strategy spent a number of years at Goldman Sachs where he headed research on Internet and media companies. It is also worth noting that Tencent's president, Martin Lau, although technically speaking not a 'foreign' employee as defined in this study, also spent a significant portion of his career at Goldman Sachs, rising to the position of Executive Director of the company's investment division in Asia and Chief Operating Officer of its Telecom, Media, and Technology group prior to joining Tencent.

The motivation of firms such as Alibaba and Tencent for hiring foreign executives with such illustrious pedigrees is both practical and symbolic. A large Chinese company with ambitious growth plans that are global in scope would naturally have complex financing requirements and to ensure a successful outcome would require the kind of expertise and network that a senior executive at a well-respected investment firm possessed. On another level, the hiring of high profile investment bankers has the effect of burnishing a Chinese company's reputation and increasing its legitimacy in the eyes of Western investors.

Henry M. ("Hank") Paulson

2006–2009 Secretary, U.S. Department of the Treasury

1999–2006 Chairman, CEO of Goldman Sachs Group

1994–1999 President and COO of Goldman Sachs Investment Banking Division
                    Born: March 28, 1946 (Palm Beach, Florida USA)

Consistently drawing support from Goldman Sachs is a reflection of the investment firm's early involvement in China under the leadership of

CEO Henry "Hank" Paulson (see profile) who engaged with China at a time when very few other investment banks recognized the potential and expended significant effort to establish a presence in the country. Evidence of Paulson's influence can be found in many leading Chinese firms and in the careers of a number of the executives profiled. As U.S. Treasury Secretary under George Bush, Paulson engaged Jim Wilkinson as his chief of staff and during his tenure as Chairman and CEO of Goldman Sachs, prior to his government post, had a direct role in steering Michael Evans towards a career in Asia (Clover 2015).

Contributing to and shaping Chinese enterprise and industries by applying their financial acumen and expertise, the Goldman investment experts bear some similarity to the NBA basketball players profiled in Chapter 3—"On the Runway" who were lured to play on teams in the Chinese Basketball Association or the Boeing aviation experts who came to China in the 1990s and contributed to the evolution of China's aviation industry. This similarity is further strengthened by the fact that these executives are experienced professionals in a later stage of their careers who may have gone about as far as they could go where they were and were looking for another opportunity (cf. Alibaba's Michael Evans who was passed over for the top job at Goldman before joining Alibaba and the company's General Counsel Tim Steinert who had been working as a partner for quite a number of years and, by his own admission, was "looking for something else to do").

Foreign Employee Development Program: AGLA

Taking its cue from the management training programs developed by American multinationals that it closely resembles, AGLA laid out a set of goals accompanied by vision and mission statements. The AGLA's stated goals—impact society, foster innovation, and establish connections—were distinctly similar in tone to the goals articulated by American multinationals. The rotations through different assignments in different operating units across the company that AGLA provided, supplemented by various team building activities, meetings and lectures from senior executives, including Jack Ma himself, further strengthen the resemblance.

The promise of AGLA, as presented to those considering the program, was that at the end of the twelve-month program trainees would be assigned to an "impactful" management role in one of Alibaba's global offices. The source of the trainees' "impact", company management reasoned, would be the close cultural (corporate and social) alignment and shorter physical and philosophical 'distance' that achieving the program's goals and participating in the rotations would ensure.

The first AGLA cohort, known as the 'Inaugural Class', comprised thirty two participants that the program's administrators selected from a pool of more than 3000 applicants. In addition to work experience, education, and an interest in China, criteria used for selection included less tangible qualities ("soft skills") such as whether candidates possessed a 'Giver' Mindset, were Open Minded and 'Mission Driven'. The selection process yielded a group of participants who represented a total of 15 countries and whose average age was 29. Despite Jack Ma's rumored antipathy towards business degrees, nearly half of the members of the 'Inaugural Class' were MBA degree holders.

> ### AGLA
> ### Candidate Profile
> ### Chloe Goncalves
>
> Nationality: French
>
> **Education**: IUT Amiens business degree. INSEEC Masters Degree in Digital Marketing
>
> **Employment**: Marketing and business development positions in Alibaba Tmall Global group
>
> **Experience**: Recruited into the AGLA program for digital marketing experience and international profile

Within the overarching goal of 'Bringing Alibaba to the World and the World to Alibaba', the participants understood their mission to involve building global bridges, transcending borders, and empowering trade. Accordingly, they understood their roles to be those of Ambassadors ('bridging cultural gaps between China and the world'), Bridge Builders ('striving to create a better world by breaking down physical/ geographical (sic)/cultural/ideological borders') and Change Agents ('across Alibaba's key strategic global initiatives')'.

Members of the second cohort of AGLA participants, known as the 'Explorer Class', maintained a view of their mission that was consistent with that of their predecessors in the 'Inaugural Class'. Their aver-age age, 29, was also consistent. Where the 'Explorer Class' departed from the 'Inaugural Class' was in its composition and in the profiles of its participants. Even though the number of applicants to the program had doubled to almost 6000 in the second year, only 20 of those who applied were accepted, a third fewer than the number who had partic-ipated in the Inaugural Class. The number of countries represented decreased proportionately from 15 to 9.[9] This change in the profiles and number of participants from the first to the second year of the program was the direct outcome of a strategic decision taken by the program's administrators to include Chinese language capability and familiarity with Chinese culture within the list of selecttion criteria. By introducing this criterion, those responsible for the program's management believed they could improve the program's success by reducing the size of the cultural gap while increasing the effectiveness of the participants.

Once this criterion was added, it had the effect of filtering out quite a number of potential candidates and increasing the number of ethnic Chinese participants.[10]

When the year-long AGLA program comes to an end some 50% of the participants remain in the company where they become part of the approx-imately 500 strong foreign staff[11] employed at company headquarters in Hangzhou[12] and in local offices in 11 countries around the world.[13]

The majority of Alibaba's foreign employees are engaged in the company's lines of business that have the greatest international exposure (see Chart 4.2).

The typical foreign employee in Alibaba headquarters is most likely to be American or German, works in a Marketing or Business Development role, is approximately 35 years of age, and has worked in the company for two to three years (Chart 4.3).

[9]This is a bit deceptive as some of those whose nationalities are listed as Korean, Indonesian, etc. actually grew up in the U.S. and are most likely U.S. citizens.

[10]40% of the Explorer class was comprised of ethnic Chinese.

[11]This number arrived at by extrapolating from the number of participants in the AGLA program who have remained following conclusion of the program.

[12]According to participants in the AGLA program interviewed, approximately 50% of AGLA participants remain in Hangzhou, a surprisingly large number given that the intent of the program is to prepare trainees for management roles in markets outside of China.

[13]France, Germany, India, Italy, Korea, Turkey, Russia, Singapore, United Arab Emirates, United Kingdom, United States.

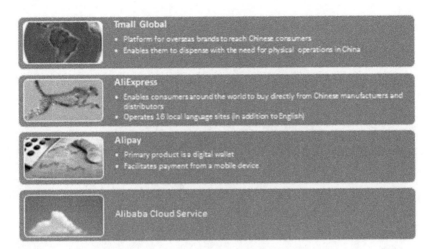

Chart 4.2 Alibaba lines of business that employ the greatest number of foreign staff (*Source* Staff interviews and LinkedIn profiles)

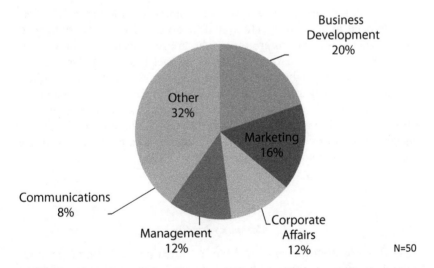

Chart 4.3 Foreign employees at Alibaba (headquarters)—Top functional roles (*Source* Staff Interviews and LinkedIn profiles)

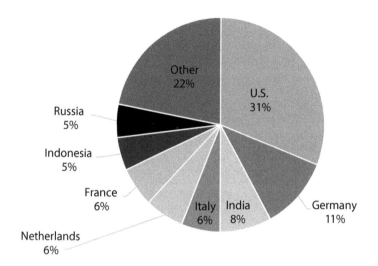

Chart 4.4   Foreign employees at Alibaba (headquarters)—Top countries of origin (*Source* Staff interviews and LinkedIn profiles)

Nearly all the foreigners who work in Alibaba corporate headquarters are employed in staff roles. The only foreign employees who hold general management positions are those who are responsible for the company's business in select markets overseas. Michael Evans and Tim Steinert (see profiles below) who occupy positions that are in the very highest echelon of the organization are notable exceptions. This phenomenon—a small group of high-profile foreign executives in the company's top echelon and a much larger group of young foreign staff who are engaged in various commercial roles is common to a number of Chinese companies that employ foreign talent (Chart 4.4).

HUAWEI

Company Profile

Huawei is a leading global provider of information and communications technology infrastructure and "smart" devices (including mobile phones) that sees its mission as creating a "fully connected, intelligent world" by bringing digital technology to every person, home and organization. The company envisions achieving this goal by providing integrated solutions across four key domains: Telecommunications Networks, Information and Communications Technology (ICT), Smart Devices, and Cloud Services.

Founded in the Southern City of Shenzhen in 1987, Huawei started out as a rural sales agent for Hong Kong-based phone and cable network enterprises. After establishing a base in the rural areas that were its primary area of coverage, Huawei began to expand into metropolitan areas. It was an initiative whose timing proved fortuitous as it occurred just as China's cities were entering into a significant period of expansion (Chart 4.5).

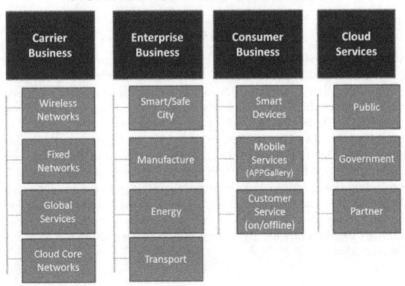

Chart 4.5 Huawei lines of business (*Source* Huawei Annual Report 2017)

Internationalization Path

Huawei's initial forays into overseas markets such as Brazil, Thailand, and a number of African countries date from the early 1990's.[14] Following a script similar to the one it had applied in growing its China domestic business, the company adopted a conservative strategy that was designed to facilitate entry into emerging markets where the low pricing on which Huawei's value proposition was based was a key competitive advantage. In 2001, a string of modest sales in Germany, the Netherlands, and France signaled the company's entry into more developed markets. At that time, the contribution of sales from overseas markets accounted for less than 10% of the company's overall revenue, but this number would increase dramatically over the next decade until it finally surpassed domestic sales in 2006 thanks to an increasing number of contracts with top-tier international telecommunications service providers such as British Telecom. These deals cemented Huawei's position as a global company, a position that was further strengthened by increasingly strong sales of mobile phones that Huawei introduced to the market in 2005 (Micheli and Carillo 2016, page 39).

Leadership Composition

Although it was some time before Huawei began to consider entry into markets outside of China in any serious way, statements that the company's founder, Ren Zhengfei, made in the company's early years expressed his conviction that the company's long term success depended on expanding its horizons and looking to overseas markets as a source of future growth. As example, Ren exhorted his leadership team to cultivate a world view: "I want you to go places where strategic resources are concentrated and broaden your horizons by exploring alongside others". Ren's rhetorical question "Someone once said, 'If you've never even seen the world, how can you possibly have a world view?'" was a thinly veiled directive to his staff that made clear the importance of getting experience outside of China. Despite Ren's best efforts, his words, it would seem, fell on deaf ears.

---

[14]In 2000, then-Chinese Vice Premier, Li Lanqing and Ren Zhengfei traveled together to various African countries and entered into contracts for the company cited in Micheli and Carillo (2016).

A review of the current leadership team's professional profiles reveals that less than 30% have spent any part of their careers in an overseas posting and not one has studied outside of China. The typical career path for a top executive at Huawei is one that is well-worn and paved with clear milestones: Obtain a technical degree from a Chinese university in the mid-1990s; upon graduation join Huawei directly; Spend the next twenty years developing a career in the company. Despite the management team's overall lack of direct international experience, Huawei has by any measure been successful at expanding its business in markets outside China and is widely considered a multinational company.

Foreign Staff Profile

To sustain its global business, the company has increased the number of foreign staff involved in its operations commensurately. The company has an estimated total of 20,000 foreign staff employed in more than 100 offices worldwide. Approximately 1000 of whom are based in company headquarters in Shenzhen.

Nearly 70% of Huawei's foreign staff are engaged in Sales and Sales-related positions—Sales Marketing, Communications (see Chart 4.6). Of note is the prominence of Corporate Affairs as a discipline where foreign employees are especially well-represented. The definition of "Corporate Affairs" as presented is fairly elastic and takes into account, for example,

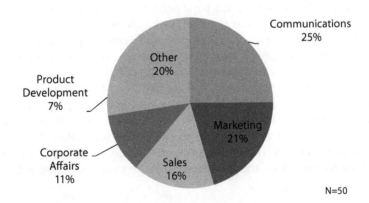

Chart 4.6 Foreign employees at Huawei (headquarters)—Top functional roles (*Source* Staff interviews and LinkedIn profiles)

Chart 4.7 Foreign
employees at Huawei
(headquarters)—Top
countries of origin
(*Source* Staff interviews
and LinkedIn profiles)

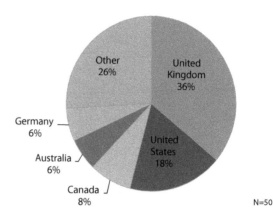

Corporate Social Responsibility (CSR) and Environmental Sustainability
(see Appendix for complete description of definitions and assumptions).
These are areas of increasing importance for Huawei as it matures as a
global company and is subject to a set of expectations that include its
level of social engagement and contribution to social causes as well as
increasingly frequent encounters and more intense engagement with
regulatory and legal affairs, especially in developed markets where it has
been expanding its presence (Chart 4.7).

These are areas where foreign staff have greater experience and are a
source of expertise whose value is increasingly important to the company's business. Not surprisingly, a large percentage of Huawei's employees
come from countries such as the U.S. and U.K. whose markets are well
developed and who possess requisite skills and experience in these areas.

To put the situation of foreigners in Huawei in proper perspective,
it is instructive to make a comparison with Alibaba. The most immediate point of difference is age. The average age of a foreign employee
working in Huawei is mid-40's. The average Alibaba employee is a full
decade younger.[15] This difference in age, considered in broader context, seems to reflect two different approaches to international business
development. Huawei is already well-established in overseas markets
and is therefore not so concerned with devising and executing a future

[15]Ages derived from university graduation dates presented in employee personal
LinkedIn profiles.

market entry program. This is a goal the company has already achieved. As a result, Huawei is focused on hiring seasoned professionals who will have an immediate impact and perhaps serve to counter-balance a domestic workforce that is reportedly much younger and very much execution-oriented. Alibaba, on the other hand, is looking to the future and realizing a strategic vision that has been articulated by company executives (see Jack Ma's vision of a company that will "last for 102 years"). It is also a fact that the business Alibaba is engaged in is relatively new and there is a recognition that younger staff who have grown up with and are well-versed in the applications and services that Alibaba provides are in best position to execute the company's long-term vision. The focus of Huawei's core business, by contrast, is on sales of telecommunications equipment to other companies (B2B), a business that places a premium on technical knowledge and experience, or sales of devices (mobile phones etc.) to consumers. This difference in business model and focus in turn leads to a difference in the types of positions that foreign employees hold and the distribution of employees across those positions. In Alibaba and Huawei, the most common role held by foreign employees is "Business Development". The position held by the greatest number of foreign employees working in Tencent is "Community Manager".

Huawei, like Alibaba, has developed a training program for foreigners called "Seeds for the Future".

Foreign Employee Development Program: Seeds of the Future

At a high level, Huawei's 'Seeds of the Future' program bears some resemblance to Alibaba's AGLA in as much as the goal of both programs is to offer young foreign talent the opportunity to learn about their respective companies, develop a better appreciation for Chinese culture, and build skills that will benefit them in their career development.

Where the programs differ, however, is in their strategic positioning, the nature of the competence they are trying to develop, and even their duration (Alibaba's AGLA is a year-long program. The "Seeds" program lasts just two-weeks).

While the objectives of AGLA are clearly linked to Alibaba's larger corporate objective of growing the company's business in markets outside of China, Huawei's 'Seeds of the Future' program is more closely aligned with broader industry and social goals. This fundamental difference in intent and strategic position has a direct influence on the structure of the programs and the experience of the young foreign professionals who are their participants.

Launched initially in 2008 and then relaunched in 2016, the 'Seeds' program's stated objective is:

> to develop local ICT talent, enhance knowledge transfer, promote a greater understanding and interest in the ICT sector and improve and encourage regional building and participation in the digital community.

This commitment to addressing social issues that is intrinsic to the 'Seeds of the Future' program provides some justification for Huawei's decision to position the program under the broader umbrella of the company's Corporate Social Responsibility (CSR) initiatives.

The underlying expectation is that an ICT-centric development program such as 'Seeds' can deliver benefits that surpass the borders of its own industry. Indeed, it holds the promise of helping to do nothing less than "solve the problem of youth unemployment and the mismatch of skills to employer demand".

Despite the loftiness of the goals the program has set for itself, its agenda exhibits an ambition that is much more conservative and more heavily weighted towards Chinese cultural enrichment than towards the development of technical skills that, at least according to its mission statement, is its raison d'être. A large part of the two-week period the program covers is occupied with visits to famous historic sites, classes in Chinese language, and seminars on cross-cultural understanding. The technical training provided, judging by the time allotted to it and the activities it comprises, is at best an appendage to the core program and so loosely attached that it seems an afterthought. However, even if the 'Seeds' program administrators reformulated and reweighted the agenda in favor of the technical training, it is questionable whether the program would come any closer to achieving the outcomes desired. The significant discrepancy that exists between aspiration and reality calls the objective of the program as stated into question and leaves one to speculate on the program's real intent.

A potential resolution of this conundrum comes in the form of a document designed to promote the benefits of the program. In the photos that accompany the document, program participants appear in the company of prominent government officials and industry leaders from their respective countries who presumably have come for a visit to

Huawei headquarters, often with the local Chinese ranking representative (ambassador, etc.) in tow. This gives the impression that the 'Seeds' bprogram's real goal is to support the company's international relationship building and cultural diffusion strategy by leveraging a set of techniques—visits to historical sites, language training, and limited duration—that are familiar and effective.

TENCENT

Company Profile

To fulfill its mission of "enhancing the quality of human life through Internet services", Tencent has developed social platforms and provides digital content to meet the various needs of Internet users including communication, information, entertainment, and financial services. From modest beginnings in 1998, Tencent has grown into a company valued at nearly $500 billion whose growth has been fueled by expansive communications platforms such as WeChat that serve nearly one billion users in China and in markets overseas (Global 2000 2018). Another indicator of the company's success is the growth in Tencent's value, from less than $2 billion when the company went public on the Hong Kong exchange in 2004 to $500 billion in 2018.[16] To ensure a consistent flow of innovative products that can sustain growth, Tencent places significant emphasis on research and development as evidenced by the nearly 25% of revenues the company allocates to this area (Chart 4.8).

Internationalization Path

Almost exclusively focused on the China domestic market for the first decade of its existence, Tencent began to take a more concerted approach to expanding its presence overseas in 2011 with investment in Riot Games (U.S.) and subsequent investments in Kakao Talk (Korea) and Epic Games (U.S.) in 2012. The company opened its first office in Korea in 2006 and has since expanded this number to more

---

[16]Towards the end of 2018 the company experienced a decline in value of more then $200 million.

TENCENT LINES OF BUSINESS

Social & Communication	Online Games	Digital Content	Online Advertising	Others
Weixin WeCHat	PC Client Games	Online Video	Media Advertising	Cloud Service
QQ	Smart Phone Games	Music Streaming	Social Advertising	Payment Service
QZone		IP Portfolio Content Library		

Chart 4.8   Tencent lines of business (*Source* Tencent Annual Report 2017)

than a dozen offices with principal locations in the U.S., Germany, the Netherlands, Japan, and India.[17]

In expanding its business internationally Tencent has adopted a cautious strategy, exemplified by the approach the company took to introducing WeChat Pay, it's digital payment service, which involved targeting Chinese tourists traveling outside of China. Tencent's guiding principle for entering markets overseas is whether it has a demonstrably better way of meeting the needs of local customers for any digital products and services ("Tencent needs to see market gap" 2018).[18] As a function of this strategy Tencent's presence outside of China is still limited. However, there are some indications that expansion of its international business underway.

In the last two years, Tencent and its affiliates have made a number of large investments and acquisitions ("Tencent Needs" 2018) outside of China in the areas of e-Commerce, Payments and Gaming valued in the

---

[17] *Source* Tencent corporate. Additional offices include—Thailand, Malaysia, Singapore, United Kingdom, Italy, Indonesia, Brazil, Australia, Philippines, South Africa, Vietnam, United Arab Emirates.

[18] Articulation of international strategy from Tencent Senior Executive Vice-President, S. Y. Lau in South China Morning Post interview (2018).

billions of dollars.[19] Three projects in particular reflect the approach the company is taking to investment overseas.

- A $8.6 billion deal in 2016 to take control of Finnish mobile games site Supercell.
- A trade deal with Britain to develop creative partnerships with organizations such as the BBC, British Fashion Council and Visit Britain, the country's tourist promotion board.
- An e-payment license in Malaysia that will enable it to support transactions for local customers, a service it plans to launch via its WeChat ecosystem, over the coming year (Jiang 2017).

This strategy of taking investments in local companies and maintaining a background presence is one that a number of other—Chinese companies in the sector have taken ("Chinese Internet giants" 2017). It is a strategy that stands in marked contrast to similarly-oriented U.S. companies such as Google, Facebook etc. whose presence in overseas markets tends to be more prominent and typically involves aggressive promotion of their own brands and the establishment of local offices that feature their names on the marquee.

In a few select markets where it sees the greatest potential, Tencent has taken a more aggressive step of opening offices. One such facility the company opened in India, referred to as a Global Publishing Center, has as its goal to take games developed in China and adapt them to the local market. The initiative in India marks a departure from Tencent's traditional strategy of acquiring licenses to adapt games from overseas and introduce them into the China market and at the same time aligns the company with a broader national effort to export culture from China to the rest of the world.

Leadership Composition

Despite following a strategy that has been largely focused on the Chinese domestic market for most of its history, Tencent has an executive team whose profiles are rounded out with significant international experience

---

[19]Tencent and its affiliates spent 38 billion yuan (US$5.1 billion) in 2017 to acquire overseas assets, followed by Alibaba and its associated units which made transactions valued at approximately 23 billion yuan (US$3.2 billion).

acquired in both academic and professional domains. Approximately 40% of Tencent's leadership team hold advanced degrees from universities overseas[20] and have worked for multinational companies such as Oracle and PWC. Nearly all (75%) of Tencent's executives have technical degrees (Computer Science and Electrical Engineering) that in quite a number of cases they have complemented with commercial degrees (i.e. MBA). Exemplary is the profile of company president, Martin Lau, whose academic pedigree includes engineering degrees from the University Michigan and Stanford University and an MBA from Northwestern University (Kellogg).

Foreign Staff Profile

From an early time in its corporate history, Tencent has had international exposure through engagement with foreign investors and the hiring of foreign staff. David Wallerstein, an American management consultant with experience in China's telecommunications and IT industries, has the distinction of having played the role of both international investor and foreign employee.[21] Wallerstein first visited Tencent as an interested investor at an early stage in the company's development. Based on his evaluation of the company's potential, he ultimately convinced Naspers, a South African company he was advising, to make an investment in the company. Naspers' $34 million investment gave the company two seats on the Tencent Board, seats it still holds (Zhang 2016).

Wallerstein eventually joined Tencent as an employee in 2001 and today plays two complementary roles. As Tencent's Senior Executive Vice-President responsible for Tencent's operations outside mainland China, Wallerstein oversees the company's international business initiatives including identifying areas of cooperation with overseas partners such as Silicon Valley startups. In his capacity as Chief Exploration Officer, Wallerstein evaluates and identifies opportunities for investment that are speculative, but that have the potential to deliver significant returns in the longer term. An example of an investment that meets these

[20] In most cases, the degrees are from American universities.

[21] David Wallerstein profile (Crunchbase), https://www.crunchbase.com/person/david-wallerstein#section-jobs.

criteria is Lilium Aviation, a startup that is developing electric flying cars to reduce travel time (Abkowitz 2018).

The other foreign member of Tencent's executive ranks, James Mitchell, joined the company in 2011 as the company's Chief Strategy Officer. Prior to joining Tencent, Mitchell, like company President Martin Lau, had a career at Goldman Sachs where he led a team that was responsible for analyzing Internet and media companies.

The presence of Wallerstein and Mitchell on Tencent's leadership team presents a foreign employee profile that is similar to Alibaba's: A couple of foreign executives who have been involved with the company and contributed to its development over a long period of time.

The presence of these foreign executives is complemented by a much larger base of younger foreign employees who are active in areas that range from game development to localization and, more recently, investment and acquisition consistent with the company's strategic direction. (see Dan Brody profile.) In comparison with the functional areas foreign employees at the other Chinese companies considered are engaged in, foreign staff at Tencent are much more active and present in product development and design. Notably, only one foreign staff member in the sample analyzed, located in the company's U.S. (Palo Alto) office, was engaged in the practice of Corporate Communications, an activity that a much larger number foreign staff at other Chinese companies are occupied with (Chart 4.9).

Dan Brody

2018– Managing Director, Tencent Investments

2014–2018 Vice-President, Business Development, Tencent

2004–2014 Various China-based Business Development and Strategy roles with Motorola, Google, Spotify, etc.

2000–2003 Director of United States Information Technology Organization (Beijing)

1993–1996 Georgetown University (BSFS Foreign Service)

Over and above contributing to product development, the typical positions that foreign employees at Tencent hold include:

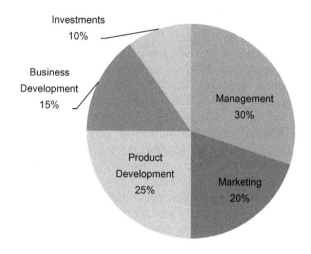

Chart 4.9   Foreign employees at Tencent (headquarters)—Top functional roles (*Source* Staff interviews and LinkedIn profiles)

Community Manager
A Community Manager in Tencent approximates a traditional Marketing Communications position and encompasses organizing and staging promotional events, launching promotions, and writing and publishing social media posts.

Business Development
A foreign employee who practices Business Development is primarily occupied with licensing games, connecting developers with publishers and sourcing deals in the IT sector. It is a role that functionally occupies an intermediary position between a team of designers who are inside the company and the ecosystem of partners, etc. who are outside the company and, in this case, outside of China.

Localization
A newly hired young foreign employee at Tencent with limited experience is typically assigned to a role that involves managing localization, a process that involves adapting game content, promotional material, etc. to the requirements of local markets overseas. Language translation is an example of a common adaptation.

Nearly all foreign staff profiled have advanced business degrees and a significant number combine technical (engineering) degrees with

Chart 4.10 Foreign
employees at Tencent
(headquarters)—Top
countries of origin
(*Source* Staff interviews
and LinkedIn profiles)

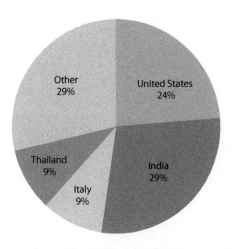

Other
29%

United States
24%

Thailand
9%

India
29%

Italy
9%

N=20

commercial degrees, a combination that is especially prevalent among the
members of the company's local team in India.[22] It is a combination of
disciplines that is consistent with, and perhaps a reflection of, the portfolio of skills featured in the profiles of the Tencent executive team.

A member of the Indian managment team in insisted that the prevalence among local staff of degrees in both technical and commercial
domains was not coincidental. He explained that Tencent favored an
organizational structure based on 'lightweight' teams that were small
and agile enough to keep pace with the fast-moving markets the company operated in and able to respond rapidly to changes that were often
sudden and unexpected. The key to success in structuring "lightweight"
teams was having members with the right temperament and also the
right set of skills that would enable them to meet both technical and
commercial demands (Chart 4.10).

Foreign staff employed at Tencent represent nine countries that, by
and large, are places where there is an entrenched gaming industry, are
strategically important to the company as a source of design and development talent in the near term and of partners and customers in the
longer-term. Nearly half of Tencent's foreign staff are from the U.S.
or India, presumably the locus of markets with the greatest potential
demand for the company's products and services as well as the greatest
sources of talent for the key parts of Tencent's business.

[22] All members of the India management team have advanced engineering degrees.

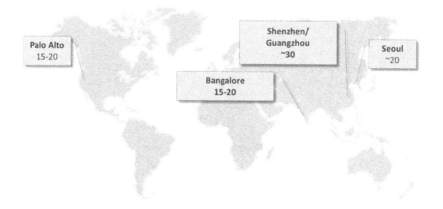

The company employs an estimated 200–300 foreign employees currently, about a quarter of whom work in company headquarters in Shenzhen (see map).[23]

A number of indicators such as number of overseas investments, applications for local operating licenses, and number of new job postings (especially in the U.S. and India), suggest there is a plan to significantly expand foreign staffing over the next twenty-four months that could double or triple the current number of foreign staff (Table 4.1).[24]

The average age of a foreign employee at Tencent is 35, which is a little higher than the average age of a foreign employee at Alibaba and quite a bit younger than the average foreign employee at Huawei. This is perhaps a reflection of the industry and business that are Tencent's focus and a function of the types of products it develops and sells as well as of the profile of its target customer base. About a quarter of the foreign employees at Tencent have previous China experience and familiarity with the Chinese language.

---

[23] The Tencent global office map was developed by the author in early 2018. The offices that appear on the map are those that have the greatest number of staff. Remaining offices not presented have, on average, fewer than 10 employees or are managed by partner organizations. Staff numbers referenced are estimates that have been derived from information resident on websites (corporate and local), provided in company documentation (e.g. annual reports and financial filings), and shared during staff interviews. Numbers are indicative and subject to change as company hiring plans take shape.

[24] These projections are based on reviews of company performance and direct interviews with foreign staff.

Table 4.1 Profiles of job postings in the U.S. for positions based primarily in the San Francisco area

Engineering	20
Business development	12
IT/HR/finance	10
Product	10
Sales	8
Marketing	6
Admin	5

Source Tencent U.S. website

Unlike Alibaba, Tencent does not offer a training program that is specifically designed for foreign staff, nor does it provide any sort of onboarding program for new foreign employees although it does offer a weekend retreat for newly hired Chinese employees that may be adapted for foreign hires in the future.

The transformation of Tencent's foreign employment strategy is a reflection of the company's larger plans to expand its international business. When the company's focus was primarily on the China domestic market, the need to employ foreign staff was less compelling and limited to those who could contribute to the development of products that could be used in China or who could help secure licenses for games developed in other markets that could be attractive to domestic Chinese customers. As Tencent's international business has moved to a place of greater prominence in the company's strategy and become more important to its future, the profile of foreign staff has shifted from those who were hired primarily for their ability to develop products/games to those who could contribute to marketing and selling those products to customers in markets outside of China.

CONCLUSION

A review of the foreign employment strategies of companies in China's tech sector reveals a number of common denominators as well as distinct differences in approach.

Commonalities

Functions

As a function of the general trend towards expansion into markets outside of China, all the companies considered employ a significant number of foreign staff and have plans to increase that number in future. As the international strategies of these companies have evolved, so too have their hiring practices and the requirements they have defined for the employment of foreign employees—from those with technical and development profiles to those with experience in disciplines such as Marketing, Communications, and Corporate Affairs.

Profiles
In general, there is a tendency among the Chinese companies considered towards hiring North American and European staff in their company headquarters. Tencent's employment of Indians who are engaged primarily in development roles is exceptional. In addition, despite the fact that these companies all have presence in Southeast Asia and Africa the number of representatives from these regions they count among their headquarters staff is very small (virtually none from Africa).

Organizations
Foreign employees in Alibaba and Tencent occupy two distinctly different tracks in the organizational structure of those two companies: rank-and-file staff who make up the majority and a select few senior executives. The senior executives of both companies have a clear and long-standing connection to the investment firm, Goldman Sachs.

Different Approaches

Differences in the position that foreign employees in each of the companies profiled occupy are reflected in the scope of their jobs and the contribution to the business that is expected of them. The nature of these differences is conveniently illustrated in a comparison of the way in which "Business Development", a function common to all companies profiled, is defined and practiced.

Alibaba
The practice of "Business Development" in Alibaba is very sales-oriented. A foreign employee who has "Business Development" in his or her job description is primarily engaged in the promotion and sales of Alibaba's value added products and services to foreign brands.

Huawei

Business Development in Huawei is understood and applied in a much more comprehensive way than in it is Alibaba. It incorporates some aspects of Marketing and involves the definition of product requirements, features, and demand. Those engaged in "Business Development" are affiliated with a number of different departments (including Finance) and operate within a number of different contexts.

Tencent

A foreign employee who practices Business Development in Tencent is primarily occupied with licensing games, connecting developers with publishers, and sourcing deals in the IT sector.

Distinct Foreign Staff Profiles

Huawei's foreign employees are on average a decade older than those of either Alibaba or Tencent. This discrepancy in age reflects a difference in strategy and perhaps even differences in the composition of each company's executive team.

Huawei's preference for hiring senior foreign employees is motivated by a need for experienced professionals who can deliver results in the near term for a company that already has a well-established international business. Alibaba's employment of younger foreign staff conceivably is a function of the company's longer-term plans for international expansion that will depend on contribution of foreign employees who have a solid understanding of the company's business and its culture. Tencent's international business is at a much earlier stage of development so less thought has been given to the position of foreign employees within that development. The composition of the executive teams in each company has some implication for the foreign employee. Although there is no way of drawing a direct connection between the profile of a company's executives and their strategy of hiring foreigners, we can see a distinct difference between the type of foreign staff Huawei has employed and that of the foreign employees of the other two companies.

Huawei's executive team, in aggregate, has very little direct international experience and very little experience outside the company.

Effectively it is a group of 'insiders' who have spent nearly their entire careers in the company. Given this profile, it is unlikely that a foreign employee would ever be considered for a senior executive position. As a consequence there is less incentive to hire young foreign talent or develop a management training program that will enable them to make a long term contribution to the company and reach an executive level.

Alibaba's executive team is more international in profile and many of its members have experience in other companies and other industries. It is reasonable to assume that the profile of the Alibaba executives and the nature of their experience made them particularly receptive to the idea of a dedicated management training program for foreign hires was an impetus for establishment of the AGLA program. Moreover, the correspondence between the gender balance that Alibaba's executive team exhibits and that also characterizes the make up of the AGLA cohorts is likely not coincidental.[25]

With the exception of Tencent which employs a number of foreign staff in basic development positions, the Chinese companies considered tend to hire foreign staff into positions that are international market facing, i.e. they involve interacting with customers, partners, etc. outside of China.

Through its description of the ways in which Chinese companies employ foreign staff and the profile of those staff it presents this chapter accounts for what foreigners employed in Chinese organizations do, where they work, and how they contribute. Building on this foundation, the following chapter will investigate the experience of foreigners employed in Chinese firms and illuminate the conditions that shape their experience. For example, where this chapter presented the outline of a foreign employee development program such as Alibaba's AGLA the following chapter will consider the reception of the program's participants and gauge its effectiveness in meeting the objectives that have been set.

---

[25] This is a statistic that is obviously important to the company as it clearly highlighted in the AGLA program's promotional material.

REFERENCES

Abkowitz, Alysa, "The Man Who Bets Tencent's Moonshot Money" *Wall Street Journal*, February 8, 2018, https://www.wsj.com/articles/the-man-who-bets-tencents-moonshot-money-1518098400.

Bradley, Diana, "Jim Wilkinson Exits Alibaba Group", *PRWeek*, April 5, 2016.

"China's Internet Giants Go Global", *Economist*, April 20, 2017.

Clover, Charles "Low-Key Michael Evans Brings Goldman Connections to Alibaba", *Financial Times*, August 7, 2015.

Erisman, Porter, *Alibaba's World: How a Remarkable Chinese Company Is Changing the Face of Global Business*, St. Martin's Press, 2015.

Faure, David. 2006. *China and Capitalism: A History of Business Enterprise in Modern China*. Hong Kong: Hong Kong University Press.

"Global 2000: Growth Champions", *Forbes*, June 2018.

Gray, Naomi, "A Look at Alibaba's International Business", *MarketRealist* (online), July 26, 2017, https://marketrealist.com/2017/07/a-look-at-alibabas-international-business/.

Jiang, Sijia, "Tencent Turns to WeChat, Games and Deals for Global Strategy", *Reuters*, November 20, 2017.

Micheli, Jordy, and Carillo, Jorge, "The Globalization Strategy of a Chinese Multinational", *Frontera Norte*, Vol. 28, No. 56, July–December 2016, pages 35–58.

Sun, Leo, "Alibaba Is Expanding Its E-Commerce Platform into These 4 Markets", Fool.com, September 1, 2018, https://www.fool.com/investing/2018/09/01/alibaba-is-expanding-its-e-commerce-platform-into.aspx.

"Tencent Needs to See Market Gap Before Expanding Further Overseas, Says Executive" [interview with Tencent Senior Executive Vice-President, S. Y. Lau], *South China Morning Post*, June 22, 2018.

Zhang, Yunan, "The Most Powerful American at Tencent Targets Silicon Valley". *The Information*, November 3, 2016, https://www.theinformation.com/articles/the-most-powerful-american-in-tencent-targets-silicon-valley.

CHAPTER 5

Living to Work

This chapter complements the previous chapter that described the roles foreign employees play in realizing a Chinese company's international aspirations by supplementing the elements already introduced with an experiential dimension. In this context, 'experience' refers to the working conditions and unique challenges foreign employees face once they have joined a Chinese company, but is defined broadly enough to encompass the very first encounter that a foreign employee, or potential employee, may have with a Chinese company and the initial impressions formed from that encounter.

EMPLOYER OF CHOICE

Are you an undergraduate STEM student looking for a life changing experience?

Are you excited by technical problems because you see them as opportunities to grow as a person?

Are you fascinated by the rise of Asia and ever wondered how to get practical experience working for a dynamic global business in China?

This opening to an informational flyer for Huawei's "Seeds for the Future" program distributed by the Career Services office at the University of Southampton in England is an example of Huawei's outreach to potential recruits overseas and may very well be the first point of

© The Author(s) 2020
P. Ross, *Barriers to Entry*,
https://doi.org/10.1007/978-981-32-9566-7_5

encounter with the company that many outside China have.[1] For those whose interest is piqued by the flyer and who would like to learn more about the company and the program advertised, Huawei has developed an accompanying brochure that provides a basic overview of the program and a statement of its objectives: (1) Developing local ICT talent; (2) Enhancing knowledge transfer; (3) Promoting a greater understanding of and interest in the ICT sector; (4) Improving and encouraging regional relationship building and participation in the digital community. Just below the statement of objectives, presented as an array of graphic images accompanied by explanatory bullet points, is an enumeration of what the program offers to those who participate. Highlighted at one end of the array are study programs in Beijing and Shenzhen, represented graphically by the image of a lecturer in suit and tie gesturing in front of a diagram-filled Powerpoint slide. Featured at the other end is an aerial view of the Great Wall bounded by the words "National Historical Sites Tour". In between the study program and the site tour are images of a bullet train, a cornucopia basket with loaves of bread, and the interior of a room with a bed designated respectively as "One-Way Air Ticket or High Speed Rail Ticket", "Food", and "Hotels", this last accompanied by a note advising that hotel rooms "may need to be shared with another [sic]". As selling points designed to stimulate the interest of a career-oriented, high-performing foreign candidate of the type the program hopes to attract these key words and their graphic representations are not particularly compelling. A one-way train ticket, for example, is a fairly trivial item whose subsidization would, under most circumstances, be taken for granted and whose provision, under any circumstance, would not warrant being called out as a program benefit. The use of low-resolution photos in the graphic images that illustrate the brochure reinforce the impression of a document still in draft. Moreover, the design of the overall layout against which the photos are set is guided by a distinctly Chinese aesthetic expressed through a juxtaposition of colors, choice of font, and use of space that may not be readily understood or appreciated by a representative of the non-Chinese audience that ostensibly is the brochure's target. Taken together, the less-than-compelling value proposition, grainy images, and unfamiliar design scheme create the image of a company that

[1] The company has recently developed and begun distributing an updated version of the brochure (see Philip Candice LinkedIn blog https://www.linkedin.com/in/philip-candice-40026a5/).

has not quite grasped the essence of what attracts and motivates the type of foreign professional it hopes to count among its recruits. A set of accompanying videos presented on the company's website that is designed to convey a sense of the program and what its participants experience hews closely in tone and effect to other similarly conceived videos reviewed in previous chapters (cf. the foreign pilot recruiting videos, promotional videos of Chinese companies operating in the U.S., etc.).

Largely composed of disjointed scenes that have been deliberately choreographed, these videos come across as stiff and awkward, an effect that diminishes their immediacy and authenticity. In one scene, for example, a group of young foreign recruits with awestruck looks on their faces stand assembled, as if in a carefully arranged tableau, around a lady dressed in ancient garb strumming classical ballads on the Guqin, a Chinese zither. Perhaps it is because the scene has been so obviously staged that one has the sense there was some specific intent behind its presentation and a specific message it was designed to convey. A clue for what this message might be can be found in the programming lineup of China's national television broadcaster, CCTV.

Foreign Impressions

CCTV regularly airs culture programs that feature foreigners who are living and working in China. Typically, the foreigners who make an appearance on these shows dress in traditional Chinese clothing, experience Chinese cultural artifacts, and sing Chinese songs much to the delight of a Chinese studio audience who greet the performances with raucous laughter and enthusiastic applause (Gorfinkel 2012).[2] Taken at face value these shows and the antics that characterize them represent nothing more than a bit of fun, albeit at foreigner expense, that inject a bit of leaven into an otherwise predictable programming lineup. Looking beneath the superficial cultural trappings and the cross-cultural pratfalls for which the foreign actors are a foil, however, sociologist Phiona Stanley finds evidence of more serious intent.

Situating these shows within the larger context of cross-cultural relations between Chinese and foreigners, Stanley takes them as exemplars for how Chinese perceive foreigners and as guides that condition

---

[2]Gorfinkel (2011, page 288). Gorfinkel, L., Performing the Chinese Nation: The Politics of Identity in China Central Television's Music-Entertainment Programs (PhD), University of Technology, Sydney, 2011.

Sino-foreign interaction (Stanley 2013). Every scene of a foreigner struggling to grasp peanuts with a pair of chopsticks, stumbling over Chinese tongue-twisters, and misidentifying Chinese provincial capitals that the television programmers dish up is a snapshot of an acculturation process. The programs, taken as a whole, present a model for how an appreciation of Chinese culture is to be instilled in foreigners, non-Chinese taking first wobbly steps along the path to adopting a set of customs whose origins and characteristics go back to the earliest time of Chinese civilization. In this context, the foreigners who don traditional forms of Chinese dress and appear awestruck as they watch performances of classical Chinese music are implicitly expressing their love for China or, to invoke Stanley's paradigm: "validating 'Chineseness' and helping to construct a China that is the envy of Outsiders" (Stanley 2013). The scenes in which foreigners are asked to feign struggling to use chopsticks and are represented as 'wide-eyed, comedic, and eager to learn and discover the wonders of a mysterious and alien, yet wise and patient China (Gorfinkel and Chubb). So in general, whether they are infantilizing foreigners as hapless and helpless characters struggling with chopsticks on television shows or presenting them as awestruck observers of Chinese cultural exhibitions in corporate videos, the Chinese programming experts who have conceived these scenes are deliberately casting the foreign actors in a position that is subordinate to Chinese whom they look up to, admire and learn from. The intent of expending so much effort in "constructing foreignness", concludes Stanley, is to "establish a more concrete and robust self-identity" (Stanley 2013, page 48).[3] And to contemporize her insights and make them more generally applicable Stanley goes one step further in asserting that "This constructs a Chinese-dominated cosmopolitanism and restores the metanarrative of China's national revival to its former, exceptional, central status under the guidance of the [Communist Party]" (Stanley 2013, page 18).

Reinforcing this impression of a traditional view of foreigners and how Chinese relate to them is the realization that there is effectively no interaction between the "Seeds" participants who appear in the videos and company employees (i.e. local Chinese staff). Moreover, participants appearing in the videos are grouped and presented strictly by nationality (Malaysian, Australian, etc.). The presentation of each group follows a common script that includes a perfunctory meeting with a delegation of

---

[3] Stanley's terminology for this is "using an 'Other' in the construction of the 'Self'".

government officials from the respective group's home country. Making a well-orchestrated reception the highlight of a promotional video undoubtedly says more about a Chinese sense of official protocol and decorum than it does about the interests and aspirations of the foreign participants they depict.

A series of videos that document the experience of foreigners in the Alibaba Global Leadership Academy (AGLA) program couldn't be more different in tone, content, and production from the videos Huawei has developed to capture and promote the experience of foreign participants in its 'Seeds' program. With their rapid scene cuts, liberal use of American business jargon, and injection of a personal angle, the Alibaba videos look and feel very much like similarly purposed videos that are typically to be found on the sites of large American multinationals. As such they serve as a visual demonstration of the extent to which Alibaba has transcended the standard model Chinese companies employ in attracting foreign staff and depicting their experience.

Clearly meant to address the specific concerns and goals of potential foreign participants and position the company as an 'employer of choice' to potential hires from overseas, each one of the half dozen videos featured on the AGLA website highlights a different facet of a foreign employee's experience in China and in the company (see Table 5.1).

Table 5.1 Index of videos depicting the experience of foreign employees in Alibaba

	VIDEO TITLE	KEY MESSAGE
❶	Rural Taobao	Social responsbility. Alibaba's suppor for the underserved in rural China and the contribution of foreign staff to that effort
❷	Hangzhou	Hangzhou is a liveable city with many attractions and good lifestyle
❸	Culture Shock	Cross-cultural challenges foreign staff at Alibaba face and how the company helps to bridge the gap.
❹	A Day In The Life	What a typical day in the life of a foreigner at Alibaba looks like
❺	Cultivating International Talent	Insight into the working environment at Alibaba and the types of projects foreign staff are engaged in

Source AGLA website

Among the videos featured, "Culture Shock" (original title: "An American at Alibaba"),[4] a video that highlights the specific challenges foreign staff face and how they succeed in adapting, is especially relevant.

FITTING IN

The Ideal Experience

"Culture Shock" chronicles a "day in the life" of an Alibaba employee named "Tom" who takes the viewer on a tour of the company. As he walks through the halls, "Tom" provides a narration for what the viewer is seeing, from time to time interrupting his running commentary to share observations drawn from personal experience and impart lessons drawn from challenges he himself has faced. There are cultural challenges ('it can be weird'), linguistic challenges ('I don't know any Chinese'), and even culinary challenges ('being a vegan, that's a whole other layer of challenges'). In addition to sharing his observations on life in China and work in a Chinese company, Tom also offers practical suggestions for ways in which a foreign employee can adapt to working in such an environment. Taking advantage of the support Chinese colleagues offer ('How do I survive? ... The kindness of Chinese colleagues') is one of them.

The scenes in the video that accompany these observations are well-aligned with the narration and feature the program's foreign participants interacting with Chinese colleagues in both formal and informal settings. The vignettes and accompanying commentary together form the base on which the chronicle of a foreign employee's experience in a Chinese company is constructed. By virtue of this format, the scenes in the videos could almost be read as a set of visual FAQs (Frequently Asked Questions), responses presented in visual form to the questions foreigners who are considering working for a Chinese company most frequently ask. The key message these responses impart to a potential foreign recruit is that working for a Chinese company is a different and sometimes challenging, but ultimately rewarding experience, or. to paraphrase. "Tom": "Don't worry. You too can survive."

In addition to the overall format and style, what distinguishes the presentation of the foreign experience in Alibaba from that of other Chinese companies as presented in these videos is its candor. In his

---

[4] "An American at Alibaba" video dated August 2016 appears on the AGLA website.

narration of the office scenes and his commentary on the experience of a foreigner in a Chinese company, Tom, for example, eschews the pleasantries and stock phrases that characterize the promotional material other Chinese companies in favor of a tone that is more forthright ("it can be very hard to accomplish the things I need to do my job well"). The sincerity that Tom conveys through what he says is reinforced in a subtle way by his decision to face the camera and address the viewer directly. It is a method of presentation that stands in sharp contrast to the more institutional, "reportage" style favored by other Chinese companies and casts the unique aspects of Alibaba's presentation, its cultural savvy, and experience, in greater relief. Yet for all the sophistication Alibaba demonstrates in depicting the experience of foreigners in the company through these videos, when one takes the context in which the videos are presented into more careful consideration, the company nevertheless reveals itself to be much closer to other Chinese companies in the way it perceives foreigners in its employ and the model it uses to guide its interactions with them.

At one point in the video, Tom gives his 'culture shock' a more concrete shape when he discloses, with his usual candor, that he can't always find the 'Western amenities' he is accustomed to ('sometimes I just wish I could go to a Whole Foods'). The irony is that Hangzhou is one of the most cosmopolitan cities in China and a place where most of the 'Western amenities' a foreigner could ever desire are relatively easy to come by. Moreover, for all their apparent candor, Tom's little confidences—his ignorance of Chinese and his dependence on the support of Chinese colleagues to meet the requirements of his job—ironically mask what foreign staff in the company actually experience.

The Real Experience

By and large, the assignments that foreigners employed by the company carry out involve dealing with customers and partners beyond China's borders, whose preferred language of communication, if communication in their own language cannot be accommodated, is English, in most cases, not Chinese. So Tom's ability to survive in the company without knowledge of Chinese is less dependent upon the support he receives from Chinese colleagues and more a function of the requirements for the job he is expected to fulfill. Moreover, given the AGLA program's use of Chinese language fluency as a selection criterion for candidates accepted into the program, it is highly unlikely that an employee with Tom's profile would correspond to any of Alibaba's real foreign staff members. As an adjunct to the requirement it has set for Chinese language fluency and cultural familiarity, Alibaba explicitly states that possession of a "global mindset" is a character trait company management prioritizes in evaluating foreign candidates for employment.[5] Given the obvious importance that the company assigns to thinking globally and the premium it places on cultural adaptability, it is therefore difficult to imagine that a young foreigner who has been accepted into the program, and presumably possesses the 'global mindset' the company has defined as a criterion for acceptance, would be the type who would pine for supposedly "unavailable" Western amenities. On the contrary, a foreign hire with a profile the company has defined as ideal would most likely welcome the lack of a Whole Foods market rather than despair over its absence.[6]

The discrepancy that exists between the profile of a foreigner presented in the promotional video and that of a real foreign employee is significant enough to raise the question of what the rationale for presenting the experience of a foreigner in the company in this way would be. It certainly would have not required any additional expense or effort to have presented Tom as an urbane, cosmopolitan foreigner with a "global mindset" who could comfortably, and in all candor, express his appreciation for local Hangzhou specialties such as West Lake soup and Dragon Well tea, and describe the pleasure he derives from being able to enjoy these delicacies at their source. In fact, a promotional video that presented a "Tom" whose profile was more closely aligned with that of the model foreign hire the company wanted to attract, would arguably be more likely to appeal to and attract those foreigners who possess the qualities the company desires.

From an execution standpoint, the Alibaba videos considered here are much more refined and coherent than the ones of European pilots and African factory workers referenced in previous chapters. However, in their depiction of foreign employees (unsophisticated people who

---

[5] Described on AGLA program website https://agla.alibaba.com/.

[6] To this point, a number of participants in the AGLA program expressed their displeasure at being taken to quintessential tourist sites (Great Wall, Tiananmen Square, Terracotta soldiers, etc.) on trips organized by the company to "acquaint" them with China's history and culture. These were places with which they were already quite familiar and that provided very little entrée into Chinese society, the aspect of China they were most interested in and curious about. Seen in the context of activities organized by other Chinese companies for foreign staff this appears to be another example of a standard fixture of corporate protocol that is not meant as an educational program.

lack familiarity with Chinese culture and need to be shepherded and instructed by their Chinese colleagues), the themes they present (indoctrination into Chinese culture, trips to tourist sites, classes in Chinese language and traditional Chinese arts) the Alibaba videos are strikingly similar to those of other companies.

The number of applications for a place in the cohort that entered the AGLA program in its second year was double that of the first year, an unequivocal measure of interest and an indication that the company was able to attract qualified talent. Inexplicably, instead of increasing the number of places in the AGLA cohort commensurate with the increase in applications, those who administer the program actually reduced the number of places by nearly a third thus engineering a scarcity that effectively sharpened demand. Under these conditions—greater demand for fewer available places—it would seem that making an investment in promotional activity would be superfluous if not unwarranted and makes the inquiry into the motivation for producing these videos in the first place an even more pertinent one. One explanation might be that the videos were not, in fact, developed to enhance recruiting, an activity that, judging by the numbers referenced above, required little additional support. It is not beyond the realm of possibility that the target audience for these videos was not external at all and that they were not, in fact, designed to stimulate interest in the program among potential foreign recruits by presenting the company as an employer of choice, but were developed instead to convince an internal audience, whose members were not entirely convinced of the program's effectiveness or even its necessity, that AGLA was making progress, meeting expectations, and achieving the goals set (i.e. earning a satisfactory return on the time, money, and resources that had been invested in its establishment).

So if these videos present an idealized view of foreign employees and their experience, what are the real foreigners saying and thinking? We can start by considering their motivations as a proxy for the response to the question: "Why work for a Chinese company in the first place?"

MOTIVATIONS

For the pilots, athletes, and models who were profiled in the preceding chapter compensation clearly played a decisive role in their consideration of an employment opportunity in China. However, for the French marketing manager, American public relations expert, or Indian software developer who is considering employment in a Chinese enterprise, compensation, although a motivating factor, is clearly not as important a consideration. Moreover, the motivations identified by foreign employees as those that influenced their decision to work in a Chinese company were distinctly different from the ones that figured in the considerations of pilots, models, and athletes. In general, the motivations that foreign employees in Chinese enterprises identified when interviewed can be grouped into four broad (yet not mutually exclusive) categories.[7]

1. Chinese Culture (Cultural Attraction)
2. Academic Study
3. Career Development
4. Personal and Social Values[8]

1. Culture

Quite a number of foreign employees in Chinese companies cited exposure to Chinese or Asian culture, and at a relatively young and impressionable age, as a motivation (or at least the spark of an interest in China that was a precursor for engaging more directly with the country at a later time) for coming to China and deciding to work for a Chinese company. The two principal sources of exposure to Chinese culture referenced were: (1) Social—early encounter with Chinese people and culture in the foreign employee's home country. This was especially the case for those who had grown up or lived for an extended period of time in the U.S. (e.g. pursuing study at an American university) especially in locations where was a high concentration of Chinese immigrants and presence of a large Chinese community. Respondents specifically mentioned interaction with members of Taiwanese communities in cities such as Washington, DC. and Los Angeles.[9] (2) Cultural Artifacts—A surprising

---

[7] Compensation as a motivator is taken for granted and not called out. However, it was not mentioned directly in the discussions conducted.

[8] By way of comparison, the top four motivations cited by foreigners (Americans) working for Japanese firms were Professional Opportunity, Chance to join a start-up team, Growth potential, Interest. In Kopp, Rochelle, *The Rice Paper Ceiling*, Stone Bridge Press, 1994, page 73.

[9] According to the TaiwaneseAmerica.org there were 358,000 Taiwanese immigrants in the U.S. in 2010.

number of respondents reported developing a fascination with Asia and Chinese culture initially through exposure to Japanese video games, art (including cartoons) and clothing (fashion). In one case, a respondent mentioned that her interest in China was triggered as a child when her father presented her with a traditional Chinese tunic and matching pants, in child's size, that he had purchased on a visit to the local Chinatown. A comparatively unique case, but perhaps a reflection of the influence and effect of globalization on younger foreign employees, was that of an American working for a Chinese company in the U.S. who identified the numerous trips to Asia (including China and Taiwan) he took as a teenager accompanying his father who often traveled there to conduct business with customers based in the region as the source of motivation for his later engagement with China and Chinese culture.

2. Academic Study

An increasing number of foreign employees working at Chinese companies stated that they had studied Chinese language and taken classes in Chinese history, culture etc. at schools in their home country prior to taking positions in Chinese companies.[10]

In addition to the standard curriculum and complement of courses they list in their catalogues, many schools in the United States and Europe offer in-country study programs typically for a Summer, a semester, or an academic year. One participant in the AGLA program who had no previous contact with China took advantage of an opportunity to study in China that his school in Europe offered.[11]

Universities, especially in the U.S., were key places where respondents were exposed to Chinese culture and not only through a formal course of study but increasingly through interaction with Chinese students.[12]

---

[10] 227,000 students in the U.S. have enrolled in Chinese language classes "Popularity of Chinese Language Learning Soaring Within U.S. Education System: Survey", *New China* (Xinhua), May 5, 2017.

[11] The school offered the opportunity to spend an academic year in China or in Russia and he chose China because of its commercial potential.

[12] There were more than 360,000 students from Mainland China studying at U.S. schools in the 2017–2018 school year (Source: International Institute of Education [IIE] Open Doors 2018 Report, "Places of Origin", https://www.iie.org/Research-and-Insights/ Open-Doors/Data/International-Students/Places-of-Origin).

A number of other programs that exist outside of the standard university curriculum such as Confucius Institutes, sponsored by the Chinese Government's Education Bureau, and Rotary International Rotary Clubs (an organization whose mission is to engage members—business, professional, and community leaders—in taking action on the world's "most persistent issues") provide supplementary paths for young people in countries around the world to learn about China and experience Chinese culture.[13] An employee in a Chinese company who was from Europe had not previously followed a course of study related to China at university. Instead her first engagement with Chinese culture and society came through participation in a Rotary International program in Taiwan. That experience led her to the conclusion that the center of economic activity was shifting towards the East and that her career path following graduation would in all likelihood have some connection to Asia.

3. Career Development

Quite a number of foreigners were motivated to work for a Chinese firm because they felt it would enable them to develop skills and knowledge that would be beneficial for their career development. The types of skills they hoped to develop were varied and included acquiring an understanding of the market conditions in China and techniques for meeting its unique challenges, gaining experience in digitally-driven commercial platforms such as e-commerce, and getting the opportunity to develop new products under conditions not present elsewhere (large scale, short timeframes, etc.). Interestingly, those motivated by the opportunity to acquire new techniques, gain product development experience, and market knowledge did not necessarily have any previous interest in or exposure to China as such (i.e. Chinese culture and language).

4. Personal and Social Values

A number of respondents—albeit small— were motivated to join the Chinese company at which they were employed because of a perceived alignment between their personal values and the company's mission.

---

[13]More than 500 Confucius Institutes in 142 countries worldwide in: "Over 500 Confucius Institutes Founded in 142 Countries, Regions", China Daily.com.cn, October 7, 2017.

This typically was expressed as a belief in the fundamental value of the company's business model and the social benefit its services or products had the potential to deliver. A foreign manager in Ant Financial, Alibaba's financing arm, acknowledged that her motivation for accepting an offer to join the company and work specifically in the company's financing division was based on a belief in the difference that a service designed to enable financing on a small scale could make in the lives and livelihoods of people who would otherwise never have had the opportunity to get such access. The manager noted that it was through a previous posting in Asia that she had experienced at firsthand the challenges those living in emerging markets face in getting access to sources of financing and developed a sympathy for their situation.

A general manager from New Zealand developing business overseas for a Chinese state-run company, who was somewhat older than other foreign employees profiled, acknowledged that at this later stage in his career he placed as much, if not more, value on the impact he could make on a company's operations as he did on the compensation package offered. Consistent with his focus on his personal legacy, he was attracted by the opportunity to work in a Chinese company because he felt he could make a greater contribution to the company's future than he could at other companies he had considered and that the impact from his contribution would be more enduring. He reasoned that the business horizon along which the state-run enterprise where he was employed oriented itself was considerably longer than that of any of the Western companies with which he was familiar. Moreover, the relative stability in the executive ranks of the Chinese company gave him the confidence that whatever he contributed to the business would have longer-lasting impact than it would at a Western company. This assessment was based on his own experience working for Western companies where every shift in the executive suite brought about a corresponding change in company strategy that overwrote or eliminated many of the programs that were associated with or that had been initiated by the previous management team.

A DAY IN THE OFFICE; A DAY IN THE LIFE

Whereas "Culture Shock" focused on the challenges that foreign employees face and the adaptations they have to make working for a Chinese company and living in China, two other videos, "A Day in the

Life" and "How Alibaba Is Cultivating Its International Talent Pool", offer a much more realistic view and greater insight into what a foreigner working at a Chinese company experiences.

"A Day in the Life", weaves together the stories of three AGLA participants, each one of whom in the course of sharing his or her experience embodies a distinct and clearly identifiable theme—"adventure and discovery" (of self and of another culture), "raising a family", "everyday life" (activities and life outside of work, including travel and exercise)—and has a key message to impart.

Loren, a young American, is the voice of adventure and discovery. The experience he gives voice to is the adventure that comes from being in a new environment, facing unexpected challenges, and learning new things. This exuberance is tempered by a more introspective segment that is much more directed inwards towards self-discovery than outwards towards the discovery of new places and new experiences.

Meng Liu, from the U.K. and of Chinese descent, is a young mother whose experience in the company is conditioned by the responsibility of raising a young family while participating in AGLA and meeting the program's requirements.

Chloe, a young woman from France with experience in social media marketing, presents the range of activities (extra-curricular) that are on offer both through the company and in the city of Hangzhou at large. The scenes that form the background for her narrative show employees inside the company playing ping-pong and practicing yoga in the company's fitness center and outside jogging along one of the many scenic paths that encircle the West Lake. A vignette that features employees using a mobile phone-based electronic payment application to make purchases rounds out the video and reinforces the message that life in China and work in a Chinese company of the new millennium is diverse, stimulating, and convenient.

"How Alibaba Is Cultivating Its International Talent Pool", in a change of pace and shift in perspective from "A Day in the Life", provides insight into the work experience of those in the program with emphasis on the program structure (rotations through two different business units) and examples of hands-on projects that AGLA participants get involved in. In addition to describing how the program works, the video communicates what participants get out of the program: Learning about "the reality of modern China"; becoming more globally minded, and working for an "iconic" Chinese company that is "pushing boundaries".

Considered together the two videos effectively form a pair in which each video highlights a distinct aspect of the foreign employee's existence in a Chinese company. "A Day in the Life" represents "life" or "lifestyle" as reflected in its various facets: Culture (personal growth), Relations (personal relations), and Activities (personal health). Its counterpart, "How Alibaba Is Cultivating Its International Talent Pool", represents work: benefits, challenges, and rewards. The key message these videos impart is that the experience of a foreign employee in Alibaba is about quality of life and quality of work and that what the participants are most concerned with is livability, working on valuable projects, and keeping fit. By drawing these diverse aspects of a foreign employee's experience in a Chinese company into a composite representation that is both credible and convincing, these videos succeed as recruiting vehicles, the use for which they presumably were intended. However, as a representation of a foreign employee's experience in a Chinese company and a presentation of issues that are of greatest concern to the employees themselves they are less faithful. For example, "Life" and "Work", the constituent elements of a foreign employee's existence in a Chinese company, are presented as two separate videos giving the impression that the two domains are clearly and cleanly delineated. Ironically, such delineation bears little relation to the reality that most foreign employees in a Chinese company experience.

WORK AND LIFE IN THE BALANCE

In a blog post entitled "Working in a Chinese Company—A Foreigner's View Point"[14] (Joseph 2018). Divya Joseph, a strategic account manager for Alibaba's TMall Global business reflects on the general reputation that Chinese companies have for being "terrible places to work". In the course of her reflections, Joseph identifies "work-life balance" and "discrimination" (i.e. discrimination of Chinese employees against foreign staff) as the specific issues that form the basis on which that reputation is founded. She then goes on to dismiss these perceptions as "myth". Given the length of Joseph's tenure at Alibaba and the track record of success she has achieved during that tenure her words should be given due attention. However, interviews conducted with a cross-section of foreign nationals employed

[14]Joseph, Divya Ann, Working in a Chinese Company—A Foreigner's View Point, blog post, June 16, 2018, https://www.linkedin.com/pulse/working-chinese-company-foreigners-view-point-divya-anne-joseph/.

by Chinese firms both in China and overseas "Work-Life Balance" and "Outsider Status" (along with "Career Development"), issues Joseph consigns to the realm of "myth", consistently surface as those that are of greatest concern and that pose the greatest challenge to a foreign employee's ability to achieve success in a Chinese organization. Moreover, the sentiments expressed in interviews are consistent with those derived from comments offered by a much larger pool of respondents on Glassdoor, a website dedicated to reviews of companies provided by current and past employees. Based on analysis of reviews for the Chinese companies profiled in this study "work-life balance" was the negative factor most frequently referenced by respondents ranging from 25% of the sample for Huawei to more than 50% for Tencent. Taken as a composite, these references attest to the fact that in a Chinese company the line between work and personal life is definitely drawn in favor of the 'work' side.

REFERENCE POINT: THE JAPANESE CORPORATE EXPERIENCE

Americans who found themselves working for Japanese companies in the 1980's were impressed and awed by the level of commitment their Japanese colleagues maintained in completing the tasks to which they were assigned and by the depth of their dedication to the company at which they were employed. "They are married to the bank. That's the only way I can describe it," pronounced an American manager employed by the local branch of a Japanese financial institution—encapsulating a sentiment representative of that which many Americans who encountered Japanese companies expressed at the time. As to the source of motivation for the extraordinary commitment and dedication to work and company the Japanese exhibited, the bank manager concluded "They [the Japanese workers] need to prove their loyalty, their love" (Kopp 1994, page 88).

Foreign employees prompted to recall their first day of work at a Chinese company, whether employed in the company's headquarters or in an office overseas, similarly commented on how impressed they were not only with their Chinese colleagues' capacity for work, but by their devotion to the company for which they were working. An American production manager working for the U.S. subsidiary of Chinese industrial glass manufacturer Fuyao, for example, found the 'perseverance' and 'dedication' of his Chinese colleagues inspiring and, after witnessing the consistently long shifts the Chinese logged on the company's production lines, pronounced them 'amazing workers'.

This assessment of the Chinese work ethic and similar evaluations offered by other foreigners who have worked with Chinese are based on the common assumption of an implicit relationship between qualitative values such as 'dedication' and 'perseverance' and a quantitative measure typically expressed as number of hours worked. However, after they have spent more time in a Chinese company, foreign employees very often find their initial assessment tempered by the realization that the investment of additional hours and a qualitatively valuable or even quantitatively tangible return from that investment are parameters whose correlation is not necessarily positive. The corresponding reëvaluation that results from this realization, bounded most often by qualifiers such as "inefficient" and "wasted time", marks a significant departure in perspective from the initial assessment, a shift in perspective that is usually accompanied by a questioning of the rationale for working such long hours and speculation on the motivations.

In her study of Americans working for Japanese companies, intercultural consultant, Rochelle Kopp, posited a number of reasons for the tendency of Japanese workers to put in long hours. She cited a fundamental tenet of Japanese culture that advocated putting in as much time as required to do a job "right" as one driver for such behavior. Another culturally significant factor was loyalty not just to one's company but, more importantly, to one's team. "Even if it just means sitting around twiddling their thumbs," Kopp observed, many Japanese would not leave work until their co-workers, superiors, or subordinates had finished for the day (Kopp 1994, page 89). Working long hours therefore, Kopp concluded, was a way that Japanese workers demonstrated "group solidarity", a concept formalized in the Japanese language through the term *sukiai nook-ri* ("staying late to keep someone company") (Kopp 1994, page 89).

Although Chinese society is often characterized as "collectivist" in nature, the Chinese language, notably, does not have a corresponding term for this concept nor does it figure into the list of reasons for which foreign employees at Chinese firms speculated their Chinese colleagues were motivated to work such long hours. The motivations foreign employees did identify fall into three categories.[15]

---

[15] The assumption is that speculations on motivations for working long hours related to full-time employees who would not receive any additional compensation for extending their time in the office.

On Call: Foreign employees observed that during much of the time their Chinese colleagues spent working late into the evening they were not actively engaged in work. However, they were clearly not waiting for their colleagues to finish, as in the case of the Japanese Kopp describes. Instead they were waiting for something to happen, as if on call. That "call" most commonly came in the form of a request from a supervisor that might require some urgent attention and was highly unpredictable.

Distractions: A foreign employee at Alibaba found that a typical work-day was punctuated by frequent distractions and disruptions that made it difficult for employees to finish projects during normal business hours. As a consequence, they were obliged to stay later to complete their assigned tasks. Typical distractions include conducting conference calls on speakerphone with colleagues who may very well be sitting just a few desks away, leaving a mobile phone unattended with its ringtone volume set to the highest level, and watching videos of children's music performances on a desktop computer with the sound unmuted.[16] The impact of these distractions is exacerbated in densely packed, open offices that are characteristic of Chinese companies.

Fear: An employee in one of Huawei's offices overseas had the sense that Chinese colleagues were motivated to work such long hours out of fear, the source of which, he speculated, was intense competition for work places. The implication was that if they didn't work such long hours the Chinese employees were convinced that they could easily be replaced by others who would be more than happy to take their places.[17]

A Case Study

In the process of considering whether or not to accept an offer of employment he had received from the Chinese gaming giant, Tencent, a product developer from India consulted half a dozen of his friends. Five out of the six advised him not to take the offer because of the impression they had formed about how low the level of respect was that Chinese companies accorded the work-life balance of their employees. Based on this impression, the developer's friends concluded that the

---

[16] In my experience, Chinese colleagues in general have a higher tolerance and threshold for ambient noise and tend to find these sounds less of a distraction.

[17] A number of Chinese interviewed suggested that the motivation for some employees who worked longer hours might be avoidance of a stressful home environment.

experience of actually working in such an environment must necessarily be a miserable one. Despite his friends' misgivings, the Indian developer eventually decided to take the job. Fearing the worst, the developer's friends spent the next few months waiting for the call from the developer that would signal his imminent departure from the company. When the developer finally called, however, it was not to inform his friends that he had given notice, but to report that the working environment, contrary to expectations, was not as terrible as his friends had imagined it to be. While it was certainly true that his Chinese colleagues worked long hours, the developer sensed that this was because their concept of time and their approach to its allocation was fundamentally different from that of the employees in Western companies with whom he had previously worked.

Time in the Chinese company, he explained to his friends, was more "continuous" than it was at a Western company, but the intensity of the work that filled out the time was not as constant. The effect that these conditions had was to create a work environment that very much reminded him of his days at university which, as he recalled it, did not adhere to strict divisions between personal and study time. Rather, the daily routine that characterized the academic curriculum was a more fluid construct within which students could find themselves working on a class project one minute and then participating in an extracurricular activity the next. Similarly, during the course of a workday in the Chinese company he would very often observe his colleagues shift frequently and seamlessly from working on a development project to playing online games and then back to the development project, behavior that was considered perfectly normal and acceptable. He allowed that, in a company whose principal business was online game development, employees who spent time playing online games during the course of the workday could legitimately be excused for carrying out product testing. However, he emphasized that playing games was just one example of the many non work-related activities employees engaged in during the course of a day. The company's willingness to tolerate this behavior and allow employees the flexibility to allocate the time as they saw fit, he surmised, was based on a common understanding and expectation that the workday would then be correspondingly longer.

The developer admitted that adapting to this less structured approach to time, accommodating the overlap of "personal life" and "work life" activities, and working longer hours had certainly been a challenge.

However, he insisted that many aspects of the working environment in the Chinese company were ones his friends back in India would nevertheless find familiar because of the distinct resemblance they bore to those characteristic of the working environment in an Indian company and a similar approach to time they reflected.

THE CULTURAL DIMENSION

The suggestion that these similarities the developer identified based on observations specific to his workplace might be representative of a larger cultural tendency is bolstered by the accounts of the experience that Indians working at other Chinese companies shared. These anecdotal accounts were formalized in an article written by an Indian working for a Chinese company in Beijing that appeared in India's Economic Times (Phadke 2018). In support of her observation, "Indians find Chinese offices often operate in very familiar ways", (Phadke 2018) that served as the article's thesis, the author offered a number of substantiating points. She identified for example, a knack the two cultures share for, what she referred to euphemistically as, "finding innovative workarounds". The "chabuduo" (Chinese for "good enough") culture she experienced in a Chinese enterprise was mirrored linguistically in the Hindi word "jargaad" and culturally in the typical office environment 'jargaad' represented. Both "chabuduo" and "jargaad", she concluded, expressed a common spirit of pragmatism whose motivation was the necessity to make do with limited resources and complete tasks in short-timeframes. She also noted that organizational particularities, such as the hierarchical structure and paternalistic management style she observed in the Chinese firm she worked for, bore a distinct resemblance to those that feature prominently in a "Bajartya film", a set Indian drama whose plot revolves around the relations between members of a quintessential family-oriented Indian company.[18]

These examples illustrate the role that culture plays in determining how a foreign employee responds to the challenge of working in a Chinese company and in so doing provide a context that makes the perspective that Divya Joseph shares in her blog posts seem somewhat less provocative. More specifically, it goes some way towards accounting for the discrepancy that exists between the experience Divya Joseph (who herself is Indian)

[18]Reference to Sooraj Bajartya, a Bollywood director whose films he himself positions as "family-orented".

describes and the experience of the large majority of employees from other cultures who consistently report finding accommodating the expectations in a Chinese company to be a challenge and struggle to determine where or how to draw the line between their work lives and their personal lives.

Divya Joseph's pronouncements notwithstanding, Chinese managers, in practice, recognize that the working habits of foreigners on their teams may be different from those of their Chinese counterparts and tend make some allowance for the differences. However, there are some who attribute the necessity for making such an accommodation to the poor work ethic of their foreign employees, regarding the insistence of foreign staff on maintaining a more equitable work-life balance as an inherent weakness and, in some cases, nothing more than a ploy for working fewer hours. Typical is the Chinese expat manager whose frustration with the work ethic of the local staff he supervised was evident in his account of how they spent their time, "on morning tea, afternoon tea, and long chats during lunch breaks rather than catching up on their slow progress" (Wang et al. 2013, page 3823). The narrative that this assessment feeds into is one according to which Chinese are, by nature, more diligent and dedicated than the foreigners who work for them, a self-characterization that hints at a belief in cultural exceptionalism.

It was the cultural superiority such statements implied that prompted an American working for Huawei to take issue and draft a rebuttal. In the memo, addressed to all employees in the company, he asked the audience to consider as example the culture in Silicon Valley the employees of whose firms are known for the long hours they work and their dedication. An American employed by Alibaba who has experience working in both environments, agrees that representatives of the respective cultures have a strong work ethic and tend to work long hours, but notes that there is a difference in approach. From the American employee's perspective, Silicon Valley firms were less consistently intense and to illustrate the point brought up the case of a Google management team agreement to reschedule a townhall meeting they planned to hold on Friday afternoons in favor of a traditional Friday afternoon 'Happy Hour' employees insisted on maintaining. By comparison, the employee noted that it would be inconceivable for management in a Chinese company to support an event like a "Happy Hour" in the first place and even if such an activity were sanctioned it would, in all likelihood, not be scheduled during working hours. Executives in a Chinese company would never consider changing the schedule of an executive meeting to accommodate a 'Happy Hour'.

Even taking these accommodations into account, the reality of the working environment for a foreign employee in Alibaba and the demands of the workplace on an employee's time bears scant resemblance to the experience of the young mother that the promotional videos on the company's website profile as she moves effortlessly from one stop on her agenda to the next, following a routine that appears to accommodate both the care of small children at home and the requirements of projects at work. The case of a European woman who moved to Hangzhou with her young family after accepting an offer employment with the company, illustrates the degree to which this idealized "day in the life" of a working mother, as depicted in the videos, departs from the challenges a real working mother experiences.

Already struggling to manage care of her young children, the young European woman felt increasing pressure to put in longer hours at work. Through her discussions with Chinese colleagues who also had small children, it became clear to her that the conditions under which her Chinese colleagues were raising their children were fundamentally different from her own. While she struggled to care for her children in the absence of family and friends who might have been a source of support and without access to the kinds of supplementary resources that were more readily available when generous expat packages were the norm, her Chinese colleagues benefited from the support of parents and other family members who shouldered a good share of the childcare burden, a practice that was expected and widely accepted. It was a simple equation: Chinese colleagues could stay later in the office because they had fewer obligations at home and therefore fewer demands on their time.

Teambuilding Through "Team-Work"

After initially resisting the pressure from Chinese management to work into the evening, the young mother finally relented and agreed to stay late two days a week as a compromise. This change in habit was duly highlighted in her next performance review and positioned by her Chinese supervisor as a positive step towards closer integration with the rest of the team. The implication that working longer hours fosters team cohesion and contributes to team spirit is made concrete in Divya Joseph's account of an evening spent working in Alibaba. "A day like today, when there is a campaign running, is a day to support each other as a team, while having a fun evening with colleagues relishing a group dinner and attending fun events organized by the HR department to keep the spirits up" (Joseph 2018).

In characterizing long hours at work as a "huge blessing", Alibaba CEO, Jack Ma, very likely had a concept of work that incorporated a social dimension and a working environment in mind that was like the one Joseph describes. This realization offers some explanation for why Ma, and others like him, might see investment of longer hours at the office as something to be celebrated as a reflection of a healthy corporate culture rather than decried as the sign of one that has lost its bearings.

The Meanings of Life and The Definitions of Work

Deciding Where to Draw the Line

The impression that Chinese "live to work" (or, perhaps, "live for work") that many of the foreign employees employed by Chinese companies have, is very often predicated on the assumption that there is a common understanding of what "work" and "life" constitute and agreement on their definition. What is evident from the accounts of foreigners grappling with the issue of where to draw the line between their "work" in a Chinese workplace and their "life" outside of work is that the Chinese they work with have a fundamentally different concept of where the position of the fulcrum lies that balances "work" and "life" and by implication a different understanding of what those terms imply. The perspectives of Amazon CEO, Jeff Bezos and Buffer CEO Nicole Miller on the relationship between "Work" and "Life" illustrate just how wide the variance in definitions and how disparate approaches to finding a way to balance them can be. Bezos maintains that instead of viewing "work" and "life" as two domains that need to be balanced it is more productive to view them as two integrated parts that can be best visualized as "a circle, not a balance" (Bernard 2019). Like Bezos, Miller doesn't conceive of a balance between work and life but she uses a very different geometry to describe the relationship of the two domains to one another. If Bezos' concept is circular, Miller's is strictly linear. "there is a place for work and a place for family" Miller insists, drawing a clear border between the two (Miller 2019). Underlying this difference in perspective on the composition and definition of work and life is the fundamental issue of what, conceptually, a "company" represents and where, functionally, the "workplace" begins and ends.

Work Imitating Life

In Western countries and societies a company is commonly viewed as a commercial enterprise whose goal is to generate profits. The tradition of enterprise in China and understanding the role a company in Chinese society occupies is very different. The Chinese 'danwei' (work unit), the place of employment for most Chinese workers through the 1980's, is an apt example that illustrates the nature and magnitude of that difference. Bjorklund defines the "danwei" as a "socio-political unit in which the livelihood and domestic and social activities of its members are carried out" (Bjorklund 1986, page 19). The "livelihood" that the work-unit was responsible for providing was basic employment. The "domestic and social activities" that fell under the *danwei*'s purview filled out a long list of welfare benefits that included free housing, schooling and healthcare. In practice, the organization of the work-unit and supervisory control of its management extended deep into the personal lives of its members and included allocating their housing, approving travel, and even authorizing marriages ("Danwei People Become Citizens" 2003). The 'danwei', as the "socio-political unit" originally conceived, has long since disappeared, but its spirit lives on, most notably in the events and activities that Chinese companies organize. These activities, whose character und function will be fleshed out more fully in Chapter 7—"All Work and Play" are organized around the individual in all dimensions and in their execution very often touch on aspects of their participants' personal lives. The Shanghai Bell company, for example, holds an annual "Family Day" and even hosts mass weddings. Alibaba also organizes an annual 'Family Day' as well as a mass wedding over which Jack Ma himself presides, proof that the organization and composition of such events is standard and not unique to a state-owned enterprise. In fact, examples of this coexistence or melding of work and life (commercial and personal) such as these are just a few of the many that can be observed across the entire spectrum of Chinese enterprises. It is common practice and considered perfectly acceptable for Chinese shop owners and restaurateurs, for example (even in a fast-food chain like McDonald's), to bring their children into the workplace and give them free rein of the premises while the proprietors conduct their business. An anecdote attributed to Huawei CEO, Ren Zhengfei, illustrates just how tightly integrated into the social fabric and how pervasive a presence in the lives of its employees a Chinese company can be. According to the anecdote,

Ren suggested that an employee based in Shenzhen who was reluctant to take a position company offered him in Beijing because his wife was opposed to the move should immediately file for divorce. The message was clear: the employee's affiliation with the company trumped his relationship with his wife as was the implication: the company was as much a family surrogate as it was a commercial entity.

As Chinese companies extend their reach and enhance their presence overseas, it becomes increasingly likely that the local laws and regulations they encounter will influence the number of hours they can expect their foreign employees to work and, by association, lead to a recalculation of the equation for work-life balance. An attorney specializing in international employment noted: "Chinese companies are often targets of many kinds of employment claims, sometimes because they are unaware of local (U.S.) employment law and, at other times, because they don't realize that what works in China's culture doesn't work in the U.S." (He 2014).

Local employees of Chinese companies in locations around the world may talk about how impressed they are with the work ethic of their Chinese colleagues, but most have no desire to work that way themselves and, if need be, will call on lawyers and unions for support to ensure that proper expectations are set and appropriate working hours and conditions are maintained. There are signs that in their attitude to work and life and approach to reconciling and balancing these two spheres of their daily existence, foreign employees may increasingly be joined by younger Chinese colleagues whose view of their place at work and the place that work occupies in their lives is undergoing a transformation.

THE NEXT GENERATION: TIRED OF OVERWORKING

"Leisure is making a comeback" trumpeted an article in the Financial Times that examined the changing perceptions of work and the workplace in China (Waldmeir 2012). This was bookended by a BBC article profiling China's younger generation that announced "ambitious millennials have had enough" (Hruby 2018). Hard evidence for the changing attitudes towards work these media publicize can be found in related statistics. Topping the list of numeric references is "996", a shorthand China's Millennials use to describe the traditional work schedule—9 in the morning until 9 at night 6 days a week—many are desperate to break free of. A turnover rate of 20–30% attributed to those who are quitting their jobs in favor of a better "lifestyle" is an equally significant data point. The change for which this statistic is a leading indicator is explained by larger social and technological trends that are redefining the Chinese employee's relationship to the workplace.

Sociologists are of two minds when it comes to providing an explanation for the changes in behavior that underlie the shift in the attitudes of Chinese towards work and coming to resolution on where work fits into a younger employee's larger view of life. On one side, are those who attribute the divergence of China's Millennial generation from their parents in their attitude towards work to their pampered upbringing as single children, a condition that has made them more self-centered and less patient. On the other side, are those who agree that the condition of being a single child is consequential, but whose analysis and interpretation of what that condition implies is very different. They argue that single children, already burdened with the dual demands of caring for children and parents, find it impossible to accommodate the traditional pace of work and demands of the typical Chinese workplace. What is motivating the change in attitude and driving demand for transformation of the work environment, these experts conclude, is the heightened risk of burnout and fear of a breakdown.

In their search for a more satisfactory relationship to work, younger Chinese are looking elsewhere for models. A Chinese expat manager in the U.S. remarks, somewhat wistfully, that many of his American colleagues also work hard, but seem to do a better job of balancing work and family. "They make sure to take vacation time with their family and children, which I highly value, but did not do so well myself" (Yu 2016, page 95).

Ironically, the push these younger employees are making for a clearer definition of the line between work and life is at the same time being offset by the pull of technologies and new modes of communication that are blurring those same lines. WeChat, for example, the social media platform that is at the heart of a Chinese Millenial's life is concurrently the prime vehicle for workplace communication and enabler of business-related interaction. The extent to which these aspects of a Chinese employee's "life" not only co-exist, but have actually merged, can be seen from a foreign employee who recounted connecting to colleagues at work via WeChat and then finding that this concurrently gave her access to "snippets of their [colleagues'] personal world" (Zhang 2018). The author of a blog addressing this conundrum advises that the most effective way to restore work-life balance is to pull back from technology and increase productivity through "more study and better time management" (Gudian 2013).

CONCLUSION

Chinese firms that employ foreign staff tend to view them in an idealized light and the image of foreigners they present in company brochures, websites, and videos is often a stereotype that bears little resemblance to the flesh-and-blood foreigners they employ nor does it reflect what real foreigners in a Chinese workplace experience. This discrepancy between the "real" and the "ideal" foreigner is a source of tension between foreign staff and their Chinese supervisors that expresses itself most frequently as a misalignment of expectations—especially in the degree of commitment to the company and its activities.

Foreign employees of Chinese companies who appear in company videos or share their thoughts in written accounts consistently emphasize the "family" atmosphere of the Chinese company they work for, and the concern that Chinese management has for their well-being. In reality, finding a balance between work and life that satisfies themselves and their Chinese supervisors is one of the most significant challenges foreign employees in a Chinese enterprise face.

However the Chinese workplace is changing and an increasing number of Chinese, especially those who represent the younger generation, are reassessing the role that work plays in their lives and recalibrating the balance between the two. In light of this trend and the reassessment that characterizes it, there conceivably will be a much closer congruence in future between the views of Chinese management and foreign staff about work and the role of the workplace.

In the meantime, satisfying the requirements of work in a Chinese company and finding a satisfactory balance between work and life remains a significant challenge for foreign employees. As we will see work life balance is, in fact, just one of many challenges that foreigners working in Chinese companies face and that pose an impediment to their success. A more detailed view of what these obstacles are and ways to overcome them is the subject of the next chapter.

REFERENCES

Bernard, Zoe, "Jeff Bezos' Advice to Amazon Employees Is to Stop Aiming for Work-Life 'Balance'—Here's What You Should Strive for Instead," Business Insider, January 9, 2019.

Bjorklund, E.M., "The 'Danwei': Socio-Spatial Characteristics of Work Units in China's Urban Society", Economic Geography, Vol. 62, No. 1, January 1986, pages 19–29.

"Danwei People Become Citizens", *Economist*, September 4, 2003.

Gorfinkel, L., Performing the Chinese Nation: The Politics of Identity in China Central Television's Music-Entertainment Programs (PhD), University of Technology, Sydney. Referenced in Stanley, Phiona, 2011.

Gorfinkel and Chubb (Gorfinkel, L., and Chubb, A. [2012, March 2–3] Foreigners Performing the Chinese Nation: Between Cosmopolitanism and a Superior Chinese Culture). Paper presented at the Television, Power, and Ideology in Postsocialist China Conference, Australian National University, Canberra. Referenced in Stanley, Phiona, 2012, page 13.

Gudian, "Gongzuo he shenghuo xuyao pingheng ma ?" sina.com.cn, June 4, 2013, http://blog.sina.com.cn/s/blog_4b09eac00102espj.html.

He, Amy, "Chinese Companies in US Urged to Learn Employment Laws", *China Daily USA*, September 18, 2014.

Hruby, Denise, "Young Chinese Are Sick of Working Long Hours", BBC, May 8, 2018.

Joseph, Divya Ann, *Working in a Chinese Company—A Foreigner's View Point* (blog post), June 16, 2018.

Kopp, Rochelle, *The Rice Paper Ceiling: Breaking Through the Japanese Corporate Culture*, Stone Bridge Press, Berkeley, CA, 1994.

Miller, Nicole, "Your Company Is Not Your Family," *Fast Company*, March 15, 2019.

Phadke, Mithila, "Chinese Workers Do This Thing at Work That Indian Offices Would Never Tolerate", *Economic Times*, August 5, 2018, //economictimes.indiatimes.com/articleshow/65274492.cms?utm_source=contentofinterest&utm_medium=text&utm_campaign=cppst.

Stanley, Phiona, *A Critical Ethnology of Westerners Teaching English in China: Shanghaied in Shanghai*, Routledge, London and New York, 2013.

Waldmeir, Patti, "China's Young Warm to the West's Work Life Balance," *Financial Times*, March 6, 2012.

Wang, Dan, Freeman, Susan, and Zhu, Cherrie Jiuhua, "Personality Traits and Cross-Cultural Competence of Chinese Expatriate Managers: A Socio-Analytic and Institutional Perspective," *International Human Resources Management*, April 29, 2013, pages 3812–3830.

Yu, Xi, "From East to West: A Phenomenological Study of Mainland Chinese Expatriates' International Adjustment Experiences in the U.S. Workplace", dissertation University of Minnesota, March 2016.

Zhang, Michelle, "WeChat Blurs Work and Life in China", *Medium|Technology*, April 6, 2018.

CHAPTER 6

Bamboo Ceiling

"Bamboo Ceiling" the term that has been used to describe the specific obstacles and barriers that Asian Americans face in reaching the upper echelons of leadership and management is a fitting term for the experience of foreign staff in Chinese companies who very often find themselves blocked and marginalized with very little room for professional advancement and career development.[1]

OFF THE TRACK

A survey conducted by human resources advisory firm, Korn Ferry, determined that potential for "career progression" was the second most important criterion (after 'company culture') that candidates for employment consider when choosing an employer (Maurer 2017). Moreover, a company's level of commitment to career development can have direct bearing on employee satisfaction and, by association, on productivity and turnover. Foreign employees working in Chinese companies, regardless of level and title, consistently report that they see very little opportunity to develop their careers and are keenly aware of limits to their progression. Even participants in programs Chinese firms have developed for

---

[1] The term 'bamboo ceiling' was coined by author June Hyun in her book: *Breaking the Bamboo Ceiling: Career Strategies for Asians*, HarperCollins, 2005 to characterize the obstacles to professional development Asian Americans face.

© The Author(s) 2020
P. Ross, *Barriers to Entry*,
https://doi.org/10.1007/978-981-32-9566-7_6

the express purpose of preparing foreign employees to take on leadership roles see little promise for development of a career as they conceive it. A case in point, Huawei's "Seeds" program makes no commitment to hire those who complete the program, much less guide them onto a long-term career path. Tencent's strict system of grade levels poses a challenge to any employee, Chinese or foreign, who wants to move up in the company that is so daunting an American game developer working for the company came to the conclusion that leaving the company for a competitor and then getting hired back later at a higher grade level was a more effective method of securing a management position than trying to advance internally. Alibaba's AGLA program, in spite of the structured rotations through key business units it provides, does not offer participants an opportunity to take on a direct management role, an experience that many consider an essential element of any training program and vital to longer-term career development. Lack of such an opportunity is a major source of disappointment for many members of the program, most of whom were recruited for the very qualities that typically would constitute a management profile—career ambition, educational excellence, and dedication. As a consequence, a number of participants who were graduates of programs in business administration (MBA) noted that they would advise classmates hoping to get direct management experience not to consider such a program and admitted that they themselves didn't view employment with the company as a long-term commitment. Rather, they saw it as a stepping stone along the way to a longer-term career that they would undoubtedly go elsewhere develop.

Identifying similar limitations and frustrations for Americans working in Japanese companies, Kopp concluded: "The consequence of a lack of opportunities for growth and advancement appears to be a very common reason for Americans leaving or wanting to leave their positions at Japanese employers". Where the Chinese and Japanese cases differ is in the degree to which these limitations are institutionalized within the corporate organizational structure. Japanese organizations codify the differences in career development and potential between Japanese and foreign staff through the use of specific designations referred to as *Seishan* (Kopp 1994, page 192)[2] and *Shokotaku* (Kopp 1994, page 192) and

---

[2] Seishan is translated as "permanent employee", but as Kopp notes this is not a meaningful or satisfactory (or adequate) translation in Kopp, Rochelle, *The Rice Paper Ceiling: Breaking Through the Japanese Corporate Culture*, Stone Bridge Press, 1994, page 192.

an employee's career prospects and progression in a Japanese company are very much dependent on and tied to the organizational category to which they have been assigned. '*Seishan*' designates an employee who has been hired directly out of university, has subsequently been trained internally, and is expected to stay with the company until retirement. The career path of a '*Seishan*' is characterized by regular rotations through different parts of the company in a slow and steady progression up the career ladder from one position of greater responsibility and one grade of increasing compensation to the next. By contrast, '*Shokotaku*', defined technically as "contract staff", is the designation for an employee who has been hired to do a specific job with no expectation or promise of any other engagement outside of the scope that has been defined. It is also the organizational designation to which foreigners hired into a Japanese company are usually assigned. An employee so designated does not have claim to the same benefits, does not enjoy the same degree of job security, nor have access to the same career development programs as one who has been classified as *Seishan*. For example, the personnel department does not usually offer *Shokotaku* employees supplementary training opportunities, evaluate their performance, or rotate them through other posts or departments. Regardless of the nature of the work they do or the value of their contribution, '*Shokotaku*' are considered "temporary" workers even though the tenure of their 'temporary' employment in a company may extend over a number of years (Kopp 1994). As a consequence of this organizational condition, a foreigner classified as a "*Shokotaku*" is destined from the outset to have a career path within the company that is very attenuated. "Zai bian" (full-time), "Fei Zai bian" (on-contract) the terms in a Chinese organization that most closely correspond to the Japanese "*Seishan*" and "*Shotaku*" are, by contrast, much more general categories that do not carry the same organizational implications as their Japanese counterparts nor is their application as rigorous or as uniform.

Like the Americans Kopp interviewed who worked in the local offices of Japanese companies in the U.S., local staff working in the overseas offices and subsidiaries of Chinese companies complain that their career prospects are limited because management roles are in most cases occupied by Chinese who have come from company headquarters or been rotated in from another representative office. These individual cases reflect a more far-reaching strategic approach Chinese firms take towards managing their operations overseas that Shen and Edwards refer to as "ethnocentric", defined as a condition where management of a local

Table 6.1   Chinese company overseas staff classification ('ethnocentric')

	POSITION TYPES		
	Executive	Other Managerial	Non-Managerial
PCN	100%	85%	3%
HCN	0%	15%	97%
TCN	0	0	0

Source Shen and Edwards, "Recruitment and Selection in Chinese MNEs", page 826

office is placed almost exclusively in the hands of Parent-Company Nationals (PCNs), in this case Chinese (Shen and Edwards 2004).

In general, companies that take an "ethnocentric" approach to management do so because they want to maintain control of key administrative functions (e.g. financial, operations, etc.) usually as a way of ensuring effective coordination of global activities and consistency. Other motivations for installing PCNs in senior management posts include being able to troubleshoot complex technical and commercial issues effectively, facilitate diffusion of company culture, develop corporate PCN management talent, and meet specific technical requirements (company headquarters as a repository of PCNs who have requisite knowledge and experience).

The majority of Chinese companies Shen and Edwards studied were guided by an 'ethnocentric' strategy in managing their overseas operations and consistently filled executive posts almost exclusively with PCNs. By contrast, nearly all non-managerial positions were held by Host Country Nationals (HCNs) (see Table 6.1)[3,4] (Shen and Edwards 2004).

A number of the other companies analyzed in the study followed a strategy referred to as 'polycentric' that accommodated greater participation of HCNs in the managerial ranks. When the profiles of these companies were taken into account there was a more equitable split of managerial positions between PCNs and HCNs in the composite that resulted. However, nearly three-quarters of the executive posts were still allocated to PCNs (see Table 6.2).

[3] This table is adapted directly from Shen and Edwards page.

[4] Shen, Jie and Edwards, Vincent, *International Journal of Human Resource Management*, Vol. 15, No. 4, August 2004, page 826.

Table 6.2 Chinese company overseas staff classification (all organizatational profiles)

	POSITION TYPES		
	Executive	Other Managerial	Non-Managerial
PCN	72%	51%	3%
HCN	28%	59%	97%
TCN	0	0	0

Source Shen and Edwards, "Recruitment and Selection in Chinese MNEs", page 827

Management ascribed the underrepresentation of local hires in senior positions to a lack of qualified local staff and noted a difficulty in finding and retaining local talent with satisfactory skills and experience. HCNs consulted stated that they had little motivation to stay in the company that had hired them because they saw no opportunity for advancement and no hope for development of a career.

Beneath this generalized picture, the opportunities for upward mobility and the potential for career progression that exist in the overseas offices of Chinese companies can vary quite significantly from one office to the next and across regions. A consultant for Huawei who visited key offices in locations around the world recognized a distinct difference in the profiles of the organizations in Canada, where a number of local employees held management positions, and Africa, where there were virtually no local hires in the senior management ranks.

While it is true that there are foreigners who hold senior management positions, these positions, staffed by local hires, are almost exclusively country or regional level positions.[5] Those few senior posts that foreigners in a Chinese company's headquarters occupy are usually functional in nature (cf. Donald Purdy, Huawei's Head of Cybersecurity and Alibaba's General Counsel, Tim Steinert) and not ones that carry profit-and-loss responsibility or have broad management purview. Nor are they at the highest level of the company organizational structure. The few exceptions to this general rule are cases referenced previously; foreigners who are members of a company's executive team thanks to a unique set of circumstances such as a large-scale investment they made at a formative stage of a company's development.

[5] Andrea Ghizzono and Srinath Ramanujan, Tencent's GM for Europe and Head of India respectively are examples.

However, in these cases the foreign executives were already "fully-formed", i.e. well along in their careers with significant industry experience and expertise in a specific domain (investments, legal, etc.). Importantly, not one of these foreign executives came up through the ranks of the Chinese company following a clear and well-defined internal career development path. In this regard, the conditions in Japanese companies are not too dissimilar. However, there are a number of cases where a Japanese company's CEO is a non-Japanese (Howard Stringer, for example, at Sony and, until recently, Carlos Ghosn at Nissan). The ranks below the CEO, however, remain steadfastly populated by Japanese managers.

Career Development Case
Fait Accompli

An AGLA participant recounted that, as the program was nearing its end, he was unexpectedly called to attend a meeting the subject of which, ostensibly, was his next step in the company. He was pleased to learn that there was some interest in the development of his career and began preparing for the discussion. First he reviewed his career goals and then gave further thought to what the definition of the job would be that would give him the experience he needed to take a step closer to achieving those goals.

It was with no small amount of anticipation that he opened the door to the conference room where the meeting was to be held. Once he stepped inside, the scene he found was one that he could hardly have anticipated. Seated around the conference table in the middle of the room was a group that included the foreign employee's direct supervisor, representatives from the Human Resources department, and, much to his amazement, at the head of the table in the position of greatest prominence, sat the head of the entire division for which he was working. As impressed as he was by the presence of such a senior executive, he questioned what contribution the head of the division could make as they had no previous interaction.

As the discussion progressed, it became clear to him why his lack of any previous interaction with the parties in attendance had not precluded their participation. Prior to the meeting, those sitting around the table had effectively decided among themselves the next step his career was to take. The employee's personal development and interest was of little or no consequence.

Job

Even before concerning themselves with career development, much less giving any thought to acquiring the experience that might eventually get them into the top echelons of a Chinese company, foreign employees in a Chinese company face the more fundamental issue of determining what the job they have been hired to do actually entails. "If there was a job description," says Bill Plummer, former Head of External Affairs for Huawei in North America, "I never saw it" (Plummer 2018). Indeed, a common complaint of foreign employees working in Chinese organizations is that they do not always understand what is expected of them nor is the guidance they receive from the Chinese who have hired them sufficient or satisfactory. Even those who believe that they had come to firm agreement on a position definition and title with representatives of the Chinese company during the contract negotiation process quite often find that the job they are asked to do on arrival bears little or no resemblance to the one that had been defined over the weeks and months of discussions that preceded their acceptance of an employment offer. "It was vague as to whom I might be reporting and as part of what of organization," notes Plummer recalling his first day on the job (Plummer 2018). This is an outcome that invariably leads to recriminations, accusations of duplicity, and, in some cases, even threats of legal action. The frequency and consistency of these cases raises the possibility that what the new foreign hire perceives to be tantamount to a bait-and-switch deal and reads as an attempt by the company's management to annoy and confuse new foreign staff is not, in fact, intentional, but may instead be symptomatic of a particular organizational state. Bouée, in his inquiry into the nature of Chinese enterprise culture, characterizes this state as one of "more or less permanent flux; as constantly moving and evolving" (Bouée 2012, page 131) Bouée's contention is that the inherently flexible nature of the organization that characterizes a Chinese enterprise reflects management's response to an overall business climate and operating environment in China that he notes is "more fluid and turbulent than it is in America, for example" (Bouée 2010, page 131) and is a manifestation, more broadly, of "the central role that movement rather than structure or shape plays in the Chinese world view". These high-level conclusions Bouée arrives at are substantiated at an organizational level by the number of foreigners employed in Chinese companies who report never having seen an organizational chart, either for their department or any other, for that matter. Consistent with these accounts is my own observation of placards designating departments and their functions posted at the entrances to offices in the Shanghai Bell company that are consistently (and hopelessly) out-of-date. Despite the discrepancy that exists between the designations on the signs and the profile of the team that actually inhabits the office, very rarely is there an attempt made to update the signs and make sure they reflect the latest change. It is conceivable, therefore, that the position of any individual employee within this fluid and malleable organizational construct is less tightly tethered and that the role he or she is meant to play is, by association, less formally defined. In recognition of this phenomenon, an American employee working for Sinochem in the U.S., when asked to validate an organizational chart, noted: "all the important stuff is in the white spaces" (Wang 2006, page 165). My own impression (corroborated by Chinese colleagues) is that a new Chinese employee would assess his or her fit in an organization and determine what he or she was supposed to be doing not by scanning the lines and boxes of a formal organization chart and parsing a carefully-crafted job description, but, a bit like a submarine equipped with sonar, would 'ping' other members of the group to find out what they were doing and then intuit, based on a composite of those 'soundings', where to plug in. Such an approach, if effective and valid, then would obviate the need for formal charts and descriptions. This evidence of a pliable organizational structure contradicts the persistent perception of a stifling hierarchy that most foreign employees have. And the work environment it creates is a much more flexible one than most foreigners are comfortable with. It would also explain why a new employee, especially a foreign one, who is not plugged into or, in many cases, not even aware of the organization's informal network, would find trying to determine what he or she was supposed to be doing and how to fit in such a difficult and frustrating exercise.

When evaluating a foreign candidate for employment, management in a Chinese company has traditionally prioritized skills and experience directly relevant to the position under consideration followed by cultural competence (sensitivity, language, etc.) and flexibility.[6] What the cases referenced make clear is that there is a range of behaviors, attitudes, and character

---

[6]Just as it does for Chinese who are being considered for expat roles in overseas locations.

traits that are as important, if not more important even, than functional expertise and cross-cultural competence as a criterion for evaluation and determinant for the success of a foreign employee in a Chinese workplace.

An American working in one of Alibaba's U.S. offices who was tasked with building a team, very early on came to the conclusion that the ideal candidate was not necessarily one who possessed a specific skill (although this was certainly an important consideration), but rather one who was comfortable with uncertainty, with rapid and unexpected change, and with taking initiative and finding his or her own direction. The most likely source for candidates who possessed the requisite combination of traits was a startup environment and those who had prior experience in such an environment were preferred. Whether they had been successful or not was of secondary importance. A foreign director of recruitment working in the company's headquarters concurred with the assessment of the director in the U.S. office, emphasizing that there is relatively little direction given, so a foreign employee needs to be very motivated and self-directed. He concluded that people who need or expect a lot of direction will not do well in such an environment. The subject of a foreign employee's career development in a Chinese organization and related issues is part of a larger universe of obstacles and challenges employees at Chinese companies face that not only impede professional development but contribute to a more general sense of exclusion and even isolation.

OUT OF THE LOOP

A few minutes before noontime, Chinese colleagues I had been meeting with suddenly shut down their computers, closed their notebooks, and headed off to lunch leaving me sitting by myself in the conference room. Prior to the conclusion of the meeting there had been no overt disagreements or apparent conflict that might have precipitated such behavior. On the contrary, the meeting had gone quite well and had ended in agreement on next steps to be taken, an outcome that would be considered positive under any other circumstance. In the months that followed, the phenomenon of colleagues leaving me behind while they headed off to lunch would become a pattern that left me feeling excluded.[7] Behavior such as the kind I experienced and the sense of exclusion I felt is not an isolated case, but a situation that foreign employees in a Chinese company frequently encounter and can find demotivating. The exclusion that a foreigner experiences in a Chinese company can take many forms.

Linguistic

In the past, Chinese staff would go to great lengths to accommodate a foreign colleague who didn't speak Chinese. If there were even one foreign attendee present at a meeting whose other participants were all Chinese, the meeting would typically be held in English. For the Chinese speakers, not all of whom were comfortable or adept at expressing themselves in English, this accommodation could be a significant inconvenience. Foreign employees currently employed in Chinese companies, even those who don't speak Chinese very fluently, report that the meetings they participate in with Chinese colleagues are increasingly held in Chinese. Moreover, other communication such as emails that are directed to them, or on which they are copied, very often are written in Chinese and this is a phenomenon that is not exclusive to a Chinese company's headquarters or restricted to its domestic Chinese offices. An employee in Huawei's U.K. office, for example, described organizing a conference call with Chinese colleagues who were based at company headquarters in Shenzhen and a number of other locations where the company has operations. After completing a few perfunctory introductions in English, the Chinese participants proceeded to conduct the rest of the call in Chinese, leaving the local employee in the U.K., whose command of Chinese was limited, completely in the dark. It wasn't until the call was nearing its conclusion that one of the Chinese colleagues noted with surprise that the local employee in the U.K. was still on the call, seemingly forgetting that it was the local employee who had organized the call in the first place. Huawei's former U.S. head of External Affairs, Bill Plummer, describes "periods of frustration" when the conversation in meetings with Chinese executives shifted

[7]Being 'invited' to lunch has significant implications. As Li Ma notes in "Employee Characteristics and Management": "One of the standards by which co-workers judge each other's trust is: 'do they ask me *to have lunch*" (Ma 2014, section 8.5.2).

into Mandarin. He makes the point that the linguistic exclusion reinforced the unstated but palpable feeling that local staff occupied a position inferior to that of Chinese colleagues and were expected to defer to them. It is a dynamic for which Plummer finds visual expression in his description of Chinese managers occupying the conference room in his office while the local staff waited in the corridor outside (Plummer 2018).

It was in recognition of this issue, and the belief that it could be addressed by hiring foreign staff who had Chinese fluency, that Alibaba made Chinese language competence a criterion for selection of participants in the second cohort of the AGLA program. The assumption behind the introduction of this criterion was a degree of confidence that a sufficient number of foreign candidates with Chinese language competence could be found. The more than 4000 primary and secondary schools in the U.S. that offer Chinese language classes, the more than 500 schools registered in the US-Chinese language school system, and the presence of over 100 Confucius Institutes, are statistics that provide some basis for this confidence (Zhan 2017).[8] Despite this trend towards more wide-spread knowledge of the Chinese language and the optimism it engenders, too few of those who have acquired some competence in the language have learned it to a degree that would be adequate for effective communication in a commercial environment (conducting negotiations, delivering executive level presentations, etc.). Given this circumstance, it is likely not coincidental that a fairly large number of the participants who made up the cohort in the AGLA's second year of operation were of Chinese ethnicity and who, in many cases, possessed a fluency in the language that approached that of native speakers.

Ironically, despite the increased insistence of Chinese employers on Chinese language competence as a criterion for employment and the greater attention that foreign candidates for employment in Chinese firms are paying to its acquisition, there is plenty of evidence to suggest that such a requirement may, in reality, not be so critical to a foreign employee's survival in a Chinese company or such an important key to effectiveness in carrying out specific tasks assigned. Moreover, there is some question as to whether Chinese management, even those who insist foreign staff be able to speak Chinese, are entirely comfortable with

[8]Zhan, Qianhui, "Chinese Language Fever Grips US Students", *The Telegraph*, July 18, 2017, https://www.telegraph.co.uk/news/world/china-watch/culture/chinese-language-studies-usa/.

foreign employees who have reached a satisfactory level of fluency in the language.

Townhall meetings in the Shanghai Bell Company are always highly-scripted affairs with even the questions to be posed by the audience prepared well in advance and carefully vetted by the staff of the company president's office. Prior to one such meeting, I was assigned the task of asking a question on behalf of our department with the proviso that I ask the question in English, a request I found odd given that the audience—some 400 strong—were all Chinese. Not to be daunted, I decided to ask the question I had prepared in Chinese when it finally came to my turn in the meeting agenda. In contrast to the looks of surprise that registered on the faces of the department's management, the face of the company president who was standing at a rostrum on stage remained impassive. After a few moments of silence during which he appeared to be gathering his thoughts, the president finally responded. "I finally get your meaning," he said in English and then proceeded to answer the question in Chinese. However, before offering his response, the president made a point of instructing the Chinese colleague seated next to me to translate his words into English, ostensibly so that I would be able to understand what he had said. Given that the question and the accompanying response were already known well in advance of the meeting and that my Chinese was more than adequate to understand the words the president subsequently delivered, the message was clear: Although fluency in Chinese language is a skill an increasing number of Chinese companies expect a foreign employee to possess and even set as a condition for employment (cf. the second cohort of the Alibaba AGLA program), its application is not always welcomed in every situation and its use very much depends on the circumstances, the environment, and, as this example illustrates, the profile of the interlocutor. As an illustration of how situationally dependent use of Chinese language in the workplace can be and a demonstration of the influence that location has on the relationship between foreign employees and Chinese colleagues, I have regularly experienced the phenomenon of starting a discussion with a Chinese colleague who insists on speaking English while we are in the office and then seamlessly switches into Chinese as soon as we walk outside the building. It is a sample size that, admittedly, does not meet the conditions for statistical significance, but is a phenomenon whose appearance is, nevertheless, consistent enough to warrant mention and further consideration.

Social

Common wisdom (cf Hofstede et al.) holds that Chinese companies, reflecting a culture that places a premium on cooperation and that privileges group harmony over individual ambition, are hives of Collectivism staffed by employees who keep the goals of the organization top of mind and consistently demonstrate a willingness to sacrifice (careers, health, time, etc.) for the greater good. This is an interlocking piece that fits neatly and conveniently into the image of a highly socially-oriented and collaborative society. It also forms an essential element of the narrative Chinese themselves have a penchant for telling that depicts Western companies (American ones, in particular) as competition-oriented and their employees as comparatively individualistic and self-interested ("what's in it for me"). This is held up as a foil for Chinese corporate culture that, according to the conventions of the narrative, is at its core a collective one with less focus and fixation on the individual and more on the organization at large. Evidence that accepted wisdom might not be applicable in practice and that there might be instances where the narrative that accompanies it departs from reality comes from a number of sources.

In the conclusion to their comparative study of metaphor use in the mission statements of Chinese and U.S. companies, Sun and Jiang note:

> ...Chinese and US companies seem to convey different values to their stakeholders, although both cooperation and competition exist regardless of whether business is conducted in China or in the US.
> The Chinese companies, which tend to describe themselves as energetic leaders and strong competitors, seem to be more competition-oriented and, thus, seem to run contrary to the conventional wisdom that Chinese companies often operate under a Confucian and cooperative model and to the consensus in the existing literature that 'cooperation' is the prevailing and vital behavior for Chinese firms. (Sun and Jiang, page 13)

Conversely, they find that Western companies, despite a reputation for competition and focus on the individual, place greater emphasis on teamwork and the development of related skills, ostensibly because they recognize that the effectiveness of a team and its ability to deliver results is much greater than that of any individual.

Sun and Jiang's conclusion is based exclusively on an analysis of external communications, but the case for its wider applicability is made by Qiu's observation that Chinese working in teams can appear to be uncooperative and disunited despite being part of a culture that is described as "collectivist" (Qiu 2014, page 288). As the following examples illustrate, the conditions inside a Chinese company that foreign employees experience are consistent with the views referenced above and can be difficult for foreign staff to accommodate and adapt to.

A foreign consultant at Huawei described the company culture as he encountered it to be very individualistic where decisions made by those in management positions and their allocation of resources motivated more by personal gain and benefit than a commitment to the larger group and team. The insight from this eyewitness account is consistent with Qiu's observation that "Chinese people's 'collectivism' is characterized by a tendency to maintain relations with others as achieving one's own goals and maximizing one own's interest rather than sacrificing personal interest for the good of the collective" (Qiu 2014, page 289).

A foreign employee at Alibaba supporting the company's TMall business confessed that he sometimes found it difficult to reconcile his day-to-day experience in the office with the company's official rhetoric about the spirit of teamwork and the degree to which employees support each other. It was all well and good for someone like Tom, narrator of the Alibaba promotional video (see Chapter 5—"Living to Work") to opine on the unstinting support he gets from Chinese colleagues, but the reality of the workplace the foreign employee experienced as he worked on the company's e-commerce programs was one in which there was a relatively low level of trust and lack of cooperation. Employees tended to withhold information from others with whom they weren't directly connected or familiar, but this reluctance to share information could even occur among members of the same team, as he himself had discovered. He recounted that on a number of occasions members of his own team refused to provide him with input he needed to complete a project he was working on claiming that the information was 'confidential'. An American game developer at Tencent described an office environment characterized by a high degree of competition not only between departments and groups, but even between teams in one department. He noted that employees, in many cases, made a pretense of collaborating, but that this "collaboration" masked an undercurrent of intense competition that coursed just below the surface.

Geographic

Maintaining relations between a field office and headquarters in any company is challenging, but in a Chinese company it is especially so because of the premium placed on face-to-face communication and the decisive role that personal relations play in determining effectiveness on the job. The case of Alibaba's previous General Manager for its North American business is an apt illustration of the issues that can arise between a foreign field office and headquarters and the decisive role that relationship building plays in ensuring alignment and overcoming the incidence of exclusion that such geographic distance naturally creates.

Prior to his appointment with Alibaba, the General Manager, a British national, had a successful track record working in management roles for U.S. companies and extensive industry experience. Given the executive's background and credentials, it came as a surprise when he was dismissed from his post in favor of a Chinese executive with long term experience in the company and who had occupied a number of management roles during his career.[9]

The rationale given for the change in leadership was multifaceted. However, the common understanding, distilled down to its essence, was that the General Manager had not adequately grasped what company leadership expected of him nor understood the requirements of the market he was charged with managing. This explanation was not an entirely satisfactory one because it merely described an outcome, but not the root cause that was its genesis.

Further investigation revealed that there were a number of occasions where the General Manager had decided not to attend executive level meetings organized at company headquarters in person, opting instead to decline the invitation outright or, if attendance was absolutely necessary, take advantage of a remote access alternative (phone, video conference, etc.). The calculation that guided his decision, and that he used to determine the extent of his participation, comprised a set of parameters that included the distance between his office and company headquarters, the flying time traveling that distance would require, and the duration of the meeting. Certainly, this method of arriving at a decision was well-conceived and understandable, especially since there were also personal issues involved. However, the flaw was that he failed to take the culural element

[9] In reality, his dismissal wasn't a complete 'surprise' as there was some prior indication although not official notice.

into sufficient account, in particular the opportunity to build the relationships crucial for achieving success in the field office of a Chinese company that such meetings afforded. Taking advantage of such opportunities was especially important for someone who had not previously spent any appreciable time in the company's headquarters. Finally, there was a political issue. A senior executive different from the one who originally brought the General Manager into the organization was now taking on a more significant role in guiding the overseas operations and had a different strategic vision and direction (conceivably one that was more "ethnocentric" and involved more direct intervention and guidance from headquarters).

Organizational

Under the guise of offering a career development opportunity and enabling foreigners to learn about a Chinese company and Chinese culture, management programs such as Alibaba's AGLA by their nature call attention to the difference between foreign staff and the rest of the company. A seemingly innocuous description of the AGLA program Peking University Professor Jeffrey Towson provides subtly reinforces this point.

> "...And you also can't really understand Chinese e-commerce without having lived a regular life in China. So the students rent regular apartments, open bank accounts, get on WeChat (sorry Alibaba mgmt. but it's true), pay their electricity bills, shop at the local market and so on. They become local (to some degree)". (Towson 2018)[10]

According to Towson, the inherent value of the Alibaba program, beyond the well-promoted induction into company culture and business, lies in the opportunity it affords its participants to experience "regular life" in China. The implication is that foreigners, in general, do not lead a "regular life" in China and have very little exposure to its operational intricacies. That the experience of renting apartments and opening bank accounts should warrant any particular mention or be called out as a program achievement is certainly out of the ordinary. It contains a hint of the exoticism conveyed in descriptions of China that appear in other contexts such as the challenging place for foreign employees to navigate and survive that the video narrator Tom presents (Chapter 5— "Living to Work").

---

[10]Towson, Jeffrey, "The Alibaba Global Leadership Academy Is Awesome. You Should Apply. Like Right Now" (Pt 2 of 3), LinkedIn blog, July 23, 2018, https://www.linkedin.com/pulse/alibaba-global-leadership-academy-awesome-you-should-apply-towson/.

It would be highly unlikely that anyone commenting on a similar program offered by a French, German, or British firm, if such a program were even on offer, would highlight the opportunity it afforded its participants to rent an apartment in Munich, say, or open a bank account in Paris (just like 'real' Parisians!) So why should the experience be any different for a participant in the management program of a Chinese company in China, especially one that is located in Shanghai, Beijing, Guangzhou or any other major city? Contrary to depictions of China such as Professor Towson's, as a place where even opening a bank account can be legitimately notched as an achievement, the real China, especially as experienced in a city like Hangzhou, is a place where renting an apartment, opening a bank account and shopping in local markets is a relatively trivial exercise, or at least no more challenging than it would be elsewhere. Furthermore, the rapid adoption and widespread use in China of applications such as WeChat makes the everyday transactions and tasks that Towson lists even easier for a foreign recruit to contemplate and to complete.

Cultural

Foreigners working in a Chinese company will often remark on how difficult it is to establish meaningful relationships with Chinese colleagues, especially outside the workplace. The blame for this inability to connect is typically placed at the feet of the Chinese who are accused of being insular and closed to outsiders, a trait that is especially pronounced when the outsiders are members of a different social and cultural group. Much less attention is paid to the behavior of the foreign employees who, in many cases, take deliberate steps to maintain distance and close themselves off from their Chinese colleagues and the local environment in which they find themselves. Perspectives such as those Professor Towson and Tom the video narrator share, reveal that it is the foreigners themselves who are guilty of calling attention to and perpetuating the degree of difference that exists between foreign employees and the Chinese they work for.

An extreme case of reclusive behavior among foreign employees is to be found among athletes who come to play on Chinese basketball and soccer teams. By their own accounts and those written by observers (cf. foreign players on a Chinese basketball team profiled in Jim Yardley's Brave Dragons), foreign players spend much their time off the court, or the field, holed up in the hotel rooms that have been booked for them. In fact, the behavior of foreign players, as described in these accounts, is so consistent that one has the impression the players are following a playbook that is as prescriptive as the one that guides their play on the court. This off-court "play book" comprises a set of standard elements that include: obsessively playing Nintendo video games, making periodic Skype calls to family and friends and ordering burgers and pizza when the mood strikes and appetite dictates. Jim Yardley's description a typical evening for Donta Smith, the ex-NBA point guard recruited by the Taiyuan Brave Dragons is a case in point:

> now 'the Life' meant nights at the World Trade[Hotel]. He [Donta Smith] ate in the hotel or at McDonald's and watched movies, played video games, or talked to friends through instant messages or Skype. (Yardley 2012)

While the behavior of these players is somewhat extreme and certainly not representative of the conditions and behavior of most foreigners working in Chinese organizations, at large, they do have some similarities and points in common.

A participant in Alibaba's AGLA management program acknowledges that he regularly takes lunch by himself outside the company or goes off campus to "get a break" from being in a Chinese work environment. Other participants in the program who by day work in different groups from one another and often exclusively with Chinese colleagues, tend to spend a good part of their time after work outside of the office socializing with each other and even living together.[11] A local manager in Chinese glass-maker Fuyao's U.S. subsidiary, when asked whether he spent any time with Chinese colleagues outside of the office, commented on the tendency of Chinese he worked with to stay to themselves and not be very inclusive. Language was cited as a significant impediment to engaging in any meaningful social interaction. Upon further reflection, the manager recognized that he, in fact, had not made much of an effort to socialize after work because of "family obligations" and "limited time".

Communication

To analyze the flow of communication in a Chinese company, let alone the complex paths informal communication follows, is an undertaking that is beyond the scope of this study. However, because a foreign

---

[11] Half a dozen members of the second AGLA cohort rented a suite of rooms in a large apartment complex.

employee's access to this mode of communication and the information it contains is usually quite limited, a review of factors that contribute to organizational exclusion that failed to make reference to it would be incomplete.

Existence of an informal mode of communication that is distinct from an organization's formal communication is characteristic of any corporate environment including a Chinese one. However, there are some aspects of the informal communication in a Chinese enterprise that are unique and worthy of further consideration. Informal communications in a Chinese company obeys a set of rules and follow a set of paths that circumvent strict levels of hierarchy and is very different from those that the formal organizational structure provides for or would seem to allow. However, in my experience, it is the informal communication that employees consider a more reliable and accurate source of information and guidance, obviating the need for formal communications of changes in positions and, by association, organizational charts. As example, at a few critical junctures in my career at the Shanghai Bell company Chinese colleagues have suggested, contacting the chairman of the company directly for guidance and support outside of the official organizational structure and actually assumed that I had already taken this step. The implication was that this approach was a standard practice and seemingly one that they themselves had taken advantage of. The existence of such communication and the characteristics that define it calls into question the notion of a strictly hierarchical Chinese organization that exists duly inscribed within the canon of common wisdom. It is a notion that persists perhaps because any related studies have focused exclusively on the more readily accessible formal communications that reinforce the image of a more hierarchically-oriented structure.

Racial

The exclusion of foreign employees and discrimination based on race or ethnicity is an ever present undercurrent in a Chinese company that takes many forms, even manifesting itself in the terms Chinese staff use to refer to their foreign colleagues. In an open letter to Huawei staff, Sean Upton-McLaughlin, an American working in the company, took issue with his Chinese colleagues' consistent and indiscriminate use of the term "Lao Wai" (a colloquial term for "foreigner" in Chinese) when

referring to foreign staff.[12] As Upton-McLaughlin made clear in his letter, it wasn't the term itself that he and other foreign employees objected
to as much as the presence of an ethnic dividing line between Chinese
and foreigners its use implied. He argued that Chinese colleagues' prevalent use of the term demotivated foreign staff by making them feel
excluded and in so doing undermined the spirit of 'teamwork' that company management actively promoted and on which the company claimed
that its success depended. "We are all Huawei employees," Upton-
McLaughlin insisted and concluded his letter by calling on the company's employees to look beyond cultural differences and join together as
one team (Upton-McLaughlin 2015). In form and sentiment, Upton-
McLaughlin's letter is the direct descendant of the "5 have- nots and
2 haves" poster the Hintons tacked to the wall of the Foreign Experts
Bureau in Beijing a half- century before. Judging by the response
Upton-McLaughlin's letter received, a single comment posted below the
online version of the letter that read: "you daoli" ("it's true"), it is not
clear whether Upton-McLaughlin found an audience that was any more
receptive to his message than the one the Hintons appealed to or that it
had an impact that was any greater.

As much as discrimination and exclusion based on ethnicity is common to the experience of foreign staff at large and is a recurring theme
that runs through the heart of this study, its effect can be even more
severe for specific racial groups and genders.[13] Discrimination against

[12]The use of the term and its reception by those it designates is the source of much
debate. At one of the spectrum are those who regard the term as neutral and point out
that "lao" when used in conjunction with a name connotes familiarity or even endearment.
At the other end are those who regard the term as offensive and even racist because it
shows a lack of sensitivity to those not ethnically or racially Chinese (cf. Mullin, Kyle, "Is
It Offensive to Be Called 'Lao Wai?'", *The Beijinger*, June 22, 2017, https://www.thebei-
jinger.com/blog/2017/06/22/mandarin-month-it-offensive-be-called-laowai).

[13]I use the plural form, "genders", here in recognition of LGBT representation among
foreign staff in Chinese companies. However, I was unable during the course of my research
to obtain data on this aspect of the foreign experience that was sufficient to give it the attention it deserves. To my knowledge, a number of foreign employees in Chinese companies
who are gay and lesbian have plans to describe their experiences and the accounts that result
from these efforts will provide the insight needed to fill the current gap in understanding.

black Africans has a long history in China that goes back to a time when China was beginning to come into contact with more of the world that lay beyond its immediate borders. During the Tang and Song Dynasties, a period in history that encompassed the latter half of the first millenium and first half of the second, Dikötter notes that "black symbolized the most remote part of the geographically known world" and that there was a very clear distinction made between "White, the center of the civilized world and Black, the negative pole of humanity" (Dikotter 1992, page 12).[14] A European pilot working for a Chinese airline recounted how he and a number of other foreign pilots were approached by the airline's management for assistance in recruiting other foreign pilots who might consider coming to work at a Chinese airline. However, there was one condition: It would be preferred if the candidates that the pilots approached were not black or female. A foreign consultant retained by Huawei to work on projects that involved a number of company offices located in regions considered strategic to the company's business, remarked that he was especially struck by the differences in the relationship of Chinese management to local staff in the company's African and North American offices as reflected in the scope of their respective responsibilities. A number of the local executives in the Canada office were regularly engaged by Chinese management in discussions on how the office was to be run. The line between the local staff and Chinese management was drawn much more sharply in Africa where there were virtually no Africans who held management level positions. A study that epitomizes those differences described cases where Chinese management representing their companys' interests in Africa maintained a dining room for their exclusive use that was not accessible to local staff. Outside of the workplace they had no interaction with local employees (Tang 2016, page 119). This just one of many cases, a number of which were presented in the introduction to this study (see Chapter 1) where African employees have suffered discrimination and even abuse at the hands of Chinese bosses. Based on these cases one might conclude that discrimination and exclusion based on race is a phenomenon exclusive to the local offices of Chinese companies operating overseas. Indeed, there are far fewer reported cases of such discrimination in the headquarters offices of

---

[14]Dikötter, Frank, "Race As Culture: Historical Background" in *The Discourse of Race in Modern China*.

Chinese companies. However, evidence suggests that Chinese headquarter offices are not immune to racially-based exclusion of this kind and that the low incidence of such cases is simply due to the fact that the number of Africans employed in these offices is so disproportionately small.[15]

Cases of racial and gender discrimination feature prominently in Kopp's study of Americans employed by Japanese companies showing that this phenomenon is not unique to Chinese enterprises. In one such case, that bears a distinct resemblance to the foreign pilot recruiting program initiated by the Chinese airline referenced above, Kopp recounts that a former human resource manager at the U.S. branch of a Japanese bank, called to testify at a hearing convened by the U.S. House Committee on Government Operations, claimed that he was told not to consider African-Americans and women for loan officer positions.[16] Discrimination based on race and gender are arguably the most common and blatant form of exclusion based on appearance. However, there are some forms this kind of exclusion takes that are more subtle and less well-documented.

A young foreign marketing manager employed by a Chinese company recounted that towards the end of his first week on the job at the company's headquarters he was invited to a dinner organized so that he could get to know his Chinese colleagues and they could get to know him. Just as the first dishes were brought to the table, following a round of introductions, one of his Chinese colleagues suddenly complimented him on his appearance. As if this weren't already awkward enough, the same colleague then proceeded to call out another member of the team sitting across the table for being "fat" and "ugly" by comparison. The exchange elicited giggles from the others seated at the table, but left the foreign employee feeling uncomfortable.

Despite the prevalence of these cases of exclusion and discrimination in varying degrees of severity and blatancy there are signs that Chinese

[15] Iyembi Nakanza a native of Zimbabwe who is a business development manager at Alibaba states in an online interview that he was the only African in the AGLA program (cf. Iyembi Nakanza public LinkedIn profile https://www.linkedin.com/in/iyembi-nkanza-25801326).

[16] Kopp, Rochelle, *The Rice Paper Ceiling: Breaking Through the Japanese Corporate Culture*, Stone Bridge Press, Berkeley, CA, 1994, page 18.

employers are becoming more sensitive to these issues and more aware of the effect they have on foreign staff. A clear sign of this change is the case of Kenyan Richard Ochieng employed by Sonlink, a Chinese motor-cycle manufacturer with offices outside of Nairobi. Insulted repeatedly by his Chinese supervisor who likened him to a monkey, Ochieng had the presence of mind to capture his boss's misdeeds on video. Presented with Ochieng's formal complaint and the incriminating video clip that accompanied it, company management moved quickly to remove the offending supervisor and sent him back to China where he was summarily dismissed (Goldstein 2018).

The case of Richard Ochieng is quite clear and the evidence of discrimination incontrovertible. However, there are some instances, where foreigners see discrimination and perceive intentional measures taken to exclude them that are not so black and white and often result from misunderstandings that result from their own lack of familiarity with Chinese culture and language. An American teacher employed at a school in Fujian Province, recounted how on a hot day a Chinese teacher who was her supervisor advised walking in the shade of the trees at the edge of the schoolyard rather than walking across it to, as she put it, avoid "becoming black" from exposure to the direct sunlight. The American teacher interpreted the Chinese teacher's use of the word "black" as a racial slur not realizing that the apparently 'inappropriate' expression was the result of a linguistic misunderstanding and not willful discrimination. Apparently not familiar with the English word "sunburn", the Chinese teacher had literally translated the corresponding Chinese expression ("shai hei") that happens to incorporate the Chinese word for "black".

Of all the challenges a foreign employee faces in achieving acceptance perhaps the most significant is determining what the employee can or should do to bridge the linguistic, cultural, and operational gaps and overcome barriers to integration. Following is a review of methods and techniques that provide some means to address issues encountered, if not resolve them outright:

Breaking Through and Building Trust

As a way of building a personal network and integrating as quickly as possible, it is common practice for a new employee who has just joined a Western company to invite a colleague for lunch or a cup of coffee. While this tactic is effective in a Western corporate environment, it is one that is almost never practiced in a Chinese company. Extending an invitation to a colleague in a Chinese company, especially a colleague with whom one has no prior relationship, even for something as casual as a cup of coffee, is bound to raise suspicions. As previously noted, Chinese employees typically take lunch together in groups formed of members from the same team. A one-on-one lunch is the exception rather than the norm. Making such an overture, especially to someone one doesn't know well, usually signals a prelude to a request that the person extending the invitation would like to make. Very often the request is one that will inconvenience the other party and might require some effort to fulfill. So if the methods that would typically be invoked in a Western company are not acceptable, effective, or appropriate in a Chinese company, what steps can and should the foreign employee take to fit in and build the trust on which successful integration into a Chinese company is founded?

Make the Effort (Take the Initiative)

Among foreign employees working in Chinese companies interviewed, there was common agreement that even a foreigner who had been specifically assigned to a team in a Chinese company and given a position that was well-defined would find the process of forming relationships with Chinese colleagues less than straightforward. Under any circumstance, making progress depended on the foreign employee's willingness to "take the initiative". However, "taking the initiative" is not to be understood as undertaking a specific or dedicated activity, such as inviting a Chinese colleague to lunch. Instead it means, what a number of foreign employees working in Chinese companies referred to as "being present". While on surface this formulation would seem nothing more than a cliché infused with a dose of the exoticism ("Orientalism") that very often characterizes pronouncements related to things Chinese, its meaning takes on a more concrete shape and appears less exotic when more clearly defined through related examples. One foreign employee working in the U.S. office of a Chinese company explained that she often felt isolated and excluded when she participated in activities with Chinese colleagues because most of the discussion was conducted in Chinese and concerned topics with which she had little to no familiarity. Nevertheless, she made a point of attending dinners with Chinese colleagues when she came to the company's headquarters for periodic meetings because she understood that even the act of appearing at the dinner itself was recognized as a demonstration of commitment to the team and an affirmation of membership that made developing relations and working with them that much easier.

Sign Up (Join In)

Foreigners working in Chinese companies very often pass up opportunities to participate in and attend corporate activities and events that are on offer. The most common reasons given for not participating are that the events impinge on personal time, are not particularly meaningful, and can even be demeaning. However, as frivolous and inconsequential as they may at times seem, such activities are integral to Chinese company culture, a connection that is examined in greater depth in Chapter 8—"All Work and Play". What this examination reveals is that it is not the activities themselves that are so important, but rather the opportunity they afford for relationship-building. By temporarily suspending the rules that would normally govern personal interactions in the day-to-day working environment, Chinese corporate events and activities are in effect a catalyst for socialization across teams and levels that established organizational structures would otherwise constrain.

Make Being Outside "In"

Alibaba's Divya Joseph, in her post on survival skills for foreigners working in a Chinese company, proposed that the best way to "whiff off the feeling [of exclusion]" was to be "mindful of the fact that you have to be aware of cultural differences" and advised foreign employees to just "stay positive".[17] Recognizing that a feeling of exclusion in a Chinese company is not something a foreign employee could just "whiff off" and that addressing such a complex issue takes more than simply being "mindful of cultural differences", an Indian who had spent a number of years working at a Chinese firm came to the conclusion that entirely eliminating the sense of exclusion was not possible and therefore overcoming it was not a realistic goal for a foreign employee to set.[18] He advised, instead,

---

[17] Joseph, Divya Anne, "Working in a Chinese Company—A Foreigner's Viewpoint," LinkedIn blog, June 16, 2018, https://www.linkedin.com/in/divya-anne-joseph-b112a44/detail/recent-activity/posts/.

[18] He made a point of distinguishing between "exclusion" and "discrimination" that in his definition implied malice which he certainly did not sense in the exclusion.

that foreign employees reconcile themselves to being outsiders and went so far as to suggest that acceptance of the role was one of the keys to a foreigner's ability to survive in a Chinese company and gain acceptance. He admitted that it might have been easier for him to adapt to such a role than it would have been for employees from other countries because he had already experienced being outsider while still in his own country. He explained that after graduation from university he had moved from his home state in Northern India to take a position with a company based in Southern India where the customs, culture and even language of his fellow employees and management were entirely different.

Based on his experience, he found that actively embracing the role of an outsider was much more effective than merely accepting the role because of the advantages it could bring. He observed that an outsider in a Chinese company, especially one from another culture, naturally arouses curiosity. Many Chinese colleagues came to speak with him because they were interested in learning more about his background. He emphasized that if Chinese colleagues wanted to benefit from the opportunity this initial encounter provides, foreign employees should make themselves available and demonstrate a willingness to meet and speak with Chinese colleagues who were interested, even in cases where doing so might be inconvenient or the topic of discussion not directly task or job-related. As an extension to making oneself available, he noted that the final ingredient for success was offering to teach a skill. He at first considered his inability to speak Chinese an impediment, but eventually came to the realization that this deficiency could actually be turned to advantage. In contrast to most foreigners working in Chinese companies who resent being obliged to teach English to Chinese colleagues and regard such requests as a burden, the developer took the initiative and made his Chinese colleagues aware that he was willing to speak English with anyone in his department who wanted to practice and improve their language skills. A number of Chinese colleagues took him up on the offer and he found that by helping them improve their English he was able to get to know them on a much more personal level. Because the colleagues he taught perceived speaking and improving their English to be an activity that fell outside the scope of their professional responsibilities, they felt more comfortable sharing details about their personal lives. Through this extracurricular activity, the developer was able to establish a much stronger and closer relationship with his Chinese colleagues and this, ironically, enabled him to be more effective in the workplace and feel much more integrated with the rest of the team.

Teach a Skill

The example of teaching English to build relationships introduced in the previous section falls under the larger rubric of offering a skill to build trust and establish a base for collaboration and cooperation, a method that Chinese assign significant importance to and consider an indispensable part of establishing relations with foreigners.

Shortly after acquiring an Australian power company, Huaneng dispatched engineers who were experts in the equipment the Australians were using. Nominally, the Chinese experts were sent to provide on-site support and troubleshooting where necessary, but Huaneng executives reasoned that by demonstrating superior technical expertise they could instill confidence in the Chinese company and its management. They believed that the trust they established would be a key to bridging the cultural gap. In a similar vein, a foreign journalist with a background in business reporting working for the English-language version of a Chinese publication found that he was able to improve relations and bridge the cultural gap by offering to teach his Chinese colleagues how to improve their business reporting skills.

Dangle a Carrot, Wield a Stick

There are some cases where foreign employees find that because of specific project requirements and related time constraints they have to take more direct or concerted action in overcoming organizational obstacles that impede access to resources or information needed to achieve a satisfactory outcome. These approaches fall into two basic categories that can be conveniently characterized as *Carrot* and *Stick*. The approach taken is usually contingent on the time available, with the 'carrot' approach typically the more time consuming of the two options.

Carrot

The 'carrot' approach usually involves actually going to the Chinese colleague and engaging him or her in conversation, most likely not related to the project, as a way of building rapport that would be a prelude to making a request. However, sometimes this was not sufficient and needed to be combined with an additional step. Two American managers employed by the Fuyao Glass company in the U.S. approached the Chinese representative of the company's purchasing department to get a requisition for additional parts they needed to complete a project they had been working on. Although the request was couched in the most polite terms the American managers could muster, the purchasing manager rejected the request. All attempts to engage her in further discussion were to no avail resulting in an increasingly tense atmosphere that was heightened as the managers became more frustrated . Sending an official e-mail on which the purchasing manager's supervisor was copied had the desired effect because it followed an accepted process that the purchasing manager was comfortable with and that her management had approved.

Stick

A foreign employee in a Chinese company who was having difficulty getting support from another department was advised to first set up a WeChat group (i.e. inviting a number of parties at the same time to join a discussion on the social media platform) that included his direct supervisor, the colleague in the department he was trying to get support from as well as the other department's director. Although the foreign employee was concerned that taking such an approach would be perceived as aggressive, he found that it was perceived as an indication of priority or urgency and considered an acceptable way of resolving inter-departmental issues such as the one he had encountered rather than a threatening gesture or sign of overt displeasure/frustration.

CONCLUSION

The day I received an invitation to join a "fan tuan", a lunch group that four of my colleagues had established, was one of my most memorable. Receiving an invitation to lunch under normal circumstance is not usually an event that would warrant any particular mention, but considered within the context of a Chinese workplace and the impediments to integration a foreign employee faces, being invited to join such a group can legitimately be claimed as an achievement of some significance and a step forward in overcoming the exclusion that foreign employees face. However, it is a step that is still too small to bring the foreign employee much further along the road to developing a longer term career in a Chinese company, much less enable the foreign employee to achieve full organizational integration, a goal that remains elusive.

Luckily, there are a number of techniques and methods foreign employees can consider that have proven useful in addressing exclusion in the workplace and improving prospects for integration. In these efforts, the foreign employee will be aided by ongoing progress Chinese firms are making. A number of Chinese companies now provide 'onboarding' programs to help new foreign hires acclimate to their respective company cultures and learn more about the resources available to them. These onboarding programs in a number of cases were developed and spearheaded by foreign employees who recognized the importance of the role such programs could play in increasing the effectiveness of foreign staff and reducing employee turnover. A foreign employee in Alibaba's human resources department found when he joined the company that the program organized for foreign hires consisted of little more than a couple meetings with company executives in which they shared basic information about the company. The more formal onboarding program he shaped from the original base is structured around a week-long series of activities that include team-building as well as insights into the company operations and even an introduction to local Hangzhou culture. As they continue to evolve and employ foreign staff in greater numbers they will continue to refine and improve how they approach, support, and integrate foreign staff who join them.

REFERENCES

Bouée, Charles-Edouard, *China's Management Revolution: Spirit, Land, Energy*, Palgrave Macmillan, 2010.

Dikötter, Frank, *The Discourse of Race in Modern China*, Hong Kong University Press, Hong Kong, 1992.

Goldstein, Joseph, "Kenyans Say Chinese Investment Brings Racism and Discrimination", *New York Times*, October 15, 2018.

Hyun, June, *Breaking the Bamboo Ceiling: Career Strategies for Asians*, HarperCollins, New York, 2005.

Joseph, Divya Anne, "Working in a Chinese Company—A Foreigner's Viewpoint," LinkedIn blog, June 16, 2018, https://www.linkedin.com/in/divya-anne-joseph-b112a44/detail/recent-activity/posts/.

Kopp, Rochelle, *The Rice Paper Ceiling: Breaking Through the Japanese Corporate Culture*, Stone Bridge Press, Berkeley, CA, 1994.

Ma, L., "Employee Characteristics and Management", In Zhang, Z.X. and Zhang, J. (eds.) *Understanding Chinese Firms from Multiple Perspectives*, Springer, Berlin and Heidelberg, 2014.

Maurer, Roy, "Candidates Choose Jobs Because of Company Culture", *Society for Human Resource Management*, February 15, 2017, https://www.shrm.org/resourcesandtools/hr-topics/talent-acquisition/pages/candidates-choose-jobs-company-culture.aspx.

Mullin, Kyle, "Is It Offensive to Be Called "Lao Wai?"", *The Beijinger*, June 22, 2017.

Plummer, William, *Huidu: Inside Huawei* (self-published), June 2018.

Qiu, Jing, "Work Teams in Chinese Enterprises", in Zhang, Z.X. and Zhang, J. (eds.) Understanding Chinese Firms from Multiple Perspectives, Springer, Berlin, Heidelberg, 2014.

Shen, Jie, and Edwards, Vincent, "Recruitment and Selection in Chinese MNEs", *International Journal of Human Resource Management*, Vol. 15, No. 4 June/15:5 August 2004, pages 814–835.

Sun, Ya and Jiang, Jinlin, "Metaphor Use in Chinese and US Corporate Mission Statements: A Cognitive Sociolinguistic Analysis", *English for Specific Purposes*, Vol. 33, 2014, pages 4–14.

Tang, Xiaoyang, "Does Chinese Employment Benefit Africans? Investigating Chinese Enterprises and Their Operations in Africa", *African Studies Quarterly*, Vol. 16, No. 3–4, December 2016, pages 114–123.

Towson, Jeffrey, "The Alibaba Global Leadership Academy Is Awesome. You Should Apply. Like Right Now" (Part 2 of 3), LinkedIn blog, July 23, 2018, https://www.linkedin.com/pulse/alibaba-global-leadership-academy-awesome-you-should-apply-towson/.

Upton-McLaughlin, Sean, "Women shi Huaweiren, bu shi 'Lao Wai'", Huaweiren, No. 306, August 19, 2015, http://app.huawei.com/paper/newspaper/newsPaperPage.do?method=showSelNewsInfo&-cateId=8565&pageId=10056&infoId=19259&sortId=1&commentLanguage=1&search_result=1.

Wang, Zhong (June), "Displaced Self and Sense of Belonging: A Chinese Researcher Studying Chinese Expatriates Working in the United States", dissertation, University of South Florida, March 24, 2006.

Yardley, Jim, *Brave Dragons: A Chinese Basketball Team, An American Coach, and Two Cultures Clashing*, Knopf, New York, 2012.

Zhan, Qianhui, "Chinese Language Fever Grips US Students", *The Telegraph*, July 18, 2017.

CHAPTER 7

All Work and Play

Like the heavyset young man on my left and the colleague wearing the pair of Nikes on my right, I've got my eye on the starter and my feet planted firmly on the makeshift starting line that's been chalked out across the pavement in front of our building. At the drop of the starter's flag we're off, half-a-dozen two-man teams tightly gripping the handles of stretchers that they juggle between them as they sprint the length of a walkway that crosses the company's campus.

It's "Fire Prevention Day" at the Shanghai Bell Company and the stretcher race is just one of the many activities that fill out the morning's program. The full complement of activities along with the bright red banners decorated with slogans in white characters stretched across the trees that line the front walk, the families strolling across the lawn in front of our building, and the firemen sounding their sirens on their trucks lend the whole event a festive air.

TAKING FUN SERIOUSLY

Making a foot race with stretchers the focal point of a serious activity like fire prevention might strike a Western audience as out of the ordinary or even inappropriate, but a foreigner working in a Chinese firm soon realizes that, when it comes to corporate activities and events, the boundary separating the realm of the "casual" from the realm of the "serious", a line drawn so sharply in a Western corporate context, is a much more fluid and malleable construct in a Chinese one. This ambiguity can be challenging for a foreign employee to negotiate and the difference in the way these concepts are

© The Author(s) 2020
P. Ross, *Barriers to Entry*,
https://doi.org/10.1007/978-981-32-9566-7_7

understood and constituted can be a source of significant misalignment in expectations between Chinese management and foreign staff. The following anecdote illustrates just how significant this misalignment can be.

A multinational company with operations in Asia organized a regional sales conference that was attended most notably by teams from Australia and China, the two countries that were home to the company's most important customers and the source of its largest market opportunities. In addition to presentations on market results and strategic plans, the conference program featured a variety show where the sales teams from each country were invited to take the stage in the hotel ballroom and perform a song, a dance, or the somewhat loosely defined, "similar routine". A panel of "judges" drawn from the company's regional executive team were charged with choosing the winning team, each of whose members would receive a token prize for their performance and honorable mention in the company's monthly newsletter.

The Australian team, a group of eight men and women, showed up less than half-an-hour before their performance was scheduled to begin. The decision to improvise a song-and-dance routine loosely based on the Rolling Stones was taken during a brief and hurried discussion along the way to the hotel's ballroom where the routines were to be performed. Preparation consisted of buying a few props—brightly colored wigs, a few plastic bangles, and half-a-dozen pairs of cheap sunglasses—at a convenience store around the corner from the hotel. The team spent the little time that remained before the start of the performance trying on the costumes and making jibes at each others' expense. Needless to say, rehearsing the songs was an afterthought. As the team clambered onto the stage it was clear they hadn't given much thought to how they were going to present themselves either.

The Chinese team could be heard long before they were seen. The sound of drums beating and cymbals clashing that echoed through the hallways outside the ballroom heralded their approach. As the Chinese reached the entrance to the ballroom, the doors swung open and in marched twenty men and women attired in matching tunics waving brightly colored banners. At the head of the procession was the Vice-President of Sales who accompanied each step forward she took with a perfectly coordinated broad sweep of a large, red flag. The members of the team filed onto the stage and proceeded to organize themselves into two neat rows. As soon they had taken up position, they parted ranks and, as if on cue, out stepped a young man and woman who proceeded to sing a medley of rousing national songs. It was a performance that was so good it could have easily passed for professional. At the conclusion of their jaw-dropping performance, the Chinese marched out of the room with the same precision as that with which they had entered it, this time accompanied by the sound of a well-deserved round of applause.

No sooner had the event ended when representatives of the Chinese team came back to the ballroom and approached the judges, aggressively lobbying them to award victory to the Chinese team. There was no doubt in anyone's mind that the performance the Chinese team had delivered was the best, by far, and if they were named the winners there was certainly no one who would object (although it was debatable whether any of the other participants even cared). The Australian team, certainly, put so little stake in the results they repaired to the hotel bar immediately after their performance to enjoy a cold beer. As far as they were concerned, a bottle of beer and a dish of peanuts was more than adequate recompense for their efforts and the best outcome that could have been expected. The only people who took issue were some of the judges who felt that the hard-driving tactics the Chinese had employed to ensure their victory were inappropriate and demonstrated a lack of understanding for what the event was all about. "They missed the point," concluded one of the judges. "They just didn't seem to realize that it wasn't about winning. It was about more important things like team spirit, networking, and having a good time." But had the Chinese really "missed the point" or was their approach motivated by a different understanding of what such an event represented and their behavior conditioned by a different set of rules?

The Chinese Cultural Dimension

The Masculine—Feminine dimension, one of six dimensions from which Dutch sociologist Geert Hofstede's model for cultural analysis is formed, reflects the way in which values are distributed between genders in a given society (see Chart 7.1). A society with a high score on this dimension, in other words a more Masculine-oriented society, is one that places significant value on achievement and success and whose members tend to be assertive, ambitious, and competitive. A society with a low score, by contrast, places a premium on caring for others and tends to assign a higher value to quality of life than to quantity of achievements.

China's position on this dimension places it firmly in the ranks of Masculine-oriented societies. In fact, at 66, China's score is higher than the scores recorded for 80% of the other cultures considered, an

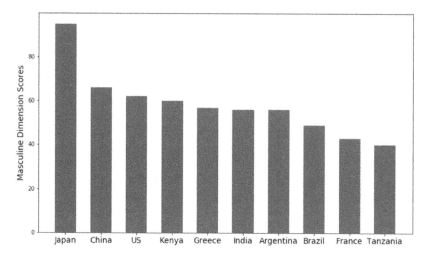

Chart 7.1 Masculine—Feminine   Dimension—Cross-cultural   comparison, www.hofstede-insights.com/country-comparison/

incontrovertible indicator for the source of a competitive streak that can surface even in activities that are as seemingly innocuous as a footrace at a company outing or a song-and-dance routine at a sales conference variety show. This investigation of deeper cultural and social influences that Hofstede's model facilitates is illuminating for what it reveals about the behavior observed. However, it does not shed any light on the curious juxtaposition of casual and formal elements that distinguished the stretcher race, nor does it adequately account for the importance such activities are clearly accorded. To fully comprehend the significance and meaning these activities and events have for those who are engaged in them requires taking a closer look at the role they play in shaping corporate culture.

CHINESE CORPORATE ACTIVITIES

Role in Shaping Corporate Culture

Sociologists Terrence Deal and Allan Kennedy's pronouncement, "a company without activities is dead," brings into sharp focus the significance of the role corporate events play in shaping what Deal and Kennedy refer to as a company's "ethos" (Deal and Kennedy 1982, page 63) However, this assessment is generally applicable, as relevant to a Western company as it is to a Chinese firm. What distinguishes Chinese corporate activities from their Western counterparts (the sales kick-off, the company picnic, etc.), observes Colin Hawes in his study of Chinese corporate culture, is that they are not just opportunities for networking, teambuilding and having a good time, but are more "purpose-oriented" (Hawes 2012). Hawes asserts that the role activities play in a Chinese corporate environment and in shaping corporate culture are related to a Chinese company's unique profile that he characterizes as a "hybrid economic-political-cultural organization devoted to national and individual renewal and improvement" (Hawes 2008, page 35) and further identifies "a strongly moralistic tone in the promotion of these activities that blurs the line between the corporation's interests and broader socio-political agendas" (Hawes 2012). Granted, the companies that are the specific focus of Hawes' study are state-owned enterprises whose corporate culture, he readily admits, "has been shaped to accommodate the Chinese Government's own policy priorities" (Hawes 2012). However, his observation that Chinese corporations devote significant budget to the organization of events and activities that are intended to bring employees together in a "harmonious way", build social and team spirit, and provide them with a platform to cultivate self-improvement and creativity is more broadly applicable (Hawes 2008, page 47). The result of this focus and investment of time,

Table 7.1 Taxonomy and classification of Chinese corporate activities

Corporate	Town hall meetings, connected with National holidays (e.g. Dragon Boat Race)
Team	Department Level: team-building, weekend trips, dinners Company Level: day and week long trips to tourist destinations
Personal	Dance, yoga, language, speaking clubs, book clubs, seminars that range from investing to child care.
Cultural	Calligraphy, Tai Chi, Peking Opera

Note Classifications based on the author's study and observations money, and manpower is that in a typical Chinese company, as "Tom", the narrator of the Alibaba promotional video in Chapter 5—"Living to Work" notes, "there's events after events after events" (Table 7.1).

Structure and Classification

The Shanghai Bell Company's "Fire Prevention Day", for example, is just one of more than one hundred activities and events the company organizes and supports during the course of any given year. The various seminars, trips and classes the company makes available to employees, and very often to their families as well, can be roughly grouped into four categories: Corporate, Team, Personal, and Cultural (see Table 7.1). A good number of these activities take place outside of standard working hours, a circumstance that does not, however, seem to pose an impediment to participation. A historical survey of Chinese art offered at the Shanghai Bell Company late one afternoon, for example, attracted an audience of over a hundred employees. With an outline that spanned the entirety of China's long cultural history, from the pre-Han age all the way to the current era, the survey seemed destined to last the entire night. Despite the ambitious agenda, the presentation nevertheless ended at 8:30 p.m. as advertised, a schedule participants considered perfectly "normal" for such an activity. It is, indeed, hard to imagine that a hundred employees in a Western company would turn out for a similar presentation, if such a presentation were even offered, and that a three-hour presentation ending at 8:30 at night would be considered "normal".

In a Chinese state-run enterprise, organization and support for such activities is typically the domain of the Communist Party office and the Labor Union. This political 'tag-team' shares responsibility for providing the funding, logistical support, and resources required to achieve a successful outcome. In a typical arrangement, the Labor Union takes the lead in organizing and providing logistical support for an activity that is then led and staffed by members of the Communist Youth League. Hawes insists that the Party's enthusiasm for promoting corporate culture and the leading role its members take in supporting company activities is not coincidental. He comes to the uncomfortable conclusion that in a Chinese context corporate culture can be considered a "political and even thought control measure" (Hawes 2012, pages 27 and 44).

With this context we can see that the events introduced through the vignettes that began the chapter are representative of a much broader spectrum of activities that a Chinese company offers. No matter what position on the spectrum they occupy, what all these events have in common is that they reflect the larger issues and themes of national culture (cf. the medley of national songs sung at the sales rally), the promotion of social values (cf. "Fire Prevention Day"), and the betterment of the self (cf. Chinese art history lecture). This lends credence to Hawes's observation that Chinese firms recognize an obligation to instill Chinese cultural values in their employees and "spread the legacy of the traditional culture of the Chinese nation" (Hawes 2012, page 21).[1]

Hawes' inquiry into the nature of Chinese corporate culture and examination of its constituent elements is expansive, but suffers from a number of inherent limitations: It depends almost exclusively on a review of company websites as the source for its analysis and considers corporate culture only within the context of general company operations. So, for example, Hawes does recognize that a Chinese company's mission includes spreading the legacy of traditional Chinese culture, but he does not specifically examine the form that the corporate culture of a Chinese firm takes when transmitted to locations overseas, much less consider how this shapes the working environment and experience of foreign employees employed at those locations, a topic that is of particular relevance to this study. The case of Huaneng, one of China's largest electricity generating companies and an early mover into overseas markets, offers a good example.

HUANENG: SPREADING THE GOSPEL

Defining Corporate Culture

Huaneng, has a well-defined and well-articulated corporate culture that is often cited as an example worthy of emulation. Dubbed "Three-Color" ("san se") because its key constituents are represented metaphorically by three colors—Red, Green, Blue—Huaneng's corporate culture strategy is designed to realize well-articulated political, social, and technological aspirations: (1) **Red**—represents the practice of "Socialism with Chinese Characteristics" (2) **Green**—represents the prioritization of technology in the service of environmental protection. (3)

[1] This statement is Hawes' citation of an excerpt from Article 12 of the State-owned Assets Supervision and Administration Commission (SASAC) "Guiding opinion on strengthening the building of corporate culture in centrally controlled corporations [i.e. State-Owned Enterprises]" issued on March 16, 2005 (Hawes 2012, page 19).

Blue—represents the study of innovation and engagement with the rest of the world (conceivably a connection exists between the color and the aspiration it designates [Huaneng Group 2013]. The sea that the color blue represents is a common Chinese iconography representing the larger world). Of the three colors, undoubtedly 'Blue' is most directly relevant to the case of the foreign employee in a Chinese firm for the insight it offers into how a Chinese company conceives transplanting its corporate culture into companies it has acquired overseas and the effect this has on the local working environment and the experience of local staff. "Let the staff in the subsidiaries understand the parent company's culture" is the explicit directive articulated by Huaneng management to express their expectation for promotion of the company's "Three-Color" culture overseas (Huaneng Group 2013).

Huaneng

Corporate Profile

- Construction, operation, and management of power generation assets.
- Production and sale of electric power.
- Founded in 1985.
- 85 Thermal and Hydro Power Plants (2015).

Promotion of corporate culture is supported by a prescriptive strategy whose formulation derives from three basic principles:

1. Develop a comprehensive cultural integration strategy.
2. Identify and address areas of cultural difference while integrating aspects that can deliver mutual benefit.
3. Make managing people a priority.

Transmitting Corporate Culture

As it moved forward with its foray into overseas markets, Huaneng closely adhered to the strategy set out in the so-called 'Going Out' ("zou chu qu") initiative, an official Chinese Government program designed to promote expansion of Chinese firms into overseas markets. The

Government reasoned that at the same time the 'Going Out' initiative provided Chinese firms with an incentive to look beyond China's borders for new market opportunities, it would also enhance the country's profile and stature in countries around the world. To guide Chinese firms as they embarked on related initiatives, the strategy prescribed a number of areas that warranted particular attention: Improve production, supply, and value chains; Cultivate a more international approach and way of thinking; Establish a solid base of technology, talent, and market assets (MOFCOM 2012). Within this larger strategic framework, a closer study of Huaneng's experience reveals just how central to the company's overseas market strategy and planning transmission of its culture is and to what extent post-acquisition success depends on it.

Australia Power: Bridging Gaps

When the Huaneng Group acquired the Australia Power Company it became one of the first Chinese companies in the power-generating sector to acquire a major overseas asset. Despite the potential it held and the importance of the role it played in the company's overseas strategy, the acquisition had not been without its challenges. The local Australian staff were initially leery of Huaneng management and, according to reports sent back to Huaneng headquarters, were less than forthcoming in sharing critical information. Faced with this challenge, Huaneng took a number of steps to improve the operating climate and strengthen relations with local staff. One of those steps was to send skilled engineers from headquarters to the Australian plant ostensibly to resolve some thorny technical problems, but also to instill confidence in Huaneng management among local staff and take an important step forward in bridging the cultural gap. It was a goal, Huaneng management was convinced, that could be achieved through a demonstration of technical competence. An excerpt from one of the management reports written at the time reads:

> The engineer in charge of the M plant did not entirely trust the Huaneng experts. He would only authorize offline work. After the work was finished, the engineer personally downloaded the program into the computer. This greatly reduced the speed with which the repairs could be implemented.... The deep technical expertise of the Huaneng experts, their perseverance, and their sense of responsibility earned respect. (Huaneng Group 2013)[2]

[2] Translation is mine.

Executives at Huaneng headquarters would undoubtedly have found this report encouraging and regarded it as a proof point for the effectiveness of the management strategy and principles they espoused. However, a closer reading of the report reveals that Huaneng was ironically sowing the same seeds—overriding and circumventing accepted practice and procedures to maximize speed—that led to conflict and misunderstandings between Chinese management and local staff in Chinese companies elsewhere in the world and ultimately undermined the efforts of Chinese management to win the hearts and minds of local staff.[3]

As a complement to the strategy of bridging the gap with local staff through a demonstration of "hard" technical competence, Huaneng management launched a series of "soft" initiatives designed to introduce local employees to Chinese culture and instill a sense of belonging ("gui shu gan"). One such initiative involved teaching local employees how to make Chinese dumplings, an activity that according to the company newsletter was well-received by the local staff and earned a positive review from Chinese management.

> Eighty-two Australian employees enjoyed authentic Chinese dumplings and many other dishes. And Beijing, the headquarters of the Huaneng Group, is one of their most desired travel destinations.
>
> Huaneng corporate newsletter—management report

In addition to teaching local staff how to make Chinese dumplings, Huaneng employees who had been assigned to work in the Australia office put together presentations designed to introduce the local employees to Chinese culture and customs ("feng tu renqing"). And to make the local employees feel a part of the Huaneng "family" ("da jiating") Huaneng management designated a day on which local employees were invited to bring their children to work, an initiative dubbed, "From Work to Life".

BY THE BOOK

The emphasis on family values incorporated into relevant activities and expressed through related messaging, promotion of Chinese culture through traditional Chinese cuisine, demonstration of technical

---

[3]A more detailed description of cases such as Fuyao in the U.S. presented in Chapter 1 ("Introduction").

competence to earn respect and gain confidence, and other techniques Huaneng employed to transmit corporate culture and bridge cultural gaps with local staff are, it turns out, not unique to Huaneng. They belong to what appears to be a standard repertoire of strategies, a sort of cross-cultural 'playbook', that Chinese companies commonly invoke to establish positive relations with local staff, no matter where in the world those staff may be. Moreover, the traditional Chinese "element" these activities contain lends credence to Hawes' assertion that the function of such events is to strengthen national spirit.

Jeff Chee, the General Manager of Greenfield Industries, a Chinese-owned, South Carolina-based industrial tool manufacturer, promotes a "family based" company culture the essence of which he distills into a single, concise message that is at the heart of his communication to his American staff: "The company is your family". Halfway around the world in Kenya, the Chinese oil conglomerate CNOOC regularly organizes Chinese cultural events for its local employees. One such program, "Sending Fortune with Fuwa", took activities that were developed in conjunction with the Beijing Olympic Games and adapted them to the local audience. As a complement to these cultural initiatives, CNOOC organizes trips for employees in Africa to visit Chinese cultural sights and supports employee exchange programs that give African staff an opportunity to work at company headquarters in China. Closer to home the company supports a wide range of sports activities for local staff, encourages them to develop hobbies and provides them with requisite venues and funding (CNOOC 2009). In Indonesia, for example, CNOOC has implemented training programs designed to help local workers improve their technical skills. Sinochem organizes annual tours of sites in China for workers at its USAC (U.S. Agri-Chemicals Corporation) subsidiary in Central Florida (Wang 2006, page 166).[4]

Introducing national culture and instilling of a sense of family among staff in overseas offices is something it would be hard to imagine management of an American or European company would occupy itself with to such a degree. This difference in focus with Western companies notwithstanding, the approach a Chinese firm such as Huaneng takes towards cultural transmission does track closely with Chinese Government policy, objectives, strategy and priorities. A program like the Chinese

[4]USAC was Chemical business of U.S. Steel subsequently acquired by Sinochem.

Government-sponsored Confucius Institutes, conceived as a platform for promoting Chinese language and culture internationally, operates according to a set of objectives and presents a portfolio of programs that are distinctly similar to those of a company like Huaneng. It is also further evidence that Hawes' general postulations about the correspondence between the government and enterprise approach to and promotion of culture are also applicable in the international arena and that, through transmission of their corporate culture overseas, Chinese firms are concurrently advancing larger national, social, and political goals. Questions of larger cultural and national significance aside, it is important to recognize that despite their diversity and number and no matter how incongruous or distracting they may be, virtually all these events and activities are carefully orchestrated and possess an underlying structure that is rigorously adhered to. This structure comprises three essential elements that are designated for convenience as: *Gab, Games,* and *Gifts.*[5]

Gab: An event always begins with an executive speech that serves two purposes. It sets the tone for the proceedings to follow and positions the event in larger context. It also serves as an opportunity to show respect for the highest executive in attendance. Similarly, the event is brought to closure with a speech structured around a series of formulaic and well-worn expressions of gratitude for support and commendation to those who contributed to the event's success. It also incorporates a recap of the event that invariably includes a critique and suggestions for improvement. In the case of "Fire Prevention Day" introduced at the beginning of this chapter, for example, the Shanghai Bell company's president, the highest level executive in attendance, highlighted the positive attitude with which the participants had approached the day's activities, commended representatives of the local fire department on the professional execution of their demonstrations, and thanked the assembled families for their ongoing support of the company and its employees. These words of praise were then balanced by a more sober assessment of the event and very candid feedback on areas for improvement. Specifically, the president noted that during the evacuation exercise (conceived as a kind of fire-drill on steroids where employees take up position at their desks and are then timed on how quickly they can file out of their offices through hallways and down stairwells to a designated gathering spot outside the building) there were a number employees who hadn't evacuated the building quickly enough

---

[5] This scheme is one I developed.

or who had failed to pay careful enough attention to instructions. "If this had been a real fire, you would most certainly have perished," the president admonished. "and we," he concluded on a sombre note, "would have borne no responsibility for your fate". In delivery and tone, this pronouncement fits a more general pattern of executive communications that is presented in Chapter 8—"Metaphorically Speaking" and a style of managerial feedback focused on highlighting fault and assessing penalties that is taken up in Chapter 9—"Reverse Angle".

Game: An event or activity is typically animated by what a Western audience would recognize as a parlour game shot through with a streak of simple and often physically-based humor that is reminiscent of slapstick. The case of a Chinese telecommunications service provider's executive level weekend retreat at a spa on the outskirts of Hangzhou offers an illustration of this phenomenon. Despite the fact that the program for the weekend was so packed with activities that timings in the agenda were calculated to the minute, the organizers nevertheless managed to shoehorn a game in between an employee rendition of the Chinese classic "Jasmine" ('Molihua') and a violin performance of the theme from Bizet's Carmen. Those who accepted the invitation to participate in the game, a group of a dozen or so company executives, appeared on stage incongruously wearing animal masks that on closer inspection were identifiable as characters from the Chinese classic "Journey to the West"—Sun Wukong—the Monkey King, Zhu Bajie—the Pig, etc. Just downstage from where the executives were gathered was a figure dressed incongruously as Santa Claus who proceeded to lead the participants in a round of what turned out to be a derivative of "Simon Says". Much to the amusement of the audience, Santa/Simon wielded a large, inflatable baseball bat that he mercilessly tapped on the heads of the unfortunates who failed to heed his instructions, quite literally knocking them out of contention. The game was such a hit that it ended up going ten rounds rather than the five advertised, irrevocably throwing off the tightly-timed agenda, but exceeding the expectations of the audience.

The reaction of a foreign employee who is witness to an activity like 'Simon Says' is typically one of disbelief or perhaps even shock, especially if the foreign employee has accepted an invitation to join the event and finds him or herself among the participants. Faced with the prospect of participating in such an event, foreign employees very often find a way to decline an invitation if one has been extended or, if no such opportunity presents itself, will attend provisionally, ducking out at the first convenient moment.

A foreign employee at Huawei shared that participation in such events the company organizes was particularly difficult for older foreign employees working in the company to stomach, especially if they hold a more senior post, because they perceive the immature nature of the events and sophomoric humor to be inappropriate and degrading for someone of their age and stature. To dismiss these activities as frivolous and inventive ways to avoid them is to underestimate their importance and misunderstand their meaning. Arriving at a satisfactory explanation for the significance these activities are accorded and a sufficient understanding of the critical role they play in Chinese corporate culture entails an investigation of social, cultural, and even linguistic sources as well as an evaluation of the larger universe of ritualistic activities that condition a Chinese company's daily routine.

RITUAL IN THE WORKPLACE

A Chinese company, on any given day, is full of ritualistic events, activities and gestures that range from the mundane to the ceremonial. As examples of activities that have ritualistic import, Mary Szto in her review of the practice of ritual in Chinese law firms, lists tea drinking, post-work Karaoke, and even mid-day napping. In these seemingly mundane activities, Szto sees connection to a more universal cosmology that touches on the domains of culture, society, and even health (Szto 2014, page 125). She singles out the communal meals that partners take at noontime for special attention because she sees in them a representation of unity of purpose and harmony, health, and well-being that is closely aligned with the Dao or "Way" (commonly referred to as 'Tao' in Western sources), embody "the distribution of blessing" that is integral to ancestor worship, and in a practical way incorporate ingredients that have medicinal properties (Szto 2014, page 123). By making the "cosmic" links intrinsic to these meals the exclusive object of her attention Szto fails to consider the more mundane, yet no less consequential, issue of the strict routine that determines their consumption.

Daily Routines

The period allotted for lunch at the Shanghai Bell company begins punctually at 11:00 and ends at 1:00 sharp, fitting a more general social pattern of taking meals within well-defined windows of time that are strictly observed. Employees take lunch nearly every day with the same group of colleagues (usually members of the same team) and almost always at the same pre-determined time and then, after taking lunch together, the groups of employees make their way up to the 3rd floor of the building where they take a walk that is always conducted in a slow and leisurely fashion and always in a counter clock-wise direction.

Meals are just one example of routine activities that fill out what Szto refers to as "a full daily ritual". There are the exercise routines carried out in the office every morning at 10:30 a.m. sharp and then once again in the afternoon at 3:00 p.m. The music never changes and even the person who turns the music on is always the same. Similarly, members of the same department sit together during company-wide meetings, a habit that is codified in a detailed seating assignment chart prominently posted at the entrance to the meeting room. Small placards bearing names of the designated departments and aligned with the seating chart, are placed at the entrances to rows and on the backs of chairs to ensure the meeting's smooth operation. Even something as innocuous as fish that swim in the small aquariums that many employees keep on their desks (all the same species—guppies!) are cogs in the wheel of a larger daily routine.[6]

Even more innocuous, but of even greater significance, are the ubiquitous bottles of water set out conveniently and unobtrusively in front of each participant at the start of a meeting. At first glance, a six-ounce bottle of water does not seem like an object that would be worthy of any particular attention and could be easily be dismissed as nothing more than a convenience. However, the fact that these bottles (always six-ounces no more no less) appear at virtually every meeting, suggests that their diminutive size belies a greater significance.

It would be reasonable to see offering water to participants at the beginning of a meeting as a gesture of hospitality or an act of gift-giving, artifact of an ancient civilization, perhaps, and related in spirit to the distribution of token gifts that marks the conclusion of a corporate event. However, if this were the case, it is not clear why such an act would need to be performed at a meeting attended by colleagues who presumably enjoy well-established relationships and towards whom extending a gesture of gratitude would otherwise be superfluous. A more intriguing explanation for this ritual does indeed have historical antecedents, but is one whose source is different than that drawn on by other studies.

---

[6]It is part of company lore that the fish occupying the bowls on the desks of employees in offices throughout the company are all descended from one original pair.

Looking to Chinese history and traditional Chinese philosophy as a source of insight for understanding modern China, Chinese corporations being no exception, is a longstanding practice (see, as example, reference to the influence of traditional Chinese thought on modern management practice in Chapter 9—"Reverse Angle"). Those studies of Chinese corporations whose subject is Chinese corporate culture and organizational behavior, almost without exception, invoke Confucius and apply the precepts for which the sage is best known to divine and define the nature of the relationship between supervisor and supervised. It is an indispensable cultural reference that lends an air of legitimacy to the study in which it is used. Conversely, a study that omits such a reference runs the risk of being judged incomplete.

There is no question that referencing Confucius and applying Confucian thought has its rightful place in the study of the modern Chinese corporation and its application to the relations between actors in a Chinese organization is relevant, but the relevance is more nuanced and refined than typical references would allow.

Confucius' Mat

Best known today for words of wisdom articulated in the Analects, Confucius in his own time distinguished himself as much for what he did as for what he said. In fact, Confucius was well known for the number and variety of rituals that he practiced. His disciples believed that these small gestures and simple acts had inherent meaning and they devoted no small amount of time to deducing the lessons they were meant to impart. One ritual in particular that attracted the disciples' attention was the Master's curious habit, upon entering a room, of devoting a significant amount of effort to adjusting the position of his mat, carefully smoothing and straightening it out before sitting down and beginning to speak. Straightening a mat in and of itself would not seem to be a very noteworthy activity. However, the strict sequence of steps Confucius followed in straightening his mat and the consistency with which he applied those steps suggested to his disciples that this otherwise insignificant act was in fact to be taken more seriously.

Taking the disciples' hypothesis as a point of departure, Harvard professor Michael Puett, has posited that Confucius' habit of smoothing and adjusting his mat upon entering a room was a technique for ensuring that the ensuing discussion was productive and led to a satisfactory conclusion. According to Puett, Confucius recognized that people naturally tend towards developing a set of behaviors and a corresponding set of patterned responses based on those behaviors that condition how they interact with others (Puett Soundcloud 2017). These behavioral patterns can become so ingrained that they make people less willing to tolerate the perspective of others and can thus impair their ability to find common ground in resolving differences. Confucius believed it was the repetition and consistency inherent in the practice of rituals that make them particularly effective at breaking entrenched patterns of behavior that foster intolerance and bias. Rituals accomplish this disruption of habit by forcing people into what Puett refers to as a different "disposition", essentially a new pattern of behavior that enables them to see others in a slightly different way and, by extension, gain a better appreciation for a point of view that may be quite different than the one they are usually most comfortable holding. Confucius' seemingly innocuous habit of straightening his mat when he came into a room, Puett argues, was in fact a subtle yet powerful mechanism for, at least temporarily, altering the atmosphere in the room he had entered and ultimately helping the people in the room to interact with one another in a different and, hopefully, more productive way than they would have normally (Puett Soundcloud 2017). Seen in this light, the act of setting out a water bottle each and every time at the beginning of a meeting can be read as a subtle way of marking a break in the daily office routine and sending a signal for a change in behavior that makes participants more receptive to the ideas and views of others as a prelude to productive discussion.

Fathers and Sons

The practice of setting out bottles of water is pervasive and is dependent neither on the size of a meeting nor on the number of its participants. A couple of subordinates meeting with a supervisor are just as likely to find small bottles of water placed on a table in front of them in the supervisor's office as a team of staff members attending a formal meeting in a large conference room. However, in the case of the meeting in the supervisor's office, it is most notably the supervisor himself who sets out the bottles of water from a store of such bottles he keeps conveniently at hand for this purpose. To understand the significance of this gesture we can again look to Confucius for guidance and insight.

In the 'Book of Rites', a treatise dedicated to the presentation of rituals and their application, Confucius devoted significant attention to the relations between fathers and sons, a relationship that when translated into a corporate context is not too dissimilar from the relationship between supervisor and subordinate. Given the importance of fathers and sons in the Chinese social order, Confucius paid considerable attention to the relationship between them and devoted significant effort to thinking about how the relationship could be improved. One of the techniques Confucius proposed for strengthening the bonds between father and son and resolving the differences that were bound to arise between them was to have them temporarily change roles. To accomplish this role reversal, Confucius prescribed inviting father and son to enter a ritual space specifically designated for this purpose and then asking each one to assume the role of the other before addressing the issues at hand. Employing this technique would, Confucius believed, enable father and son to gain a better appreciation for each other's position. The expectation was that, by invoking this technique, father and son would be able to successfully reduce the incidence of conflict and misunderstandings while, at the same time, increase the level of humility and respect (Puett and Gross-Loh 2016). Although the technique used in the case is admittedly different from that of straightening the mat and the approach is more clear, direct and prescriptive, the ultimate goal is consistent: Make use of ritual to engineer a break in the usual pattern of behavior and take advantage of that break to create a greater sensitivity for someone else's point of view.

Like Confucius, the philosopher Xunzi (300 B.C.–230 B.C.) recognized the potential of ritual to influence patterns of human behavior and improve inter personal relations. However, where Confucius considered the general application of ritual in getting different parties to see each other's point of view, Xunzi's concept of ritual was much more circumscribed. Its application was specific to the relations between a ruler and his subjects and its potential focused on what philosophy professor Daniel Bell calls 'egalitarian consequences' (Bell 2008). Reducing the inequity that existed between those in power and those of lower social status was one of the most pressing issues of Xunzi's day. The philosopher believed that ritual, correctly applied, could effectively address social inequity and restore society to a more 'harmonious' state by creating the emotional disposition that would curb the excesses of those who held positions of power and make them more considerate of those less privileged and of lower rank. Bell concludes that the real value of Xunzi's philosophy "lies in its ability to show

how ritual – more than laws and more than verbal exhortation – has the effect of promoting the interests of those most vulnerable" (Bell 2008).

Viewed through the lens of both Xunzi's and Confucius' concept of ritual, a supervisor's simple act of presenting his subordinates with bottles of water can be seen as a subtle gesture that is nevertheless powerful enough to temporarily invert the customary hierarchically-defined relationship between supervisor and subordinate. Through this transposition of roles the sensitivity of each side for the other's point of view is heightened. Supervisors are predisposed to demonstrate greater humility and be more tolerant in their treatment of subordinates and subordinates are encouraged to be more open and at ease in sharing their opinions.

This interplay between the roles of Chinese supervisor and subordinate reveals the relationship to be more complex than the rigidly hierarchical relationship that is commonly depicted. In so doing, it also gives a more nuanced picture of the Chinese "boss" as a more benevolent leader concerned with the welfare of his staff and capable of a certain degree of humility that is greater than the more common portrayal of the boss as dictator and tyrant would allow (a more comprehensive profile of the Chinese "boss" is presented in Chapter 9—"Reverse Angle").

Echoing Puett, ritual theorist Victor Turner has observed that when people perform rituals they separate themselves, at least partially, from their traditional roles and status. However, where Turner differs from Puett and, by extrapolation, from the traditional view espoused by Confucius, is in his concept of the effect that ritual has on its participants, i.e. what participants in ritual activity do after they have stepped outside their normally prescribed roles. Turner's contention is that rituals serve as a "portal" through which those who participate in them can enter into "a state of play" (Turner 1982 quoted in Raj 2010). This pairing of "ritual", an activity imbued with solemnity, and "play", an activity that the ritual in its usual practice would normally preclude, strikes one as incongruous and out of the ordinary. However, this association of ritual with solemnity is, it bears mentioning, an association that is conditioned by Judeo-Christian religious practice and, as we will see, not absolute. Within the context of religions native to the Asia-Pacific region (Buddhism, Hinduism, and their various derivatives) the relationship between these two activities, 'ritual' and 'play', is much more proximate. "Ritual Levity", the term coined by anthropologists and sociologists to describe this uncommon juxtaposition, is an apt expression for the nature of this relationship.

"Ritual Levity" defines and conceptualizes a mechanism for challenging, defying, or even subverting established social, cultural and religious conventions. Those who engage in such activities do so outside the boundaries of normal order, whether divine or human, and take advantage of the liberty this out-of-boundary foray affords to, as Raj and Dempsey put it, "play with gods and sacred realities with certain temporary impunity" (Raj and Dempsey 2010, page 5). By collapsing or overturning the order of the existing cosmology, Ritual Levity narrows the difference between human and divine realms and "softens" (at least temporarily) the distinctions between people and gods.

RITUAL LEVITY

Studies of Ritual Levity have focused their investigation almost exclusively on its manifestation in social, religious, and even psychological domains. However, the potential application of Ritual Levity in a commercial context is one that, to date, has not been raised as a topic for exploration and, as a consequence, has not been the object of any dedicated consideration. Yet, seen from the perspective of this study, the incorporation of the dual if somewhat contradictory qualities of light-heartedness and gravity within the activities that "Ritual Levity" enlivens, recalls the unique and sometimes surprising nature of Chinese corporate activities, a resemblance whose presence provocatively suggests that a more through investigation of this connection has merit.

Driver's depiction of ritual as "playful work" and his observation that work is "actualized" through play suggests that the domains *ritual*, *work*, and *play* intersect, at least on a metaphysical plane (Driver 1998, page 98 quoted in Raj and Dempsey). The observation that "work" and "play" are both present and often closely intertwined in the tribal and agrarian rituals of peoples who inhabit Southeast Asia suggests that these three domains, *ritual*, *work*, and *play*, can and do co-exist on an earthly level as well (Turner 1982, page 34 quoted in Raj and Dempsey). China's shared heritage with Southeast Asian societies, history of cultural exchange, and geographic proximity strengthens the plausibility of a connection to China and by extension heightens the probability that there is application for Ritual Levity in a Chinese corporate environment. Moreover, the wide acceptance of the role that classical philosophical precepts and principles (Confucianism, Daoism, etc.) play in a Chinese corporate context is an apt precedent for entertaining the possibility of an influence from a socio-religious source.

A PLAY ON WORDS

If "ritual" and "levity" at times seem to stand in antithesis to one another, "play" is the glue that binds them. "Play", as understood in this context, is a multi-faceted concept that, depending on the context in which it is invoked, can refer to a range of activities, from spontaneous revelry to highly scripted performances that are executed through "make-believe" play-acting. The Chinese word for 'play', encompassing as it does both serious and casual meaning within its semantic scope, is uniquely capable of expressing the dual nature of these activities.

Someone who is just beginning study of the Chinese language is invariably given to understand that there is a one-to-one correspondence between the meaning of the Chinese word 'wan' and 'play', its English-language counterpart. Both Chinese and English words do indeed convey similar meaning when used in reference to games, sports, and related activities. However, the Chinese word can also be applied in a more formal and serious context. It would not be considered out of place for a Chinese executive, for example, to invite a friend or colleague to his home using the expression "dao women jiali lai *wan*", a phrase that a Chinese speaker, unfamiliar with the nuances of the semantic difference between English and their own language, will typically render as: "Come to our home to 'play'". An amused English speaker in receipt of such an invitation might anticipate an evening of football or ping-pong or imagine it to be a misdirected invitation whose originally intended recipient was a child of six. This is certainly not the Chinese speaker's intention. The phrase, in this context, is meant as a polite and thoroughly acceptable expression of Chinese etiquette that is open-ended enough to include more formal activities such as dinner, discussion, etc.

Ritual Play, broadly defined, can take a number of different forms (restorative, redemptive, transformative, etc.). Of these dimensions, "messy fun" and "competitive play" are the two that are of most direct relevance to a Chinese company and have the potential to make the most compelling case for the presence of Ritual Levity in a corporate context.

Messy Fun Activities that merit the distinction of being labeled "messy fun" are extreme in their irreverence and correspondingly even more extreme than other forms of play in the degree to which they overturn established norms. Activities characterized by "messy fun" have as their goal to "mend" the divide that exists between humans and the divine by creating a more intense sense of intimacy than it would be possible to achieve under normal circumstances (Dempsey and Duryappah 2010, page 85). Dempsey and Duryappah cite the Buddhist practice of *maha abhishekam*, a playful ritual that centers on the deity of the temple in which it is practiced, as an example of "messy fun" in action (Dempsey and Duryappah 2010). On one occasion, Dempsey and Duryappah observed practitioners of *maha abhishekam* take pails of milk and unceremoniously empty them out over the statues of revered deities as part of a ritual ceremony. On another occasion, a temple's planned ritualistic program was disrupted without warning by a mud-fight that the monks themselves initiated. Characteristic of all these events is that, while they may appear to be highly spontaneous and disorderly, they are, in reality, carefully conceived and orchestrated by those who initiate them (Dempsey and Duryappah 2010, page 76). "The job of linking worlds," Dempsey and Duryappah explain, depends on "skillfully applied mischief."

If one were to imagine a *Maha abhishekam* ritual taken out of its socio-religious context and transplanted into a corporate one, it might look very much like the executive 'Simon Says' event that the Chinese telecommunications company staged as part of the program of activities organized for its weekend retreat (see description above). There is admittedly nothing very "messy" about the 'Simon Says' activity. However, 'Simon Says' bears a sufficiently close resemblance to activities that embody Ritual Levity in so many other respects as to make it worthy of qualification as a legitimate exponent. It is certainly irreverent and shocking enough and, even though it is not overturning an existing *cosmological* order per se, by putting executives in what are ludicrous, uncomfortable and, ultimately, vulnerable positions 'Simon Says' is implicitly overturning an existing *organizational* order. The "softening" of distinctions this accomplishes is not between deities and humans, but between their corporate counterparts, senior executives and rank-and-file employees. Masks, a standard feature of activities associated with Ritual Levity, feature prominently in the 'Simon Says' event and serve a similar function. They afford the participants an opportunity to engage in 'play' and act as 'symbol-vehicles' that transport the activity in which they are used from the realm of the mundane to the realm of the fantastic (Turner 1982, page 85). A final point of similarity is the commitment of both religious and corporate practitioners of these events to thorough and intense preparation. Like the monks who initiated the mudfight in their temple or dumped pails of milk over the statues of their most revered deities, the telecommunications company executives spent hours in advance of their appearance on stage rehearsing 'Simon Says' to ensure that "mischief" was "skillfully applied" and that no *coup de bâton* missed its mark. In sum, as different the context is in which they are practiced the basic form and effect of both socio-religious and corporate applications of "messy fun" are effectively the same. They suspend the rules of hierarchy through outrageous, irreverent, and ludicrous activities whose effect is to change the balance of power and narrow the gap that separates what under normal circumstances are two distinct realms, and in so doing "soften" the distinctions between those who inhabit those realms.

Competitive Play A characteristic of all activities that merit inclusion under the "Ritual Levity" umbrella, is that they incorporate "competitive play", an aspect that combines the light-hearted with the serious. Also characteristic is that the "serious" element is hardened with a competitive edge. This competitive undercurrent comes to the surface most often in contests of display between rival participants within a religious group, or between competing, if not conflicting, traditions. These contests produce winners and losers who often have much at stake (Raj and Dempsey 2010, page 11).

McDermott finds evidence of "Competitive Play" in a festival held annually in Calcutta to honor Durga, a warrior goddess who is a central figure in Hinduism (McDermott 2010). The "Megafestival" celebrates the exploits of the goddess by displaying her likeness in humorous, creative, and even irreverent house-like settings, called 'pandals' that lend a carnival atmosphere to the festival. Lurking just below the surface of this "Megafestival" and the spirit of playfulness that pervades it, is the specter of artistic, social, and political competition among individuals and groups who seek to distinguish themselves from—and prove themselves better than—one another. What is nominally a religious event that takes the form of a casual festival is, in reality, a highly-charged contest whose participants are focused on edging out the competition and winning.

On surface, there is no apparent connection between the Durga festival and house displays that are the focus of McDermott's account and the 'Stretcher Race' event that was the focus of the Shanghai Bell company's "Fire Prevention Day" featured earlier in the chapter. Closer investigation reveals a number of characteristics the events share that transcend the specific contexts in which they took place.

The 'Stretcher Race' was similarly conceived within the context of a festive occasion and positioned as a fun activity designed to inject energy and novelty into "Fire Prevention Day". As a race, however, it maintained an ill-concealed competitive edge and those who participated were very much focused on getting the prizes and accolades that awaited the winners, a fitting recompense for the time and effort they had invested in preparation over the weeks leading up to the event.

CONCLUSION

As quirky, impromptu, and disorderly as they may appear, Chinese corporate activities are not organized just 'for the fun of it'. They play a central role in shaping company culture and are the primary vehicles for transmitting the essence of that culture to the company's employees, including those who represent the company's operations overseas.

Apparently offbeat events such as the executive version of "Simon Says", the 'Stretcher Race', the 'Sales Variety Show', etc. follow a set of conventions that situate them within a much larger system of political, social, cultural values and beliefs. They also incorporate a number of characteristic elements that define them and account for their unique nature:

- **Serious Fun**: Chinese corporate activities pair seemingly antithetical casual and serious elements. They very often incorporate games and, as a result, take on an air of frivolity that borders on the sophomoric. Yet underlying this simplistic humor is always a sense of serious intent.
- **Competitive Edge**: Consistent with the unique juxtaposition of casual and serious, Chinese corporate events almost always incorporate an element of competition even when competition, to a foreign employee, would seem misplaced, or out of place.
- **Intense Preparation**: Even seemingly casual events are always well-rehearsed and carefully orchestrated. Every day over the three weeks prior to "Fire Prevention Day", the two-person teams that participated in the stretcher race spent their lunch hour practicing how to keep a stretcher balanced while running and, more

importantly, learning how to adjust their running style to accommodate the weight of a "patient" lying prone in the bottom.

Activities in a Chinese company are governed by routines that establish the company's internal rhythm and lend a clear structure to an environment that in many respects lacks structure (absence of organizational charts, nebulously defined job descriptions, etc.) and, according to Deal and Kennedy, "give employees a sense of belonging while making their work more meaningful" (Deal and Kennedy 1982).

In conclusion, events and activities in a Chinese company carry a much greater significance than they do in a Western company, a point of distinction that foreign employees of a Chinese company need to be mindful of if they are to succeed in adapting to the company culture and understanding management expectations.

The advent of management theories that advocate "gamification", incorporating games into a firm's operations to stimulate employee engagement, marks a shift in the way Western companies view the relationship between business and entertainment and a softening of the borders that has traditionally separated them. If, over time, 'gamification' is widely adopted and accepted as standard business practice, it is possible that the differences between Chinese and Western corporate activities, that today seem so significant, will be less pronounced and that foreign employees of Chinese firms in future will find the nature of the activities they encounter more familiar and, as a result, be less likely to decline an invitation to join them.

REFERENCES

Bell, Daniel A. *China's Neo Confucianism: Politics and Everyday Life in a Changing Society*, Princeton University Press, Princeton, NJ, 2008.

CNOOC Annual Report 2009.

Deal, Terrence E. and Kennedy, Allan A., *Corporate Cultures: The Rites and Rituals of Corporate Life*, Penguin Books, London, 1982.

Dempsey, Corinne and Duryappah, Sudharshan, "The 'Artful Trick'", in Selva, Raj and Dempsey, C.G. (eds.) *Sacred Play: Ritual Levity and Humor in South Asian Religions*, 2010.

Driver, Tom F. 1998. *Liberating Rites: Understanding the Transformative Power of Ritual.* Boulder, CO: Westview Press quoted in: Sacred Play: Ritual Levity and Humor in South Asian Religions, edited by Selva J. Raj, and Corinne G. Dempsey, State University of New York Press, 2010.

"Guojihua jingying zhong kua wenhua guanli de shijian yu yanjiu", Huaneng Group, March 26, 2013, pages 1–15.

Hawes, Colin, "Representing Corporate Culture in China: Official, Academic, and Corporate Perspectives", *The China Journal*, No. 59, January 2008, pages 33–61.

Hawes, Colin, *The Chinese Transformation of Corporate Culture*, Routledge Contemporary China Series Book 82, 2012.

McDermott, Rachel F., "Playing with the Durga in Bengal", in Selva, Raj and Dempsey, C.G. (eds.), *Sacred Play: Ritual Levity and Humor in South Asian Religions*, 2010.

"Shangwubu deng qi guanyu yinfa <<zhongguo jingwai qiye wenhua jianshe ruo-gan yijian>> de tongzhi", Ministry of Commerce of the People's Republic of China (MOFCOM) research office (zhonghua renmin gonghe guo shang-wubu zhenyanshi), May 16, 2012.

"Chinese Philosophy—Michael Puett" Program on Snow, Dan, "History Hit", Soundcloud Recording—Podcast, 2017. https://soundcloud.com/historyhit/chinese-philosophy-michael.

Puett, Michael and Gross-Loh, Christine, *The Path: What Chinese Philosophers Can Teach Us About the Good Life*, Simon & Schuster, 2016.

Raj, Selva and Dempsey, C.G. (eds.) *Sacred Play: Ritual Levity and Humor in South Asian Religions*, State University of New York Press, 2010.

Szto, Mary, "Chinese Ritual and the Practice of Law", *Touro Law Review*, Vol. 30, No. 1, Article 8, 2014.

Turner, Victor, *From Ritual to Theater*, Performing Arts Journal Publications, New York, 1982.

Wang, Zhong (June), *Displaced Self and Sense of Belonging: A Chinese Researcher Studying Chinese Expatriates Working in the United States*, dissertation, University of South Florida, March 24 2006.

CHAPTER 8

Metaphorically Speaking

The foreign employee who has achieved some degree of fluency in Chinese will most likely have developed this competence through a dedicated course of study, but conceivably also in an environment that is less structured. Regardless of the circumstances under which he or she learned how to speak Chinese, the foreign employee will discover that the language of communications in a Chinese company follows a very different set of rules than the ones with which the foreign employee may be familiar or conversant and that being able to communicate in Chinese language is no guarantee for being able to communicate effectively in a Chinese corporate environment.

A foreign employee's ability to make a contribution and succeed on the job in a Chinese company depends implicitly on an ability to communicate, yet there are few resources available that describe the practice of Chinese corporate communications and can serve as a guide. This chapter is designed to serve that purpose and ensure that the foreign employee is able to be as effective at communicating in a Chinese corporate environment as he or she is at communicating in Chinese language.

Despite the vital role communications plays in shaping a Chinese company's culture—ensuring organizational cohesion and enhancing management effectiveness—its practice and application in this context has previously received little critical attention either inside or outside China. Members of the Chinese academic community who study the discipline of communications in China have, for historical reasons, traditionally focused their attention on its manifestation in mass media and explored

© The Author(s) 2020
P. Ross, *Barriers to Entry*,
https://doi.org/10.1007/978-981-32-9566-7_8

its socio-political consequences rather than examined its application in a corporate environment (Lu et al. 2002). Those studies that do address the subject of Chinese corporate communications focus almost exclusively on those methods and vehicles of communication (company messages, addresses, and presentations) that are most 'visible', i.e. specifically oriented towards an external audience and transmitted through a company's website or other publicly accessible channel. To gain insight into the particular company cultures of Chinese state-run enterprises, for example, Colin Hawes examined information made available on the websites of companies whose profiles met his criteria (Hawes 2012). Similarly, in support of their comparative study of metaphor use and application in Chinese and U.S. firms, Sun and Jiang analyzed mission statements presented on the websites of firms included in the Fortune Global 500, an annual ranking of the highest revenue generating corporations worldwide (Sun and Jiang 2014). Moreover, the sources of communication these studies consult are predominantly ones that are available in English. However, as Sing-Bik Ngai and Singh demonstrate in their comprehensive study of corporate messages Chinese CEOs direct to their constituents (customers, shareholders, partners, etc.), these sources cannot be taken as representations of a Chinese company's communications that are either faithful or complete (Sing-Bik Ngai and Singh 2014, pages 369–370).[1] Even less can they be taken as a proxy for a Chinese company's internal communications. However, it is the communications within a Chinese company that are of greatest relevance to the foreign employee given the degree to which effectiveness on the job is contingent on the employee's ability to make sense and use of a Chinese company's communications in all its modes. In filling the gap that exists in the current research on Chinese enterprise communication, this study also serves as a guide for the foreign employee in a Chinese company who needs to know what to say and how to say it.

As a mechanism to frame the study and approximate as closely as possible the conditions the foreign employee is most likely to encounter while working in a Chinese company, the study takes as its premise and point of departure a hypothetical assignment to develop a corporate presentation that the foreign employee has received from their supervisor.

---

[1] Sing-Bik Ngai and Singh compare CEO messages in Chinese and English and demonstrate there can, in fact, be a substantial difference between the content, messaging, and even branding a Chinese company presents to a local audience in Chinese and what it communicates in English to a target audience outside China.

THE ESSENCE OF A CORPORATE PRESENTATION

Consistent with the general lack of attention that has been paid to the practice of communications within a Chinese company, there has been little rigorous analysis conducted of presentations delivered by its executives. Not only is such an analysis of intrinsic interest for what it reveals about Chinese management practice and corporate culture, but it is also of practical application for foreign employees in a Chinese company who want to make sense of presentations delivered by the Chinese executives they work for and ultimately need to be able to deliver an effective presentation themselves. Accordingly, the study is organized around the basic components from which such a presentation would normally be built: *Content, Messaging, Design, Delivery,* and *Feedback,* and examines each one in turn. To bring into sharper relief those aspects of communications in a Chinese company that are unique, the study draws on cases and examples drawn, by way of comparison, from the executive communications of Western companies with which the foreign employee is likely to have some familiarity.

To assist the foreign employee in evaluating the characteristics of a Chinese executive presentation and identifying what makes it unique, the employee's supervisor has compiled a set of representative Western and Chinese executive speeches as well as a few reference presentations that have been prepared for him in the past and made them available to the employee as a resource. As an additional aid, the supervisor's assistant has created a directory for the presentations (see Table 8.1). A note appended to the file explains that, to facilitate a more coherent comparison, the presentations have all been drawn from CEOs representing companies in the U.S. and Chinese hi-tech industries.[2] With the intent of approximating as closely as possible the experience of the foreign employee working in a Chinese company, the speeches provided for consideration are ones that the respective executives delivered to internal audiences (i.e. audiences comprising employees) of the respective companies they represent.[3]

[2]For sake of consistency and to make the comparison more meaningful speeches have been drawn from Chinese executives whose companies are profiled in Chapter 4 (Enterprise Experience).

[3]This claim comes with the caveat that although the speeches have been designated 'internal' the fact that they have been made publicly available raises the question about the original intent of the speech and the suspicion that the speaker had some sense that his words would find wider circulation and be exposed to a broader audience than the strictly internal one it was nominally intended for.

Table 8.1   Index of Western and Chinese executive speeches (internal) analyzed

CEO Name	Company	Presentation Title	Target Audience	Key Message
Ma Huateng	Tencent	Tencent should focus on service and differentiatiors	Product Managers	Developing services and creativity and innovation
Ren Zhengfei	Huawei	Huawei is not United Airlines	Corporate strategy staff	Maintaining customer focus.
Ma Yun	Alibaba	"102 Years" is more than just a slogan	Longer term employees	Cultivating a positive attitude and not resting on your laurels.
John Chambers	Cisco	Welcome to Cisco	New employees	Key ingredients for a successful and exciting career
Jeff Weiner	LinkedIn	Acquisition by Microsoft	General	Keeping a positive attitude in a changing environment
Satya Nadella	Microsoft	First day as CEO	all employees	Microsoft is positioned well for the future and is poised to make a great contribution to society

See Appendix for complete text of speeches listed

As a first step, the foreign employee will most likely review the openings to the speeches of the CEOs listed above. This is a good starting point as these openings contain many of the basic elements that differentiate the speeches they introduce and make them unique.

OPENINGS

I was thinking about the last time we had an All Hands that was not on a Wednesday morning, this is shaping up to be a little bit of LinkedIn trivia. Anyone know the answer? Anyone but Dee know the answer? IPO, very good. For bonus points, where was it broadcast from live? Empire State Building. Correct.

Jeff Weiner—LinkedIn

Hello, I'm John Chambers, chairman and CEO at Cisco and I want to welcome each of you as a new hire to Cisco. Some of you will be coming out of college some of you will be in the industry for multiple decades. But what you are about to find out is going to be the most exciting job you've ever had in your life. It's one of the best places to work in every country in the world, we are a family in a very unique way and we're going to change the way the world works, lives, learns, and plays.

John Chambers—Cisco

Today is a very humbling day for me. It reminds me of my very first day at Microsoft, 22 years ago. Like you, I had a choice about where to come to work. I came here because I believed Microsoft was the best company in the world. I saw then how clearly we empower people to do magical things with our creations and ultimately make the world a better place. I knew there was no better company to join if I wanted to make a difference. This is the very same inspiration that continues to drive me today.

Satya Nadella—Microsoft

But in fact we should be talking less about 'products' and 'features' and more about 'service' and 'characteristics'. We should be less often saying "I want a product that should have these features" and rather be saying "I want to offer a service with the following characteristics". The entire service process is and the total cost for the service is how much

Ma Huateng—Tencent

You should be like seeds, going to those places where you are most needed, putting down roots, sprouting buds, blossoming and finally carpeting the ground with flowers. A few brave souls who go to those places where it is most difficult to grow will mature quickly

Ren Zhengfei—Huawei

On the road to where it is today Alibaba has hit its share of potholes. I'm very glad Alibaba has a salesforce. It's thanks to your hard work that Alibaba today is as influential as it is. There may be a few of you who started with the company right out of school.

Ma Yun (Jack Ma)—Alibaba[4]

As abbreviated as they are, these excerpts nevertheless convey a sense for what distinguishes a Chinese corporate presentation from a Western (in this case, American) one and for what they reveal about how the executive presenters relate to their employees and to the companies they represent.

Making a Personal Statement

The profile of a multinational CEO and the role they are expected to play has undergone a metamorphosis, from hard-driving commander to coach and mentor, a leader who is valued as much for their Emotional Quotient (EQ) as for their Intelligent (IQ). Consistent with the cultivation of this more empathic persona, modern CEOs are expected to reveal more of their personal lives and expose more of their vulnerabilities to those who work in the company they preside over. "Talking about the

---

[4]Unless otherwise noted, translations of Chinese executive speeches are my own.

things that happen in their [CEOs] lives outside of work", an article in the Los Angeles Times observes, "makes them both more accessible and more credible" (McGregor 2015).

In keeping with the times, Satya Nadella begins his presentation on a personal note (see excerpt above): "Today is a very humbling day for me. It reminds me of my very first day at Microsoft, 22 years ago.". Nadella then uses the words "Like you...", that begin the next sentence, as a subtle way to strengthen his rapport with the employees he is addressing. A device applied with similar intent but in somewhat different form are the jokes and humorous asides with which Jeff Weiner begins his speech and that punctuate much of the presentation that follows.

The Chinese executives profiled don't reveal anywhere near as many personal details in their presentations as the Western CEOs, yet each one of the Chinese leaders speaks in a distinctive and readily identifiable voice that clearly conveys his unique character and personality traits. Tencent's Ma Huateng is recognizable as the engineer and product developer ("we should be talking less about 'products' and 'features' and more about 'service' and 'characteristics'") who revels in getting his hands dirty with the inner workings of an ATM machine; Huawei's CEO Ren Zhengfei is the mystic who has a distinct penchant for delivering homilies and dispensing home-spun aphorisms ("You should be like seeds..."). Alibaba's Jack Ma is a man of the people, a humble leader who is quick to praise others and thank them for their contribution to the success of the company ("It's thanks to your hard work that Alibaba today is as influential as it is").

The speeches of the Western CEOs, for the all the lengths their creators go to personalize them, are virtually indistinguishable from one another. Perhaps this is because by all adopting the same strategy of sharing explicit personal details the Western CEOs have inevitably made their presentations generic. The Chinese CEOs, by sharing fewer personal details, unexpectedly reveal more of their personalities.

CONTENT: GLOBAL VISIONS; LOCAL MISSIONS

The mission and vision statements that are the stalwarts of communications in Western companies feature prominently in executive presentations and are the glue that holds their parts together.

Perhaps a reflection of how they see the role they play as statesmen who are able to make an impact on society and as the stewards of organizations that impact the world, the missions of the Western CEOs as

presented in their speeches extend far beyond the walls of their companies. Satya Nadella makes very clear that he sees his mission as "making
the world a better place". John Chambers speaks about being on a mission to "change the way the world works, lives, learns, and plays". "The
world needs what we do more than ever before," says Jeff Weiner in one
instance of the more than thirty references to the "world" he makes in
his speech to LinkedIn employees. This concept of changing the world
and making it a better place is often coupled with the theme of giving
back to Society which is, in essence, an effective vehicle for improving
the state of the world. Consistent with their mission of making the world
a better place, these CEOs articulate a vision that is equally all-encompassing and, as a vision, very much oriented towards the future.

As important as expressions of mission and vision are to the Western
CEOs they do not merit a single reference in the presentations of their
Chinese counterparts whose aspirations are much more mundane (see
Table 8.2). Tencent's Ma Huateng, who devotes his presentation to parsing through the details of how products are built, marketed, and sold, is
a perfect example of the Chinese CEO's preoccupation with tightening
the operational nuts and financial bolts that are the key to running a successful business and making money. The Chinese CEOs are clearly less
concerned with saving the world than with serving those who purchase
their products and services, a distinction that is reflected in the number
of times they make reference to the "customer" in their presentations.
Remarkably, the number of times the Western CEOs refer to the customer is so small that the word does not even qualify for a ranking within
the ten most frequently terms their presentations contain (see Table 8.2).

If Chinese CEOs, based on the way they present themselves in their
speeches, can be said to have any mission or play any particular role, it is
that of a teacher whose mission is to improve the performance of those
who work for them. It is a goal they accomplish by imparting words of
wisdom that are distinguished both by their degree of specificity and by
their consistent appearance in the last third of a given executive's presentation, a consistency that marks them as a standard and indispensable
feature of a Chinese executive's rhetorical repertoire.

Huawei's CEO Ren Zhengfei, for example, towards the end of his
speech dedicated to the importance of customer service, instructs the
employees who make up his audience to download company cases relevant to market strategy. Then, as if the instructions weren't already specific
enough, he advises employees, as a precautionary measure, to copy the

Table 8.2 Comparative study of usage frequency for the words "World" and "Customer" in select Western and Chinese executive speeches

	"World" References	"Customer" References
Chambers	4	2
Nadella	13	1
Weiner	34	5
Jack Ma	-	7
Ma Huateng	-	2
Ren Zhengfei	-	29

relevant materials to the hard drives of their computers.[5] To ensure that the product managers he is addressing stay current with developments in the market and deepen their understanding of customer requirements, Tencent's Ma Huateng, exhorts them to complete 10 customer surveys a month, look at 100 customer blogs, and review feedback from 1000 customers. Employees at a Western company would be likely to dismiss such prescriptive instructions as superfluous or even patronizing. However, given that the speeches and the words of wisdom they contain are so prescriptive it is clear that those who offer them expect them to be followed.

Consistent with their less expansive missions and more pragmatic approach to the management of their businesses, the Chinese CEOs whose presentations are considered here tend to situate themselves firmly in the present, forego visions of the future, and take their cue from the past. (cf. Ren Zhengfei: "A hundred years ago trains, telegrams, barges were the mechanisms of competition"; Jack Ma: reference to characters from the Chinese classic "Journey to the West" as a model for the ideal corporate team, etc.)[6]

Sing-Bik Ngai and Singh's finding that CEOs in the study they conducted tended to center the messages they communicated to their constituents on past issues rather than on future developments (Sing-Bik Ngai and Singh 2014, page 372) suggests that this temporal positioning is characteristic of Chinese executive communication more broadly.

[5] "Shoucang dao ziji de chucun" 收藏到自己的储存.
[6] 过去的一百多年,经济的竞争方式是以火车、轮船、电报、传真等手段来进行的 (Ren Zhengfei speech to party members) "Ma Yun tan 'Xi You Ji' tuandui ruhe chengong",

Sing-Bik Ngai and Singh attribute this grounding of messages in the past to a general respect for history that is intrinsic to Chinese culture. In support of Sing-Bik Ngai and Singh's conclusion, but more precise in the identification of its source, Zhang suggests that the preference Chinese exhibit for past-oriented communication is cultivated at a young age by educators who encourage them when writing to cite extensively from the works of the sages ("yin jing ju dian"). As a result of this pedagogical orientation, Zhang notes, Chinese in their communications tend to regard themselves as less reliable sources than the sages and historical figures they have been taught to revere and surmises that Chinese speakers orient themselves towards the past when they communicate for the simple reason that "citing from history is more credible" (Zhang 2011, page 76).

Another rhetorical habit the Chinese education system cultivates in the students that pass through it and that conceivably has a bearing on the way its executives communicate is the use of allusion, proverb, analogy and metaphor. Judicious application of these rhetorical devices is considered an expression of the Chinese language's beauty and a criterion for stylistic elegance (Chen and Chung 1994).[7] These usage habits are so ingrained that Chinese students, even when writing in English, make use of such fixed patterns four times more often than native English speakers do. (Xing et al. 2008, page 80).

MESSAGING: METAPHOR USE AND APPLICATION

More Than Just Rhetorical

There is no shortage of studies that compare the usage of metaphor in Chinese and Western cultures. Their most common objects of focus are metaphors that relate to a part of the human body, a color, or an animal (Wang et al. 2011; Han 2017, etc.). There are relatively few studies that have undertaken a comparative analysis of metaphor in a commercial context (Hu and Xu 2017; Sun and Jiang 2014). The following analysis of metaphor usage in the presentations of the CEOs featured deepens understanding of this phenomenon by adding a new dimension to the existing body of research.

Sohu, June 15, 2018 (www.sohu.com/a/19360353_130673) (article on Jack Ma's discussion of "Journey to the West" and corporate teams.

[7] Cited in: (Xing et al. 2008, page 76).

Sprawson has proposed that each culture draws on its own particular set of metaphors to express its attitude to life. The ancient Romans, for example, tended towards use of swimming metaphors. The English favor cricket or boxing terms (Sprawson 1992). Chinese culture, or its corporate culture to be precise, exhibits a distinct preference for military metaphor.

Fighting Words

"The soldiers of the Red Army spent nearly fourteen years battling their way through the worst terrain on the way to Beijing. Along the way they grew up: from children to young adults and when they eventually got to Beijing they became heads of ministries …" Seemingly an account lifted from a history of the Chinese People's Liberation Army, this excerpt is, in fact, a parable used by Huawei's CEO, Ren Zhengfei, to justify privileges granted to employees with longer tenure in the company.[8] This application of military metaphor as a rhetorical device appears consistently in speeches Ren delivered over a twenty-year period beginning at the end of the 1990's and is therefore not unique to the speech under consideration here.[9] It would be tempting to ascribe Ren's expansive use of military references to the influence of his tenure as an officer in China's People's Liberation Army and regard its application as a calculated technique engaged to sustain the image of a company renowned for its hard-driving culture. However, this application is not unique to Ren. Such metaphors appear just as frequently and consistently in the presentations of other Chinese CEOs, including the ones considered in this study.

As the close to a Chinese New Year speech in which he shares his view on Baidu's prospects over the upcoming year, CEO Robin Li calls on employees to, "do what it takes to win every war, every battle, and every fight".[10] Xiaomi CEO, Lei Jun, recapping company performance

---

[8] 红军从爬雪山过草地,到了北京,这过程仅仅经历了十四年。他们从一个少年才变成一个青年,到北京就当了部长. From Ren Zhengfei speech to Party members entitled "A Soldier's Life Is The Most Rewarding and The Most Challenging".

[9] "Ren Zhengfei neibu wenzhang quanji", Huawei, 1994–2012.

[10] 我们要做好准备,打好每一场战争、战役和战斗.

Li, Yanhong (Robin Li), "Ushering in the Modern Era", Tencent Web, February 7, 2017, http://tech.qq.com/a/20170207/020968.htm?t=1486457334699.

over a year just ended, highlights the victory "on all our battle fronts" employees have achieved.[11] Even Alibaba's CEO, Jack Ma, the epitome of a cooperative, collaborative, and empathetic leader, does not shy away from employing overtly confrontational and combative language in his speeches to internal audiences. At a ceremony held to recognize employees who had been with Alibaba for more than five years, Ma suggested that the transformation of the company, from the start-up it had been when the employees in the audience first joined to the corporation it had since become, could be likeneed to the transformation of a band of fighters "engaging in hand-to-hand combat" into a battalion of soldiers "waging battle as an organized army."[12] A poster at the Shanghai Bell Corporation that featured a slogan exhorting sales teams to 'fight' for year-end sales results superimposed over the image of a Chinese aircraft carrier decked out with a full complement of fighter planes, offers yet another point of reference for the consistency with which military rhetoric is used in Chinese corporate communication and an illustration for the pervasiveness of its application across all modes of communication: written, spoken, and visual.

Despite the prevalence of military references in Chinese corporate communication there have been relatively few studies that have undertaken a dedicated analysis of its application or endeavored to understand the motivation for its use (Hu and Xu's "WAR Metaphor in the Chinese Economic Media Discourse" being one of the exceptions). Those studies that address the subject do so in a broader context, considering the use of military reference in popular and general communication rather than specifically in a corporate context. They are, nevertheless, useful references from which conclusions about the corporate application of military metaphor and related allusions can be drawn. These studies take one of two approaches: There are those that concern themselves with investigating the origin of military references, an investigation that usually involves a look to Chinese history as the source. Others concern themselves with the function of such references and consider the motivation for their use and intended effect.

[11] Lei Jun, "在刚刚过去的一年里,我们在每一条战线上都取得了非常了不起的业绩.
[12] 因为在中国,像我们这样的公司真的不多,你们会经历很多。五六年前是肉搏战,今天是军团作战. Ma, Yun, "'102' years' Is Not Just a Slogan".

Source
Hu and Xu attribute the use of military reference in Chinese commercial discourse to the essential nature of Chinese civilization. "The five-thousand year history of the civilization of China is also the five-thousand year history of warfare," they state emphatically, as if the mere invocation of China's lengthy history is sufficient on its own merit to obviate the need for any further explanation (Hu and Xu 2017, page 104).

Lu, more credibly, pinpoints China's Cultural Revolution, a tumultuous period in China's modern history marked by pervasive use of militaristic terms and rhetoric, as the source for military references. He demonstrates that, even though the rhetoric that was pervasive during the Cultural Revolution has long since disappeared from general discourse, quite a number of words and phrases in use at that time were subsequently absorbed into the common vernacular and are still in current use. As one example among many, Lu cites the phrase "annihilate the dishes", a colloquialism used to invite or encourage someone to finish the food that has been set before them (Lu 2016). Lu attributes the popularization of bellicose rhetoric in Chinese society to Mao's putative successor, Vice-Premier Lin Biao, who was particularly aggressive in promoting the use of military slogans and metaphors during the Cultural Revolution (Lu 2016, page 159). Although the validity of such specific attribution is debatable, the effect that this rhetoric had in galvanizing and stimulating acts of violence and brutality is unquestionable. Another particularly relevant reason for which the rhetoric from that time may have been retained in executive communication, specifically, is that many Chinese CEOs came of age during this time of turmoil and conflict and it is plausible that the way they express themselves was formed by the experience. (see more detailed discussion of this effect in Chapter 9—"Reverse Angle").

Function
A number of other scholars, less historically-oriented, have speculated that military expressions are such a fixture of communication in a Chinese corporate environment because they can be readily mapped to a variety of commercial domains. Another point of attraction is their demonstrated ability to make concrete for a general audience some of the more abstract commercial and economic concepts executives would like to convey and ensure that their employees retain. Above all, the military idiom is such a favored form of Chinese executive communication because its vivid imagery sustains attention and because of its proven

effectiveness at boosting morale within a group and rallying the group's members to unite against a common enemy.

DESIGN: OUT OF BOUNDS

The foreign employee reviewing a Chinese corporate presentation for the first time will no doubt be struck by the cluttered appearance of the slides that comprise it. There is much more information—both data and text—than any slide can reasonably accommodate or that any viewer can hope to process (Image 8.1).[13] The colors, overly bright and oddly paired, distract attention from the information they are meant to highlight (Image 8.2). The graphic images that augment the text are similarly mismatched both in size and color with the overall layout of the slide and the seemingly haphazard application of animated images is at cross-purposes with the direction and intent of the slides on which they appear (Image 8.3).

Image 8.1   Example of cluttered, text and graphics-heavy presentation slide

[13] This image and the ones that follow are drawn from actual corporate presentations. However, as the intent is to illustrate aesthetic and design principles, only relevant elements have been retained. All content has been removed to maintain confidentiality and preserve anonymity.

ENTERPRISE GUIDANCE

Image 8.2 Example of 'uncommonly' paired color scheme

Image 8.3 Example of disjointed graphic images

"Lack of sophistication," the critique that a Western marketing expert offers to account for these design quirks and aesthetic anomalies, is an assessment that is shared by many (Rajeck 2016). The implication of the critique, if not directly expressed, is that the Chinese who developed these presentations lack the requisite experience or training necessary to develop more "sophisticated" presentations and would do well to invest time in the study of standard presentation guides. Typical of the basic principles laid out in these guides are ones such as the following:

• Eliminate as many words as possible and use graphics.
• Just use one graphic that illustrates a point or a graphic and a word or two.
• Don't just take a standard Excel table and copy it into a presentation.
• Simplify down to the essential elements that matter.

(Theriault 2011)

Adhering to these principles and following the accompanying guidelines in developing a presentation for my Chinese supervisor, I was taken aback when he concluded, following review, that the presentation had fallen short of expectations. He noted specifically that the slides had too much empty space and not enough detail. Moreover, the muted colors I had applied as a thematic element designed to lend the slides a coherent look and feel, detracted from the overall reception of the content because they were "much too dark". The dreary pall these somber colors cast over the presentation was exacerbated by the presence of black boxes that I, following 'accepted practice', had used to delineate key points of information from the rest of the figures on the slide. He explained that the appearance of text enclosed in boxes reminded him of the way the names of the deceased were typically presented on a Chinese death notice. In drawing a connection between an aesthetic device and a *momento mori*, the supervisor, whether he realized it or not, was reprising the Qing emperor Qianlong's reaction to the application of *chiaroscuro* in the paintings of the Jesuit artist Giuseppe Castiglione who had taken up residence at the emperor's court more than two hundred years before (see Chapter 2—"History Lessons"). Similarly, my supervisor's antipathy towards what he perceived as excessive use of white space and the sparsity of information in the slides I presented, mirrored a common reaction many Chinese viewers have to the use of space on the websites of Western companies, the following comment as representative: "A

Western site wastes space. It's simple, clean.... But the problem is, while it doesn't have any useless information, it also has less useful information" (Cheng and Nielsen 2016). The coincidence of these associations and the consistency of the reactions they inform, strengthens the case for the existence and application of a coherent set of aesthetic principles in the design of Chinese corporate presentations that are different from those that the foreign employee is accustomed to and from those that standard presentation guides present as "universals".

Recognizing that the presentation design standards and aesthetic principles he or she has studied and appropriated are not cast in stone or universally respected, the foreign employee who has been charged with developing a presentation for a Chinese executive faces a conundrum. To meet expectations and complete the assignment successfully, the employee needs to gain a better understanding of the principles that govern the design of Chinese corporate presentations and some appreciation for how to apply them in developing the presentation requested. However, as few formal studies have been undertaken that are specifically dedicated to the evaluation of Chinese corporate presentations the availability of references that could serve the foreign employee as a guide is limited.

An alternative source of insight that presents itself for the foreign employee's consideration is to be found in the aesthetic principles that form the basis for the composition of Chinese corporate websites that are similar enough to corporate presentations in the design issues they seek to address to qualify them as an appropriate proxy and valid frame of reference. Moreover, since the aesthetics and design of Chinese websites has been the object of much more concentrated attention and thorough study than corporate presentations there are many more resources available that the foreign employee can draw on for guidance. Following a preliminary review of these guides and resources, the foreign employee will find that the most applicable and relevant elements fall into three categories: Social, Cognitive, and Linguistic.

Design Elements

Social

There is plenty of evidence to suggest that the tendency of Chinese developers towards conceiving presentations whose slides are packed with information is less the consequence of a haphazard approach to design or a poorly-tuned aesthetic sense than a product of strategic intent calculated to achieve two potentially incompatible goals: attracting attention and establishing credibility.

Sensing in the design and layout of the typical Chinese website a look-and-feel that was reminiscent of a "Wet Market", the colloquial reference for a traditional Chinese open air bazaar, a web designer speculated that the effect that website and market were designed to achieve was the same. The designer posited that the cluttered webpages, flashy graphics and animations that populate a Chinese website, similar to the raucous atmosphere and, to the uninitiated, disorganization that characterize the Wet Market, serve as an effective mechanism for creating a sense of excitement and activity that attracts attention and ultimately generates business. Accordingly, he dubbed this phenomenon he had identified the "Wet Market Effect" (Thibaud 2016).

As a corollary to the "Wet Market Effect" is a complementary effect here dubbed the "Credibility Quotient",[14] for convenience. Like the "Wet Market Effect" the "Credibility Quotient" is about presenting a large volume of information. However, whereas the intent of the Wet Market Effect was to present a large volume of information—in the form of text, graphic elements, and animations—to create a specific visual impact, attract attention and create a sense of excitement, the emphasis of the "Credibility Quotient" is on the content (in the form of data points) and the intent is to establish credibility rather than achieve a specific visual effect. The assumed positive correlation between the volume of information presented and the level of credibility achieved derives from Chinese viewers' evaluation of Western websites and subsequent accusations that by maintaining a ratio of open space to text and information that is orders of magnitude greater than those of Chinese counterparts these [Western] sites are "just playing with words, with no real meat, no real content at all" (Cheng and Nielsen 2016).

Linguistic

Over and above the "Wet Market Effect" and the "Credibility Quotient", another reason Chinese websites and slides in Chinese corporate presentations often appear so packed with information to foreign employees as to be "dense and impenetrable" may quite practically be due to the intrinsic nature and form of Chinese characters and

---

[14]The term 'Credibility Quotient' is a concept devised by the author to describe this phenomenon.

extrinsically to the relation of Chinese characters to the writing systems of other languages to which the foreign employee may be more accustomed (Thibaud 2016; Rajeck 2016; Taylor 2018).

Intrinsic—Chinese characters in their composition, especially those formed from a greater number of strokes, can appear complex, especially to the uninitiated. In their application, there are typically no spaces that separate characters from one another and there is no concept of capital and lower-case that might further differentiate them, features that both add to the sense of crowdedness and density that the foreign employee may perceive.

Extrinsic—Parameters for the correspondence between Chinese and English, such as the rule-of-thumb ratio of three Chinese characters to two English words and the observation that a Chinese character takes up a space roughly equivalent to that of two English letters make it clear why the layout and look-and-feel of a Chinese website and, by association, a Chinese presentation would be significantly different from that of an English language-based one.

Cognitive

Recent advances in neuroscience have illuminated deeper cognitive structures that underlie observed cultural tendencies and aesthetic preferences. There is a growing body of research that suggests the way in which viewers perceive and process the information on websites (and in presentations) is culturally-determined.

One such study that analyzed the viewing habits of American, Chinese, and Korean subjects (Dong and Lee—"A Cross-Cultural Comparative Study of Users' Perceptions of a Webpage") came to the conclusion that the way a visitor to a given website perceives information on a website and processes it can vary quite significantly across cultures, a conclusion whose implication for website design and composition is undeniable. The American subjects who participated in the experiments exhibited a tendency to proceed sequentially when viewing information on a website and were primed for that information to be organized in categories, an approach that the researchers who conducted the study designated "analytic". Chinese visitors had a tendency to scan "back and forth" when viewing information on a site, an approach the researchers designated "holistic" (Dong and Lee 2008, page 28).

Both in concept and terminology, the difference in viewing habits the study identified recalls the distinction comparative studies of rhetoric, known as "contrastive rhetoric", make between the logic Westerners and

Chinese use to structure essays and presentations. Proponents of contrastive rhetoric traditionally characterize the rhetorical logic Chinese use to structure presentations and essays as "Inductive" and the method of reasoning representatives of Western cultures apply as "Deductive" (Xing et al. 2008, pages 73–74). What this means in practice is that a Chinese writer would normally structure a presentation by introducing the background material at the beginning and then use it to guide the reader to the main point whereas the representative of a Western culture would typically prioritize the main idea and accordingly place the statement of the argument or thesis at the beginning of a presentation (Xing et al. 2008, page 74). The corresponding terms used to describe the respective ways in which the information between the beginning and the end are organized (determined by the number of topic changes or average number of topic sentences in a paragraph) "circular" for inductive and "linear" for deductive (Xing, Wang, and Spencer), are strikingly similar conceptually to the approaches ("holistic" and "linear") of Western and Chinese visitors to information on websites described in Dong and Lee's comparative study of cross-cultural viewing habits (Dong and Lee).

Some scholars (Smith and Kirkpatrick) consider the logic on which rhetorical structure is based to be a linguistic phenomenon and ascribe the distinguishing features of Chinese rhetoric to a "penchant for relational thinking" (Smith 1983, page 92) that is a function of the "iconic and natural word order of Chinese [language]" (Kirkpatrick 2002, page 253).[15] This view of the connection between Chinese language and the way information is structured complements the previous discussion about the influence Chinese language has on the way information on websites is presented. So these are two dimensions of the same thing. One is about the underlying logic of Chinese language and the other is about its form.

DELIVERY: CLOSE TO THE VEST

American courses in public speaking emphasize the importance of engaging an audience and present numerous techniques speakers can employ— making eye contact, executing a strategically timed gesture, and moving energetically—to ensure that what is said produces the desired effect and achieves the greatest impact.

---

[15]This reference comes from "Literary Background and Rhetorical Styles" in Kirkpatrick, page 43.

Invited to speak to an audience of students and faculty at Tsinghua University, one of China's most prestigious institutions of higher learning, Facebook CEO Mark Zuckerberg revealed himself an adept of this school of presentation from the moment he bounded onto the stage of the university's auditorium. To maintain audience engagement and sustain interest in what he was saying, Zuckerberg then spent the balance of the presentation moving from one end of the stage to the other as he spoke.

Zuckerberg made headlines that day in the Fall of 2014 but it wasn't because of his presentation skill or even his stature that he attracted attention (there were certainly plenty of other foreign executives and even heads of state who had taken the stage at Tsinghua long before he had). The point of attraction was that he delivered his presentation in Chinese. In the ensuing discussion that played itself out on blogs, websites, and articles over the days that followed Zuckerberg's visit, there were those who commended Facebook's CEO on his willingness to deliver a public speech in a language whose degree of difficulty for native speakers of Western languages is legend. Others were curious about his level of proficiency and about how much the audience actually understood. Because they were so intently focused on the linguistic aspect of Zuckerberg's presentation not one of those who commented paid the slightest attention to how Zuckerberg had delivered his presentation.

From the moment he bounded onto the stage and addressed the audience with his rendering in Chinese of a rousing "How are you all doing today?" ("Ni hao ma!") Zuckerberg revealed just how quintessentially American his style of presentation was and, by the same token, just how unfamiliar he was with the Chinese practice of delivering corporate presentations. A Chinese executive making a similar presentation, especially in such a formal setting, would have taken a much more measured approach when stepping on to the stage and would never have made an entry that was as dynamic as Zuckerberg's. Once on stage, the Chinese executive would have then walked purposefully to the rostrum and used it to anchor himself for the balance of the presentation. As an opening he would not have used such a casual and all-encompassing "How are you all doing"! but, by convention, would have addressed the most important and esteemed members of the audience by name and title as a sign of respect and then, using a standard formulation befitting the circumstance, expressed his gratitude for the effort they made to attend his presentation.[16] The words would have been delivered in an evenly modulated tone and any accompanying gestures would have been spare and executed within a limited range of motion. The principle of making eye contact with the audience that features so prominently in any Western presentation style guide is one that Chinese presenters tend to ignore, preferring instead the increasingly common practice of reading the text of the presentation they have prepared off the screens of laptops that they have brought on stage with them. A foreign presenter who fails to take these conditions into account and make necessary adaptations runs the risk of losing the audience's attention and diminishing the presentation's impact.

Unaware of these differences in delivery I, like Zuckerberg, devoted most of the time I spent preparing my first Chinese presentation to practicing the language, convinced that the audience's ability to understand what I said was directly dependent on the accuracy of my pronunciation. Even with such intense and focused preparation, I learned at the conclusion of the presentation that, while the audience had appreciated my effort, its members had not understood much of what I had said. Based on this feedback, I concluded that my language skill was still at a level that was too low to be effective. I later learned it was not my linguistic shortcoming that had been the cause of the audience's difficulty but my delivery. My movement on stage, use of gesture, and eye contact were perceived by the audience as excessive. Ironically, by applying these techniques I had distracted the members of the audience from what I was saying rather than engaged them.

More than simply examples that illustrate what makes the Chinese delivery of presentations unique, these anecdotes reflect a more fundamental difference in the way Chinese and Western cultures perceive the goal of such presentations and purpose of the rhetoric on which they are based. It is a difference that has its origins in ancient history.

From earliest times, rhetoric in Western culture was conceived as an "artificer of persuasion" most commonly applied in the resolution of disputes (Kirkpatrick and Xu 2012, page 15). The proceedings that conditioned such disputes typically engaged three actors: a protagonist and an antagonist who presented their respective cases and a third party whose role

---

[16]"Zai bai mang zhi zhong chou chu shijian" (在百忙之中抽出时间), one of the more commonly used of these formulations is an expression of gratitude to the members of the audience for taking time out of their busy schedules to attend the event.

was to evaluate the cases as they were argued and then pass judgement. By convention, the participants presented their cases orally and in public. This application of rhetoric and practice of oral argumentation that was a product of the Greco-Roman tradition was completely unknown in China. This was largely because the system of adjudication in China was much more hierarchical and usually involved only two parties, an individual who delivered a plea and an official (e.g. an emperor or governor) who heard the plea and rendered a decision. Because of the significant disparity in power and stature that existed between the supplicant and the official to whom the supplicant was appealing, those pleading their cases tended to proceed with a good deal of caution that was reflected most obviously in the way they presented their grievances. The indirect manner of presentation and the highly-nuanced language they adopted were all calculated to keep from "ruffling the scales of the dragon" and provoking a confrontation that could have a negative influence on the outcome (Kirkpatrick and Xu 2012, page 28).

FEEDBACK: GETTING PERSONAL

"Thank you for such a great presentation!" ("feichang ganxie ni hen jingcai de yanjiang"), an expression of gratitude typically delivered by a member of the audience as a prelude to asking the presenter a question, is very often the initial feedback that a presenter will receive at the conclusion of a presentation and exemplifies a style of communication that Hwang characterizes as "harmonious, non-argumentative, mild, humble, nurturing, and modest".[17]

Foreigners who have the opportunity to participate in meetings with Chinese come away impressed by how cordial and civil those meetings are and typically find the Chinese attendees to be positive, respectful, and encouraging in their feedback. Indeed, the expression "thank you for such a great presentation" has all the appearance of the type of "positive feedback" that a Western speaker would find familiar and welcome. In reality, however, the phrase is nothing more than a platitude that is invoked more as a matter of convention than intended as a source of any significant meaning or relevance. Moreover, the "harmonious style" of communication that observers find so impressive may be as much an attempt to avoid revealing divisions in front of an outsider, especially a foreigner, as the expression of a unique cultural tendency and reflection

---

[17]Hwang, John C., "Masculinity Index and Communications Style", *Chinese Communications Theory*, Chapter 5.

of a "normal" state of affairs. Under normal circumstances, the atmosphere in meetings that are conducted in a Chinese company can be highly charged and feedback can be uncomfortably direct.

"Constructive Criticism", the name given to the type of feedback employees in Western companies are encouraged to provide and expect to receive, involves offering words of encouragement and highlighting the positive aspects of a presentation before sharing suggestions for areas of improvement. Feedback in a Chinese setting typically takes the form of a critique whose focus is on identifying shortcomings and highlighting areas of failure. It is often delivered in a language that is direct and often quite personal (for related examples, see Brave Dragons "Boss" Wang's postgame diatribes described in Chapter 3—"On the Runway" and feedback of the Shanghai Bell Corporation's president at the conclusion of "Fire Prevention Day" in Chapter 7—"All Work and Play").

The feedback that I received following one of the very first times I delivered a presentation to a Chinese audience was that, in addition to being disorganized, the presentation had been all but impossible to follow because of various inconsistencies in my pronunciation and numerous grammatical errors. After the critique was concluded, members of the audience then turned their attention to speculating on the root cause of my less than satisfactory performance. The object of speculation was the method I had used to learn Chinese and the specific course of study I had followed. The conclusion the audience came to was that my approach to learning the language had not been sufficiently systematic ("xitongxing"). My admission that I had learned the language on my own outside of any formal curriculum ("wu shi zi tong") satisfied the members of the audience who felt vindicated in rendering the judgement they had. The recommendation that followed was that I undertake a more formal course of instruction and hire a tutor.

A Chinese colleague who gave a presentation on another occasion was given to understand, in no uncertain terms, that his presentation had been much too rambling and that the conclusion he presented did not follow from the rest of the presentation. These faults, the members of the audience reasoned, had resulted from a lack of focus. As in my case, the audience then began to engage in speculation on the reasons for my colleague's shortcomings. The hypothesis that the audience found most plausible was that his inability to deliver a satisfactory presentation was due to some lack in his Middle School education, a time when basic skills for organizing essays would normally have been taught. Conceivably, this was a part of the curriculum he had somehow missed or, more likely the case, to which he had not paid careful enough attention. This habit of delivering feedback with a personal edge is another example of where the line between private and public and between the employee's personal life and life in the company is much more fluid than it is in a Western corporate environment.

VECTORS OF CHANGE

The first part of this chapter offered a comparative assessment of Chinese and Western rhetorical traditions and highlighted differences between Chinese and Western (American) executive presentations, treating them as two separate and distinct systems. However, the most recent evolution of the two rhetorical systems, marked by the collapse of the imperial order in China at the end of the nineteenth century and the failure of the Republic in the early twentieth, has been characterized by their interaction. The catalyst for this interaction was the so-called "New Culture Movement" that took shape in the 1920s. The Movement's stated objective was to find replacements for traditional Chinese social, economic, political, and even rhetorical models that had proven ineffective or were woefully outdated. The group of intellectuals who launched and led the "New Culture Movement", many of whom had studied overseas, looked to the countries where they had lived and studied (e.g. Japan and the United States) as a source for new models and new ideas. One of the most pressing issues those focused on the reform of language and rhetoric faced was finding appropriate terms for innovations that were previously unavailable in China or expressions for concepts that simply did not exist. The framework for a new rhetorical system took shape in a series of presentations that John Dewey, a professor of social science at Columbia University, delivered during a lecture tour in China he undertook between 1919 and 1920. In his lectures, Dewey advocated the application of scientific method to the practice of rhetoric, an approach that stimulated new thinking about the purpose and practice of rhetoric in China and its application to composition and presentation. (Chang 2002, pages 51–53). The subsequent appearance of books such as Tang Yueh's "Rhetorical Style" ("xiucige") that introduced and promoted these new methods was concrete evidence for the influence of Anglo-American rhetoric in China in the early part of the twentieth century (Wu 2009, page 157).

Beginning in the early part of the twenty-first century, a hundred years later, we can discern the outlines of the next chapter in the story of interaction between Western rhetorical theory and Chinese practice. The focus of this chapter is on public speaking and presentation skills, competences that, for historical reasons, were not paid much heed within the Chinese rhetorical tradition (Kirkpatrick and Xu 2012, page 16). This change in focus and increase in exposure to Western methods of presentation, both written and spoken, tracks with a larger surge in demand for English language training. It also reflects a sharp increase in the employment of Chinese professionals in multinational corporations and participation in international conferences. At the forefront of the diffusion, communication, and adoption of these presentation methods and new rhetorical models are organizations dedicated to the promotion of public speaking, high-profile personalities regarded for their rhetorical acumen, and consultants engaged for the methods they have devised to enhance presentation skills.

Organizations

Founded in Santa Ana, California in 1924 by an educator named Ralph Smedley, the public speaking organization, Toastmasters, was originally conceived by Smedley as a set of classes designed to improve the communication skills of the young men he was responsible for educating. Today, the organization claims more than 300,000 members who have formed nearly 15,000 clubs in 126 countries (Brennan 2014). In China, Toastmasters has expanded rapidly, especially in major metropolitan areas (Beijing, Shanghai, Shenzhen, etc.), establishing hundreds of new chapters that have attracted thousands of new members eager to better their career prospects by improving their English language presentation skills. The "Shanghai #1 Toastmasters Club", one of the first clubs to open in China was chartered in 1999. Today, Shanghai hosts more than 150 Toastmaster clubs all of which adhere to a rigorous and consistent format that consists of structured presentations followed by evaluations and critiques.

Personalities

The degree to which Steve Jobs is revered in China verges on a cult. His image has been captured in media as august as marble statues and as pedestrian as rubber mousepads and he has been held up as a model for emulation by members of China's business community, especially the country's hi-tech industry whose executives imitate his products (smart phone knock-offs), dress (Xiaomi CEO, Lei Jun who has adopted Jobs signature turtleneck sweater), and speaking style (the presentation Jobs delivered at the Stanford University graduation ceremony in 2005 has been translated into Chinese and viewed by thousands). And as a measure of Jobs' impact on corporate communication, his presentation techniques have been analyzed, copied and adopted into the standard repertoire of presentation training consultants.

Consultants

There are hundreds of corporate trainers and coaches in China who preach the gospel of Western (American) presentation methods and principles such as making eye contact, use of gestures, and expressions (see Image 8.4) and, like their "New Culture Movement" predecessors, have introduced new terms, many adopted from English, to describe techniques and concepts that were not represented in the the traditional Chinese rhetorical canon.[18] The effect these influences are having on Chinese rhetoric and presentation can be detected in a marked trend; visually, towards more minimal design and greater ratio of images (graphics)

Image 8.4 Slide from presentation consultant guide (*Source* Choize Management Consulting Shanghai Co., Ltd.)

[18]Examples: "shenti yuyan" (body language), "pobing yanjiang" (ice breaker speech") etc.

to text in corporate presentations and on corporate websites and logically, in the way they are structured (Blondeau 2017).[19] Wang Chaobo's study of scientific articles submitted by Chinese and Western scientists to Mainland Chinese and American academic journals reveals that Chinese scientists in an increasing number of cases have adopted an approach to structuring presentations based on the "deductive" logic that was traditionally considered characteristic of Western rhetoric and composition (Kirkpatrick and Xu 2012 page 159).

CONCLUSION

A foreign employee who is tasked with developing a presentation for a Chinese executive should be aware that principles for communication are not universal and that a Chinese executive presentation follows rules and guidelines that depart from and, in some cases, even contradict what are considered "best practices" for presentation design in a Western corporate context. Some of the key principles the foreign employee should keep in mind when developing a presentation for a Chinese supervisor include.

Content and Delivery

- Portraying the Chinese executive as focused on the customer and on the immediate task of running a business.
- Positioning the Chinese executive as a teacher who has practical advice and words of wisdom to impart not as a statesman who is out to make the world a better place. Accordingly, the voice of the executive and the tone of the presentation should be pragmatic not visionary.
- Making liberal use of military metaphors and idioms that the presenter can draw on to exhort, galvanize, and encourage the members of the audience, an effect that a Western executive would typically achieve through the use of more physical methods, i.e. body language, eye contact, and gesture.

---

[19] However, this should not be interpreted as a complete abandoning of the information and data on a webpage.

Structure and Design

- Err on the side of including more text in a presentation under the understanding that the presentation is a source of information and reference for the members of the audience. Providing more data points and support information will increase the speaker's credibility and make the presentation more convincing.
- Dispense with subdued, neutral hues in favor of brighter colors whose desired effect is to create a more engaging and energetic presentation.
- Increase familiarity with Chinese symbolism and iconography to avoid references and design techniques that would be considered inappropriate (cf. positioning text within boxes delineated by dark borders).

Finally, the foreign employee should not be surprised if the supervisor's feedback following review of the presentation is direct, critical, and even personal.

To increase the likelihood that feedback will be positive by helping the foreign employee improve his or her understanding of the Chinese supervisor's expectations, the next chapter will consider the relationship between employee and supervisor from the supervisor's perspective.

REFERENCES

Blondeau, Jason, "Web Design Trends in China in 2018", *QPSoftware*, November 1, 2017, https://qpsoftware.net/webdesign-trends-china.

Brennan, Molly, "Toastmaster's Heads to Asia", *PCMA Convene*, November 1, 2014.

Chang, Changfu, "The Problem of the Public: John Dewey's Theory of Communication and Its Influence on Modern Chinese Communication", in Lu et al. (eds.) *Chinese Communications Studies:Contexts and Comparisons*, Chapter 3, 2002, pages 47–63.

Chen, G. H., and Chung, J., "The Impact of Confucianism on Organizational Communication", *Communication Quarterly*, Vol. 42, No. 2, 1994, pages 93–105 cited in Xing, Mingjie, Wang, Jinghui, and Spencer, Kenneth, "Raising Students Awareness of Cross-Cultural Contrastive Rhetoric in English Writing via and e-Learning Course", *Journal of Language Teaching and Technology*, Vol. 12, No. 2, June 2008, page 82.

Cheng, Yunnuo, and Nielsen, Jakob, "Are Chinese Websites too Complex ?", NN/g Nielsen Norman Group, November 6, 2016. https://www.nngroup.com/articles/china-website-complexity/.

Dong, Ying, and Lee, Kun-Pyo, "A Cross-Cultural Comparative Study of Users' Perceptions of a Webpage: With a Focus on the Cognitive Styles of Chinese, Koreans, and Americans", *International Journal of Design*, Vol. 2, No. 2, 2008.

Han, Feifei, "Metaphors in English and Chinese", *Academic Exchange Quarterly*, Vol. 21, No. 1, Spring 2017, pages 1–6.

Hawes, Colin, *The Chinese Transformation of Corporate Culture*, Routledge Contemporary China Series Book 82, Routledge, 2012.

Hu, Chunyu, and Xu, Yuting, "WAR Metaphor in the Chinese Economic Media Discourse", *Higher Education Studies* (Canadian Center of Science and Education), Vol. 7, No. 1, February 20, 2017, pages 94–106.

Kirkpatrick, Andy, "Chinese Rhetoric Through Chinese Texbooks: Uniquely Chinese ?", in Lu et al. (eds.) *Chinese Communications Studies*, Chapter 15, 2002, pages 244–260.

Kirkpatrick, Andy, and Xu, Zhichang, *Chinese Rhetoric and Writing: An Introduction for Language Teachers*, The WAC Clearinghouse and Parlor Press, Fort Collins, CO, 2012.

Lu, Xing, *Rhetoric of the Chinese Cultural Revolution: The Impact on Chinese Thought, Culture, and Communication*, University of South Carolina Press, 2016.

Lu, Xing, Jia, Wenshan, Heisey, D. Ray. (eds.), *Chinese Communications Studies: Contexts and Comparisons*, Praeger, Westport, 2002.

McGregor, Jena, "Executives Are Sharing More Details About Their Personal Lives", *Los Angeles Times*, December 20, 2015, https://www.latimes.com/business/la-fi-on-leadership-new-ceos-20151218-story.html.

Rajeck, Jeff, "Why Does Chinese Web Design Look so Busy ?" Econsultancy, February 10, 2016, https://econsultancy.com/why-does-chinese-web-design-look-so-busy-part-two/.

Sing-Bik Ngai, Cindy, and Singh, Rita Gill, "Communication with Stakeholders Through Corporate Websites: An Exploratory Study on the CEO Messages of Major Corporations in Greater China", *Journal of Business and Technical Communication*, Vol. 28, No. 3, 2014, pages 352–394.

Smith, Richard J., *China's Cultural Heritage: The Ch'ing Dynasty 1644–1912*, Westview Press, Boulder, CO, 1983 cited in: Kirkpatrick, Andy, and Xu, Zhichang, *Chinese Rhetoric and Writing: An Introduction for Language Teachers*, The WAC Clearinghouse and Parlor Press, Fort Collins, CO, 2012 (Chapter 2: Literary Background and Rhetorical Styles).

Sprawson, Charles. *Haunts of the Black Masseur: The Swimmer as Hero*, Pantheon, New York 1992.

Sun, Ya, and Jiang, Jilin, "Metaphor Use in Chinese and US Corporate Mission Statements: A Cognitive Sociolinguistic Analysis", *English for Specific Purposes*, Vol. 33, 2014, Pages 4–14.

Taylor, Dan, "Why Are Chinese Website Designs so Different ?" (blog), December 13, 2018.

Theriault, Michael, "5 Principles for Making Powerpoint Slides with Impact", *Forbes*, November, 25, 2011.

Thibaud, "Chinese Website Design vs. Western Website Design", Daxue Consulting (blog), July 20, 2016. https://daxueconsulting.com/market-analysis-chinese-website-design/.

Wang, Dongshuo, Wang, Jinghui, and Xing, Minjie, "Metaphorical Thinking in Engilsh and Chinese Languages", *Asian Culture and History*, Vol. 3, No. 2, 2011.

Wu, Hui, "Lost and Found in Transnation: Modern Conceptualization of Chinese Rhetoric", *Rhetoric Review*, Vol. 28, No. 2, 2009, Pages 148–166.

Xing, Minjie, Wang, Jinghui, and Spencer, Kenneth, "Raising Students' Awareness of Cross-Cultural Contrastive Rhetoric in English Writing via an e-Learning Course", *Journal of Language Learning and Technology*, Vol.12, No. 2, June 2008, pages 71–96.

Zhang, Jie, "Linguistic, Ideological, and Cultural Issues in Chinese and English Argumentative Writings" *Journal of Language Teaching and Research*, Vol. 2, No. 1, January 2011, pages 73–80.

CHAPTER 9

Reverse Angle

The picture that has emerged from previous chapters is a composite drawn from the historical record, from profiles of industries and companies, and from the day-to-day experiences of foreign employees. In current form, it is a source of background, context, and insight that the foreign employee can apply to negotiate challenges in the workplace, be an effective communicator, and even come out on top in a stretcher race. What it doesn't do is offer any insight into the relationship with a Chinese supervisor, undoubtedly the most consequential relationship that a foreign employee in a Chinese company is likely to have. The goal of this chapter, then, is to complete the picture by bringing the Chinese boss's profile into clearer focus and in so doing provide the foreign employee with an appreciation for the boss's view of the world. However, before engaging in a more detailed study of the supervisor's expectations, challenges, concerns and motivations there is the basic and very practical issue of how to approach the Chinese boss and take first critical steps on the road to building a satisfactory relationship.

THE RIGHT FOOT

Like any new hire, the foreigner who has just begun working at a Chinese company will want to get their relationship with a Chinese supervisor off on the right foot. To ensure a good first impression the foreign employee can turn to one of a number of resources that offer tips

© The Author(s) 2020
P. Ross, *Barriers to Entry*,
https://doi.org/10.1007/978-981-32-9566-7_9

on the best approach to take. These 'prescriptions for success' generally fall into one of three basic categories: *Etiquette*, *Respect* and *Protocol*:

Etiquette: Reach for your boss's hand first. "A high-ranking person in the company should never, ever initiate a handshake," counsels Brian Su, the head of a global market consulting firm (Spitznagel 2012).

Respect: Maintain a limp grip. "Most Chinese think of handshakes as excessive touching," cautions Lyudmila Bloch an expert on cross-cultural etiquette. A limp grip connotes humility and respect (Spitznagel 2012).

Protocol: The foreign employee who has successfully negotiated the first handshake and wants to remain in the good graces of a Chinese boss can refer to a number of guides that describe proper protocol, typically presented as a set of proscriptions:

- Do not escalate every question you have up to your boss, especially in a company that has a clear management structure. Rather, discuss the matter with your direct supervisor first; he or she may report to the boss and speak on your behalf.
- Do not challenge your boss too often, as it will make them think that you are deliberately questioning their authority, and cause them to lose face.
- Do not shoot down your boss's ideas too quickly, especially not in front of a group. Avoid definitive statements such as "No," "It's not practical," "It won't work," and so on. Explain your opinion by blaming outside issues or other factors; never imply that it is your boss's fault, even if it really, blatantly is.

Anticipating that in their eagerness to establish good relations with their Chinese boss foreign employees may go too far in applying such proscriptions, cultural consultant Claudia Ju admonishes foreign employees not to confuse 'sucking up' with 'building rapport' (Ju 2017). She cautions that the foreign employee who mistakes one for the other is bound to fail because "they [Chinese bosses]", according to Ju, "can tell your intention easily" (Ju 2017). This pronouncement, and others like it, that profess to lift the veil on the mind of the Chinese boss, ironically perpetuate the myth within which the boss is shrouded. In this case the boss is depicted as an omniscient being vested with powers of cognition so evolved that he can 'easily' intuit an employee's intentions (and a foreign one, at that!). Of potentially greater value to the foreign employee is Ju's subsequent revelation that there is a much easier way to maintain good relations with a Chinese boss. "All you have to do," she confides, "is work on your job well as it is after all your boss's KPI" (Key Performance Indicator). This attempt to distill all the complexity of a relationship that spans very different cultures and organizational levels into a single kernel of wisdom, unfortunately, yields a statement so generic that it could just as easily pass for a description of the relationship between employee and manager in a Western company. It also lays bare the inherent limitations of the epigrammatic form that such guides favor as a vehicle for imparting words of wisdom. The statements are so condensed that they offer little practical insight and so short on detail that they gloss over issues that should be given more serious attention. A foreign employee's ability to deliver the kind of job performance that is good enough to satisfy a Chinese supervisor and meet the requirements of a Chinese supervisor's KPI assumes that the employee has a clear definition of what the job entails and a clear understanding of the supervisor's expectations. As cases introduced in previous chapters have demonstrated, neither a clear definition nor clear expectations can be taken for granted. To assume otherwise would be to make an assumption that is ill-advised.

Arguably more essential to building rapport with a Chinese supervisor than ruminating over the intricacies of managerial protocol and obsessing over the most appropriate grip to apply when shaking hands is the issue of how to address the boss, an item that escapes the attention of the guides referenced. In any organization, especially one as complex as that of a Chinese enterprise, a familiarity with forms of address is important because their correct usage demonstrates an understanding of organizational dynamics and enables the employee to navigate more effectively within that organizational structure. In fact, a Chinese corporate organization has many designations for executives, each one of which conveys a specific meaning while defining a scope of responsibility.

THE RIGHT ADDRESS

Given that providing instruction did not feature anywhere in the definition of my boss's scope of responsibilities, "Teacher Zhu", the title everyone in the organization used to address him, seemed to be a misnomer. By way of explanation, a colleague who had worked with 'Teacher Zhu' for years suggested that the title was the vestige of a role he had played earlier in his career as a subject matter expert called upon when and as needed to advise those who were engaged in the preparation of complex commercial bids. Over time I came to understand that "Teacher", in this context, was meant as a term of respect rather than a reference to a particular calling. It was at once a testament to the length of my boss's tenure in the company (a career that spanned more than two decades) and a recognition of his seniority (in his 50's he was somewhat older than those for whom he worked and those who worked for him).

From personal names to official designations, Chinese titles are rich in meaning and variety. In a society notorious for its complexity, titles serve as a convenient and indispensable index that enables members of the society to understand where they fit in and divine the nature of the relationships that connect them with others. Even the most elemental units of Chinese social nomenclature—an individual's family name ('Xing') and given name ('Ming')—can contain a layer of deictic 'meta-data' that fixes the individual's position within an immediate family structure as well as within the larger generational cohort into which they have been born. In traditional society, it was not uncommon for Chinese to adopt a supplementary 'courtesy name' ('Hao') that was used as a common form of address among acquaintances and associates. Orders of magnitude more complex and varied than the naming conventions individuals adhered to were the titles used in the Chinese civil service to designate the ranks and levels of the officials who staffed its various bureaus and ministries. At more than 8000 entries, historian Charles Hucker's monumental dictionary of Chinese bureaucratic organizational structures and official titles is still considered by some to be incomplete (Hucker 1995). In a corporate organization, titles, if not nearly as complex and varied as their counterparts in the civil service and imperial administration, are nevertheless just as meaningful and worthy of further consideration (see Table 9.1 for common corporate titles in Chinese with English equivalent).

The honorifics and titles that fill out these lists are convenient placeholders for the organizational structures they represent and, if for no other reason than this, should be part of the Chinese corporate vocabulary with which any foreign employee is acquainted. In the end, however, it is nothing more than a two-dimensional list that offers no insight into the appropriate way to address the holder of one of these titles. Nor does it provide any understanding of the organizational and political subtleties that a title implies. This is a critical reference for the foreign employee to

Table 9.1 Common corporate titles (Chinese–English)

CORPORATE ORGANIZATION TITLES		
English	**Chinese**	**Chinese Transcription (Pinyin)**
Chairman of the Board	董事会主席	dǒngshìhuìzhǔxí
President of the Board	董事长	dǒngshìzhǎng
Vice President of the Board	副董事长	fù dǒng shì zhǎng
Board Director	董事	dǒngshì
President	总裁	zǒngcái
Executive Vice President	执行副总裁	zhíxíng fùzǒngcái
CEO	首席执行官/执行总监	shǒuxí zhíxíngguān/zhíxíng zǒngjiān
COO	首席营运官/营运总监	shǒuxí yíngyùnguān/yíngyùn zǒngjiān
CFO	首席财务官/财务总监	shǒuxí cáiwùguān/cáiwù zǒngjiān
CTO	首席技术官/技术总监	shǒuxí jìshùguān/jìshù zǒngjiān
CMO	首席营销官/营销总监	shǒuxí yíngxiāoguān/yíngxiāo zǒngjiān
General Manager	总经理	zǒngjīnglǐ
Vice-general Manager	副总经理	fùzǒngjīnglǐ
Manager	经理	jīnglǐ
Operations Manager	营运经理	yíngyùnjīnglǐ

https://www.hierarchystructure.com/chinese-business-hierarchy/

have, especially if the holder happens to be the foreign employee's supervisor. As a guide and aid for the foreign employee, an introduction to a few of the more common and, for the foreign employee, most pertinent forms of address follow:

"Zong"

Even a cursory review of the common executive titles listed in the accompanying table (Table 9.1) reveals a preponderance in use of the term 'Zong'. Indeed, 'Zong' appears in literally every Chinese version of a 'C-Suite' title (e.g. 'Zong Jingli', 'Zongcai', etc.). In a Chinese corporate organization, 'Zong' is the most common form of executive address and is broadly applied to virtually every executive, regardless of the executive's level, rank or position. In standard usage the term is appended to the executive's family name. An executive whose family name is "Wang", for example, is appropriately addressed as "Wang Zong". The case where the title is used in conjunction with the executive's given name also exists (e.g. 'Lixin Zong'), but this usage is exceptional and only invoked to avoid confusion when two executives in an organization have the same surname.

Considered in its own right, "Zong" is an adjective most frequently used to convey comprehensiveness, completeness, and entirety. When used in a corporate environment to designate a member of the organization who has managerial responsibility, it conveys a sense of complete or comprehensive authority. The application of 'Zong' in this context predates the founding of the People's Republic of China. Already in use during China's Republic Era (1912–1949) the term appeared most commonly in the titles of senior officials in the Chinese Civil Service who held a post of some responsibility and consequence.

"Lao Ban"

Usage of the term "Lao Ban", the general term by which employees in a Chinese organization both refer to and address their boss, is not confined exclusively to a large enterprise but is more broadly applied to designate the proprietor of any commercial establishment (restaurant, small shop, etc.) irrespective of size or stature. Important for the foreign employee to bear in mind is that in a meeting the "Lao Ban" always occupies a place at the head of the table and that when the 'Lao Ban' stops by an employee's desk, even if just for a quick update or brief discussion, the employee by habit and convention stands in the Lao Ban's presence.

According to a number of sources, the term 'Lao Ban' had its origins in the print shops of the Qing Dynasty, but made its first public appearance in the theater. "Ban", in the printers' taxonomy of the nineteenth century, referred to the plates used in the production of printed material,[1] Despite its mundane application the printing plate captured the imagination of a

---

[1] *Note* an alternative derivation is based on use of the "ban" to refer to the covers that proprietors of stalls in markets would draw down over their wares to protect them from thieves

local theater troupe who saw in the role that the plate played in the printing process a meaning that transcended its basic functionality. Because the printing plate was, in effect, the template from which all subsequent copies were made, the actors recognized it as the embodiment of 'authenticity' and 'originality'. As such the they decided it was an apt metaphor for their master Cheng Zhanggeng, one of the foremost interpreters of Peking Opera at the time, whose unique talent was a model for others to copy. To eliminate the potential for any confusion or any implication of impropriety that might arise from likening their esteemed master to a lowly printing plate, the actors took the precaution of adding the honorific "Lao", thereby imbuing the form of address with the degree of respect befitting a master and ensuring that "Ban" was understood in its metaphoric sense, not its functional one.

Like other actors of his stature and experience, Cheng was also responsible for the troupe's overall management and direction. As a form of address, 'Lao Ban' adapted itself to this dual role and was applied agnostically to both "Master Cheng" the actor and "Master Cheng" the director. Over time it was the managerial application of the term that become the predominant one with the theatrical reference eventually relegated to an intriguing historical footnote.

"Laoshi"

Although most commonly used as a term of respect that recognizes a member's seniority and tenure, 'Laoshi' can in fact be used more broadly as a form of address for anyone in the organization who instructs others and imparts knowledge. However, when used in this broader context the title is conferred only for the duration of time within which the instruction is conducted and not maintained as a form of address after the period of instruction has ended. This more restrictive application of the term "Laoshi", in a corporate context, comes closest to its original use as a designator for someone who instructed others in a given subject area. In ancient times, the subject in question was, very often, of a religious nature. During the Cultural Revolution, when teaching in its traditional form was denigrated and those who engaged in its practice reviled, the term was shunned or, if used, had pejorative connotations.

and from the elements. The metoymy to stand for the proprietor. There is more direct connection to commerce, but less intriguing (see Li, Mingjie, "Zhui Gen Su Jue" 6:45).

In the aftermath of the Cultural Revolution, 'Laoshi' as a form of respectful address was reinstated consistent with the overall restoration of China's educational system. Coincident with its re-emergence as a positive term, "laoshi" underwent a semantic transformation. In its post-revolutionary incarnation 'Laoshi' became fashionable as a form of address by those who were members of intellectual circles and denoted someone who possessed an artistic or literary skill or talent.

Titles That Are Off the Charts

The use of nicknames or alternative names, to be more precise, has a rich tradition in China. These names very often ranged from familiar to offbeat, but they could also be quite thoughtful and sophisticated. Artists and scholars were known to adopt names that included reference to a place that was meaningful or relevant to the person it designated, typically the location of the artist's studio or a scholar's residence. Employees in a Chinese workplace don't have a habit of taking alternative names that incorporate the corporate brand, but in keeping with tradition and social convention they do very often adopt nicknames that can take many different forms and guises.

Many Chinese executives have adopted English names and will often use those names when introducing themselves to foreign staff, expecting in return that foreign staff will use these adopted names when addressing them. This usage is a sign of how widespread and popular English has become in China, a mark of sophistication, and perhaps an attempt to make life easier for the foreign employee.

A less common but no less intriguing case that illustrates the way in which alternative names are used in the workplace is that of Alibaba whose management, inspired and encouraged by founder Jack Ma, have adopted names drawn from Chinese traditional martial arts ("Wuxia"). Feng Qingyang, Xiaoyaozi, Tiemuzhen, the names for Jack Ma and senior executives Daniel Zhang and Jonathan Lu respectively demonstrate how essential the martial arts culture is to the company's culture. The intent behind the adoption of these alternative names is to instill a sense of belonging and team spirit. Despite the enthusiasm with which management and staff have adopted these names, there are some who caution that this usage is reminiscent of techniques used by cults to secure the allegiance of their followers (Lee 2018).

Knowing how to approach and address the Chinese boss is a good first step, for getting things off on the right foot, but to sustain the relationship and meet a Chinese supervisor's expectations, the foreign employee needs to have a better understanding of the supervisor's motivations, concerns, and aspirations.

DIMENSIONS OF LEADERSHIP

"You should be like seeds going to places where you are most needed, put down roots, germinate, flower and bear fruit." Ren Zhengfei's vision for international expansion has inspired generations of Huawei managers to go out into the world and evangelize the company's products and services to customers in countries from Algeria to Zimbabwe.[2] Articulating such a vision is one thing; realizing it quite another.

As Ren himself would admit, managers who have the personal qualities and professional qualifications that would make them suitable candidates for overseas assignments don't just grow on trees. Identifying appropriate candidates, assessing their potential, and providing them with adequate training is a significant challenge for any company and often beyond the reach of the average Chinese enterprise whose overseas operations are of modest scale and whose Human Resources department typically lacks personnel with the experience necessary to adapt the company's domestic human resource management system to an international environment (Shen and Edwards 2004, page 816).

Consistent with research conducted into other aspects of Chinese society, studies of Chinese management and evaluations of Chinese leadership are, as a rule, rife with references to traditional Chinese culture and philosophy. However, there are a number that have made an assessment of traditional Chinese thought's impact on modern management practice a more exclusive focus (Ma and Tsui 2015; Miedtank 2017, page 82, Chen and Lee 2008). Ma and Tsui, as representative, draw a direct line from the precepts of Daoism, Confucianism, and Legalism to the principles of Chinese corporate management and posit that the style of management a Chinese leader practices bears the imprint of the particular philosophical school to which he or she adheres (Ma and Tsui 2015, page 14). The brand of management to which a leader who is

[2]Ren, Zhengfei, 你们要像种子一样,到最需要的地方去,生根、发芽、开花、结果,再成片开成花海。部分勇敢的人,要到最艰苦的地方去快速成长.

an adherent of Daoism subscribes, for example, is likely to be authentic, empowering, or 'laissez-faire' (Ma and Tsui 2015, page 16). A leader who is of a more Confucian persuasion has an inclination for a leadership style that is transformational, paternalistic, and differentiated (LMX)[3] (Ma and Tsui 2015, page 16). A variation on this tradition-centric approach are studies that refine the basic premise of a correspondence between ancient wisdom and modern management practice with a demographic overlay, drawing out distinctions between the management practice of Chinese executives who took on leadership roles on either side of the economic reforms initiated in the 1980's (Ralston 1999; Zhang et al. 2014, page 206; Cheng et al. 2004, page 97). The general conclusion these studies arrive at is that the cohort of Chinese corporate executives who moved into positions of leadership prior to the period of opening and reform have demonstrated a preference for a management practice guided by traditional values. By contrast, executives who have assumed leadership roles during the reform period have shown themselves to be less beholden to the past and more overtly "individualistic". Ralston closes the circle that connects the behavioral tendency of the younger generation with their attitude towards the past through his observation that their desire for independence comes "at some cost to their Confucian values" (Ralston et al. 1999, page 424).

Perhaps inspired by the departure from traditional practice this younger generation of Chinese leaders has taken, more recent studies of managerial behavior consider Chinese management in relation to management as practiced in corporate environments that are depicted as more "advanced" or "mature", an oblique reference to Western multinationals. Analyzing the effect that management theories tempered in the halls of Western academic institutions and management principles burnished in the boardrooms of MNCs have had on the leadership style of Chinese executives occupies a place of highest attention (Warner and Rowley 2010, page 282; Gao et al. 2011; Zhang et al. 2008; Wang et al. 2014). The general conclusion these studies come to is that Western theories bring greater "scientific rigor" to traditional Chinese management practice and introduce a more 'structured' approach to corporate disciplines such as Marketing. Fang's examination of the factors and characteristics

---

[3] *Leader-Member Exchange* (LMX)—analyzes how leaders and managers develop relationships with members of their teams and explains how those relationships can either contribute to or constrain growth by encouraging employees or holding them back.

that shape and define the management practice of younger Chinese managers—greater access to sources of information, new commercial models, and educational opportunities outside of China—bridges demographic-based studies with those that consider the impact on Chinese management of Western theory and practice (Fang et al. 2008, page 143).

A more recent permutation on the assessment of the relationship between Chinese and Western business practice, presumably a function of China's increasing economic power and leadership in a growing number of industrial sectors, are studies that promote a re-evaluation of Chinese management principles, valorizing them as an effective, acceptable, and appropriate style of management within the context of local corporate organizations (Sanchez-Runde et al. 2011) and positioning them as a source of lessons and emulation for Western managers, leaders and companies (Lynton 2013). Looking to the future, King and Zhang find evidence for the convergence of Eastern (Chinese) and Western management practice, a phenomenon that is becoming increasingly prevalent as executives who stand on one side of the cultural fence gain an appreciation for the advantages and applicability of the management practice of those on the other (King and Zhang 2014, page 13).

Conspicuous by their absence from the manifest of formative influences on Chinese management practice are references to the Cultural Revolution. This omission is especially glaring since many of those who today hold senior leadership positions in Chinese companies would have spent their formative years in its shadow and presumably been imprinted by the experience. Ralston's general observation that "the generation in which one grew up appears to be crucial to understanding the values of Chinese managers" implies, by extrapolation, that the Cultural Revolution is relevant to the management practice of Chinese executives now in mid-career who came of age during this decade of social turmoil. All but one of the Chinese CEOs Shaomin Li interviewed as part of his analysis of Mao's influence on the management practice of Chinese corporate leaders (one of a very few such studies), admitted that they turned regularly to Mao's teachings for management guidance. The way that guidance manifested itself, Li found, was as a tendency towards secrecy and a habit of bypassing formal decision making processes (Li and Yeh 2007, page 1). These tendencies and habits translated into actions that could be quite disruptive to the organization. An example of an action that CEOs who fit the profile initiated, involved mobilizing lower-level employees to criticize and undermine upper level executives as a way of keeping the executives in a state of uncertainty and therefore more pliant. Taking these points to their logical conclusion it is hard to imagine that executives who experienced nearly a decade of aggressive attacks on traditional Chinese values would have emerged from that ten-year period with Confucian principles intact much less looked to Confucius as a primary source for management guidance as many of the studies previously referenced suggest.

Of particular relevance to the foreign employee whose Chinese supervisor fits this demographic profile, is the recognition that the boss, in all likelihood, experienced direct attacks on foreign value systems that, assuming the previous discussion and hypothesis is valid, presumably would have had a similar effect on their management practice. The effect of this exposure to anti-foreign rhetoric would have been reinforced through exposure to similarly oriented follow-on campaigns that persist even into the current era[4] and exacerbated by an overall erosion of trust that a number of studies have highlighted as one of the Cultural Reviolution's most common and long-lasting psychological effects (Wang 2017, page 23). The conclusion one draws from these references is that it is quite likely the number of executives in Chinese companies who harbor, even if subconsciously, a lingering distrust of foreigners is not small and that this deeply embedded lack of trust could have an influence on the way they manage foreign staff. This is a discussion that is undeniably speculative and validation of the hypothesis on which it is based would require further study. Whether or not Chinese firms recognize the existence of such an issue, it is clear they are refining the criteria they use to select managers who are comfortable managing non-Chinese staff and whose efforts are most likely to bear fruit in environments that may be quite foreign to them.

SELECTION CRITERIA

Based on What and Who You Know

Consistent with the central role that cultural adaptation and transmission play in Huaneng's international strategy, the company stipulates that any candidate under consideration for an overseas posting be thoroughly

---

[4](Cf. advisories that have appeared prominently in public venues (metro stations, bus stops, etc.) exhorting passengers, pedestrians, and drivers to be vigilant and exercise caution when interacting with foreign nationals whom the advisories caution may, despite appearances to the contrary, be spies seeking to extract sensitive information from unsuspecting Chinese citizens).

familiar with the company's culture. The underlying assumption is that employees who meet these conditions can effectively communicate the company's corporate culture to local staff in offices overseas. Implicit in this requirement is that the ideal candidate has achieved significant tenure in the company. Huawei prioritizes the following competences as the ones those taking up posts in overseas locations should possess: (1) Language skill (2) Ability to work cross culturally (3) Ability to handle challenges arising from globalization (Peng 2013). A survey conducted with a broader cross-section of Chinese companies with international ambitions ranked the following criteria as among the most important: (1) Domestic track record (2) Management skill or technical competence (3) Language ability (4) Education (Shen and Edwards 2004, page 827). Not appearing in any formal list, but considered by many to be the most decisive factor for selection is, not surprisingly, the candidate's relationship to senior management.[5] Selection based on the strength of relationships is, of course, not entirely unknown in Western companies. However, there are a number of ways in which the conditions in Chinese companies differ.

There is a tendency among those in Chinese firms charged with determining a manager's candidacy and fitness for an overseas assignment to take a "one-size-fits-all" approach. In other words, the same set of parameters are used as criteria for evaluation in each case regardless of the specific characteristics of the market and conditions of the assignment or the background, knowledge, experience or particular interests of the participants.

Based on How You Feel

A growing trend among Asian companies towards assigning heavier weighting to a more "human touch" when evaluating the profile of potential expat managers is somewhat less pronounced among Chinese companies studied (Allen et al. 2013, page 2). In addition, Chinese companies tended to attribute less importance than a Western multinational would, to traits such as creativity, cultural empathy, emotional stability

---

[5] Shen and Edwards note that in many cases top management is under "great pressure to assign employees who have a good relationship with senior management" in Shen and Edwards, "Recruitment and Selection in Chinese MNEs", *International Journal of Human Resource Management*, Vol. 15, No. 4, August 2004, page 828.

and maturity when assessing a candidate's fitness for an overseas post. (Shen and Edwards 2004, page 831). As another point of difference, the candidate's family circumstances, considered within the scope of the assessment conducted by Western multinationals, typically fall outside the scope of assessments conducted by Chinese firms. Many Chinese firms consider family arrangements to be the sole responsibility and concern of the candidate and, strictly speaking, outside the perimeter of the assignment as defined (Shen and Edwards 2004, page 831; Zhong et al., page 294).[6] This inclusion of personal criteria in the considerations of the Western firms and their exclusion from those of the Chinese is a curious reversal of position given the tendency among Chinese firms, in general, to see personal and work realms as more integral parts of a larger whole rather than more clearly demarcated as they are in Western firms (see Chapter 5—"Living To Work". It is an anomaly that is perhaps explained by the expectation, implicit in the conditions of the assignment, that the manager will be taking the assignment alone and the tendency of Chinese firms to prioritize candidates in the selection process who will not be distracted from the job at hand by family-related concerns (Fei 2015, page 34). The presumption that Chinese managers who take overseas postings under such circumstances are not as affected by an absence of family as Western expatriates might because Chinese managers are "used to it" is revealed to be faulty when direct feedback from the Chinese expatriates themselves is solicited. A study of Chinese expatriates working in offices overseas noted that those interviewed who had spouses and children to take care of made mention of the related challenges they face and anxieties they experience (Yu 2016, page 94). The burden of family care weighs especially heavily on younger expatriates who, as a consequence of the "One Child" policy China enacted in the 1980's, are predominantly single children who are, therefore, solely responsible for aging parents in addition to spouse and children. In interviews conducted with Chinese expats, it becomes clear that family issues are consequential and have a direct impact on an expat manager's performance and level of satisfaction. The presence of family can be a significant source of both emotional

---

[6]Both Shen and Edwards and Zhong et al. emphasize lack of consideration for family situations in the expatriate selection process of Chinese companies. Zhong et al. cite Stone (2010) for evidence of a similar tendency among Japanese firms. Shen and Edwards cite Tung's finding (1982) that 41% of European MNEs "interviewed both candidate and spouse".

and practical support: "My wife came here with me and stayed with me for two months, which was extremely helpful. She helped to deal with the living issues..." (Yu 2016). Conversely, a family's absence can be a significant source of stress and dissatisfaction: "It was challenging for the entire family to balance out the expatriate's professional career and personal life, which was one of the main sources of stress and worries for the Chinese expatriates" (Yu 2016, page 97). One reason the personal circumstances of a candidate under consideration for an overseas assignment in a Chinese company gets such short shrift is that the candidate has much less input into the conditions for their assignment than a Western expatriate would expect to have.

No Right of Refusal

In their study of the conditions under which Chinese managers are selected for overseas postings, Shen and Edwards found that, in many cases, the identification and evaluation of candidates was assigned to a small committee referred to as a 'work-group'. At the conclusion of its deliberations, the 'work group' invited the candidate it deemed worthy of such an assignment to an 'interview'. However, the intent of the 'interview' was not to solicit the candidate's views and supplement the assessment already conducted, standard practice in a Western multinational, but rather to inform the candidate of the committee's decision, effectively a *fait accompli*, and communicate the expectations associated with the post and related conditions. The candidate's agreement was usually not solicited, but taken as a foregone conclusion. This practice of entrusting the decision for an overseas assignment to a small workgroup that comes to resolution without taking the candidate's input into consideration recalls the account of the AGLA participant in Chapter 6—"Bamboo Ceiling" who was invited to a meeting ostensibly convened to discuss his career progression only to find that the members of the small workgroup assembled had already decided among themselves the next career step he would take with little regard for his perspective or thoughts. Given the circumstances, the turnover rate for Chinese expat managers is surprisingly low. At 4% it is substantially lower than the turnover rates among expat managers of Western multinationals (Shen and Edwards 2004, page 828). Some explanation for this low turnover rate can be found in the motivations of Chinese expatriate managers for taking overseas assignments:

Prestige: In many Chinese enterprises an overseas assignment carries a certain amount of prestige. A key attractor and primary source of value is the higher compensation that such a posting typically carries. In addition to this immediate benefit is the prospect of a promotion or a position with more responsibility in the longer term.[7] **Skills and Experience**: In line with the view of many Chinese companies that foreign assignments are a training ground for high potentials and their active support for "learning by doing", there is also the general benefit of getting a different cultural experience, learning new skills, and broadening horizons. The clear benefits, both tangible and perceived, that those assigned to overseas posts associate with them offers some explanation for why the workgroup charged with selection of candidates doesn't feel an obligation to solicit their agreement. It's taken for granted.

GAPS IN EDUCATION

The author of a position paper entitled "Human Resources Challenge of Huawei—Culture Clash", perhaps motivated by aspiration of becoming a cross-cultural training consultant, offered a set of recommendations for ways in which Huawei could structure its expatriate management training program "to more effectively promote communication and understanding among people of different cultural backgrounds" ("Human resources challenge"). The crux of the proposal, that Huawei should consider offering "seminars, language training, books, websites, and discussion", reads more like a laundry list than anything actionable or of much value to a Human Resources manager facing the challenge of ensuring that managers have what they need prior to departing for an overseas office. Luckily, Huawei, and other Chinese companies, give much more thought to preparing their managers for overseas assignments than those who draft 'recommendations' such as these.

The standard training that Huawei offers expatriate managers consists of three phases: *Pre-departure*—that covers language instruction, cross-cultural training, and functional briefing; *On-site*—supplemental local cultural briefing and mentorship. *Repatriation*—The company supplements training in the classroom (especially for language improvement)

---

[7] *Note* despite the potential for future promotions that overseas postings carry, there some studies that indicate repatriation for expat managers in Chinese companies does not always end well and often fails to meet expectations.

with online courses offered through the company's internal "Huawei University" platform (Fei 2015, page 34)

The training program Huaneng has developed to support those who will be managing foreign staff in locations overseas features a curriculum that is designed to supplement the base of acquired knowledge and experience participants already possess with instruction in cross-cultural management, leadership, and language. In line with company strategy, the training program is optimized for cultural transmission. Striking the right balance between transmitting the company's culture while adapting to local conditions is a theme common to all elements of the curriculum. It reflects the company's recognition of the likelihood that a management model employed by a Chinese state-owned enterprise will encounter resistance when applied overseas and realization that foreign staff may never have worked with Chinese people, let alone for them. To guide its expat managers the company is very prescriptive in its definition of where the point of equilibrium lies. "Take advantage of strength in product knowledge and technical expertise and follow the foreign companies for financial matters, risk management, and strategic planning" is the expression of a general principle based on the common wisdom that the most effective way to gain the respect and confidence of foreign staff is to demonstrate superior technical skills and competence while demonstrating a willingness to learn. In line with the balance they are trying to achieve, Huaneng management encourages expat managers, who are striving for the optimal congruence of "demonstrating" and "learning" the company advocates, to take an "open, innovative, and confident approach" to their work overseas. At the same time it cautions them against adopting a 'Western' management style (Huaneng 2013).

An Accenture report on the globalization of Asian multinationals highlights the Eagle Training Program of Chinese electronics maker TCL as a success case. The effectiveness of the program lies in its integration of four areas deemed critical to success in managing business overseas: International operations, Strategic thinking, Leadership, Business group management (Allen et al. 2013, page 6). In recognition of what Wang et al. refer to as "institutional factors" (Wang et al. 2013, page 3821) the Eagle Training Program is structured in tiers that correspond to the diverse needs and competences of its participants.

Despite the progress that has been made in developing these programs (as exemplified by Huawei, Huaneng, and TCL) and the best efforts of those who are charged with their delivery, the training for overseas assignments provided by the vast majority of Chinese companies is not sufficiently adequate or effective. The managers who are the recipients of these training programs very often find that what they are taught in the classroom does not adequately prepare them for what they encounter in the field. "The lecturers keep on talking pure theory and that gives us little help in solving our managerial problems at work" (Sun and Ross 2009, page 105), is a comment lifted from the feedback provided by a group of Chinese managers sent to the U.K. for intensive cross-cultural training. The frustration it expresses is symptomatic of what Sun and Ross identify as a "consistent" insufficient assessment of needs and poor coordination between the company management and training staff as well as the intermediaries who serve as organizers and agents (Sun and Ross 2009, page 112). The practical consequence that this pedagogical disconnect has for the Chinese expatriate's ability to work effectively in an overseas post is most clearly evident in the area of communications. "Many American people are not quite direct sometimes, which is different from what I learned about the 'direct' communications in America. I made a lot of mistakes because of that notion" (Yu 2016, page 80), said one Chinese expat manager interviewed, representative of many. A candid remark from another: "The other day during a meeting with the team...I made some comments that seemed too critical" (Yu 2016, page 92) is another instance of inadequate awareness of the local environment and conditions. It raises the possibility that persistent characterizations of 'bad' Chinese bosses may, in fact, be a misperception that results from a misunderstanding of the situation the Chinese boss finds themselves in and the challenges he or she faces. A boss who comes across as too critical, or exhibits some other behavior that appears inappropriate. may, in reality, just be struggling to find their footing and not consciously trying to antagonize or insult the foreign staff who work for them.

Culture

Another area where a discrepancy between theory and practice exists is in the degree of cultural difference that Chinese expatriate managers believe separates them from the local staff they will be working with. The training that Chinese expatriate managers participate in prior to assuming their overseas assignments tends to focus on the cultural difference they are likely to encounter and present strategies they can invoke to address them. It can therefore be a revelation to many Chinese managers, once they are on the ground, to discover how many points in common they have with the local staff who are working for them. An expatriate manager working for Huawei in Belgium noted that he had "mentally prepared" for a culture shock only to find he "didn't meet any[culture shock], or not much" (Fei 2015, page 35). Similarities range from broader social characteristics: "American culture is complicated just like the Chinese culture" (Yu 2016, page 92) and a common prioritization of family relationships: "family values are also very important in Portugal, they often have family parties" (Liu 2015, page 35) to the more mundane such as the discovery of Chinese expat managers in Portugal that their Portuguese staff also ate rice and even enjoyed sunflower seeds (Liu 2015, page 35).

Language

Language instruction, at or near the top of the priority list of any training program for Chinese managers, is commonly cited by expatriates as the competence on which their effectiveness in an overseas post was most directly dependent. However, it was also the area where they felt they were consistently least prepared for experience in the field. In offices where English was the native language of the country to which they has been posted, Chinese expatriate managers found that daily usage bore little resemblance to the formal English they were exposed to in the classroom. The speed at which the language was spoken posed an additional impediment to comprehension. More often than not managers were assigned to offices in countries where English was not the local language. In these cases, English was invariably the language Chinese management and local staff had in common and was therefore the most expedient means of communication. The challenge the Chinese expatriate managers encountered was that the English the local staff spoke was often a non-standard variant whose idiosyncratic grammar and pronunciation could deviate quite significantly from the standard with which the Chinese managers were more familiar.

In light of these challenges and the degree of difficulty involved in developing and structuring a satisfactory training program, quite a number of Chinese companies with operations overseas have simply opted for a 'learning-through-doing' approach and expect that the manager will develop global capabilities and acquire international experience "on the job" (Zhong et al. 2015, page 295). A general manager at USAC, Sinochem's chemical subsidiary in the U.S. stated that one of the motivations for the acquisition was to have a "solid training base" (Wang 2006, page 153). In these cases, and many others like them, the local office that is the Chinese expatriate's place of work doubles as a cross-cultural training center and laboratory that the manager can take advantage of to develop skills and competence in this area.

Despite the best preparation and the most well-conceived training, Chinese managers suffer from a high rate of turnover among the foreign staff who work for them. One of the most often cited sources of dissatisfaction, attributable more to general organizational circumstance than to a specific lapse in management is the tendency of Chinese firms to follow an "ethnocentric" strategy in managing their overseas operations, a strategy that puts Chinese executives in leadership positions and leaves little room for local staff to advance their careers and have any hope of promotion (see Chapter 6—"Bamboo Ceiling"). In addition to organizational circumstance, there are other drivers of foreign staff turnover whose source can be traced more directly to management ineptitude and lack of familiarity with the expectations and needs of foreign staff.

FEEDBACK ERROR

Faced with a high turnover rate among its foreign staff, Huawei conducted an internal survey to determine the root cause. The reason most frequently cited by foreign staff for their decision to leave was poor management. Specifically identified as the key points of dissatisfaction were a lack of clear job definition and responsibilities, lack of encouragement, and lack of communication (Peng 2013). Inadequate job definition and insufficient communication are issues that are commonly raised and previously addressed (see Chapter 6—"Bamboo Ceiling"). Lack of encouragement, although perhaps implied within the other areas of dissatisfaction, is usually not called out as a separate item. The experience detailed in the commentsof the foreign staff employed by Huawei surveyed is consistent with previous observations from diverse sources that a Chinese supervisor's feedback tends to be critical and direct, emphasizing errors and failures rather than offering encouragement and support. Whether foreign pilots employed by Chinese airlines or Thai workers employed at Chinese manufacturing sites, foreign staff consistently highlighted the Chinese supervisor's tendency to find fault, assign blame, and assess penalties and offer feedback that was positive only in the rarest of circumstances

(Piansoongnern 2016, page 21). Presented with the results of the survey during the course of interviews conducted with them, Chinese managers offered, by way of explanation, that if a manager didn't find fault with the employee's work or criticize an employee's performance, the foreign employee should assume, by default, that performance was satisfactory. A number of managers interviewed noted, in the course of discussion, that they themselves had been treated in similar fashion by their management. The implication was that they were simply modeling behavior they themselves had observed and experienced (Peng 2013).

In practice, a Chinese manager who is satisfied with a subordinate's performance will offer a favorable comment only sparingly, if at all, and under no circumstance with the effusiveness that is characteristic of a Western (read American) manager's response to a job well done. "Our Hart", the expression of praise Prince Kung of the Tsungli Yamen lavished on Robert Hart (see Chapter 2—"History Lessons", similar in sound and in spirit to "women zhe ge Paul" ("That's our Paul!") the expression my boss has used on occasion to recognize my positive contribution and express his satisfaction, is a study in minimalism that is so non-specific as to appear devoid of meaning. Yet, if understood in context, these spare phrases speak volumes. First, the scarcity of such feedback itself means that, on the rare occasion that it is given, it is that much more meaningful. Second is that the use of the first person plural ("our") in the expression is a subtle affirmation of the recipient's affiliation with the rest of the team and a sign of acceptance. A less experienced foreign employee might not recognize these expressions for what they are and find the praise and implied encouragement too faint to be detected as such. However, to the foreign employee who has longer tenure and struggled with exclusion and overcoming barriers to acceptance, such an expression is especially meaningful because of the crossing of a cultural boundary it implies and change in status within the team it signals.

In addition to not getting the encouragement and positive feedback from the Chinese supervisor they expect, foreign employees are also challenged by what they perceive as a Chinese supervisor's lack of respect for what employees consider their "personal space". Work-life balance, presented in Chapter 5—"Living to Work", is perhaps the most obvious example of where personal boundaries are infringed on. However, there many instances in the course of the everyday work day where foreign employees feel their supervisor has crossed a line, even though the transgression may be unintended or unwitting. Moreover, what the foreign employee might regard as insulting, intrusive, and outside the bounds of a supervisor's area of concern, the Chinese manager may very well consider an expression of care and attention. A number of representative examples follow:

Care and Attention

- A foreign employee who had caught a cold in the middle of Winter was called into his supervisor's office and reprimanded for not wearing warm enough clothing. The supervisor proceeded to point to his padded vest and ask the foreign employee, undoubtedly rhetorically, to describe what it was the supervisor was wearing. Satisfied with the response he received, the boss then gave the foreign employee explicit instructions on where to find the shop from which the same vest could be purchased and an indication of the purchase price.
- A Chinese manager observing that a foreign employee on his team was taking notes in a notebook that was of a different format from the one the manager himself was using went to his office and came back with another notebook that was exactly the same as the one the manager had in hand. The manager proceeded to hand the notebook over to the foreign employee with the instruction that foreign employee make use of the notebook from then on.
- A foreign employee and his Chinese supervisor had been working all day and into the night on an urgent project. At a certain point the supervisor came to the conclusion that the investment of effort in the project they were making was reaching a point of diminishing returns and decided they would continue first thing the next morning (a Saturday). He then instructed the foreign employee to go home, take a shower, have a bowl of soup, and "go to bed by 10:30 or 11:00, at the latest".

Crossing the Line

- A local employee in the overseas office of a Chinese multinational received a request from his Chinese manager to connect on LinkedIn and duly accepted the request. In the days that followed, the employee discovered that his boss was harvesting the employee's LinkedIn contacts to accelerate his recruiting efforts and achieve the target that had been set.

- Perhaps as much illustration of an attitude towards time as a management style, a foreign employee received a notification for a 10:00 AM conference call at 8:30 AM on a Sunday morning sent by the assistant of a senior executive in the company he worked for. 15 minutes before the appointed time, the foreign employee received another message informing him that the meeting had been rescheduled to 2:00 PM. An hour later, at five minutes to 10:00 AM, a third message arrived informing the foreign employee that the conference call had been re-scheduled for the original 10:00 AM time. At 10:00 AM half a dozen participants were on the conference bridge waiting dutifully for the call to start. The executive who called the meeting arrived on the conference call bridge 15 minutes later.
- A Chinese boss will on occasion ask or expect staff to run errands or do small, personal jobs. William Plummer recounts that during his time as head of external affairs for Huawei in the U.S. his Chinese boss asked him to take him to get a haircut (Plummer 2018).

CONCLUSION

The most consequential relationship a foreign employee in a Chinese company is likely to have is with a supervisor and the employee's success in the company depends implicitly on being able to build a strong relationship with the supervisor and meet expectations. The employee can achieve this by behaving in an appropriate and respectful way and demonstrating a sensitivity for the supervisor's challenges and concerns.

Awareness

In building rapport with a Chinese supervisor, the foreign employee needs to understand the appropriate way of addressing management in a Chinese company as a way of demonstrating respect and organizational awareness. Titles illuminate underlying organizational structures and can give foreign employees an idea of where they fit in and how they should relate to others with whom they work.

Understanding

A Chinese manager's tendency to refrain from delivering positive feedback and providing encouragement is less related to the quality of the foreign employee's performance than it is to cultural habit, formative experience (the Chinese supervisor's own boss managed in a similar way and served as a model), and behavioral profile (empathy, emotional stability, etc. are character traits that are given less weight and attention in the assignment of Chinese managers to overseas posts). Finally, the foreign employee needs to consider that the Chinese supervisor for whom he or she works may have been assigned to the post without having had any choice in the matter.

Sensitivity

The foreign employee needs to recognize that on those occasions when a Chinese supervisor does or says something that is perceived by foreign staff as inappropriate or politically incorrect, the misstep may in fact be a consequence of inadequate training, not necessarily the result of some malicious or willful intent. The foreign employee also needs to recognize that the source of a Chinese manager's pressure and stress may not be work-related. The absence of family is one example.

REFERENCES

Allen, Arika M., Gosling, Paul, Powell, Grant D., and Yang, Claire, "The Human Touch Behind Asia Inc's Global Push", *Accenture-Outlook*, Issue 2, 2013, pages 1–10.
Bloch, Lyudmilla, Cross-Cultural Etiquette Expert, quoted in Spitznagel, Eric, "How to Impress Your Chinese Boss: A Guide to Sino-American Business Relations", *Bloomberg BusinessWeek*, January 6, 2012.
Cheng, Bor-Shiuan, Chou, Li-Fang, Wu, Tsung-Yu, Huang, Min-Ping, and Farh, Jiing-Lih, "Paternalistic Leadership and Subordinate Responses: Establishing a Leadership Model in CHINESE Organizations," *Asian Journal of Social Psychology*, Vol. 7, 2004, Pages 89–117.
Chen, Chao-Chuan and Lee, Yueh-Ting, "The Diversity and Dynamism of Chinese Philosophies on Leadership", in Chen, Chao-Chuan and Lee, Yueh-Ting (eds.), *Leadership and Management in China*. Cambridge University Press, 2008 (online version May, 2010), Pages 1–28.
Fang, Tony, Zhao, Shuming, and Worm, Verner, "The Changing Chinese Culture and Business Behavior", *International Business Review*, Vol. 17, 2008, pages 141–145.
Fei, Xing, "Expat Training Effectiveness in Chinese MNCs: Four Case Studies", Louvain School of Management (Master's thesis), 2014–2015.

Gao, Jinsong, Arnulf, Jan Ketil, and Kristofferson, Henning, "Western Leadership Development and Chinese Managers: Exploring the Need for Contextualization", *Scandinavian Journal of Management*, Vol. 27, 2011, Pages 55–65.

Huaneng Group, "Guojihua jingyingzhong kua wenhua guanli de shijian yu yanjiu", March 26, 2013.

Hucker, Charles O., *A Dictionary of Official Titles in Imperial China*, Stanford University Press, Stanford, CA, 1995.

"Human Resources Challenge of Huawei—Culture Clash" (unattributed).

Ju, Claudia, "Building Rapport with Your Boss" in "How to Work for Chinese Companies" (blog), October 18, 2017, https://www.linkedin.com/pulse/how-work-chinese-companies-claudia-ju/.

King, Peter, and Zhang, Wei, "Chinese and Western Leadership Models", *Journal of Management Research*, Vol. 6, No. 2, April 1, 2014.

Lee, Emma, "Cute or Cult? Inside Alibaba's Curious Nickname Culture", TechNode, October 9, 2018.

Li, Mingjie "Zhui Gen Su Jue", 6:45.

Li, Mingjie, "Dexue wei gaohua 'Laoshi'", *Ciyu Qunqiu*, Vol. 12, China Electronic Publishing, 2015, pages 24–25.

Li, Mingjie, and Xu, Jing, "'Zong' de yuyi bianyan ji xiangguan wenti", *Yuwen Yanjiu*, Vol. 1, No. 142, 2017, pages 26–31. Jiangxi Shifan Daxue.

Li, Shaomin, and Yeh, Kuang S., "Mao's Pervasive Influence on Chinese CEOs", *Harvard Business Review*, December 5, 2007, Page 16.

Liu, Hongyu, "Cross-Cultural Adjustment Factors of Chinese Expats in Portugal", ISCTE—University Institute of Lisbon Business School (Postdoctoral Dissertation), May 2015.

Lynton, Nandani, "Managing the Chinese Way", *McKinsey Quarterly*, July 2013.

Ma, Li, and Tsui, Anne S., "Traditional Chinese Philosophies, and Contemporary Leadership", *The Leadership Quarterly*, January 26, 2015, Pages 13–24.

Miedtank, Tina, "International Human Resource Management and Employment Relations of Chinese MNCs", in Drahokoupil, Jan (ed.) *Chinese Investment in Europe: Corporate Strategies and Labor Relations*, Chapter 4, Etui, Brussels, 2017.

Peng, Bo, "Foreign Talent Management at Huawei", *Huawei People* (online Magazine), Issue 244, March 13, 2013.

Piansoongnern, Opas, "Chinese Leadership and Its Impacts on Innovative Work Behavior of the Thai Employees", *Global Journal of Flexible Systems Management*, Vol. 17, no. 1, March 2016, pages 15–27.

Plummer, William, *Huidu: Inside Huawei* (self-published), June 2018.

Ralston, David A., Egri, Carolyn P., Stewart, Sally, Terpstra, Robert H., and Yu, Kaicheng, "Doing Business in the 21st Century with the New Generation of Chinese Managers: A Study of Generational Shifts in Work Values in

China," *Journal of International Business Studies*, Vol. 30, No. 2, 1999, Pages 415–427.

Sanchez-Runde, Carlos, Nardon, Luciara, and Steers, Richard M., "Looking Beyond Western Leadership Models: Implications for Global Managers, *Organizational Dynamics*, Vol. 40, 2011, pages 207–213.

Shen, Jie, and Edwards, "Vincent, Recruitment and Selection in Chinese MNE's", *International Journal of Human Resource Management*, Vol. 15, June 4/August 5, 2004, Pages 814–835.

Spitznagel, Eric. "How to Impress Your Chinese Boss: A Guide to Sino-American Business Relations", *Bloomberg BusinessWeek*, January 6, 2012.

Sun, Xiao, and Ross, Catherine, "Training of Chinese Managers: A Critical Analysis of Using Overseas Training for Management Development," *Journal of Chinese Economic and Business Studies*, Vol. 7, No. 1, 2009, Pages 95–113.

Wang, Dan, Freeman, Susan, and Zhu, Cherrie Juhua, "Personality Traits and Cross Cultural Competence of Chinese Expatriate Managers: A Socio-Analytic and Institutional Perspective", *International Journal of Human Resource Management*, Vol. 24, No. 20, 2013, Pages 3812–3830.

Wang, Lake, James, Kim Turnbull, Denyer, David, and Bailey, Catherine, "Western Views and Chinese Whispers: Rethinking Global Leadership Competency in Multinational Corporations", *Leadership*, Vol 10, No. 4, 2014, Pages 471–495.

Wang, Yuhua, "For Whom the Bell Tolls: The Political Legacy of China's Cultural Revolution" (abstract), Harvard University, January 19, 2017, pages 1–37.

Wang, Zhong (June) "Displaced Self and Sense of Belonging: A Chinese Researcher Studying Chinese Expatriates Working in the United States", University of South Florida (dissertation), March 2006.

Warner, Malcolm, and Rowley, Chris, "Chinese Management at the Crossroads", *Asia Pacific Business Review*, Vol. 16, No. 3, July 2010, Pages 273–284.

Yu, Xi, "From East to West: A Phenomenological Study of Mainland Chinese Expatriates' International Adjustment Experiences in the U.S. Workplace", University of Minnesota (dissertation), March 2016.

Zhang, Zhi-Xue, Chen Chao-Chuan, Liu, Leigh Anne, and Liu, Xue-Feng, "Chinese Traditions and Western Theories: Influences on Business Leaders in China", in *Leadership and Management in China: Philosophies, Theories, and Practices*. Cambridge University Press, 2008, pages 239–271.

Zhang, Zhi-Xue, Chen, Zhen Xong (George), Chen, Ya-Ru, and Ang, Soon, "Business Leadership in the Chinese Context: Trends, Findings, and Implications", *Management and Organization Review*, Vol. 10, No. 2, July 2014, Pages 199–221.

Zhong, Yifan, Zhu, Cherrie Juhua, and Zhang, Mike Mingqiong, "The Management of Chinese Expatriates: The Current Status and Future Research Agenda", *Journal of Global Mobility*, Vol. 3, No. 3, 2015, Pages 289–302.

CHAPTER 10

A View to the Future

It's noontime at a construction site in a large industrial city somewhere in China's interior and two young Frenchmen in bright yellow hard hats have knocked off work for a few minutes to escape the midday heat. Around the corner, a young man from Spain is hawking watermelons by the side of a busy thoroughfare. The price list, scrawled in crudely formed Chinese characters on a dog-eared scrap of cardboard, is propped up against the side of his cart. And as night falls a young British woman, provocatively dressed in high heels and mini skirt, begins her shift in a local KTV bar that caters to Chinese businessmen. These jarring vignettes of young Westerners eking out a living in China as manual laborers and low-level service staff represent a harsh reality that Benoit Cezard, the French photographer who staged them, conceived as a view of what the future may hold for foreigners seeking employment in China (Photo 10.1).

Whether Cezard's vision for the employment of foreigners is one that will ever be realized is open to debate and indeed there are many who have taken issue with its basic premise. For some, the images of foreigners selling watermelons by the side of Chinese roads or working shifts on Chinese construction sites are a portent for the irrevocable decline of the West. Others, more nationalistically-minded perhaps, view the images in a satirical light and regard the series as a thinly-veiled slight on the plight of poor Chinese citizens. Finally, there are those who dismiss such a view of the future as pure fantasy because of the degree to which it diverges from the experience of foreigners currently in the employ of Chinese. In coming

© The Author(s) 2020
P. Ross, *Barriers to Entry*,
https://doi.org/10.1007/978-981-32-9566-7_10

Photo 10.1   Credit Benoit Cezard—"China 2050"

to resolution on whether such a vision should be viewed as portent, satire, or fantasy it is instructive, as is often the case when one tries to make prognostications about China's future, to look first to China's past.

The legacy of foreigners in the employ of Chinese as depicted in the accounts of Brady and even Spence, to some extent, is a story of exploitation and manipulation. Seen against this historical backdrop, Cezard's images are the visual extension of a narrative that Spence concludes is "more cautionary tale than inspirational tract". However, the story that Spence and Brady recount reaches its conclusion not long after the founding of the People's Republic of China, well before the most recent chapter in China's history that begins with the economic reforms of the 1980's. It is a chapter that chronicles the massive social, economic, and political changes those reforms have unleashed and, most relevant to this study, charts the formation and evolution of modern enterprises whose business has grown in China and overseas.

As we have seen, the story of foreigners in the employ of Chinese organizations in the current era marks a departure from the past most notably in the conditions of their employment and the type of work in which they are engaged. Undoubtedly, a Jesuit missionary serving at the Ming court in the seventeenth century, a British clerk working in Hart's customs office a century ago, or even a foreign doctor like Bethune operating on the front lines in the 1940's could hardly have imagined that one day Europeans, Africans, Southeast Asians, and North Americans would be employed in the thousands by Chinese firms in China and, most strikingly, in locations around the world. As the number of foreigners working in Chinese organizations has grown and the range of roles they play expanded, their perception of what they contribute to the Chinese organizations that employ them and the way in which those organizations perceive them has undergone a significant transformation.

Spence notes that many foreigners who worked for Chinese in the past engaged China within the embrace of a relationship that quite often was "emotionally charged" (Spence 2002, page 290). Within the context of that relationship they very often viewed their work as a means to an end, a stepping stone on the road to a vision that they were desperate to realize rather than merely as a way to put bread on the table.

How disillusioned they were to discover that the Chinese viewed the relationship in much more contractual terms and, as Spence observes, "maintained, as nominal employers, the right to terminate the agreement" (Spence 2002, page 290). In contrast to their more idealistic predecessors, the foreigners working for Chinese today view the relationship they maintain with their employers as a much more transactional one where contracts determine the conditions of employment and monetary compensation serves as the motivation. As such, the relationship between Employer and Employed is a much more symmetric one and the expectations of the parties more closely aligned. Viewed through the lens of this present, Cezard's vision of the future appears even less solidly grounded in reality and more proximate to the realm of the fantastic.

The young foreign marketing and development professionals participating in a program like Alibaba's Global Leadership program present an undeniably positive counterpoint to the construction workers and fruit sellers who inhabit the photos that are the visual expression of Cezard's vision. However, as we have seen, although a program like AGLA is a promising sign for the future to come it is nevertheless subject to the tension that arises from taking steps to break with the past on one level while on another remaining steadfastly beholden to it. This tension that exists between present and past that the AGLA program exemplifies is one of a number of themes that together form a comprehensive narrative whose arc encompasses the experience of foreigners working for Chinese management in the twenty-first century. The sections that follow present a summary and review of key themes identified and developed within this study:

AGENTS OF TRANSFORMATION

The social and economic reforms China has undertaken over the past forty years have created new employment opportunities for foreigners from around the world in areas and industries such as Aviation, Sports, and Fashion that previously did not exist. As diverse as these professions are, and as varied the countries those who work in them represent, what they have in common is that they have all contributed to a transformation in the way that China presents itself to the world and in the way the world views China.

Foreigners are not just working for Chinese organizations in the professions and industries presented, they are playing an active role in contributing to their evolution. Instances of this phenomenon include foreign basketball stars who transformed Chinese basketball into a more physical game guided by a more coherent strategy; the foreign aviation experts who made significant contributions to the definition of safety regulations for China's aviation industry and maintenance conditions for its commercial airlines; and finally there are the investment executives primarily from the U.S. who helped Chinese enterprises gain access to the sources of capital they needed to grow. Then, when those companies had grown to a satisfactory size and reached a sufficient level of maturity, those investment experts helped to take them public, a critical step that set the stage for their global expansion.

A PAST THAT IS NOT SO DISTANT

Even those professions that appear to be products of the modern area nevertheless reveal traces of the past when they are pared down to their essence. For example, the job description and profile of foreign athletes who have joined Chinese sports teams in the recent past is completely unlike that of the doctors, soldiers, and scientists who came to China for employment in previous centuries. However, if one goes back much further in the historical record, to the Tang Dynasty, one can discern in the performances of the Kuchan dancers, musicians, and other entertainers roles that are certainly similar in spirit to those of today's basketball players and soccer stars even if not in exact form. The presence of foreigners in many other areas of Tang society, military and commerce, etc. lends further support for the view of the Tang as a template for the full range of roles that foreigners play in the current era and have played in the centuries in between.

EVOLVING EMPLOYMENT STRATEGIES

The strategies Chinese companies follow as a guide for their employment of foreign staff can differ quite substantially from one company to another. The shape that these employment strategies takes depends on a number of factors such as business model, industry, and corporate culture. As Chinese companies have evolved, so to have their expectations of foreign staff. An increasing number of Chinese companies, for example, expect that foreign staff have some understanding of Chinese language and culture and consider this a basic criterion for employment. Yet at the same time the large majority of the jobs Chinese hire foreigners to do are oriented towards other foreigners and markets overseas and are therefore not entirely dependent on fluency in Chinese language for their successful execution.

EMPLOYMENT CHALLENGES

Misalignment of Expectations

There is often a discrepancy between what Chinese management expect of their foreign staff and say they need them to do and the actual requirements of the projects to which they assign them. This discrepancy stems in large part from a lack of clarity around what those jobs entail and what foreign staff expect from them, especially around career development and scope of responsibility.

Barriers to Entry

Even though today the number of employment opportunities in a Chinese company for which foreigners qualify and can take advantage of is far greater than it has ever been before, a foreign employee's potential for integration into a Chinese company's core operations and prospects for long-term career development is still quite limited. Moreover, limitations to which foreigners in general are subject can be even more restrictive for foreign employees who belong to certain gender or racial groups. This condition is one whose effect may be mitigated, to some extent, over time as Chinese companies operating in countries overseas make changes to organizational behavior and company culture in compliance with local legislation and in response to pressure exerted by local organizations (e.g. unions) that are dedicated to promoting and guaranteeing employee rights.

Finding Equilibrium

Arguably, the most significant challenge a foreigner faces working in a Chinese company and making an effort to integrate into its operations is finding a satisfactory balance between work and life and a way to overcome organizational and cultural exclusion. These are significant impediments that keep a foreign employee from contributing as much as they could and from realizing their full potential.

Following review of the current conditions for foreigners in the employ of Chinese that has been the focus of this study and reflection on how the current state of affairs has been shaped by the past, we will now turn our attention to the future.

FUTURE TRENDS: DISPLACEMENT AND REPLACEMENT

A thorough examination of recent developments and emerging trends leads to the conclusion that the future for employment of foreigners by Chinese will be shaped by three factors:

- Policy (encompassing trade agreements, sanctions, etc.).
- Technology (advent of Artificial Intelligence and related applications).
- Demographics (including not only age distribution, but changes in the experience profiles motivations, goals and ambitions of younger generations).

Policy Effect: Prospects for Foreign Employment

Increasing trade tensions, retreat from the global system that has defined commercial relations over the last quarter of a century, and growing resistance to immigration are recent and interrelated developments that threaten to curb the international aspirations of Chinese firms and, in the process, reduce their demand for employment of foreign staff. The climate of uncertainty these tensions have created are already starting to take a toll on companies such as Alibaba whose CEO reduced revenue growth estimates for the 2018 fiscal year after conceding that trade tensions were creating an "increased risk of instability" (Zhong 2018). The decision of the U.S. and Australian governments to exclude Chinese telecommunications equipment providers Huawei and ZTE from their respective markets is a consequence of these recent developments and an example of the type of action that will slow the expansion of Chinese firms overseas if sustained over a longer period of time (Williams and Zhong 2019). In addition to these global developments, there are a number of changes taking place within China that have the potential to reduce the employment of foreign nationals and diminish the career aspirations of foreign workers seeking employment in Chinese companies.

Revisions to China's visa policy that came into force in 2016 specify a stricter set of conditions to be applied in evaluating applicant eligibility that reflect a more exclusive regime. An applicant's degree of fluency in Chinese language, level of education, and even academic institution attended are examples of the criteria that Chinese authorities take into account when determining the type of visa for which an applicant can qualify. Despite the potential for an unfavorable outcome that such developments suggest, their impact is mitigated by indicators that point to a more positive future for the employment of foreigners by Chinese companies both in China and overseas.

In China: Philippines Case

Relations between China and the Philippines have been undergoing change on a number of levels since the election of Rodrigo Duterte as President of the Philippines in 2016. An increase in cultural exchanges such as the China-Philippines Youth Friendly Exchange Program held in mid-October 2018 (Austria 2018), planning of joint military exercises such as the one organized with ASEAN countries, including the Philippines, that also took place in October 2018, and trade agreements such as the series of bi-lateral agreements the two countries concluded in April of 2018 are signs of a transformation in progress (Republic of the Philippines Report 2018).[1] Within the scope of these broader trade agreements are conditions that pave the way for the employment of 300,000 Filipinos in China, a number that is orders of magnitude greater than the 12,000 officially registered today.[2] It is anticipated that Filipinos who come to China for employment under the terms agreed upon will be engaged in a number of sectors: cooks, household service workers, musicians, caregivers, and nurses. China's Ministry of Labor expects that the largest number, approximately one third of the total, will be employed as English teachers who will play a consequential role in satisfying the Chinese middle class's seemingly unquenchable thirst for English language instruction. The prospects for ongoing and future employment that this forecast of sustained demand implies have been well received by Filipino teachers who stand to earn the equivalent of at least $1500 a month, the amount that has been specified as a reference compensation level ("China's Deal to Hire 300,000 Filipinos" 2018).[3] It is also welcome news to the Philippine Government whose success in maintaining stable economic development is directly dependent on the consistent flow of remittances to which Filipino citizens working abroad contribute. In 2017, the magnitude of that contribution to GDP was estimated to be 10% (Cuaresma 2018).

If the case of the Philippines gives some indication of the shape foreign employment in China might take in future, there is evidence to suggest that the potential for employment of foreigners outside of China is

---

[1] Of the agreements signed it is the fifth agreement, the Memorandum of Understanding on the Employment of Filipino Teachers of English Language in China, that is the most relevant.

[2] The number of Filipinos working in unofficial capacity in China far exceeds the official number and it is not clear whether these currently unregistered workers will be able to take advantage of the employment opportunities provided for in the agreement.

[3] The base compensation amount is specified in a Memorandum of Understanding signed by China's ambassador to the Philippines, Zhang Jianghua and presented in a statement by Philippine Labor Secretary, Bello III. Reported in: "China's Deal to Hire 300,000 Filipinos Finalized", *China Daily.com.cn(Forum)*, April 20, 2018.

poised for growth as well. Current political headwinds and the cases of individual firms notwithstanding, Chinese enterprises as a whole have made great strides over the past decade in expanding their market presence and growing their business overseas. In 2017, Chinese firms on average generated more than 13% of total revenues from markets outside of China, an increase of more than 30% over less than a decade ago (Nishizawa 2018).[4] Nowhere are China's ambitions for global trade more prominently displayed than in the country's signature trade program, the "Belt and Road Initiative" (BRI).[5]

Outside of China: Belt and Road Case

Officially launched in 2013 the BRI and its constituent elements, the Silk Road Economic Belt and 21st Century Maritime Silk Road together describe a vision of the future in which 4.4 Billion people who inhabit more than 70 countries will be connected with China culturally, logistically, and commercially. The "win-win" arrangement that is the premise and promise of the Belt and Road Initiative, as presented, entails bringing needed infrastructure to participant countries while opening up new trade opportunities for Chinese enterprise.

As much as BRI looks to the future it is firmly grounded in the past, drawing as it does on the experience China has accumulated implementing large-scale infrastructure projects over the past seventy years in many of the countries that its scope encompasses. Through reference to the Silk Road it reaches even further back in history to evoke a perceived Golden Age for the flow of goods, people, and ideas across regions that "Belt and Road" aspires to serve. If BRI lives up to expectations and succeeds in channeling the glories of the past to realize the ambitions of the future, the commercial activity that new deep water ports, high-speed rail lines, and power plants generates will be a stimulus for employment and a source of new jobs in countries that are the Initiative's stated beneficiaries.

---

[4] *Note* A growing number of firms such as Huawei, ZTE, China Molybdenum Co., China Communications Construction Co. generate more than fifty percent of total revenues from markets outside of China.

[5] The "Belt and Road Initiative" has also been referred to as the "One Belt and One Road" program (OBOR).

Estimates for the number of jobs that "Belt and Road" and its related projects have the potential to create vary widely, from a conservative estimate of less than a quarter-of-a million to a more optimistic forecast of three to four million[6] (Lu and Tu 2018; Shepard 2016; Kanak 2016; Dai 2017; "yidai yilu maoyi touze luntan" 2018). Many of the opportunities for employment anticipated will, at least in the near term, likely be generated by infrastructure projects initiated in countries that are in proximity to China and that, thanks to a successful record of such projects previously completed, offer a ready base on which the larger scale, longer-term programs BRI envisions can be established. Pakistan and Kazakhstan are two such countries and a closer examination of their commercial relations with China and their fit within the Belt and Road Initiative yields some clues to how the future for employment of locals with Chinese enterprises operating in those countries might unfold.

Pakistan
In his speech at the 2017 Belt and Road Summit held in Beijing, then Pakistani Prime Minister, Nawaz Sharif, expressed admiration for China's vision and praised the leadership's ingenuity in developing new trade initiatives across the regions outlined (Ilyas Rana 2019). Highlighted was the so-called China-Pakistan Economic Corridor (CPEC), the Belt and Road program of most direct relevance to Pakistan. This large-scale infrastructure program is undergirded by an investment of $62 Billion, roughly half of which has been earmarked for the development of transportation infrastructure (e.g. rail and motorways) and the deployment of new hydroelectric power plants. The balance will be put towards expansion of the Gwadar port on Pakistan's Southern coast including extension of the road and rail links that will sustain the port's logistics ecosystem and enable Gwadar to achieve its full potential as conceived ("Pakistan Rethinks Its Role" 2018). Still in an initial stage of implementation, these projects are already beginning to generate local employment opportunities. In June 2016, China's ambassador to Pakistan stated that ancillary projects initiated through the CPEC already employ more than

---

[6]This wide variance in estimates is a function of the stage of development BRI is in, differing levels of confidence in the Initiative's ability to achieve its stated goals, and the proportion of Chinese employed to local hires.

6000 Pakistanis (Jacob 2017).[7] He also pointed to a number of other projects Chinese companies are undertaking outside the perimeter of the Economic Corridor that are generating additional opportunities. The Thar ignite mining and power plant that the China Machine Engineering Corp (CMEC) is building out, for example, is reported to have created an additional 1000 local jobs to date (Jacob 2017).

As a complement to the projects these companies have initiated, the Chinese Government has taken an active role in encouraging young Pakistanis to study Chinese language and enhance their familiarity with Chinese culture most notably by opening Confucius Institutes[8] in key metropolitan centers such as Karachi, Lahore, and Islamabad. In addition to these initiatives, the Chinese Government also sponsors Pakistani students to undertake formal courses of study at universities in China. In 2017, 22,000 Pakistanis were studying in Chinese institutions of higher learning. Nearly a quarter received Chinese Government scholarships in support of their studies (Dan Zhang 2018). The nominal intent of all these education-oriented programs and the overarching goal they share is to prepare Pakistanis for future jobs and careers with Chinese companies operating in Pakistan.

Kazakhstan

Khorgos, a town of about 80,000 on the border between China and Kazakhstan would not appear to be the most likely place to situate the hub for an initiative whose scale is as grand as that of "Belt and Road". Even less plausible is the Kazakh Government's ambition to position Kazakhstan as a regional trade nexus whose connecting logistics and distribution spokes will radiate out across Central Asia, ultimately extending as far as Europe. In fact, within the context of "Belt and Road" and in consideration of the Initiative's stated objectives, Kazakhstan has much to recommend it. Even though Khorgos is nowhere near a body of water of the size that would be conducive to shipping in large-volume,

---

[7] Pakistan's Applied Economics Research Center and Planning Commission project that over the next 15 years 700,000–800,000 jobs will be created under the CPEC program. In 2018 China's ambassador to Pakistan claimed CPEC had already created 75,000 jobs for Pakistanis (Toppa 2018).

[8] China's Bureau of Education-sponsored centers dedicated to the promotion of Chinese language and culture.

its fortuitous positioning somewhat equidistant from China, Russia, Iran and Eastern Europe is the "value proposition" on which its aspiration to become the world's largest dry-shipping port in the world is founded. Once fully operational, Khorgos will provide an overland shipping option that, at 14 days, is more rapid than transport by sea and less costly than transport by air (Mouk 2019, page 40).

As an affirmation of the role it envisions Kazakhstan will play within the larger BRI scheme, China has emphasized the alignment of the two countries' visions and, as a demonstration of its commitment, has invested a total of $43 billion in Kazakhstan over the past five years (Xiao Zhang 2018). A recent announcement from Kazakh Invest, Kazakhstan's national export and foreign investment agency, confirmed that 67 projects involving $7.1 billion in foreign investment will be initiated in 2018, creating more than 13,500 jobs (Beer 2018). To ensure it makes the most of the opportunities that participation in "Belt and Road" promises, Kazakhstan, like Pakistan, hosts a number of Confucius Institutes. It also currently counts some 15,000 of its nationals as students in Chinese institutions of higher learning, triple the number who were enrolled in 2013. Many of these students have their studies subsidized through scholarships that China's Ministry of Education makes available (Le Corre 2018).

Despite the positive developments for foreigners in the employ of Chinese companies that the cases described here presage, there is significant and ongoing debate not only about the number of jobs that will be generated but also about the quality of those jobs and the level of compensation associated with them. Indeed, there are some who suspect that, despite the "win-win" rhetoric that has accompanied its launch, the Belt and Road Initiative is nothing more than an elaborate ploy the Chinese Government has conceived to absorb an excess of Chinese workers, a situation that has received greater attention and whose resolution has taken on greater urgency as China's economy has slowed. The skeptics voice concerns that, as these BRI-related projects grow in scale and stature over the longer term, they will be staffed increasingly by Chinese workers whom the Chinese Government has encouraged to look abroad for jobs as prospects for employment at home diminish.

The changes that are transforming China's economic landscape are mirrored in corresponding changes that have occurred in the political landscapes of a number of countries that feature prominently on the list of those that anchor the Belt and Road Initiative such as Malaysia, and

Pakistan. The recent elections of new governments in both these countries have been accompanied by revisions to policy agendas that reflect a change in perspective on BRI and reëvaluation of domestic projects that have been initiated under its banner. Following a thorough review of China-related projects, representatives of these new governments have concluded that the economic and commercial futures of their respective countries have become overly dependent on China and, on the road to realizing that future, have taken on a level of debt that is unsustainable. As a step towards reducing that dependence, they have made clear their intention to renegotiate existing agreements or, in some cases, even cancel them outright. In Malaysia, the Mahatir government has terminated a number of planned pipeline projects and reduced the scope of the signature East Coast Rail Line that will link the South China Sea in the East coast of Peninsular Malaysia with strategic shipping routes in the West. In Pakistan, the government Imran Khan installed after his election has suspended a number of development projects that Chinese firms are engaged in and is revising some of the agreements previously concluded under the CPEC umbrella (Aamir 2018).

Technology Effect: Reducing Language Barriers

A constant in the history of foreigners employed by Chinese has been the role foreigners have played as mediators between Chinese and other foreigners. It is a role that has appeared and reappeared in many guises: interpreters, emissaries, and, most recently, marketing and sales practitioners. From the rebel general An Lushan and the Sogdians who served the Tang military in the eighth century to Jesuit missionaries such as Verbiest and Schall who headed the Astronomical Bureau in the Ming and Qing Dynasties, promoters such as Rittenberg in the twentieth century, and young foreigners working in companies such as Alibaba and Tencent today.

Traditionally, the motivation for employing foreign staff, and the value they bring in the eyes of Chinese who hire them, is the cultural sensitivity and linguistic ability they possess that can compensate for a Chinese employer's own perceived lack in these areas and enable the company to increase its effectiveness in engaging with foreign clients and partners. New technologies, such as Artificial Intelligence, that enable applications capable of real-time language translation, have the potential to reduce and, in some cases, even eliminate roles that depend primarily on linguistic fluency and cross-cultural mediation for their execution. However, to suggest that Chinese companies armed with these technologies might, at some point in the future dispense with foreign staff entirely, is a bit far-fetched. As the head of Alibaba's North American business discovered, Chinese, in a corporate environment, still place a premium on face-to-face communication no matter how efficient a proxy basic technologies such as phone and videoconferencing may be. Practically speaking, there are very few positions foreigners hold today that depend solely on language fluency and cultural mediation. In most cases, these competences are seen as an adjunct to jobs that encompass other duties and functions. However, even if they are not putting jobs that foreigners hold today at immediate risk, new technologies are already having an impact on the way foreigners in Chinese companies work. Ongoing improvement in the accuracy of these applications coupled with a decrease in the investment required to deploy them at scale increases their potential to transform the employment prospects of foreigners in Chinese organizations.

Motivated by China's growing commercial and cultural influence, experts in Natural Language Processing (an application of Machine Learning that helps computers understand, interpret, and manipulate human language) have put considerable effort over the last few years into improving translation between Chinese and other languages and this effort is beginning to yield impressive results. Researchers in Microsoft's U.S. and Asia labs announced in March 2018 that the Chinese-English translation application they developed making use of the latest advances in Artificial Intelligence had achieved a level of accuracy that was on a par with that of humans. This breakthrough, albeit, was achieved using a circumscribed set of test data drawn from "newstest2017", a digest of news stories. However, experts have widely hailed it as a milestone whose application will broaden to include other areas in the near future (Linn 2018). While such a development does indeed have the potential to eliminate the jobs of some foreign employees whose primary contribution is linguistic and cross cultural, it might at the same time open doors for others who lack fluency in Chinese language, but have an applicable skill to offer.

By his own admission the Australian director of the overseas sales support division in a Chinese State-Owned Enterprise lacks competence in speaking Chinese, let alone reading it. To compensate for his lack of Chinese fluency and increase his effectiveness he makes frequent and liberal use of a language translation function that the ubiquitous Chinese social media platform, WeChat, makes available. At the push of a button, the director can take the messages his colleagues send in Chinese and convert them into an English that is good enough for him to get the gist of the pricing requirements and requested terms and conditions for bids that are at the heart of the most relevant communications he receives. Like the Australian sales director, an Indian journalist employed at the *China Daily*, an English-language daily newspaper owned by the Publicity Department of the Chinese Communist Party, finds that new technologies are making their presence felt in his daily work environment. The journalist noted that new technologies are transforming the media industry by changing the way information is produced, consumed, and delivered. As a byproduct, they are also having a transformative effect on the media industry's employment landscape. As a result of these changes, the journalist predicted that in the next few years the number of foreign journalists employed by the *China Daily* and other Chinese publications would be much smaller than it is today. However, he noted that the impact on employment prospects was not specific to foreign journalists employed by Chinese media organizations, but was a global phenomenon that did not distinguish nationality or culture and would have an effect on the employment prospects of Chinese journalists as well. More specific to the media industry in China and of more direct relevance to the employment prospects of foreign professionals working for Chinese media organizations, was an increase in the number of Chinese who had acquired skills, through education and experience, that qualified them for jobs previously considered the exclusive domain of foreign experts. "China Global Television Network" (CGTN) the rebranded foreign-language broadcast of China Central Television (CCTV) is an example of a news organization where this displacement is already taking place.

Demographic Effect: Transforming Supply and Demand

Millenials with New Skills

As part of its rebranding, CGTN also expanded the services it provides and increased the number staff who support programming in the languages it offers. In the past, an expansion of foreign language programming would have translated into an increase in foreign staff. However, a good number of the new staff hired are young Chinese who have studied abroad and, during the course of their studies, developed a proficiency in one of the network's five languages—English, French, Spanish, Arabic,

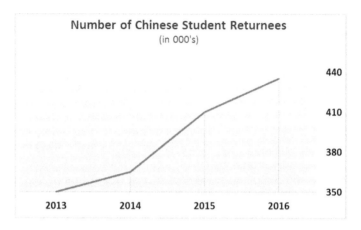

Chart 10.1 Number of Chinese student returnees (*Note* this is a visual representation of numbers provided by China's Ministry of Human Resources and Social Security)

and Russian ("China Spending Billions" 2018). Given recent trends, it is clear there will be many more cases like CGTN in future.

China's Millenials, who are just now starting work, getting married, and buying apartments, are known for being more open-minded, individualistic and rebellious than their parents ("Understanding Chinese Millenials" 2016). They are also known as the generation that has taken greatest advantage of the opportunity to spend time outside China, typically for travel and study. Millenials made up nearly two-thirds of Chinese traveling outside of China in 2017 and they traveled to places further afield and more exotic than any their parents ever visited. Moreover, their travel-related spending in that year increased by 80% over the year prior to an amount equivalent to 35% of their total annual income (Liang 2018). More than five million are completing their studies in other countries. Half-a-million went abroad to further their education in 2017 alone[9] ("Number of Student Returnees on the Rise" 2019). Even more tellingly, more than 75% of those who went abroad for studies are now coming back and this number is expected to increase as opportunities for well-compensated and high-growth employment especially in China's hi-tech and financial sectors become more plentiful ("Turtles and Seagulls" 2018) (see Chart 10.1).

[9] *Note* In 2016 430,000 returned, 60% more than in 2011.

It is important to note that at the same time CGTN was hiring young Chinese returning from overseas for roles that conceivably would have been held by foreigners, the organization was taking steps to expand its presence in the local markets overseas and as part of that effort recruited 300 local journalists to staff its London office with similar plans for other key markets (Moore 2018).

In recruiting young Chinese to do work that foreign staff would traditionally have handled, CGTN exemplifies a broader 'structural change' that is taking hold. Characteristic of this change is that Chinese companies are developing their own competence to satisfy demand in a given industry that has historically depended on inputs—products, expertise, and people—from outside of China and this will have a direct impact on the employment of foreigners in the future. The airline industry, profiled in Chapter 3—"On the Runway", is an example of an industry where this structural change is already having an effect.

Today foreign pilots are employed in significant numbers and at a high level of compensation because of a significant gap that exists between the domestic supply of available pilots and demand of Chinese airlines. However, all parties involved—the Chinese airlines, the foreign pilots, and their intermediaries—recognize that this current condition is of limited duration. To ease the shortage and the financial pressure it imposes, Chinese airlines are taking steps to train local pilots. It is expected that as the number of local pilots who complete training and are flight-qualified increases, the demand of Chinese airlines for foreign pilots will decrease accordingly. There were already a total of 5053 Chinese pilots in training in 2017 and signs that some of China's larger airlines, at least, are already scaling back their recruiting efforts and revising targeted numbers of foreign recruits (Smyth and Blend 2018).

Retirees with Old Ills
Despite the increase in the number of young Chinese who possess skills that will enable them to secure employment and displace foreigners in relevant industries and professions, their number will still not be sufficient to satisfy the demand created by a population at large that is rapidly aging ("Chinas's Debt Bomb" 2010).[10] The projected effect this aging phenomenon will

---

[10]China's State Council projects that by 2030 more than a quarter of China's population will be over 60 (nearly double the share in 2010) as referenced in: "China's Next Debt Bomb Is An Aging Population", *Straits Times*, February 6, 2018.

have on the workforce is already becoming apparent. In the U.S., workforce growth is projected to increase at a steady 0.5% per year for the next decade, an exceedingly small number that nevertheless represents an increase (Bureau of Labor Statistics 2015). In China that same indicator is already falling (Orszag 2018). The impact of an aging population (compounded by the effects of the one child policy) on the workforce and available resources is already being felt. Decreases in birth and marriage rates is exacerbating the effect of these already worrying trends[11] (Chen and Zhuang 2018). To get a sense for the effect these demographic changes might have on China's immigration policy and on Chinese attitudes towards the employment of foreigners, we can turn to Japan as a convenient reference point because many of the conditions inform the way in which the two countries perceive their respective futures are similar.

By any measure, Japan is at, or near, the top of the list of countries whose populations are aging most rapidly. Today more than 25% of Japan's nearly 130 Million citizens are more than 65 years old, a percentage that has increased by nearly 4 percentage points over the little more than 20% the segment made up just six years ago (Weller 2018). Moreover, life expectancy in Japan, at 80 for men and 87 for women, is the highest among developed countries. As in the case of China, the trend towards aging in Japan is compounded by a falling birth rate ("Japan Has the Highest Life Expectancy Rate" 2014). Considered in the absence of additional context, however, this statistic is not very meaningful. The more consequential indicator of the demographic challenge this trend represents is Japan's fertility rate[12] which at 1.42 is well below the 2.1 replacement rate.[13] For most countries the fertility rate is a statistic that is more widely referenced because it succinctly reflects the profound effect that increased life expectancy and a lower birth rate will have on the composition of a country's population and ultimately on the country's future. Caught in the grip of this demographic vice, Japanese companies are already struggling to find enough qualified workers. A recent improvement in the country's economic conditions that has resulted in an unemployment rate of less than 3%, the lowest

[11]The birth rate fell from 12.95 Million per 1000 people in 2016 to 12.43 Million in 2017 (in absolute terms a decrease from 18.5 Million to 17.2 Million) accompanied by a 30% decline in marriages as cited in Chen, M., and Zhuang, L., "China's Aging Population Worsens as Birth and Marriage Rates Fall", *South China Morning Post*, July 16, 2018.

[12]The average number of babies born per woman.

[13]i.e. The total fertility rate at which a population exactly replaces itself.

in 25 years, is putting additional pressure on enterprises unable to fill open positions. In response to the challenge created by these reinforcing trends and to ward off the "perfect storm" that is brewing, Japan has become much more amenable to welcoming foreign workers who can potentially fill the gap that unfavorable demographics and favorable economics has created. As a concrete step forward, the Japanese Government has initiated a number of programs designed to help foreign workers find available jobs and these initiatives are beginning to yield results. The number of foreign workers in Japan has doubled over the last five years to more than one-and-a-quarter million, a key milestone on the road to reaching the Government's target of adding 500,000 new overseas workers by 2025 (Obe 2018). The number of foreign workers in Japan, although still quite small relative to the size of the total population, is a number that is increasing. However, as indicative as these statistics are, they mask a distinct dichotomy in the employment of foreign workers who come to Japan.

EMERGENCE OF A TWO-TRACK SOLUTION

With an eye towards facilitating the employment of low-skilled foreign workers in areas such as construction, the Japanese Government has devised dedicated trainee programs for foreign workers. The majority of the nearly quarter-of-a-million foreign workers the programs have already attracted come from China and Vietnam. At the same time, the Government has identified a need for skilled workers in areas deemed strategic to Japan's future, such as hi-tech to ensure that the country can maintain its competitive edge and healthcare to ensure that the country can maintain its aging population. To attract hi-tech workers, the Government has instituted a "fast-track" permanent resident visa program; to attract healthcare workers the Government has entered into economic agreements with a number of countries that would allow up to 900 caregivers a year to work in Japan for up to four or five years (Mitsuru 2018).

Because it is uniquely positioned to meet the unique demands that this two-track policy the Philippines provides an instructive case. The country is a source of workers for low-skilled jobs such as those commonly found on construction sites.[14] (Marcelo 2017). At the same it is

---

[14]Memorandum of Cooperation signed during the first Philippines—Japan Conference on Construction as reported in demonstrates a commitment to developing the Philippines construction manpower sector referenced in: Marcelo, Patrizia Paola, "Japan to Train Filipino Construction Workers", *Business World Online*, November 25, 2017.

also a source of more highly-skilled workers, specifically in the area of healthcare where it has become a worldwide provider of nurses and home healthcare givers.[15] As example, take the case of Ruby Abriol, a young Filipino healthcare worker who joined a Japanese-Philippine inter-governmental program that involved six months of training in Japanese culture and language in Manila that then continued for six months in Japan (Colunsod 2016). After completion of the program, Abriol was then assigned to rotate through a number of Japanese health-care facilities while she prepared for the Japanese licensing examination for healthcare practitioners, an examination she eventually passed in 2014. Ruby Abriol (and others like her) is the face of a larger trend whose outline is beginning to shape in China.

Although there is no explicit reference to a "two-track" approach in any of the trade agreements that stipulate employment opportunities in China for Filipinos who qualify, those who drafted the agreements made such an outcome plausible by referencing 'homecare workers' in the statements they issued that specified the professions in which they foresee Filipino workers engaged. As China's aging population creates more demand for such services, the availability of Filipinos who have requisite experience and can meet the demand seems like a natural fit and a foregone conclusion that makes such an outcome inevitable. Unbdoubtedly, there will be more agreements like the one already signed in the offing that are not just concluded for political purposes but also for more practical reasons to meet the needs of an aging population. In fact, there are already more than 200,000 Filipinos working in Healthcare as nurses, aides, and caregivers worldwide ("Philippine Statistics Authority" 2019).

"Foreign" in Name Only

In speculating on what the future holds for the employment of foreigners in Chinese companies and studying relevant cases, the underlying assumption has been that the "employment" part of the expression

---

[15] The Philippines is home to 400 training programs that graduate 20,000 healthcare practitioners a year, a number greater than that of any other country. The attraction is that they can in some cases earn overseas more than five times what they can earn at home in Trines, Stefan, "Mobile Nurses: Trends in International Labor Migration in the Nursing Field", *World Education News+Reviews*, March 6, 2018.

"employment of foreigners" is variable, subject as it is to changes in the demographic, economic, and political landscape as the previous discussion has demonstrated. The "foreigners" part of the expression is taken to be immutable. However, in light of social changes that have been underway since the founding of the People's Republic of China in 1949, the definition of what or who a "foreigner" is perhaps needs to be reconsidered and the underlying assumptions revisited.

If citizenship is used as the criterion, then the definition of a "foreigner" or, more precisely, a "non-Chinese" is clear. China recognizes an individual as a Chinese citizen if at least one parent is a Chinese national. By the same token, a candidate for citizenship can be disqualified for concurrently holding citizenship of another country (i.e. dual citizenship), a condition that is becoming more rigorously enforced. However, when the criterion for determination is culturally, ethnically, or linguistically based then the term 'foreigner' does not lend itself so easily to a clear definition. Some of the most obviuous examples of those whose profiles situate them in this semantic and ethnic gray area are the children of William Hinton, Erwin Engst, and David Crook profiled in profiled in Chapter 2—"History Lessons".

Carmelita Hinton, Fred Engst, and Carl Crook, were all born in China, spent their formative years in the country, and speak Chinese as a first language. The conditions under which these 'foreigners' in China came to consider themselves first-generation 'immigrants' are, admittedly, somewhat out of the ordinary and, some would argue, nothing more than a quirk of historical circumstance. In the intervening half-century, there has been a whole generation of "Hintons", "Crooks", "Engsts", children of non-Chinese parents who were born in China, grew up in China and consider the country 'home'. Their particular circumstances make formulating an answer to the question "who is a foreigner?" more than just an academic exercise. Accompanying the increase in the incidence of foreigners who fit this profile has been an increase in the number of its permutations: Children born to mixed marriages where one parent is a Chinese citizen; Children born to non-Chinese who attend Chinese public schools, Children who are born and grow up in China, but attend schools in China whose curriculum is foreign. However they are defined and classified, these 'foreigners' belong to a very different linguistic and cultural category from, for example, the 'foreigners' inducted into Alibaba's AGLA program.

CONCLUSION

After a review of the cases presented in this chapter, we can now see that the debate Cezard's photo series provoked was inevitable given the number of dimensions that come into play in determining the shape the future of foreigners in the employ of Chinese will take:

Structural (an effect that is not partial to ethnicity or culture and affects the employment Chinese and foreigners alike).

Demographic (Younger Chinese who have the skills requisite to do jobs that were previously the domain of foreign "experts". An aging population whose demand will be the engine for the creation of new employment opportunities).

Technological (the potential of new technologies to make some work more accessible to foreign employees and at the same time make others irrelevant).

Geographic (an increase in employment opportunities for foreign staff outside of China commensurate with overseas expansion of Chinese firms and broader Chinese government programs such as the "Belt and Road" Initiative).

Simply identifying the dimensions that will define how Chinese and their organizations will employ foreign talent does not provide the insight necessary to develop an accurate or full assessment of the opportunities and prospects for foreigners in the employment of Chinese organizations. For this we need to consider the vectors of change for any given dimension, expressed as the number of jobs that will be created and the number that will be lost. This requires taking into account factors such as industry, skill, demand, etc. The CGTN case is a good illustration. In China, CGTN is hiring Chinese with requisite skills and experience into positions in the organization that would traditionally have been the domain of foreign staff. Yet, at the same time the organization's expansion of its operations overseas is creating new employment opportunities for locals in the places where the expansion is taking place.

The accuracy of Cezard's vision and the likelihood that it will be realized will undoubtedly be debated for some time to come. Although those who participate in those debates may never come to resolution on exactly what the future for the employment of foreign staff in Chinese organizations will look like, they will most certainly agree that the images on which Cezard's vision is based present just one side of a much more complex picture. While it is clear that there will be foreigners engaged in the kinds of jobs that the actors in Cezard's photos represent, there will certainly be others, like Ruby Abriol, who will occupy offices in the corporate towers that Cezard's foreign laborers are building.

REFERENCES

Aamir, Adnan, "Why Pakistan Is Backing Away From China-Funded Infrastructure Projects", *South China Morning Post*, October 18, 2018.

Austria, Hilda, *China-PH Hold 1st Youth Exchange Program*, Philippines News Agency, October 21, 2018.

Beer, Mark, *Belt and Road Initiative: One Vision of Justice*, *The Astana Times*, April 20, 2018.

Chen, Minnie, and Zhuang Linghuai. "China's Aging Population Worsens as Birth and Marriage Rates Fall", *South China Morning Post*, July 16, 2018.

"China's Deal to Hire 300,000 Filipinos Finalized", *ChinaDaily.com.cn (Forum)*, April 20, 2018.

"China Is Spending Billions on Its Foreign-Language Media", *Economist*, June 4, 2018.

"China's Next Debt Bomb Is An Aging Population", *Straits Times*, February 6, 2018.

Colunsod, Ronron, "Filipino Healthcare Workers Tout Program Offering Careers in Japan", *Japan Times*, May 16, 2016.

Cuaresma, Bianca, "OFW Remittances Hit US$ 28.1 Billion in 2017", *The Business Mirror*, February 15, 2018.

Dai, Tian, "180,000 jobs created by Belt and Road Initiative", *China Daily* (online), March 11, 2017.

"Japan Has the Highest Life Expectancy Rate of Any Major Country", *NBC News*, June 14, 2014.

Ilyas Rana, Aamir, "Belt and Road Forum: 'CPEC must not be politicized', Says Nawaz", Islamabad, Pakistan, *Express Tribune*, May 15, 2019.

Jacob, Jabin T., "Deciphering the Numbers: Employment in the China-Pakistan Economic Corridor", E-International Relations (online), August 22, 2017, www.e-irinfo/2017/08/21/deciphering-the-numbers-employment-in-the-china-pakistan-economic-corridor.

Kanak, Don, "China's Belt and Road Initiative vital to Asia Job Creation", *Nikkei Asian Review*, December 28, 2016.

Le Corre, Philippe, "China Must Look Beyond Belt and Road", *Nikkei Asian Review*, May 4, 2018.

Liang, Lu Hai, "Spreading Their Wings: How Chinese Millenials Turn the World of Travel Upside Down", CKSB Knowledge, September 19, 2018.

Linn, Alison, "Microsoft Reaches a Historic Milestone, Using AI to Match Human Performance in Translating News from Chinese to English", March 14, 2018.

Lu, Yue, and Tu, Xinquan, "The Effect of the Belt and Road Initiative on Countries' Employment", in Chaisse, J. and Gorski, J. (eds.) *The Belt and Road Initiative: Law, Economics, Politics* (online), Brill, The Netherlands, September 2018, www.brill.com/view/title38740.

Marcelo, Patrizia Paola, "Japan to Train Filipino Construction Workers", *Business World Online*, November 25, 2017.

Mitsuru, Obe, "Famous for Its Resistance to Immigration, Japan Opens Its Doors: Number of Foreign Workers Doubles in 5 Years as Nation Faces Labor Crisis", *Nikkei Asian Review*, May 30, 2018.

Moore, Matthew, "Beijing to Hire 300 Journalists for CGTN's New UK Headquarters", *The Times*, June 15, 2018.

Mouk, Ben, "Is This the Center of the Global Economy? China Thinks It Will Be", *New York Times*, February 3, 2019, pages 37–45.

Nishizawa, Kana, "Chinese Firms Have Never Been This Reliant on Foreign Revenue", *Bloomberg*, April 20, 2018.

"Number of Student Returnees on the Rise", *China Daily*, January 15, 2019.

Obe, Mitsuru, "Famous for Its Resistance to Immigration, Japan Opens Its Doors. Number of Foreign Workers Doubles as Nation Faces Labor Crisis", *Nikkei Asian Review*, May 30, 2018.

Orszag, Peter, "China's Aging Population Is a Serious Threat to Growth", *Bloomberg*, November 29, 2018.

"Pakistan Rethinks Its Role in China's Belt and Road Plan", *Straits Times*, September 10, 2018.

"Philippines Statistics Authority, 2018 Survey on Overseas Filipinos," June 27, 2019 (release date), https://psa.gov.ph/content/statistical-tables-overseas-filipino-workers-ofw-2018.

Republic of the Philippines Presidential Communications Operations Office, "PH, China Sign Six Bilateral Agreements", April 10, 2018.

Shepard, Wade, "How the New Silk Road Is Stimulating Local Economies and Changing Lives from China to Europe", *Forbes*, August 3, 2016.

Smyth, Jamie, and Blend, Ben, "China Buys Up Flying Schools as Pilot Demand Rises", *Financial Times*, May 11, 2018.

Spence, Jonathan, *To Change China: Western Advisers in China*, Penguin, 2002 (reprint).

Toppa, Sabrina, "Why Young Pakistanis Are Learning Chinese", *The Atlantic*, November 14, 2018.

"Turtles and Seagulls, What Happens When Chinese Students Abroad Return Home", *Economist*, May 17, 2018.

Trines, Stefan, "Mobile Nurses: Trends in International Labor Migration in the Nursing Field", *World Education News+Reviews*, March 6, 2018.

Travel Daily Media. "Chinese Millenials Travel Expenditures Increase by 80% YoY", August 15, 2018.

"Understanding Chinese Millenials", Marketing to China", July 29, 2016, www. marketingtochina.com/understanding-Chinese-millenials.

U.S. Bureau of Labor Statistics Monthly Labor Review, December 2015.

Weller, Chris, "9 Signs Japan Has Become a Demographic Time Bomb", Business Insider, January 5, 2018.

Williams, Jacqueline, and Zhong, Raymond, "Huawei's New Front in the Global Technology Cold War: Australia", The New York Times, June 19, 2019.

"yidai yilu" maoyi touze luntan: changyi wei you guan guojia chuangzao 20 wan jiuye gangwei", China News Network, April 12, 2018.

Zhang, Dan, "Hardworking Pakistani Students Claim a Large Share of Chinese Scholarships", Global Times, June 20, 2018.

Zhang, Xiao, "China, Kazakhstan to Deepen Cooperation on Belt and Road Construction", People's Daily, September 10, 2018.

Zhong, Raymond, "Alibaba Feels the Pinch from China's Slowing Growth," The New York Times, November 18, 2018.

Appendix A: Foreign Employee Interview Scope and Methodology

Scope:

- 28 respondents representing Chinese companies in China and overseas By phone, e-mail and face-to-face. Most of them conducted over an 18-month period from the middle of 2017 to the end of 2018
- Interviews conducted by phone and in person typically lasted for an hour but ranged from as short as thirty minutes to as long as two hours.

Questions:

Interviews typically began with basic questions whose responses could be used to develop a profile of the respondent that included current position. professional experience, education, etc.

The following questions were formulated to guide the discussion that ensued. However, depending on the respondent's availability, willingness, and own ideas about what was important, these questions were not always strictly adhered to

© The Editor(s) (if applicable) and The Author(s), under exclusive license to Springer Nature Singapore Pte Ltd. 2020
P. Ross, *Barriers to Entry*,
https://doi.org/10.1007/978-981-32-9566-7

1. How did you come to work in a Chinese company and what was your motivation?
2. To what extent has your experience in the Chinese company where you are employed differed from what you expected and in what ways?
3. How has your experience changed over time?
4. What, based on your experience, does it take for a foreign employee to be effective and successful in a Chinese company.
5. Highlight the greatest challenges you have faced and the most important lessons you have learned working for a Chinese supervisor?
6. How would you characterize "communication" (both official and unofficial") in the company where you are working and how does it compare with what is communicated and how it is communicated in any other (non-Chinese) companies where you have worked?

Appendix B: Data Methodology and Assumptions

Supporting foreign employee profiles presented in Chapter 3 (Roles and Responsibilities)

Description: Methodology and assumptions for employee profile analysis used to support conclusions presented in Chapter 3 ("Roles and Responsibilities")

Source

- Profiles considered were of foreign employees at Alibaba, Huawei, and Tencent.
- The sources of employee profile data included: LinkedIn, articles and interviews available online, and interviews conducted as part of the research for this study the respective company.
- Profiles considered were drawn randomly from the respective company headquarters and overseas locations of the respective companies referenced above.
- The size of the set of profiles for foreign employees of Huawei and Alibaba consisted of 50 samples each.
- The size of the Tencent sample at 20 profiles was somewhat smaller than those of Alibaba and Huawei reflecting the relatively smaller total number of foreign employees Tencent employs.

Technique and Methodology

- Used Google's OpenRefine tool to clean the data and perform a preliminary analysis.
- Designed a 16-field frame to accommodate profile data fields. The frame covered four areas: [Name (Last, First)], [Position, Dates of Employment (Start Date–End Date), Location] (with enough space to accommodate two previous jobs) [School, Degree, Dates Attended (Start Date–End Date)] with enough space to accommodate two degrees) [Age].
- Applied cell padding to make each entry a consistent 16 field length that facilitated coherent analysis.

Assumptions and Conditions

- LinkedIn profiles used were current as of mid- 2018.
- Country of Origin (nationality) assumed based on location of university attended, workplace, etc. Clearly this is not a fail-safe method as a number of those whose profiles were analyzed studied outside of their native countries, for example. However, in some cases, it was possible to supplement information available through profiles with that available through other sources. (e.g. on line interviews in which the subject introduced themselves and included country of origin in that introduction, in-person interviews where the question was asked, etc.)
- To achieve consistency needed for relevant comparison between companies as well as meaningful analysis within any given company, profile information related to positions and titles was categorized and normalized. For example, different designations for management (Director, General Manager, etc.) were summarized under the general category "Management". Positions related to Corporate Social Responsibility (CSR), Environmental Sustainability, etc. were grouped under the more elastic "Corporate Affairs".
- As a general principle, the designations for roles and functions were evaluated according to a given company's practice which was then used as a criterion for grouping them. For example, a Community Manager in Alibaba was similar in function to staff engaged in Business Development in Alibaba and the roles were subsequently categorized as "Marketing" based on the descriptions of their scope and areas of responsibility.

Appendix C: Executive Speeches

Internal communication (speech) from Tencent CEO Ma Huateng to employees

Date: 31 December 2014

马化腾:腾讯应该多谈服务和特性

【TechWeb报道】12月31日消息,近日马化腾在对腾讯员工内部演讲时表示:腾讯应该少提"产品"和"功能",多谈"服务"和"特性"。他指出:"我们要少谈,我要一个产品,它要包括哪些功能。应该多想,我要提供一个服务,这个服务有哪些特性,它的整体服务流程是怎样的,它的整体服务成本是多少。"

马化腾表示:过分强调显性特性的,是初级的想法。"过去,我最怕的就是听谁说,我们要改版了,新版哪天……显性特性很重要,但是显性特性救不了你。把核心资源与时间,放在一次次优化显性特性上,基本上是互联网初级从业者的狂热症。"

"我们很多人觉得自己是乔布斯传人,大神的子孙。会以自己为中心,以自己的认知和感受来设计一个产品该是什么样子。而腾讯,最应该谈的是服务。"马化腾说道。

服务是以服务对象的需求和满意度为中心,定义所做的一切。放下自己,研究服务对象。如何研究我们的用户,我们的对象,我们应该有一套科学的方法,及硬性指标。(阿茹汗)

P. Ross, *Barriers to Entry*,
https://doi.org/10.1007/978-981-32-9566-7

以下为原文:

腾讯善于做产品,世人皆知。但其实我们更多时候应该少提"产品"和"功能",多谈"服务"和"特性"。我们要少谈,我要一个产品,它要包括哪些功能。应该多想,我要提供一个服务,这个服务有哪些特性,它的整体服务流程是怎样的,它的整体服务成本是多少。

我举个例子,以一台ATM机为例。

第一个问题:ATM机提供什么服务?

ATM机的核心服务:取现金。

第二个问题:一台ATM机的设计,有哪些特性?

在这个问题上,很多产品经理,会有这样的想法。

他经过深刻观察与思考之后的用专业态度来回答:ATM机的前端界面,是公司形象,还是操作提醒;从第一次操作,到拿到钞票,需要几步达成;提醒放在哪个环节出现,声音提醒还是字幕提醒;先取卡,还是先取钞……

这些特性,叫显性特性。

ATM机,还有关键特性。是隐形特性。

比如,一台ATM机里要放20万现金。也就是说,如果一个银行提供100台ATM机,那么他要把2000万现金放在外面。所以,看似ATM机分流了银行的营业压力,提升了品牌曝光,同时也分流了公司的核心资源。

因此,如何统计数据同步数据,支持决策,让ATM机发挥战略价值,同时不让资金过多闲置,是一台ATM机设计的隐形特性。也是核心服务。

第三个问题:一台ATM机,服务的全流程是什么?

作为一个用户体会到的一台ATM机的服务是,查卡,输密码,输金额,取钞,打印凭条,退卡。如果有问题,拨打服务热线。

作为一个ATM机的服务提供者,为了让用户持续稳定的获得上述简单的服务,日常操作性的服务流程包括:

现金管理:保证ATM机里随时有钱。包括了数据、现金出库、运送等复杂流程。

硬件管理:电源工作正常,打印机工作正常,打印机的纸、油墨耗材正常…

客服管理:遇到客户问题或者投诉的处理全流程。

这时,回到更重要的问题:战略问题。

银行为什么要提供ATM机的服务?

第一是为了分流营业网点的取现压力。第二是更多的品牌曝光机会。

因此,每一台ATM机,对银行这个服务提供者来说,必须具备战略价值。

这就是数据统计的运营意义,不单纯是让管理运营的人知道,某台机器没钱了,再不补现金进去,客户要投诉了。还要按照数据了解,这个服务点的设置,是否有足够的客流,是否达到战略要求。该增加服务,还是裁撤这个网点。

因此,我们觉得象空气一样简单流畅的ATM机,正常运转的背后,有7个以上岗位,在保证它的持续稳定服务。

如果以每次取款2元收入计,一台ATM机的总体成本回收期大约是10年。

过分强调显性特性的,是初级的想法。过去,我最怕的就是听谁说,我们要改版了,新版哪天……显性特性很重要,但是显性特性救不了你。把核心资源与时间,放在一次次优化显性特性上,基本上是互联网初级从业者的狂热症。

不能由衷有兴趣有热情地研究用户的,我们的产品经理就没机会长成产品专家。

我觉得腾讯内部以"服务"来定位自己做的每件事!

我们很多人觉得自己是乔布斯传人,大神的子孙。会以自己为中心,以自己的认知和感受来设计一个产品该是什么样子。

而腾讯,最应该谈的是服务。

服务是以服务对象的需求和满意度为中心,定义所做的一切。

放下自己,研究服务对象。如何研究我们的用户,我们的对象,我们应该有一套科学的方法,及硬性指标。

我们的每个产品经理每个月是不是要做10个用户调查,关注100个用户博客,收集反馈1000个用户体验?我觉得,是非常有必要的。怎么做?比如通过我们自己的反馈工具,或者通过像问卷网这样的第三方平台。

这是2014年腾讯内部一次会议马总的分享,他认为:研究用户,听取用户反馈,多做用户调查,这是每个产品经理的必修课。

Internal Communication (e-mail speech transcript) from Huawei CEO, Ren Zhengfei to Huawei corporate strategy managers

Date: 18 April 2017

4月18日,华为内部召开了一个战略预备队的座谈会,任正非在会上发表讲话,并提出了一个问题:华为会不会是下一个美联航?

任正非说,美联航不以客户为中心,而以员工为中心,导致他们对客户这样恶劣的经营作风。"我们认为最宝贵的财富是客户,一定要尊重客户。我们以客户为中心的文化,要坚持下去,越富越要不忘初心。"

"现在有些客户不远万里来到坂田,很多专家和主官都不愿意去展厅为客户提供讲解咨询,不愿多抽一些时间粘粘客户。这是否标识着华为正滑向美联航的道路?"任正非说到。

此外,任正非还表示"华为已经进入产业的世界领先行列,我们的事业呼唤领导,华为的优秀员工要树立领导世界的雄心壮志"。

任正非内部讲话曝光:华为不做美联航!

以下是微信公众号"心声社区"4月20日发表的《任总在战略预备队座谈会上的讲话》全文:

总裁办电子邮件

电邮讲话【2017】044号 签发人:任正非

任总在战略预备队座谈会上的讲话

2017年4月18日

一、你们要像种子一样,到最需要的地方去,生根、发芽、开花、结果,再成片开成花海。部分勇敢的人,要到最艰苦的地方去快速成长。

虽然目前战略预备队的训战规模还不大,但在我心目中,将来每年应该要训战1-2万人。我们抽出这么多时间,花费这么大代价,培养出种子,是希望你们到全球各地去生根、发芽、开花、结果,推动变革进步。对于少数特别优秀员工,还可以到最艰苦的国家去快速成长,除了提升技能,更能磨炼意志。希望你们能实现这个目标,但是"大江东去浪淘沙",我们不能保证人人都能成为将军、人人都是英雄。六十年代的电影《大浪淘沙》讲述四个青年人走进黄埔军校,最后走向完全不同的人生道路。起点相同,人生不同。相信在座各位会走向不同的领域,但是期望你们都能走向我们希望的目标,为未来作出较大的贡献。

1、你们不管资格多老、经历多丰富,如果这件事你不明白,就是新兵一个,以这种姿态投入训战,围绕目标创造性开展工作。

在训战过程中,最重要是靠自己努力,最好的训战结合是在实践中,而不是在课堂上。实战无论何时何地都随时存在的,如何自我培养,学学毛泽东、邓小平,他们可没有进过任何队。你们作为选出来的优秀分子参加集中训练,要安心接受赋能。华大不能过分强调条件,黄埔军校只有两条绑腿,抗大只有一条小板凳,但它们是真正的世界名校,培养出大量人才。参加集训可能也是你们人生的一次宝贵机会,看你们自己如何把握。

尽管华为公司引进了西方管理,提供了各种表格,你们要通过自己创造性的理解,在项目中因时因地去运用,不断优化。其实我们的作业表格并非大量抄顾问公司的PPT,是结合自己的实际归纳整理的。什么是训战?就是训练时所用的表格、代码……与作战的表格与操作是一样的。你们最贴近项目,老师贴近共同规律,你们相差100米,要互相探索前进。在没有深刻体会、充分实践的情况下,你不要提意见,自显高明。应削足适履,按规定的表格作业,端正学风。在作业过程中,你们总会有感悟,可以总结发表出来,也许在这个项目中已无法改进,但可以在下一个项目中或者别人吸取经验后继续改进。我们最需要的还是你的感悟。

当然,对于未能参加课堂培训的人,也可以通过互联网学习,公司案例都是全开放的。公司有很多案例,不知道哪类最适合你,如果你认为这类案例对自己启发很大,收藏到自己的储存,因为IT是通过日落法来简化案例管理,不会长期保留的。

2、学班是混合联队建制。不同专业、不同职级、不同年龄组成的联队,互相取长补短。

大家各自来自研发、财经、人力资源……,参加训战时,可能会感到"鸡同鸭讲",如果对话不上,可能那就是你更需要去理解的内容。高、中级干部需要跨流程、跨区域成长,如果不具有全流程的知识结构,就当不好领袖。冲突文化,其实是相互最好的教育。

进入学班后,没有军衔高低。当你们进入这个团队,就没有职级之分,在一起工作,平等交流。在差异中冲突,在冲突中井喷,一杯咖啡吸收宇宙能量。互相交流对案例、执行、项目、流程……的看法,总结出精华要点,在最基层项目起步时,就能客观掌握作业的方法。

3、学会用科学的方法工作来管理项目,不是僵化地照搬流程。

既然已贴近项目,无论项目大小,应该都是有作为的。以项目管理为中心,理解、解剖,真正明白项目管理的内核。

以考促训,贴身鉴定。在变革过程中,很多不同专业的团队跟着项目前进。比如,人力资源团队也需要知道"螺丝钉怎么拧",贴近我们的业务层考核,才能给每个人做出科学合理的鉴定。也许这个鉴定不会给他的人生产生多大作用,但是未来大数据扫描,扫描几个关键词,可能我们就会发现这个苗子。又如,在混合作战团队,财经应充分发挥项目核算、项目精算、工程概算......的引导作用,也要去感知合同场景。要精通自己的业务,也要熟悉相关的业务。

二、坚持以客户为中心的路线不动摇。

1、从美联航事件看,企业必需以客户为中心。

美联航不以客户为中心, 而以员工为中心,导致他们对客户这样恶劣的经营作风。华为会不会是下一个美联航?我们认为最宝贵的财富是客户,一定要尊重客户。我们以客户为中心的文化,要坚持下去,越富越要不忘初心。

2、巴塞的火爆与坂田的冷清,标志着华为正在淡化以客户为中心的文化。

现在有些客户不远万里来到坂田,很多专家和主官都不愿意去展厅为客户提供讲解咨询,不愿多抽一些时间粘粘客户。这是否标识着华为正滑向美联航的道路?如果每个人不热心见客户,坐而论道,这类人群要从专家队伍和主官队伍退到职员岗位上去,将来人力资源会做相关考核。富了就惰怠,难道是必归之路吗?

3、产品经理与客户经理的主责,要与客户有粘性,没有这种热情及成功渴望的人,不能担任主官。

每个代表处都要明确"如何以客户为中心",干部、专家要考核与客户交流的数量与质量。考核是全流程,从机会、获得、交付、服务......。缺失这个热情的要改正,以后的考核要量化、要公开。

公司机关既然不愿意好好为客户服务,为什么机关要建立这么庞大的机构。每年管理者的末位淘汰比为10%,但淘汰不是辞退,他可以进入战略预备队重新去竞争其他岗位。通过淘汰主官,将压力传递下去。在这个时代,每个人都要进步,时代不会保护任何人。不要认为华为公司是五彩光环,我们已处于风口浪尖,未来将走向何方?没人知道。因此,我们各项工作都要导向多产粮食、增加土地肥力。

三、各环节都要关注端到端的流程打通,任何变革都要有目标方向。变革者不要站在自我欣赏的角度,把流程弄复杂了。

1、所有变革都要有目标,主干流程要以多产粮食与增加土地肥力为中心。

你们要科学性、创造性地理解项目管理,在项目中,所有流程都要端到端横向打通。流程是拿来用的,变革是为了实现业务及管理目标的。没有目标会越改越复杂,变革会成为以自我为中心的完美体系,一个个完美的癌症,会阻碍业务发展。财经2009年确立了变革目标"准确确认收入,加速现金流入,项目损益可见,经营风险可控。"为IFS成功关闭,为账实相符的流程变革关闭,作了很好的引导,"山沟里的马列主义"。我们的变革项目群和变革项目,要学习IFS用简洁的语言,准确地阐述变革的目标,用明确的目标来指引变革的方向和举措。允许没做好,不允许说不清。我们要推行"变革项目化、IT产品化、流程版本化",在持续运营中不断改进。

2、研发、供应……都要关注以客户为中心。要关注端到端的协同与流程贯通。

研发是为客户服务的,应该多与客户交流。"可生产、易交付、免维护"的设计要纳入研发立项流程,从立项开始改变。将产品研究成功后,再去做适配性的生产,这种方法要改变。研发必须是客户需求导向的,商业成功导向的。

3、成为领袖的人,胸怀宽广,视野远大,但都是从小事做起的。晋升到17级的台阶,应有完成一个项目的全流程交付。

华为已经进入产业的世界领先行列,我们的事业呼唤领导,华为的优秀员工要树立领导世界的雄心壮志。"天将降大任于斯人也,必先苦其心志,劳其筋骨,饿其体肤,空乏其身,行拂乱其所为,所以动心忍性,曾益其所不能。"应该成为华为优秀员工的座右铭。

Internal communication to employees from Alibaba CEO, Ma Yun (Jack Ma)

Source: "From Sales to Service" in: *Ma Yun Neibu Jianghua:Xiangxin Mingtian*, Beijing: Hongqi Chubanshe (Red Flag Publishing Company), 2015, pages 67–77

102 年不是一句口号

阿里巴巴走到现在,经历了很多坎坷,我非常感谢阿里巴巴有销售人员,是你们一点一滴有努力,使阿里巴巴有了今天这样的影响力,或许有些人大学一毕业就加入了我们公司。一做就是这么多年,我们相信大家一定感到疲惫,感到过厌烦,或许还遭到过家庭的埋怨,经受了很多诱惑,能坚持下来,而且做得这么好,真的很不容易,我看到有些人老了很多,也成熟了很多,你们是阿里巴巴最珍贵的希望,很多人看到你们还在我们公司,心里就有了底气,我也是如此,如果我到各个办公室,看到的还是你们这些人的脸的话,我就知道,不管遇到什么困难,阿里巴巴都会扛过去的。

在阿里巴巴上市之前,我跟我们"五年陈"的员工有过一次交流,我跟他们说,感谢你们坚持了五年,你们挡住了很多诱惑,其实我觉得,绝大部分"五年陈"的员工留下来,不是因为有远见。那时候就看好B2B,就知道阿里巴巴会发展得这么好,而是因为绝大多数人都没有地方可去,阿里巴巴也不算太糟糕,就留来了,那些自以为聪明的人都离开了,自己创业去了,还有一些人被猎头公司挖去了,出去的人默默无闻,脚踏实地地干了五年之后,我们突然发现阿里巴巴变成了一家成功的公司,个人不错,公司也不错,原因是什么?我们坚持下来了,挡住了很多诱惑。

公司取得今天的成绩,我觉得每个人都有功劳,但功劳都是过去的,我们离成功还太遥远,如果按照一些民营企业的七老板的相法,我们这些人都不用干了,换个工作、轻松一点,这一辈子都不用愁,就像20世纪七八十年代的万元户,家里养鱼养猪的、特有钱,女孩子都愿意嫁给这样的万元户,但是今天,万元户已经不行了,乡镇企业的发展非常之快,到今天为止、乡镇企业没有倒掉的只有鲁冠球的万向一家,我特别不希望阿里巴巴的老员工、老干部像当年的万元户一样,我不希望我们这些人熬了五年八年,一下了就没有了,我们挣的钱,虽然现在看来不少,但从未来来看,根本不算什么,我们公司现在还在布局中、我们要做102年,这不是一句口号,我每天都在想那些百年企业具有最重要的基因是什么,我们已经走了八年,还要走94年,全世界的电子商务才做了20年,如果我们也想做20年,光靠B2B是不行的,要把淘宝、支付宝都叠合起来,把整个产业链都打通,才有可能走20年、30年,30年以后,我们可能会进入一个新的行业,比如生物科技或是月球探索。

今年,我们集团开了两次战略会议,确定下一个目标,虽然这个目标有点大,但我觉得实现的可能性很大,从公司的市值来看,我当时希望阿里巴巴成为中国第一家市值超过100亿美元的互联网公司,但没有想到我们上市之前、腾讯和百度先做到了100亿美元,尽管我们是中国第一家市值超过200亿美元的民营公司,但我觉得这已经没有意义了,我们必须做到1000亿美元的市值,是100亿到1000亿,是一个大的台阶,中国诞生一家市值1000亿美无的民营企业,才是我们这辈子最大的梦想,这是很难做到的,如果真的做到了,我相信我们一辈子都会很高兴。

在美国很难做电子商务

其实,大家要注意一点,今天阿里巴巴的市值是200亿美元,实际上不止200亿美元,因为我们口袋里已经有货了,我们从零做到200亿美元的时候,难度是非常大的,既然我们能从零做到200亿美元,那么从200亿美元做到1000亿美元,就应该更有把握。所以我觉得,我们今天提出的目标更有可能实现,当我们真正做到的时候,我们每个人都应该为此感到骄傲,因为我们这家公司没有向银行贷款一分钱,没有拿政府一分钱,我们也没有请很多优秀的高才生,我们就是靠普普通通的每个人一点一滴地去做,凭本事去做。

我参加过全世界的很多论坛,人家说,现在全世界市值排名前十位的企业中,有三家是中国的,都是国有企业。他们不看好中国的企业,说国有企业就上垄断的,交给傻子做都差不到哪里去。所以,我们要让中国诞生一家市值超过1000亿美元的民营企业,让全世界对我们肃然起敬,这是我们的目标。我希望我们能在五年以内实现这个目标,这样,我们就有可能创造一个奇迹。为什么我们有机会创造奇迹呢?因为我们处在一个很好的行业,在互联网这个行业,一定会诞生伟大的公司。虽然中国绝大部分的民营企业是制造业的公司,但中国不可能成为制造业大国,大家要承认这一点,因为我们国家缺乏能源,缺乏原材料,而且劳动力成本越来越高,环境污染越来越来严重,这些因素都会阻碍中国制造业的发展。我认为,制造业公司要进入世界五百强,成为市值超过1000亿美元的企业,难度是很大的,而互联网企业有这个机会。

在互联网行业,中国和美国、欧洲、日本几乎是在同一起跑线上。互联网行业有三大板块、一是新闻媒体、二是娱乐、三是电子商务。八年以前,我们决定去做电子商务。虽然今天阿里巴巴的市值达到了200多亿美元,但我想告诉大家,电子商务在中国的发展还没有正式开始,整个电子商务的环境还没有建立起来,20年以后,人类社会才会真正感觉到我们今天所做的东西。我相信,未来在电子商务领域,一定会诞生一家优秀的企业。

应该说,我们比较幸运的。如果是在美国,就很难做电子商务,这什么呢?因为美国的基础建设非常好,有很好的信用体系、支付体系和网络体系,每家中小企业都有很好的IT人才。而在中国,这些东西都没有,所以我们才有机会。我们建立了一个阿里巴巴的生态体系——建立了两个交易市场,一个阿里巴巴B2B、一个是淘宝。如果我们运气好,做得不错的话,五年、十年之后,这些体系可能会成为全亚洲电子商务的基础体系,所以企业都会用我们的服务。到今天为止,已经有40万个网站在用我们的支付宝。

而且,我们比中国任何一家互联网公司都有钱,现在有160亿美元的现金储备。另外,中国互联网公司从事电子商务的人才一共12,000人,其中有8000人是阿里巴巴的。12,000个电子商务人才,我们占了8000个。钱我们有,人我们有,而且我们的布局也不错,从B2B、C2C到阿里软件,到阿里妈妈,我们的整个布局是中国电子商务的公司中最好的。所以,我们是有机会的。

但是,有一样最关键的东西不能忘——组织的建设,七八年前加入阿里巴巴的时候,就算再大胆预想,可能也想不到我们今天能成为市值200亿美元的公司。我们公司到底值多少钱,阿里巴巴B2B到底值多少钱?我们千万不要认为我们今天的股票会值三十几块钱,在我看来,我们的股票只值十三块五。为什么只值十三块五?做任何事情,都要有理性。在中国,比我们挣钱多、利润高的公司多得很,腾讯就比我们收入高,利润高,用户群也多,凭什么它只有100亿美元的市值,而我们有200亿美元?人们对我们的期望值太高了,大家把中国经济的高速发展,互联网的高速发展,电子商务的高速发展的期望都寄托在我们身上了。

十三块五是一个真实的数字,超出的部分都是人们对我们的期望,是需要我们努力做出来的。跟五年前相比,我们现在有足够的钱,有足够的人才,我们的布局不错,全世界也开始关注我们,这是好事。坏事呢?你做任何事情,人家都认为你做得不够好,有这样的资源,还可以做得更好。五年前,你跟人家说你是阿里巴巴的员工,人家可能会往地上吐痰;而今天,你说自己是阿里巴巴"五年陈"的员工,你拥有多少股票,人家看你的眼光就彻底不一样了,但是,你没有变,你还是你。要我说,阿里巴巴今年跟去年有什么区别?没有区别,今年我们的股票值200亿美元,看起来很伟大的样子,其实去年也差不多。虽然我们今天是市值200亿美元的公司,我们有股票值三十几块钱,但我们要很理性地知道自己值多少钱,我们还是昨天的我们。我们的责任更大了,以前我们只对两三个股东的负责,现在光香港本地就有19万股民买我们的股票。

我们的美国机构投资者共有1300多家,其中有600多家从来没有买过中国和亚洲的股票,他们为了我们来到亚洲,来买我们的股票,这是老外对中国人和信心,也是我们的责任。所以,千万不要觉得我们已经富裕了,也千万不要认为我们值200亿美元了,其实我们跟当年万元户没有什么区别。

企业的成长要靠员工的成长

企业的成长要靠员工的成长。我在北京碰到几个老员工,当年阿里巴巴的老销售出去以后都是去当副总经理、总监。一个老员工出去经后做了四家公司,做一家死一家,到现在公司只有三个人——他、他老婆,还有一个客户。创业真的是这样,100家公司,99家死掉,还有一家半死不活。阿里巴巴的运气太好了,前面说过,我们成功是因为我们能干吗?大家看看周围,比我们能干的人有多少。你说你很勤奋,我们是很辛苦,但是比我们辛苦的人不知道有多少,很多人比我们更起早贪黑,他们什么也没有得到。

所以,我们是运气很好,我们有好的团队、好的文化、好的行业,所有东西凑在一起,就是凑成了今天这个样子,千万别觉得自己能力强,我到今天都没有觉得自己能力强,没有每个员工实实在在的努力,阿里巴巴是不会成功的,我今天说了,五年以后,我们这家公司要成为中国第一家打进世界五百强的市值超过1000亿美元的公司,不拿政府一分钱,实实在在地打进去的公司,这需要所有阿里巴巴的员工一起努力,正因为有大家的努力,我讲的很多话才能变成现实,今天一样,否则以后这种狂话我在外面也不讲了。

我们要认清阿里巴巴今天的市值是多少,我们真正的市值是80亿美元到100亿美元。我们不要因为股票的下跌而心里发慌,哪怕是跌到20块,哪怕是跌到13块,都没有关系,因为我们看的不是半年一年,而是五年以后谁是英雄。五年以后谁牛,才是真的牛。如果五年以后,我们的市值真的变成了1000多亿美元,那你就可能休息了,你可以对自己说,对公司说,我对得起自己,对得起公司,对得起公司给我的机会。今天做成这样,你还不能说对得起自己。包括我在内,任何一个人在这个集团里说我真辛苦,我是通过自己有努力赢得这么多财富的,这是胡扯。

我不相信就凭我们这点努力,这点聪明,可以取得今天这样的成功,我们碰到了很多机遇,在最困难的时候,我们刚好凑到了2000万美元,就熬过去了,后来又碰上雅虎被我们买过来,碰上eBay犯了一个大错误,才使得我们有了今天、绝对不是因为我们伟大。当然,我们也没有那么愚蠢,我们抓住了很多机会。但是,今后的机会,我们个个都能抓住吗?很难说。我认为《三国演义》中最伟大的人是赵云,据说他到70多岁的时候,身上一处伤疤都没有,那才是不得了。

五年以前,没人有知道我们,我们是在水下面。今天,我们浮出水面了,所有的弓箭枪炮都对准了我们。我们遇到了很多困难,但我们都熬过来了。今后五年,我们会更精彩。等你到了50岁或60岁的时候,你对自己的孙子讲,你爷爷当年加入了这家公司的时候,它只是一个小房间,现在它已经成为世界上非常强大的公司,这种骄傲的感受是完全不一样的。

丰田公司的伟大不在于领导者的伟大,而在于每个员工、每个老员工的伟大,每个老员工都捍卫自己公司的荣誉,大家想想,汽车行业被美国人垄断了多少年?丰田居然把美国所有的汽车公司都打败了,现在美国最厉害的汽车公司是丰田,欧洲最厉害汽车公司也是丰田,我们阿里巴巴就缺一批这样的老员工,我们征战八年,很多人半路退出了,如果我们的老员工不能再往前进一步,不能再熬一两年的话,那我们公司就不可能成为伟大的公司。

这两年来,我有些愧疚,大家受委屈的时候,我没有来安慰大家,不过,话说回来,大家都这么大了,应该自己添伤口。我受委屈的时候也是自己添伤口,不知道谁讲,这三四年,我们做得还是不错,阿里巴巴B2B、淘宝、支付宝都做得很好,整个布局也不错,但未来我们还有很长的路要走。

我们很多员工说要去创业,在我看来,你们这些人去创业真的很难,可能会全军覆没,因为你们没有这个机会了,年龄、眼光等各方面都不如年轻人,我们公司是幸运的,每次我们遇到倒霉的事情时,就会有好运气,如果你今天加入另外一家公司,我觉得你可能不会那么舒服,因为别人对阿里巴巴的人的期望是非常高的。为什么会对你产生很高的期望?因为你可能有很好和主管,很好的老板,阿里巴巴有很好的品牌。所以,如果你离开这家公司,可能就遇到麻烦,就像你天天呼吸新鲜空气,突然到了毒气很多的地方,就麻烦了:

不提升,就不能带下面的兵

当然,有好的机会,大家可以走,每个人都自己的职业规划,要养家糊口、养父母,这都很正常。但是,如果我是你们,我会求稳健、求发展、求成长,阿里的平台还是很不错的,最怕就是头脑发热。当年有一家公司跟我们竞争,他们说,阿里巴巴的人过去,工资翻两倍。我觉得两倍低了一点,四倍可以去,我也去。大家记住,天下没有那个人傻到白白出钱请你去,他给你四五倍的工资,对你的期望也是四五倍,期望越高,失望越大。我们并不需要坐在那里不干活的人,我是老员工,我有军功,很多有军功的人都死得特别快,必须转型、必须提升,不转型,不提升,就不能带下面的兵。

你们是阿里巴巴最精英的前线销售人员,我并不希望大家回去以后跟下面的人说,同志们加油干,每个人的业绩必须翻一倍。毕竟是人,就算做死也不能翻一倍。我希望大家做一件事情——传递文化,这才是你们需要做的。如果你们希望把自己的股票留给子孙后代,将来股价能几十倍、上百倍地增长,那你们就要传递文化,培养新人,让新员去帮你们赚钱,因为他们有使不完的力气。你们要把以前的文化传递给他们,帮助他们成长,这样,你们也会成长得越来越快。

当然,我也知道我们这家公司存在很多问题。大家肯定觉得我们的反馈怎么那么差,如果反馈很好,这家公司就不存在了,今天反馈数量跟五年前比多了很多,五年前没有反馈都卖得很好,因为五年前买家没有那么多,我可以跟大家讲,哪怕十年以后,反馈也不会像你们想象的那么好,反馈意味着什么?意味着订单,订单是利润,明年我们要完成任务,这中间本来就有很多偶然,我们公司不断往前走,从一年内只有一万个反馈到几十万个反馈,客户越多买家就越多,买家就越多卖家就越多,所以,反馈好不好,关键在于跟谁比,是跟昨天比,还是跟同行比,或者是跟未来比。

把反馈做好需要一个过程。我们的网站要开放、要提升、要成长,相对其他公司来讲,我们公司今天有更多的资本和能力去做这件事,大家要相信公司一定会努力。但是,把反馈做好不是那么容易的,如果那么容易,还轮得到阿里巴巴吗?从10,000个增加到10,100个都是很艰难的,需要一点一滴地往前推进,需要五年、十年的磨炼过程,我们今天的这些客户反馈,是我们咬牙切齿坚持八年的结果,中间我们犯了很多错误,走了很多弯路。

但是,我不想找理由,我的意思不是说我们的反馈就应该永远差下去,我们必须承担这样的责任,我们必须有信心和毅力坚持下去,三四年以前,我们的战略有些问题,有人担心直销发展下去会成为公司的负担,所以我们的战略变成维持直销,不多做直销,迅速向新的模式转型。今天我们发现,当时的决定是一个错误。我们的直销跟TCL的直销是完全不一样的,我们的销售人员更像是电子商务咨询师,我们认为中国需要10万这样的人才,中国有多少企业?4000多万家企业,在中国的内贸电子商务市场,将来每家企业每月在电子商务和IT商务上的投入至少五万块钱,,一定需要培养大量的直销人员,前几年我们在培训方面的投入不够,今天我们要调整过来,继续大力建设我们的铁军直销团队,培训优秀人才。我们需要的不是纯粹的直销人员,而是电子商务咨询师,告诉别人怎么在网上促销,怎么在网上卖关键字,怎么在网上做网页。

给自己一个承诺

另外,我们这两年也没有把很多的精力放在制度创新、奖励创新上,所以我们现在的套路确实需要调整一下,我们必须面对今天的形势,我们有好的东西,也有很坏的东西,你们疲惫了,我也疲惫了,真的很累,但我希望大家能再往前挪动一步,伟大的人和不伟大的人的区别是什么?大家都要死的时候,你再往前挪一步,大家都倒下去了,你还站在那儿,你就是伟大的人,你们比绝大多数人都厉害和伟大。因为当时加入阿里巴巴的那么多人都放弃了,而你们没有放弃,既然不放弃,为什么不让自己往前走 在我们公司上市之前,我最担心的就是你们这些老员工,我理解你们,你们跟我一样,真的很累,但我希望这种累不要变成心里上的累,行为上的累。

很多人看着你们,如果有人说这个老员工每天不干活儿,还占着位置不肯走,当这种情况出现的时候,公司的灾难就来了,如果你们真的觉得自己没有动力,那就像普通人一样,当个万元户,过过日子,红军当年过草地,很多人是饿死的,还有很多人坚持不下去了,就娶个老婆在当地过了,所以,你们也一样,一但掉队,就再也跟不上了,今天,我们回过头去看看当年离开的那些员工,他们跟你们有很大的区别,这种区别不是钱多少的区别,而是对文化的认同,对团队的认同的区别,我感谢大家前面几年所做的努力,后面的路更长,如果你们相信公司,相信自己,我们在一起再奋斗五年,看看可不可以做出一家伟大的公司,五年以后,如果大家想离开,跟我讲,我一定让你们舒舒服服的离开。

我给阿里巴巴定位是一家现代服务业公司,我不希望每个员工都是销售人员,我们做的是服务性行业,我们没有把自己定位为制造业,而是定位服务业,每个员工为自己的公司,为自己的客户服务,也许你们过去的动力和服务不如五年前了,但是有两样东西,你们现在比五年前更行,一是对现有客户和潜在客户的服务,你们。。。,你们会用心去服务,二是对。。。员工的帮助,只有老员工成长了,公司才能成长,当你们把自己和功力传给别人的时候,你们的功力就增强了,很多行业没有大师,销售大师实际上只是销售员,只能称为专家,而服务业是有大师的,六七年前,你们不断交流销售经验,今天,你们要从销售走向服务,服务客户才是最重要的,给自己一个承诺非常重要。大学毕业的时候,我答应我的校长在学校教五年书,结果我教了六年半。今天,我们不是为了钱,不是为了名,不是为了利,我们就是想做一件事情,这是对社会,对团队,对所有阿里巴巴的员工,对父母的承诺。也是对自己的承诺。给自己一个五年的承诺,承诺再干五年。我相信,如果五年之后你们真的离开这家公司,你们的功力一定会更强,而不会更弱,因为在中国,像我们这样的公司真的不多,你们会经历很多。五六年前是肉搏战,今天是军团作战,未来五年公司将现面临的挑战和你们每个人将面临的挑战,跟五年前完全不一样。

从销售走向服务,又是一种新的经历。千万记住,我们不能小看自己。我们已经熬了五年了,咬牙切齿再熬五年,我们就会不一样,因为伟大是熬出来的。我希望大家给自己一个承诺,我也给自己一个承诺,让我们忘掉股份,继续往前走,往前看,做出中国第一家市值超过1000亿元的民营企业。

Internal communication to new hires from Cisco CEO, John Chambers (video transcript)

Date: 4 March 2010

Hello, I'm John Chambers, chairman and CEO at Cisco and I want to welcome each of you as a new hire to Cisco. Some of you will be coming out of college some of you will be in the industry for multiple decades. But what you are about to find out is going to be the most exciting job you've ever had in your life. It's one of the best places to work in every country in the world, we are a family in a very unique way and we're going to change the way the world works, lives, learns, and plays. This year we are celebrating our 25 year anniversary. We saw more growth both from a financial point of view, from a customer satisfaction point of view, but also from a corporate social responsibility point of view than almost any company have ever done in history during our first 25 years. And the exciting thing is we built the foundation for the next 25. We are the global leader in high tech and innovation but we are also very effective at execution.

So as you join Cisco, a couple of areas I'd like to ask you to help us keep as a key part of our culture; On your culture badge, at the very base is what we are and who we are. We put the customer success first in everything we do. In the middle is catching market transitions, we don't focus on competition although it is fun to compete, we focus on getting transitions right. Either transitions of data voice video over a single network, transitions in the consumer world with video, or data center virtualization and clouds. We focus our base in terms of organization structure around social groups, or communities, we call them councils, boards and working groups, you will hear more about that. And business models built on vision thinking 5–10 years out, strategy, execution. This allows us to move with speed, scale, flexibility and replication.

While we are family we also believe in using our own technology to really drive collaboration across the company, moving from command and control to a collaborative leadership style. And I can't emphasize enough our belief in terms of the most successful companies or individuals in the world should be the best in giving back. While we're not a perfect organization and we do regularly remind each other of that, we are a family. We watch out for each others in ways that, as you will find out over your time at Cisco, is very unique.

We set long term goals and we almost always achieve those. We have no fear about entering a new markets or taking on new peers in the industry but we have a lot of healthy paranoia about what could go wrong. And we are setting an aspirational goal that many will say is impossible to achieve but I think we can; to become the best in the world and the best for the world.

I wish you success here at Cisco. I can tell you it will be your best job of your life and I want to welcome you to the Cisco family. It's a great time to be at Cisco, I look forward to personally meeting you in years to come.

Internal communication ("All Hands" meeting) of LinkedIn CEO Jeff Weiner to employees (transcript)

Date: 13 June 2016

Jeff Weiner: A hush falls over the crowd. Welcome to All Hands special edition. I was thinking about the last time we had an All Hands that was not on a Wednesday morning, this is shaping up to be a little bit of LinkedIn trivia. Anyone know the answer? Anyone but Dee know the answer? IPO, very good. For bonus points, where was it broadcast from live? Empire State Building. Correct. It was the day of our IPO, a very memorable day, and I find some parallels between the events, I will come back to that later on. For those of you who were able to get a seat, congratulations. We have a little bit of an unusual dynamic today. Oh, dynamic, that's a little play on words now that we're with Microsoft, I didn't catch that. I have to get used to that pun.

The All Hands starts at 10:30, I was in the building across the way and at about 9:45, I started to see a line going into the building here in Mountain View where the all hands is, I was looking to myself, I wonder who is here speaking today? Like a rockstar or something, this is amazing! And I was like, oh yeah. So for those of you, I don't know if this was also the case in other locales around the world where there were long lines and unfortunately we ran out of seating capacity, but for those of you now watching from the cafeteria here in Mountain View or from your desks, thank you so much for showing up this morning and waiting in line, we appreciate your patience, and we hope this comes through loud and clear.

We have some news to discuss, I'm assuming by now everyone is aware of what that is. We will be joining forces with Microsoft to do some pretty incredible things going forward. And we are here today to talk about the rationale, I'm going to go specifically into the way I'm thinking about this personally, I shared that in the email, talk about what it means for us as a company, I will turn it over to Reid, and as our founder and chairman he will share his thoughts, and we will welcome up Satya, and as the CEO of Microsoft he will share why he is so excited, and the deal rationale.

So let's start with the facts of that email I sent this morning, I'm going to be touching on many of the same points and just a little preface—if I get a little emotional as I go through the content, please don't misinterpret it, it is not coming from a place of sadness. I promise you, it's not. Not that there's anything wrong with that. It is coming from a place of deep appreciation and gratitude to all of you. You know how much—it's happening already, Jesus, two minutes in. It's going to be a long all hands. It's coming from a place of heartfelt appreciation and gratitude. You know how I feel about this company, you know how I feel about all of you, but it is beyond a privilege to be working alongside of you to build what we have built, and we will keep building. If I do get a little verklempt, my team has instructions as always to lob in a really bad joke to reel me back in, hopefully that will work. Speaking of emotion and feeling a little verklempt, some of you in the audience here today are probably going through your own emotional roller coaster. I want you to know it is completely normal and natural. You may be excited, I know there is a lot of excitement, you may be surprised, there is some of that too—I think woke up this morning like, what? Some of you may be a bit fearful of the unknown, and all of this is just part of the process. Everyone is going to process this differently, and you should process it, you should take the time to process it. Don't walk out of here feeling you like you need to feel a certain way, because you don't. You are you, and what this means to you is up to you.

With that, let's get started, I want to start by saying thank you. Don't need the joke yet. Thank you for the best job I've ever had. We may need a joke now. No, I'm okay. I joined the company in December of 2008, and I joined the company for a few different reasons. One was Reid, and the opportunity to work with a legend, a true visionary, one of the most thoughtful human beings I've ever met, way too good to pass up. I joined the company because of the talent. The talent in December 2008 was small enough in the aggregate to fit in the break room in 2029, that is where we used to conduct All Hands. It's hard to believe, take a look at the screens broadcasting this around the world, 30 cities. And I joined because of the value we could bring to people, connecting them to opportunity in ways that had never been done before. Never in my wildest imagination could I have dreamt of what would follow over the next 7 1/2 years. From 338 employees to 10,000 today, from $78 million of revenue in 2008 to this year our guidance is for roughly $3.7 billion dollars. From somewhere from 32 to 33 million members, today we are north of 430 million, I could go on and on. I hope you take some time to reflect on what we have been able to build because it is extraordinary, and so are you for helping to make that happen. So please give yourselves a big round of applause. You're giving yourselves a lot of applause there, that was long—maybe a little extra long. Kevin said we are awesome, Pat said we are amazing. Despite everything that we have accomplished, what is particularly noteworthy is in many ways we are just getting started, just getting started in terms of the fulfillment of our potential and purpose, to connect the world's professionals, make them more productive and successful, and create economic opportunity for every member of the global workforce. Today's news, this combination with Microsoft, is another step along the way, another step along the journey, collectively, for all of us together. It is another stepping stone towards realizing our mission and vision, and for me it is the next chapter in what has been the most extraordinary professional experience that I've ever had.

So let's talk about the why. It starts with the things that I think about day in and day out on my way to work, throughout the day. Two simple things, first is mission and vision and second is our culture and values. And with regards to mission and vision, there are no strangers in this audience today to how strongly we feel about it, it is why we are here. And as strong as my conviction has been historically, it has never been stronger than it is today. And there is good reason for that—the world needs what we do more than ever before. And if you don't believe me, just take a look at the headlines on a daily basis. In the last three weeks alone, for those of you who follow the news in this area, let's start with Foxconn, a manufacturer in Asia, announced they will be displacing 60,000 factory workers with robots. 60,000 people are going to lose their jobs because of robots. Within 24 hours, a former CEO of McDonald's said that if the minimum wage continues to increase they're going to have to replace all of their franchise staff members with robots. Not sure if he was being provocative or not, but it certainly got my attention. Within another week or so, Walmart said it was going to begin rolling out tests of drone technology within their warehouses to replace all of the people who do pick, pack, and ship there. Then, within a week or so after that, Elon Musk got up at Code and said that 100% driverless technology will be ready in two years' time.

That dystopian future where robots replace people, that has been predicted in science fiction for decades, it's happening. It has begun. And what amounted to headlines over a three-week period at some point will turn into a torrent of daily news. Whether it is the displacement of individuals and people by virtue of new technologies, whether it is the widening skills gap, whether it is the growing problem with youth based unemployment, or record levels of socioeconomic stratification, creating economic opportunity will be the defining issue of our time. That's why we are here, that is why we do what we do. And I know you all believe in that deeply. So we understand the mission and vision components of this, that is the what. You also understand something that is unique to LinkedIn, and that is the fact that we care equally as much about the what as we do the how. Our culture and values, the way we do business, the way we conduct ourselves. Had you asked me about culture and values 10 or 12 years ago, before I got here, I would have rolled my eyes and I would have cited a Dilbert comic strip, like most of us. And had you asked me about the importance of culture and values after I took over as CEO, I would've said, you know what? I have a different appreciation, the stuff is important, it matters. Ask me today and I will tell you it is our ultimate competitive advantage, and it's not cheerleading, I mean it. Because I've seen up close what you are capable of doing when you believe in how we do it. It's what makes LinkedIn LinkedIn. And you know the values as well as anybody. Members first. Relationships matter. Be open and honest and constructive. Demand excellence. Take intelligent risks and act like an owner. I think one of the things that separates us from other companies is not that we have codified our values, other companies have done that. It is that we spent a lot of time and energy not just talking the talk but walking the walk. We want to raise up to the bar we have set for ourselves and the company we aspire to be, and not play down to our fears and the lowest common denominator. I will give you a shining example, something Satya and I have both been fielding today because repeatedly we get the question, how in the world did this not leak? One of the largest internet and technology deals in history, how did it not leak? And what I didn't provide them details of was the number of people who have been brought over the wall. And by the way, to every one of you who has been working tirelessly around the clock to make today as successful as it's been thus far, from Satya and I and the entire team, thank you so much. Big round of applause.

When we originally were talking about the number of people, I thought it would be appropriate to bring over the wall, consistent with our culture and values of transparency, open, honest and constructive, I was told you can't do that, it will leak. It is an inevitability. You bring a certain critical mass of people over the wall, it will leak. And that is the same playing down to the lowest common denominator that we are trying to defy, and sure enough, look at what happened. That is such a special quality. That is a competitive advantage. So we've got the what in terms of our mission and vision, the how in terms of culture and values.

Why are these things so important to me personally? Because when I was in your shoes it mattered to me, it mattered to me a great deal. I always wanted to be set up to be successful, I wanted my teams to have a chance to accomplish what we were setting out to accomplish. And I vowed that if I was ever in a role where I could do something about it, that's what I would focus on. And now, sure enough, in this capacity I can do something about it. And what has become increasingly obvious to me is that to continue to focus on our mission and vision and our long-term objectives and the role we play in the world and the value we can bring to our members and customers lives, and to do it in a way that is consistent with our culture and values, and what makes us truly LinkedIn, we need to be able to control our own destiny. This is vital. Not just in any quarter, this quarter is going as well as the last quarter did, everyone is doing a nice job, but looking out two, three, five years down the road, understanding the potential challenges, and not denying that we are sticking our heads in the sand, but confronting them head-on. And doing so in a way that enables us to do the things we dream of doing. That is what I want for us.

Some of you in the audience may be saying, hang on a second, you just said we need to control our own destiny and you are here talking about acquired by Microsoft. How do you reconcile those two things? And for me it's a byproduct of the world we live in today and how that world is evolving, and the structure in which this deal will be executed. With regard to the world and the evolution of the world, imagine a world where, rather than looking up at tech titans like Apple, Google, Microsoft, Amazon, and Facebook, and dreaming or wondering what it is like to operate at that scale—not hundreds of millions of members or customers but billions, not billions of dollars in market capitalization but hundreds of billions—you don't wonder anymore, because you are one of them. Imagine a world where, rather than react to competitive pressures, and increasing competitive intensity by virtue of the growing number of business lines that we are in, we are leading from the front, and leveraging advantages that other companies can only dream of. Imagine a world where, rather than be hamstrung in terms of our ability to invest in our people and disrupt ourselves and take intelligent risks by virtue of short-term market pressures, we can always invest intelligently in the realization of our mission vision and long-term objectives. And imagine a world where the inevitable cyclical downturns of the macroeconomics on a global basis don't weaken us, but strengthen our resolve, make us more essential to the people we need to help when it matters most to them. With today's announcement, we don't need to imagine those things anymore because it's our reality. Let's turn now to why Microsoft, and I want to provide just a little bit of context because the why Microsoft question, the answer to that starts before Satya and I sat down together a few months ago. How many of you have been following the evolution of Microsoft under Satya over the last two years? Show of hands. You can't see it Satya, but a lot of hands. They may just be saying that because of what is happening, we will talk later, everybody. I've been in the industry for over 20 years, I'm a student of great management, I like to watch great examples and learn from them, and I'm fascinated by this stuff, as you guys know. And I'm not saying this because of the situation and because Satya is essentially a one person board for me now, I'm saying this because it's true, and it's been documented, I was sharing it publicly via LinkedIn, via Twitter, over the last two years. You can check it out. I believe that what Satya has been doing as the CEO of one of the largest and most valuable companies in the world is extraordinary. He has made the company more open, more agile, more innovative, and perhaps most importantly, more purpose driven, and I give you kudos for that because it ain't easy. Satya is like, you've got that right. [LAUGHTER] And it was against that backdrop that Satya and I had a chance to meet a few months ago. He and Reid and Bill Gates already have a relationship, they would spend time over the last few years brainstorming about how we could potentially work together, and the way the world is evolving. You can imagine being a fly on the wall in a meeting between Reid and Bill Gates, by the way, that would be interesting stuff, and one I'm looking forward to joining I might add. That will be kind of fun, actually. And when Satya came in and sat down we started talking about the various ways in which the combination might make sense. We started riffing and brainstorming, I will get to some of those examples in a moment, because for those of you watching the press today, that is not rehearsed. Get us talking about what is possible and it's the easiest thing in the world for the two of us to do, because it is all true. In the throes of that brainstorming, Satya said to me, you know Jeff if we are going to get serious about this we have to have alignment on two dimensions. The first is purpose and the second is structure. I said okay, let's talk about that. And it turns out, our sense of purpose is far more similar than I ever could have imagined, than I ever could have guessed.

So, we all know our mission statement, connect the world's professionals to make them more productive and successful. How many of you know Microsoft's mission statement? Anyone? I thought you were wearing a Windows shirt for a second, like, yes, I know you do. You are ineligible for this one buddy. And by the way, not a lot of hands went up, I didn't know the mission statement, I had a sense of what it was by virtue of some pretty effective television advertising, and I knew about this idea of empowerment—so Satya said it was to empower individuals and organizations all over the planet to achieve more. I was like, really? He was like, yep. I was like, achieve more, be more productive and successful—these are almost identical. I mean the words are different but the underlying message is the same. And we were struck by the strength of the alignment, and we were also struck by the fact that we have gone at it in different ways and as a result of that, combining the two companies, it is really interesting. So we've gone at making people more productive and successful by virtue of building the world's largest and most valuable professional network. Microsoft has done it by building the professional cloud and the services that live within that cloud. And when you combine those things, it is not only unique, it is unprecedented at this level of scale. So what is possible when you start to combine these assets? Well, for starters, you could take our network and you could seamlessly integrate that within Microsoft's global footprint of over 1 billion individuals. You got that number right, 1 billion. So LinkedIn becomes the social fabric, the connective tissue, the single source of professional identity, and you deeply integrate that into things like Outlook and Calendar and Office and Windows and Skype and Dynamics and Active Directory, and pretty soon you are taking our network and you are growing it 10× in terms of what is possible with regard to meaningful engagement in connecting our members to opportunity. One example, I would also add along those lines, Satya characterizes Microsoft as essentially being a corporate graph. Sound familiar? When you marry that corporate graph with our professional graph, you take the economic graph, and it grows by leaps and bounds in terms of the reality and in terms of the value it can create. Think about that, and think about what other company or marriage of companies could come anywhere close to doing that. The answer I came up with is, there are none. Second example, everyone here I know understands how passionate we are as a company, and Satya shares this, about education, and more specifically continuing education, vocational training, and enabling individuals throughout the global workforce to acquire the skills they need for the jobs that are and will be, and not just the jobs that once were. The days of learning a skill or certification and having a job the rest of your life are nearing an end, if not already over. So what happens when you take our Lynda coursework, the LinkedIn learning stack, and you begin to deeply integrate that alongside some of the most popular productivity applications on earth? Excel, PowerPoint, Word, and how about adding a new tab within office called learning? Imagine what's possible. You are in PowerPoint, you need help with either the presentation itself or actual subject matter you are working on, we have a contextual messaging overlay our team has been working on, I can't wait to show you, you go to help and you see this. You see who within your network could help you. You see who within LinkedIn could help you, you see which freelancers through ProFinder you can generate a lead for and provide business for, and of course you see the coursework that enables you to learn on your own. That is pretty powerful stuff, especially when you consider that six of the top 25 Lynda courses are all related to Microsoft product. Third, with regard to the member experience, for years now the most commonly asked question I get is what is LinkedIn's play with in the enterprise, not higher markets, we get that. That's for customers. For the individual, what are you guys going to do? There is Facebook at work, what are you guys doing? And I've always said because we understand the importance of focus at our scale, I've always said we've got to stay with where we are already focused, we've got to play our own game. We've got to swim in our own lane. Whatever metaphor you want to inject there will work just fine. When you combine two companies and these assets—take your pick. You want to disrupt the directory? The internet? Productivity? Collaboration? Dissemination of company news? Distribution of business intelligence, and you want to do those things in a way that has never been done before? Game on. With regard to our business lines, we become the leader in hiring solutions but we've always recognized the enormity of the opportunity with regard to human capital management. Together, we can go after that.

Tens upon tens of billions of dollars of true addressable opportunity that we can start to go after by virtue of our product, our application, the platform we're building, our salesforce that is focused in this area, and combined with Microsoft's deep workflow relationships with their customers, a completely new business opportunity. Speaking of new business opportunities we can take our fastest growing businesses to scale sponsored content, and look to unlock new forms of inventory throughout Microsoft's ecosystem. Windows, Office, Skype, etc. We've already identified some pretty meaningful opportunities there. You talk about changing the game, there is perhaps no better example than thinking about how to integrate sales navigator and our sales intelligence tools with Dynamics and a proprietary CRM. That is social selling, that is changing the game. And with regard to the millions upon millions, tens of millions, of freelancers and independent service providers that live within Microsoft's applications to be able to function and do business, imagine bringing ProFinder and new leads to them where they work in those applications. I could literally go on and on, Satya and Reid could do the same. You should know those were just the ideas we discussed in the first meeting. And I say that without exaggeration. Okay, there was clear alignment of purpose and lots of opportunities to work together. We then turned to the all-important question of structure, and on this I had no idea what to expect. Was he going to propose fully integrating LinkedIn, were we going to become a division, would I need to move up north? Were those nervous laughs in the audience, like, what the f— is he about to say? I had no idea what he was going to say, so my excitement was tempered up until that point. I knew how powerful this combination could be, but as we all know it is not about the theory when it comes to M&A, it is about true alignment in terms of execution, that is almost all that matters. And Satya had me at independence. I said excuse me? He said, Jeff, we are going to do something different. We will let LinkedIn operate as an independent entity. Haven't done it before, we will do it with you. WhatsApp, YouTube, Instagram, three examples of companies that were acquired and grew to extra ordinary heights after the acquisition and unlocked incredible value by virtue of remaining independent. The beauty of our independence is that the alignment between the two companies in terms of sense of purpose, strategy, what we are trying to accomplish, how we create value for members and customers, doesn't require that top-down mandate. As Satya likes to say we are going to write our own rules. I like to think how powerful it can be, this new model. And Satya went on to provide a little bit more in the way of detail, I would continue to be the CEO, I would report to Satya, Satya for all intents and purposes would replace our board, going from seven people to one person, which will be easier to navigate. Satya, myself, Reid, Bill Gates, and Satya's two day-to-day operating leaders, Qi Lu and Scott Guthrie, productivity and the cloud, would partner together to figure out how to chart a course and maximize the value of this unique, combination of efforts. So you can see why my excitement continued to build and why I allowed myself to start dreaming big. And it's been interesting, bringing some of our leaders over the wall, seeing their responses, allowing them to go through their process and then challenging them to dream big. Because that is what I want each of you to do, but I want to provide a quick example so you can get your arms around the opportunity here. Just the other day I was on the phone with Akshay in India who came on board with our Pulse acquisition. He is now or our country manager, and we were talking about the opportunities. For those who don't know, Microsoft is extraordinarily well regarded in India, as is Satya. Satya has a vision to bring Microsoft's Advanced Technologies to every corner of the country regardless of socioeconomic position, so you can understand why they are so well received there. And Akshay was relaying to me the story of how during Satya's most recent trip where in the span of a day or a half a day he met with the Prime Minister and all of his key deputies, and Akshay was saying, I wish that was us. He and Olivier who run Asia-Pacific have always wanted to be in that position. I said Akshay, with this deal, it will be. The next time Satya is there, I'm envisioning you side-by-side with him pitching your vision to the Prime Minister to ensure that every kid graduating from an Indian school has the skills and certifications they need to get the jobs they want. That got his attention. That is what I want for each one of you, to dream big, to write your own rules here in terms of what is possible.

Okay, let's talk about you. What does this mean for you? Honestly speaking, that is probably top of mind for every individual who read the news today, how does this impact me? You will have the same titles, by virtue of this independent structure, you are going to have the same managers. You're going to have the same roles and responsibilities with one notable exception, and I want us to be as compassionate as possible here, for the group of folks at LinkedIn whose jobs were 100% dedicated to maintaining LinkedIn as a publicly traded company, everything that goes along with that, the administration of that we are going to work very hard to help you with your next play. Outside of that, it is largely going to be business as usual. We have the same mission and vision, it's more important than ever. We have the same culture and values, and you are going to be stuck with me. I'm still the CEO. I want to end on a more familiar note—I talked at the onset about the fact that over five years ago we went public, we run the bell at the New York Stock Exchange and ended up moving over to our offices in the Empire State building for an All Hands special edition, just like this one. And I remember than talking about the importance of reinforcing that the IPO was not the end game, that is not why we were here, that was not what we were playing for. It was a tactic, a steppingstone, towards the realization of our long-term objectives. Of our mission, of our vision. At the end of that meeting we finished with two words that became our unofficial mantra, you guys remember what was? Next play. For those of you less familiar with the expression, it is a turn of phrase I picked up from

Mike Krzyzewski, arguably one of the great coaches in American sports history, I'm not suggesting I endorse the Duke Blue Devils, so please no hissing and booing from people who went to other schools, but I'm a huge fan of coach K, I think the guy is extraordinary, and it turns out unbeknownst to most people, every time the Duke Blue Devils finish a play on either the offensive or defensive end of the court, no matter what happens, he says the exact same thing, next play. Next play. Don't linger too long on celebrating an amazing 360 dunk, and don't linger too long on messing up and having the opposing team steal the ball and get an easy lay-up on the other end. Spend one moment to reflect on it and then turn to the next play. This idea of next play, it served us very well then, and it will serve us very well now. So here's to the next stepping-stone. Next Play. Thank you. Okay, with that, I mentioned earlier that one of the primary reasons that I joined LinkedIn was because of a guy named Reid Hoffman who may be familiar hopefully to all of you, he was the founder of the company, he was the company's first CEO. He is our executive chairman, he is the largest controlling shareholder. And none of this happens without him, and when I say none of this, I mean all of it. You know the expression we wouldn't be here if it weren't for such and such? That is Reid. We wouldn't be here if it wasn't for Reid and his cofounders, Allen Blue and Jean-Luc Vaillant. Reid has become much more to me than a figure I admire and respect. He is much more to me than our executive chairman. He has grown to be my mentor—I almost needed a bad joke there—and he has grown to be one of my closest friends, like an extended member of my family, and my children refer to him as their uncle and Lisette adores him. I have nothing but the utmost respect and admiration for Reid, he has been an extraordinary partner throughout all of this, and by this I am referring to both developing and building LinkedIn and this decision. And with that, I wanted to invite Reid up here to tell you about the way he came to that decision. Our founder, Reid Hoffman.

Reid Hoffman: Note to self, don't follow Jeff. I think this is maybe the first time I followed you in public speaking, it was like oh s-—. So, I'm going to be reasonably brief because Jeff has covered nearly everything that I was thinking about saying. There are a few things I think I can add in for some youthful color. It's always about the mission. Part of what makes great leadership is service to the mission. It isn't, oh, come work for me, it is work for what we are doing in the world, and that is always what has mattered. The other thing people are frequently kind of not realizing is, companies have many founding moments. There is the original founding moment with Alan, who I see in the back, and I, and a few people in a room it wasn't that far from here, it was just down Shoreline—but then there are many. One of them is hiring Jeff, another one is the IPO—these founding moments are the inflection points by which you are making key decisions in order to realize the mission. Which is, as Jeff went on very eloquently to point out, is, how do you empower people to be productive and successful? How do you do that in a massive and effective way? Every decision we have done, it is never been about control. If it was about control I would be more hung up about being CEO. No, I wanted Jeff to be CEO because of realizing the mission. It's never about a question of well, do we have nominal independence, are people going to be lauding us because we are a public company? That is not relevant, what is relevant is what we do in the world. The reason this make sense is because we have the opportunity to do amazing things, and here is one of the things I can add in from something that Jeff doesn't know—in the first month when we were talking about what are the things that would make us be successful, we kicked around, what would it take to get integrated in Outlook? Literally in the first month. Like, that is the thing we would most want. Well, it only took 13 years, but here we are.

So the mission is critical, and both organizations are essentially in service of the same mission. They have complementary assets where one plus one isn't two, it isn't even four, it is probably 10. It's an amazing combination when you literally look down the list of the different possible things these two things together make them both stronger, and they are relatively straightforward to do, the list literally—we couldn't spend this entire meeting just covering the list.

Next thing is leadership. Part of what you do is you look for leaders who essentially have the product vision, have the mission vision, have the notion of culture, have the notion of what it is we are doing, we are being in service to the mission. I'm reasonably good at picking who I work with. You guys have had a lot of experience with Jeff, I also am delighted to start working with Satya, this is going to be awesome. He is exactly—not to barrow you into our organization—our kind of person. We are going to love this. And I think the possibilities are literally—we are not going public with his video, We are? Oh! We can accomplish great things, I'm just going to say that. [LAUGHTER] Next index card, yes. So when people ask me why it is that I am so strongly in support of this—mission, people, what we can do in the world. That is what matters. You go home and you think what did I do, why was my activity, why was my work worth it? I haven't been an employee here for six or seven years, I work here because it is the right thing to do. And I plan to continue doing that, so just as Jeff said, this is my mission as well. And so this doesn't change anything for me other than the fact that, well, in some number of months I won't be controlling shareholder—that is fine. It's not about control, it's about what we accomplish, and that is what matters to me, I think that is what matters to all of us. With that, I think it's been a great pleasure over the last couple years getting to know Satya quite well, I can't think of a better person that I would rather be joining forces with in order to realize this mission, and so with that, Satya.

Satya Nadella: Thank you so much, Reid and Jeff. You know, the first words that come to me is admiration. Admiration for what Reid has created, what Jeff has created and built, and all of you have built. Really, I thought Jeff talked about the different emotions that could be all going through. I'm hoping that one of those emotions is real pride. You all absolutely deserve to be very, very proud of having created LinkedIn, made LinkedIn into what it is, and that sense of purpose with which you've built this—that to me is what I admire the most in people, and what I admire the most in the institutions that people build. So this time around, give yourselves a round of applause that can go as long as you want.

So what I thought I will do is just give you a little bit of a feel for how I think we at Microsoft think, and what is our excitement of having this chance to work with you all. It starts with the mission. That's the first thing. When Reid and I started talking and when I first met Jeff, the sense of purpose to me is everything. At Microsoft I talk about our mission is empowering every person and every organization on the planet to achieve more—it has real deep meaning for all of us and for me. Because when you think about ultimately how does all of this digital technology make a difference, it has to be about empowering people and organizations. In fact, I think a lot about going beyond individual people, because quite frankly it is the institutions that move societies, that make economies, and if you don't have digital technology, software, help people build institutions that outlast them, then you've not accomplished much, so that's what I think about. I think about, how can we as Microsoft really empower people to build things that can even outlast them? And when you think about that as the mission, and what LinkedIn has done, what LinkedIn has built, what LinkedIn has always aspired to create, of connecting the world's professionals to be more productive and successful—Jeff said this super well, these two missions are exactly isomorphic. They are the same. They are the realization of how technology can shape people and the institutions they build, and that is really, really exciting, because I think a lot of technologies will come and go but that sense of identity, sense of purpose, is what will give us that energy to keep reinventing ourselves. So talking about reinvention—Microsoft—this is our 41st year. We have had a tremendous history of success, here we are, north of $400 billion of market cap, 90+ billion dollars in revenue, and behind all that stuff though, each time, in each era, you have to start with high ambition for what you can do going forward. So I want to give you a little bit of a flavor of how we think about Microsoft going forward. The first thing I talk a lot about, and Qi who is here. We dream a lot about, what we call reinventing productivity and business process. The way I come to it is by saying in all this abundance, computing is becoming ubiquitous and we have multiple devices per person and what have you, but what is scarce is human attention and time. So how can we get people to capture that back? How can they be more productive, how can they get more out of every moment of their lives? That is what I think, it is not just building another version of any tool or app or service, it is, how can we truly empower people to be able to capture more out of every moment of their life? And when you think about that and you think about the combination of what we do in Office and Office 365 and LinkedIn, I told Jeff in one of the interviews we just did, you don't go to LinkedIn to waste time, you go to LinkedIn to gain time. I thought that was a fantastic way to capture the realization of what both of us really seek. Today we have these two graphs, Microsoft graph which is the information fabric underneath all of the activity that happens inside the enterprise. People, the relationships with other people that's captured in active directory, the calendars, the schedules, work artifacts, in fact you can extend that graph, you have needs in CRM, prospects—all of that inside this information graph, which we call Microsoft graph, that is something our team has been building. We also have another graph which is the world's graph inside of Bing. Now just imagine we connect all of that with the professional graph that you have, and the dream you have, the vision you have for creating the true economic opportunity. That ability to connect these two worlds is fairly unique. We've got to realize it in tasteful, natural ways for the LinkedIn members, for all the professionals who use Office, Office tools, and LinkedIn, whether it is to be a salesperson, a recruiter, someone who is trying to learn some new skill—there is plenty of great user experience work you have to do in order to make this stuff really tasteful, natural. But our ability to change the professional world, of connecting this professional cloud and the professional network is the most unbounded opportunity that there is, and Jeff captured this. Because if you look at the world today—I get to travel the world, meet many leaders across the world, what is the number one issue for everyone? Skills. How are they going to enable their population, their societies, to be ready for this digital economy? Everyone wants employment growth in a world with a lot of displacement, and the only solution to that is this continuous up-skilling of your people, and to me that is what we encompass by bringing dynamics, Office 365, and LinkedIn together. So we have got to have very high ambition. You represent that already with what you have built with LinkedIn, but let's take that to the one billion+ users today who use our tools and bring this economic opportunity in a digital world to every corner of the world, that is the ambition. The second thing we are up to, that is also very related to, I think, what we will do is a combination is building up this cloud infrastructure, which we refer to as the Intelligent Cloud. I have known Kevin for a while and I'm already thinking about, when will I get that first look at, hey where are my GPUs to do my machine learning? The way we measure is per capita per developer in terms of machine power, because to be able to bring that AI capability to your newsfeed relevance, we are building out not simply as in the structure stack but we want to bring the power of a set of cognitive services, whether it is computer vision, speech, natural language understanding, whether it is the knowledge graph, and making that available as a set of APIs, as well as the full data platform for you to do machine learning at scale. That rich infrastructure, coupled with the kinds of things you are doing at LinkedIn, it's very exciting. I want you to be able to tell you what you need to do in the infrastructure, because platform companies are all about a feedback loop from people pushing the envelope when it comes to the outside, pushing what needs to happen in the infrastructure side, and I mean infrastructure all the way to silicon. At this point we spend over $5 billion of capital building out infrastructure, we build our own network, we build anything and everything needed in order to build essentially a global scale cloud infrastructure, but all that is only interesting if there are apps like LinkedIn or networks like LinkedIn pushing it, pushing it, so I'm so excited about that opportunity. The last thing I want to talk about is what we are trying to do in personal computing, after all we are a Windows company, we started there. We started as a tools company, the first product that Bill and Paul built was a basic printer for the Altair, then we built apps for the Mac, that was the second, and here we are. [LAUGHTER] The other thing about it, you should know is, that just down the road is the PowerPoint team, one of the first acquisitions of Microsoft in 1987. Of course now PowerPoint is what you all love and know. But it is so interesting to think about what is going to happen in personal computing. We are not building an operating system for just a single device, when I think about even Windows 10, the way we conceptualized it is, we are building an operating system for the user across all the devices. It is a service, that is how I think of it. Windows update is probably the biggest service we have because it touches 1.5 billion machines every day, and our goal is to really change what is the definition of an operating system, and operating systems for personal computing are always about inventing the next big change in input/output. And it is no question that we really missed the mobile one, therefore we understand it, we have a particular position in mobile today which is more about enterprise and where we can have more security, more management, more productivity, we will focus on that, but we are on to the next big thing. And if you look at what is happening even today, I don't know when exactly the Xbox event is, but it must be happening in parallel, hopefully I don't disclose anything before them or what have you— but the idea that we can bring AR and VR into this one continuum of what we talk about as mixed reality, is something we are very excited about. Think about this, the field-of-view becoming an infinite display where what you see is not just the analog world, but it is a world into which you can superimpose digital artifacts. That is a completely new medium, that is what HoloLens is, and Jeff said, hey where is my HoloLens? He will get one in a couple of days, and I'm really looking forward to all of you having—[unintelligible yelling offstage] [LAUGHTER].

It is the most mind-blowing new medium I have ever seen, because it changes all your assumptions about what you will do with computing. You can have your 80-inch screen wherever and whenever you want, and what it means for—think about professions. What it means for architecture. It will never be—my wife is an architect and she looks at it and says, wow, that means I can design and see what I'm designing as a holographic output right there. Think about industrial design. Completely changes. Medical education. Some of the work that Cleveland Clinic is doing, where medical students that are trying to understand the human body can look at the human body, inspect it, along with their teacher. Education changes dramatically. So there isn't a field or vertical industry—by the way, gaming too—we are excited about what Minecraft, on HoloLens could be. So to break new ground, underneath all this is amazing gesture recognition, amazing computer vision, because you have to essentially look at a scene, reconstruct the scene, understand every object and position it, and then to be able to place other objects in it, and do it in real time. That is the level of innovation that we are excited about. These are the three ambitions, we refer to them as reinventing business process and productivity, building up this intelligent cloud, and more personal computing. But besides all the technology, what I think a lot about, and I thought Jeff captured it so well when describing what you have done, which is, your competitive advantage is your culture. And that is what we think ours is as well. That sense of identity—to me the two bookends is that sense of identity and purpose and mission and culture. Those are the things that are constant, and then, technologies will constantly be renewed. And for culture—the way I think about this is not as a static model, there are values that are enduring, but the culture itself that I thought about is, what is a way for us to continuously question and improve and evolve? What is that learning, ultimate learning culture? And the meme and metaphor we picked is inspired by a professor who works at Stanford who has written a book called Mindset, which is more about child psychology, her name is Carol Duak, and her work basically says that the simple way to understand it is, if you take two people in school, one of them is a know-it-all and the other is a learn it all. Even if the know-it-all start with more innate capability, the learn-it-all will ultimately outperform them. That is true for the boys and girls in school, it is true for CEOs like me, it is true for all of us in the organizations we build. So that growth mindset is what we refer to as the cultural high ground we want. And when I think about that it starts with individual mindsets—see that is what I love about it, it is not about abdicating responsibility for culture to somebody else, it is about being able to grab hold of it individually and thinking about it in our mindset. Sometimes people say I found find people who have a growth mindset. I say, that is not the job. The idea of a growth mindset is for me to recognize individually where have I had a fixed mindset today and to push and say, how can I improve? How can I learn from this person? And that is what is sort of to me, today, is humbling, because I think there is a ton I can learn from LinkedIn. I'm really looking forward to what Microsoft, what I individually, can learn from LinkedIn, and make Microsoft a better place. So thank you all very much, I couldn't be more excited to join forces with you in really taking the mission you have to help realize the Microsoft mission of empowering every person and organization on the planet, thanks a lot. Thank you.

Additional Information and Where to Find It
In connection with the transaction described above, LinkedIn Corporation (the "Company") will file relevant materials with the Securities and Exchange Commission (the "SEC"), including a proxy statement on Schedule 14A. Promptly after filing its definitive proxy statement with the SEC, the Company will mail the definitive proxy statement and a proxy card to each stockholder entitled to vote at the special meeting relating to the transaction. INVESTORS AND SECURITY HOLDERS OF THE COMPANY ARE URGED TO READ THESE MATERIALS (INCLUDING ANY AMENDMENTS OR SUPPLEMENTS THERETO) AND ANY OTHER RELEVANT DOCUMENTS IN CONNECTION WITH THE TRANSACTION THAT THE COMPANY WILL FILE WITH THE SEC WHEN THEY BECOME AVAILABLE BECAUSE THEY WILL CONTAIN IMPORTANT INFORMATION ABOUT THE COMPANY AND THE TRANSACTION. The definitive proxy statement, the preliminary proxy statement and other relevant materials in connection with the transaction (when they become available), and any other documents filed by the Company with the SEC, may be obtained free of charge at the SEC's website (http://www.sec.gov) or at LinkedIn's website (http://investors.linkedin.com) or by writing to LinkedIn Corporation, Investor Relations, 2029 Stierlin Court, Mountain View, California 94043.

The Company and its directors and executive officers are participants in the solicitation of proxies from the Company's stockholders with respect to the transaction. Information about the Company's directors and executive officers and their ownership of the Company's common stock is set forth in the Company's proxy statement on Schedule 14A filed with the SEC on April 22, 2016. To the extent that holdings of the Company's securities have changed since the amounts printed in the

Company's proxy statement, such changes have been or will be reflected on Statements of Change in Ownership on Form 4 filed with the SEC. Information regarding the identity of the participants, and their direct or indirect interests in the transaction, by security holdings or otherwise, will be set forth in the proxy statement and other materials to be filed with SEC in connection with the transaction.

Forward-Looking Statements
This document contains certain forward-looking statements within the meaning of the Private Securities Litigation Reform Act of 1995 with respect to the proposed transaction and business combination between Microsoft and LinkedIn, including statements regarding the benefits of the transaction, the anticipated timing of the transaction and the products and markets of each company. These forward-looking statements generally are identified by the words "believe," "project," "expect," "anticipate," "estimate," "intend," "strategy," "future," "opportunity," "plan," "may," "should," "will," "would," "will be," "will continue," "will likely result," and similar expressions. Forward-looking statements are predictions, projections and other statements about future events that are based on current expectations and assumptions and, as a result, are subject to risks and uncertainties. Many factors could cause actual future events to differ materially from the forward-looking statements in this document, including but not limited to: (i) the risk that the transaction may not be completed in a timely manner or at all, which may adversely affect LinkedIn's business and the price of the common stock of LinkedIn, (ii) the failure to satisfy the conditions to the consummation of the transaction, including the adoption of the merger agreement by the stockholders of LinkedIn and the receipt of certain governmental and regulatory approvals, (iii) the occurrence of any event, change or other circumstance that could give rise to the termination of the merger agreement, (iv) the effect of the announcement or pendency of the transaction on LinkedIn's business relationships, operating results, and business generally, (v) risks that the proposed transaction disrupts current plans and operations of LinkedIn or Microsoft and potential difficulties in LinkedIn employee retention as a result of the transaction, (vi) risks related to diverting management's attention from LinkedIn's ongoing business operations, (vii) the outcome of any legal proceedings that may be instituted against us or against LinkedIn related to the merger agreement or the transaction, (viii) the ability of Microsoft to successfully

integrate LinkedIn's operations, product lines, and technology, and (ix) the ability of Microsoft to implement its plans, forecasts, and other expectations with respect to LinkedIn's business after the completion of the proposed merger and realize additional opportunities for growth and innovation. In addition, please refer to the documents that Microsoft and LinkedIn file with the SEC on Forms 10-K, 10-Q and 8-K. These filings identify and address other important risks and uncertainties that could cause events and results to differ materially from those contained in the forward-looking statements set forth in this document. Forward-looking statements speak only as of the date they are made. Readers are cautioned not to put undue reliance on forward-looking statements, and Microsoft and LinkedIn assume no obligation and do not intend to update or revise these forward-looking statements, whether as a result of new information, future events, or otherwise.

Internal communication from Microsoft CEO, Satya Nadella, to employees

Date: 4 February 2014

Today is a very humbling day for me. It reminds me of my very first day at Microsoft, 22 years ago. Like you, I had a choice about where to come to work. I came here because I believed Microsoft was the best company in the world. I saw then how clearly we empower people to do magical things with our creations and ultimately make the world a better place. I knew there was no better company to join if I wanted to make a difference. This is the very same inspiration that continues to drive me today.

It is an incredible honor for me to lead and serve this great company of ours. Steve and Bill have taken it from an idea to one of the greatest and most universally admired companies in the world. I've been fortunate to work closely with both Bill and Steve in my different roles at Microsoft, and as I step in as CEO, I've asked Bill to devote additional time to the company, focused on technology and products. I'm also looking forward to working with John Thompson as our new Chairman of the Board.

While we have seen great success, we are hungry to do more. Our industry does not respect tradition—it only respects innovation. This is a critical time for the industry and for Microsoft. Make no mistake, we are headed for greater places—as technology evolves and we evolve with and ahead of it. Our job is to ensure that Microsoft thrives in a mobile and cloud-first world.

As we start a new phase of our journey together, I wanted to share some background on myself and what inspires and motivates me.

Who am I?

I am 46. I've been married for 22 years and we have 3 kids. And like anyone else, a lot of what I do and how I think has been shaped by my family and my overall life experiences. Many who know me say I am also defined by my curiosity and thirst for learning. I buy more books than I can finish. I sign up for more online courses than I can complete. I fundamentally believe that if you are not learning new things, you stop doing great and useful things. So family, curiosity and hunger for knowledge all define me.

Why am I here?

I am here for the same reason I think most people join Microsoft—to change the world through technology that empowers people to do amazing things. I know it can sound hyperbolic—and yet it's true. We have done it, we're doing it today, and we are the team that will do it again.

I believe over the next decade computing will become even more ubiquitous and intelligence will become ambient. The coevolution of software and new hardware form factors will intermediate and digitize—many of the things we do and experience in business, life and our world. This will be made possible by an ever-growing network of connected devices, incredible computing capacity from the cloud, insights from big data, and intelligence from machine learning.

This is a software-powered world.

It will better connect us to our friends and families and help us see, express, and share our world in ways never before possible. It will enable businesses to engage customers in more meaningful ways.

I am here because we have unparalleled capability to make an impact.

Why are we here?

In our early history, our mission was about the PC on every desk and home, a goal we have mostly achieved in the developed world. Today we're focused on a broader range of devices. While the deal is not yet complete, we will welcome to our family Nokia devices and services and the new mobile capabilities they bring us.

As we look forward, we must zero in on what Microsoft can uniquely contribute to the world. The opportunity ahead will require us to

APPENDIX C: EXECUTIVE SPEECHES

reimagine a lot of what we have done in the past for a mobile and cloud-first world, and do new things.

We are the only ones who can harness the power of software and deliver it through devices and services that truly empower every individual and every organization. We are the only company with history and continued focus in building platforms and ecosystems that create broad opportunity.

Qi Lu captured it well in a recent meeting when he said that Microsoft uniquely empowers people to "do more." This doesn't mean that we need to do more things, but that the work we do empowers the world to do more of what they care about—get stuff done, have fun, communicate and accomplish great things. This is the core of who we are, and driving this core value in all that we do—be it the cloud or device experiences—is why we are here.

What do we do next?

To paraphrase a quote from Oscar Wilde—we need to believe in the impossible and remove the improbable.

This starts with clarity of purpose and sense of mission that will lead us to imagine the impossible and deliver it. We need to prioritize innovation that is centered on our core value of empowering users and organizations to "do more." We have picked a set of high-value activities as part of our One Microsoft strategy. And with every service and device launch going forward we need to bring more innovation to bear around these scenarios.

Next, every one of us needs to do our best work, lead and help drive cultural change. We sometimes underestimate what we each can do to make things happen and overestimate what others need to do to move us forward. We must change this.

Finally, I truly believe that each of us must find meaning in our work. The best work happens when you know that it's not just work, but something that will improve other people's lives. This is the opportunity that drives each of us at this company.

Many companies aspire to change the world. But very few have all the elements required: talent, resources, and perseverance. Microsoft has proven that it has all three in abundance. And as the new CEO, I can't ask for a better foundation.

Let's build on this foundation together.

Satya

INDEX

© The Editor(s) (if applicable) and The Author(s), under exclusive
license to Springer Nature Singapore Pte Ltd. 2020
P. Ross, *Barriers to Entry*,
https://doi.org/10.1007/978-981-32-9566-7

CPSIA information can be obtained
at www.ICGtesting.com
Printed in the USA
LVHW030025071219
639749LV00007B/329/P